✳

The Riddle of Latin America

※

The Riddle of Latin America

KRIS LANE
Tulane University

MATTHEW RESTALL
Pennsylvania State University

WADSWORTH
CENGAGE Learning

Australia • Brazil • Japan • Korea • Mexico • Singapore • Spain • United Kingdom • United States

WADSWORTH
CENGAGE Learning™

The Riddle of Latin America
Kris Lane and Matthew Restall

Senior Publisher: Suzanne Jeans

Senior Sponsoring Editor:
Ann West

Development Editor: Barrett Lyon

Assistant Editor: Megan Chrisman

Media Editor: Lisa Ciccolo

Marketing Coordinator: Lorreen
Towle

Program Manager: Caitlin Green

Content Project Management:
PreMediaGlobal

Senior Art Director: Cate
Rickard Barr

Print Buyer: Mary Beth
Hennebury

Rights Acquisition Specialist,
(Image, Text): Jennifer Meyer
Dare

Production Service:
PreMediaGlobal

Cover Image: *Mural, on a wall*,
La Hoyada, Caracas, Venezuela
© Panoramic Images/
Getty Images

Compositor: PreMediaGlobal

For product information and
technology assistance, contact us at **Cengage Learning
Customer & Sales Support, 1-800-354-9706**
For permission to use material from this text or product,
submit all requests online at **cengage.com/permissions**

Further permissions questions can be emailed to
permissionrequest@cengage.com

Library of Congress Control Number: 2011928770

Student Edition:
ISBN-13: 978-0-618-15306-0
ISBN-10: 0-618-15306-3

Wadsworth
20 Channel Center Street
Boston, MA, 02210
USA

Cengage Learning is a leading provider of customized learning solutions with office locations around the globe, including Singapore, the United Kingdom, Australia, Mexico, Brazil, and Japan. Locate your local office at **international.cengage.com/region**.

Cengage Learning products are represented in Canada by Nelson Education, Ltd.

For your course and learning solutions, visit **www.cengage.com**

Purchase any of our products at your local college store or at our preferred online store **www.cengagebrain.com**.

Instructors: Please visit **login.cengage.com** and log in to access instructor-specific resources.

Printed in the United States of America
1 2 3 4 5 6 7 14 15 13 12 11

Contents

Introduction

What is the riddle of Latin America? For over five hundred years, Latin America has been a land of promise and paradox, its promise still to be fully realized, its paradoxes yet to be reconciled. It remains among the least understood and most often misrepresented regions of the world.

Latin America's twenty mainland and island nations are home to nearly half a billion people, and several million more Latin Americans live outside the region, primarily in the United States but also in Canada, Europe, Japan, and elsewhere. Latin American economies now range in size and complexity from miniscule to mammoth, while the region's politics have generally shifted from colonial to autocratic to democratic. Originally named for the predominance of Romance languages and the Catholic faith rather than any natural geographical feature or political boundary, Latin America is now noted for its linguistic and religious diversity. Indigenous, African-descended, and other oppressed populations have resurged in recent decades, asserting their identities and demanding equal rights. Latin American women – comprising just over half the total population – have also made great strides, and have now held presidential seats in several countries. Latin America's vast reserves of petroleum, minerals, timber, and farmland continue to attract massive capital investment despite centuries of careless exploitation and violent competition. Several countries have used export-generated wealth to create technically sophisticated manufacturing centers. Brazil now exports full-size passenger jets and launches rockets.

The great Latin American riddle, or paradox, evident since colonial times, is most visible in the form of widespread poverty – of stark social and economic inequality in a seeming land of plenty. The riddle extends as well to include endemic problems such as political corruption, state and criminal violence, racism, environmental degradation, and economic instability. One result of this paradox of widespread poverty amid natural bounty is that Latin America, for centuries considered a promised land, has become a mass exporter of people.

But Latin America is not simply a historical problem in search of a solution. Over the past five centuries, Latin Americans have developed a unique and complex civilization, one that transcends national and even linguistic boundaries. The region's diverse cultures invite exploration, and its dynamic societies offer attitudes and practices from which we might learn a great deal.

This book explores the riddle of Latin America in a novel way by giving roughly equal weight to the colonial and national periods. This is essential in part because in Latin America, unlike the United States, colonialism started early and independence came late. Simply put, three centuries of colonial rule demand close examination. The book's first six chapters tell the story of the astonishing encounter between Iberians, Africans, and native Americans—and all that developed in its aftermath. The riddles of these early centuries are these: Why did native American civilizations remain isolated from the rest of the world, and why did they not discover Europeans before Europeans discovered them? What brought Iberians to western Africa, and soon after to the Americas, and how were they able to establish and rule such vast American colonies, for so many generations, while so greatly outnumbered?

With as many motivations as there were individuals, men and women sailed across the Atlantic Ocean seeking administrative power, material gain, social status, religious mission, scientific knowledge, and personal adventure. The lands they settled were already occupied by sophisticated peoples who were organized into societies from which they profited, and often learned, a great deal. Despite Iberian attempts to give those lands the form of their own, native Americans—and the Africans brought against their will by Europeans—contributed as much as the colonists to the formation of new colonial societies.

It is easy to assume that the legacy of the colonial period explains the events of the past two centuries. Today's Latin America is not, however, best understood in terms of colonial continuities, a common teleology. We argue that the story of modern Latin America is far more complex than a mere outgrowth of its colonial past. There are some large questions that demand broad-brush answers. For example, two of the biggest riddles of the nineteenth and twentieth centuries are the following: Why did wealth and power shift to North America, when it had been concentrated in Mesoamerica and the Andes for millennia? And why, if Latin American nations were so rich in natural resources, could they not harness these endowments to develop and improve the lot of average citizens? But the modern period also requires sensitivity to regional variations in the pace and depth of change. Latin American national trajectories, like those of neighbors such as the United States or Canada, appear predictable only in retrospect. As Latin America becomes more politically and culturally diverse, so does its civilization become more complex and more central to the larger development of human history.

The aim of this book is to provide unfamiliar readers with a balanced yet interpretive view of Latin America's long and complex history by identifying key patterns and trends and tracing them across time and space. Within chapters we take a regional rather than country-by-country approach, treating, for example, the Greater Caribbean, Mexico and Central America, the Andes, the

Southern Cone, and Brazil. Some overlaps will necessarily occur as well. In keeping with most histories of the region, we treat Haiti and other parts of the francophone Caribbean more in terms of exemplary events than long-range trends. We have also chosen to exclude French Canada, as its story is usually told in a different context. Many details worthy of study have inevitably been sacrificed in the processes of selection and highlighting, but it is our belief that the end result will be a more satisfactory and stimulating introduction to this perplexing yet fascinating part of the world.

PART I

✳

When Worlds Collide
(1450–1550)

The year 1492 marks a major watershed in world history. From this date forward Native Americans, Europeans, and Africans came into sustained contact, and often conflict. The Spanish conquest of the two largest empires in the Americas, from the 1510s–1530s, and the Portuguese initiation of the transatlantic trade in enslaved Africans just after Columbus's voyage mark only the most cataclysmic of these conflicts. Both sequences of events have long struck historians as riddles to be solved. Why was it southern Europeans, and not northern Europeans or West Africans or Native Americans, who initiated transatlantic contact? Why did it happen in the fifteenth century, rather than earlier or later? And why was the meeting of worlds a collision marked by so much violence and mortality, characterized for centuries not as a "meeting" but as a "discovery" and "conquest"?

To observers at the time, these phenomena were hardly considered as earth-shattering or portentous as they seem to us in retrospect. This was in large part due to ancient historical and cultural traditions in the Americas, Europe, and Africa that helped explain abrupt turns of events and readily incorporated new peoples, commodities, and geographic spaces, even quite distant and strange ones. In describing the unfamiliar in familiar terms, none of these societies saw themselves as fated to fail, or to be relegated to permanent victimhood. As a result, all fought on.

1

Native American Trajectories

Societies and Civilizations

Mesoamericans and Andeans

The Aztec and Inka Empires

Human beings did not evolve independently in the Americas, but human civilizations did.

The sole surviving human species, *Homo sapiens*, evolved in Africa and expanded into Europe and Asia about 100,000 years ago, perhaps more. Human beings reached North America across a land bridge from Asia at least 20,000 years ago. By 12,000 years ago, there were hunting bands of humans throughout most of the Americas, from Alaska to the tip of South America. Around this time, the land bridge from Asia ceased to exist, as the end of the last Ice Age brought rising water levels, leaving the peoples whom we call Native Americans isolated from the rest of the world until the European invasion that began in 1492.

This isolation was not absolute; around 1000 AD the Vikings that had shortly before established a colony in Greenland created a settlement in Newfoundland that persisted for several decades. There may have been other visitors to the Americas from Asia, Africa, and Europe, but there is no firm evidence of the effect of such voyages on Native Americans—or that they ever took place. Even the Viking settlement shows no signs of having had any impact on the development of Native American societies and civilizations.

Between about 6000 and 3000 BC populations in many regions of the Americas made the transition from hunting and gathering to a more settled life-style. The next 3,000 years saw the development of complex and permanently settled societies, including the first great civilizations of the Americas, such as the **Chavín** in the northern Andes and the **Olmec** in **Mesoamerica**. Scholars used

---

Mesoamerica [may-zo-a-MEH-rica] civilizational area stretching from northern Mexico down to the middle of Central America

TIMELINE	
20,000–12,000 BC	People cross the land bridge from Asia into the Americas
6000–3000 BC	People make the transition from hunting and gathering to sedentary lifestyles in many regions
200 BC–1300 AD	Great civilizations develop in Mesoamerica and the Andes
1325	The Mexica found their city of Mexico-Tenochtitlán
1427	Itzcoatl founds Mexica or Aztec Empire
1438	Pachacuti founds Inka Empire
1420s–1520s	Rise and expansion of Aztec (Mexica) Empire in Mesoamerica and Inka Empire in the Andes
1502–1520	Reign of Mexica emperor, Moctezuma Xocoyotl (Montezuma)
Late 1520s	The Inka Huayna Capac dies, leading to civil war between his successors, Atawallpa and Huascar

to call Olmec civilization "the mother culture" because its influence seems to have spread west into central Mexico and east into the Maya region. The millennium and a half that ran from about 200 BC to 1300 AD saw the rise and fall of a series of civilizations in Mesoamerica and the Andes, each one building upon the previous one in the region, and some of them featuring impressive empires. In northern Peru, the most notable of these were the **Moche** and the **Sicán**, and to the south, they were the **Nazca**, **Huari**, and (in Bolivia) **Tiahuanaco**. Meanwhile, in Mesoamerica, two great civilizations developed, that of **Teotihuacán** in central Mexico and that of the Classic Maya. The city of Teotihuacán, with over 100,000 inhabitants living over 33 square miles, was in its heyday the largest in the Americas; its political and cultural influence was felt throughout Mesoamerica. The Maya were never controlled by a single empire or city-state, but during their Classic period (250–900 AD) they built a number of powerful kingdoms centered on dozens of large cities across southern Mesoamerica. Classic Maya civilization was one of the most culturally dynamic in human history.

   In the centuries before Europeans arrived, a variety of cultures flourished in Mesoamerica and the Andes, with the Aztec and Inka empires rising more or less simultaneously in the early fifteenth century and dominating central Mexico and the Andes, respectively, by the time of Columbus's first voyage in 1492. In this chapter we look first at how we might understand the variety of cultures in the Americas through a typology of societies; then, we offer a general comparison of Mesoamerican and Andean civilizations, before turning finally to examine the Aztec and Inka empires.

Olmec [OL-mek], Teotihuacán [tay-o-tee-wah-KAHN], Chavín [cha-VEEN], Moche [MOH-cheh], Sicán [see-KAHN], Nazca [NAS-cah], Huari [WAH-ree], Tiahuanaco [tee-ah-wan-AH-ko]   names of places and cultures in Mesoamerica and the Andes

SOCIETIES AND CIVILIZATIONS

By 1492 Native Americans had created an immense quantity and variety of societies and civilizations that can be placed into four categories or types. These are important to our understanding of Native America before the European invasion, but they are also crucial to our understanding of native reactions to the European invasion and to the patterns of Spanish and Portuguese colonial activity.

We have called these four categories *concentrated sedentary*, *segmented sedentary*, *semi-sedentary*, and *non-sedentary*. The first two of these are types of sedentary societies, meaning that the members of these societies were permanently settled in built communities of some kind—villages, towns, and, in some cases, cities. Such communities tended to be located in fertile valleys or on high plateaus, rather than in heavily forested areas. Above all, sedentary societies were sustained through permanent, intensive agriculture. Complex food production not only made cities possible—before its destruction, the 250,000 inhabitants of the Aztec capital of Tenochtitlán made it one of the largest cities in the world— but also resulted in social stratification. In other words, the agricultural activities of the majority allowed a minority to live and work as artisans, merchants, warriors, nobles, and royalty—permitting the development of writing, metallurgy, bureaucracy, and other features of high civilization.

Sedentary societies throughout the world have shown a tendency toward expansion, and this was no less true of the two most densely settled areas of the Americas, Mesoamerica and the Andes. For almost 2,000 years before the European invasion, these two areas witnessed empires rise and fall. The fifteenth-century empires of the Inkas in the Andes (greater Peru) and the Aztecs in Mesoamerica were the latest in these series. There were also some smaller kingdoms in Mesoamerica that exhibited expansionist tendencies and might be classified as incipient or mini-empires, namely, the Tarascans in western Mexico and the **Quiché** Mayas and **Cakchiquel** Mayas in highland Guatemala. Sedentary peoples of Brazil's lower Amazon may have formed incipient empires as well, although less is known about them.

All of these groups comprise our category of *concentrated*—that is, sedentary peoples organized into a large kingdom or empire of some kind. But there were also other groups of sedentary peoples who lived in regions where there were no empires or large kingdoms; we have called these societies *segmented*. The best examples of segmented sedentary societies lay to the north of the Inka Empire—principally the **Muisca**, or Chibcha, of the greater Bogotá region of highland Colombia—and in southern Mesoamerica. These included the Zapotecs, Mixtecs, and other smaller groups to the south of the Aztec Empire, and the Mayas of the Yucatan peninsula as well as smaller Maya groups in Guatemala.

All Maya peoples were fully sedentary. They played a central role in the development of Mesoamerican civilization; for example, Mayas created the most complete of the three Mesoamerican writing systems, one that was still in use in the early sixteenth century. Many Mayas had in previous centuries been

M A P 1.1   Native Americans before 1492

part of larger regional kingdoms, some of which had developed into incipient empires of sorts, centered on such cities as **Tikal** (at Yucatan's southern end) and **Chichén Itzá** (to its north). Seven centuries before Spaniards invaded Maya regions, Tikal had been a spectacular, sprawling center of some 120,000 people. But at the time of the Spanish invasion the Mayas were at the segmented stage of a cycle marked by periods of expansion and centralization followed by periods of political and demographic collapse. In Yucatan, Spaniards encountered two million Mayas divided among two dozen loosely delineated city-states (i.e., segmented societies). To the south of Yucatan, in what is today Chiapas and

Guatemala, there were another two million, divided not only into numerous kingdoms but also into dozens of separate ethnic or linguistic groups. Among them only the Cakchiquel and Quiché Mayas controlled significant territories; in the century before the Spanish invasion, and in competition with each other, the Cakchiquels and Quichés had developed networks of tribute-paying subject towns that were echoes of ancient Maya traditions and that mirrored on a far smaller scale contemporaneous Aztec imperial expansion.

Although most Native Americans at the time of European contact lived in sedentary societies, semi-sedentary peoples covered the greatest geographical area of the Americas. Semi-sedentary societies were sustained only partially by agriculture, with hunting and foraging being equally important to meeting dietary needs. Semi-sedentary peoples lived in settled communities, but these were subject to seasonal movement or to periodic resettlement to areas of fresh land. Consequently, such settlements never achieved the population density of sedentary communities, nor did they contain such stratified societies. Semi-sedentary groups could and did expand—the Caribs, for example, were still moving north from the South American mainland along the chain of Caribbean islands when Columbus reached them in the 1490s. But without the agricultural base and political organization characteristic of sedentary kingdoms, semi-sedentary peoples tended to expand their reach in a mobile way, rather than an imperial one. They absorbed aspects of sedentary societies, sometimes influencing them in turn, rather than incorporating neighboring peoples.

Hundreds of distinct ethnic and language groups of semi-sedentary peoples lived in two great swaths across the Americas. In the north, they occupied much of North America between the Atlantic and the Rockies and between the Hudson's Bay and central Mexico. To the south, semi-sedentary peoples lived throughout the Caribbean islands and down eastern and central South America. Some semi-sedentary groups came close to developing sedentary societies. Northern examples are the Ancestral Pueblo, whose largest urban cluster, Chaco Canyon in present-day New Mexico, contained several thousand inhabitants, and the Mississippian culture centered on Cahokia, whose city and surrounding settlements comprised some 30,000 people. Both cultures peaked in the thirteenth century, and both traded with Mesoamerica, from whose civilization they may have been influenced.

The **Taínos** also appear to have been influenced by Mesoamerica. Dominating the large, northern islands of the Caribbean, the Taínos built towns with central plazas, ball courts (see Image and Word 1.1), and up to several thousand inhabitants. Their diet was based on **manioc** and fish, with maize—the Mesoamerican staple—a secondary food. A comparable diet sustained similar-sized towns built by **Tupis** and other peoples of eastern Brazil and the Amazon River

---

Taíno [ta-EE-no], Quiché [key-CHAY], Cakchiquel [kak-chee-KEL], Tikal [tee-KAHL], Chichén Itzá [chee-CHEN eet-SAH], Muisca [MWEE-skah], Tupi [TOO-pee] places and cultures in Native America

Manioc [MAN-ee-ok] also called cassava; a tuber, similar to a potato, whose root is edible

basin. The first Europeans to travel down the Amazon, Spanish survivors of an expedition from Peru in 1541, saw extensive settlements along the river's banks—evidence of a native population soon after decimated by Old World diseases and yet to recover even today.

In what is today Colombia and Venezuela, the Spanish encountered peoples whose material lives ranged from non-sedentary hunting and gathering to intensive maize farming, complex metallurgy, weaving, and pottery-making. Some groups, such as the Tairona, built stone palaces and temples of considerable size. The Muisca of the high plains around Bogotá also built sizeable temples and traded gold, emeralds, and fine cotton textiles with surrounding peoples. As in Maya country around 1500, warfare was common here, sometimes between complex chiefdoms, sometimes against more mobile hunters inhabiting the ecological fringes. In hot coastal and inter-Andean valleys, non-sedentary and semi-sedentary peoples proliferated, and their frequent belligerence and complex terrain made conquest difficult.

Farther south, forest peoples whom the Inkas had never managed to defeat—such as the Shuar, or Jívaro, of eastern Ecuador and Peru and the Mapuche of Chile—proved still more indomitable. These semi-sedentary cultures sometimes recognized chiefs, but mostly they prized independence of individual warriors and their extended families. Only when faced with outside threats did they join forces. In general, sedentary Andeans such as the Inkas and Muisca felt that these and other neighboring forest, desert, and mountain peoples were barbarians whose dietary and other customs were despicable. Such hostile feelings were mutual.

The Amazon basin, the Orinoco basin to its north, and the rainforests and vast marshes to its south were occupied by a complex mixture of semi-sedentary and non-sedentary, or nomadic, peoples. Farther south, especially in the southern cone of South America, non-sedentary peoples predominated, as they did in the far west and north of North America. Non-sedentary societies can most easily be defined in opposition to sedentary ones: They lacked the trappings of sedentary societies, living in small, itinerant, hunting or fishing bands; they were less sophisticated than sedentary ones, yet they tended to develop complex spiritual beliefs and they survived through a skillful adaptation to local environments.

In coastal Brazil several hundred thousand Tupi speakers subsisted on a rich variety of marine, agricultural, and forest resources. Despite close cultural and linguistic similarities spanning hundreds and even thousands of miles of coastline, the Tupi were constantly at war with one another. Instead of giving rise to an empire, as had happened with the Aztecs and Inkas, the warrior ethic in Brazil led to cultural splintering. When Portuguese and French traders and missionaries encountered the Tupi in the early 1500s, they found themselves quickly drawn into alliances with one group against another.

The location of different settlement types or categories of Native Americans might be imagined, therefore, as ripples on two great ponds. The two points where the stones enter the ponds are the two core areas of sedentary population—Mesoamerica, with about 30 million people at the time of European contact, most of them in central Mexico, and the Andes, with some 15 million people, most within the Inka empire. The first great ripples are those of semi-sedentary peoples, surrounding Mesoamerica to the north (North America), to the east (the Caribbean), and the south (the lower half of Central America), and adjacent to the Andes to the north and east. The second ring of ripples consisted of non-sedentary peoples, who lived primarily in the most interior regions of South America and at the most southern and northern edges of the Americas. All these ripples, the semi-sedentary and nomadic populations of the Americas, comprised roughly another 20 million (making the total Native American population approximately 65 million by the late fifteenth century, similar to that of western and central Europe at that time).

Why were Native Americans so different from each other? Why did some build empires and others live as forest nomads? Were the nomads inferior peoples, as we may be tempted to assume, or were all native peoples simply at different levels of cultural sophistication or "barbarism," as colonial-era Europeans tended to assume? The analogy of the ripples in the pond should not be taken to suggest that civilization emanated out from the Aztec and Inka empires. Nor should Spaniards, Inkas, Taínos, and Tupis be placed on some kind of judgmental spectrum, with one end superior and civilized and the other end inferior and savage.

Instead, the differences between native groups (and between them and Europeans) should be seen in terms of their geographical environment. As with human groups elsewhere in the world, Native Americans created the kinds of societies that their environments best sustained—often resorting to ingenious methods, such as the raised fields or **chinampas** of central Mexico and the terraced slopes of the Andes, to make the environment productive. Archaeologists are finding that there was far more settlement and trade across Amazonia than was previously realized. Still, there was no great empire in northern Mexico or central Brazil because the deserts and rainforests were not conducive to the kinds of permanent, intensive agriculture needed to develop a dense and stratified sedentary population.

This point is important not just to understanding the nature and variety of native cultures in the Americas before European contact but also to understanding the colonial period. For just as the geographical environment determined what kind of societies native peoples constructed, so did the geographical and human environment determine where and how invading Spaniards and Portuguese could build colonies.

MESOAMERICANS AND ANDEANS

In the two main regions of sedentary societies—Mesoamerica and the Andes—two great Native American civilizations developed. We look at them now in more detail by identifying ten characteristics of Mesoamerican civilization, comparing these defining features to those of Andean civilization (see Table 1.1).

Many Mesoamericans lived in cities that featured (1) monumental architecture, in particular pyramids and other large structures facing large, open plazas. These cities also tended to contain (2) ball courts (see Image and Word 1.1), and

---

Chinampa [chee-NAM-pa]   raised fields built by the Nahuas in central Mexico

TABLE 1.1   A comparison of the ten main features of Mesoamerican and Andean civilizations

	Mesoamerica	Andes
(1) Monumental architecture	pyramids with plazas	U-shaped temples
(2) Ball game	widespread and important	nonexistent
(3) Public markets	highly specialized	specialized; some suppressed
(4) Precious market goods	jade, obsidian, cacao	shells, textiles, metal goods
(5) Diet base	maize, squash, beans	potatoes, maize, squash
(6) Landscape seen in	terms of cardinal directions	radial terms
(7) Religion	pantheistic, tied to politics	pantheistic, tied to politics
(8) Sacrificial rituals	of animals; human sacrifice minor except under the Aztecs	animals, rarely humans; offerings to mummies
(9) Planetary knowledge	considerable	considerable
(10) Writing system	complex hieroglyphic writing	*khipus*, but no writing

(3) specialized markets, which operated both at local and regional levels. Such markets featured numerous items, but (4) several had particular cultural and economic importance—jade (used decoratively), obsidian (used decoratively and to create blades for tools and weapons), and **cacao** (the chocolate bean, used both as money, in bean form, and as a highly prized beverage, in liquid form). Equally significant, but as the everyday items that formed the basis of the Mesoamerican diet, were (5) maize (corn), squash, and beans. Of these, maize was the most important; over millennia, Mesoamericans had not only domesticated maize but developed a method of preparing it that released niacin, a crucial vitamin.

The Mesoamerican worldview (6) was oriented toward two principles, that of the cardinal directions and that of duality (whereby everything in the universe formed part of a pair, such as day and night, life and death, supernatural and natural, and male and female; see Image and Word 1.1). These principles were also part of (7) Mesoamerica's complex **pantheistic** religion (a religion of many gods), which included such features as nature deities, deified royal ancestors, and a multitiered heaven and underworld. At times, human communication with the gods involved (8) sacrificial rituals, ranging from the offering of animals to self-sacrificial bloodletting to the ritualized execution of human captives through decapitation or heart removal.

Cacao [ka-KA-oh]   the cocoa bean, used by Mesoamericans as currency and to make chocolate drinks

Pantheism   the belief in and worship of many deities or gods (all Native American religions were pantheistic)

IMAGE AND WORD 1.1   Playing Ball

Werner Forman/Art Resource, NY

When Spaniards invaded in the sixteenth century, Mesoamericans had been playing rubber ballgames for almost three millennia. Ballgames were played across a vast region—from Puerto Rico to Honduras, across Mexico to Arizona. Almost 1,600 ancient ballcourts have been discovered so far. Called *ullamaliztli* (the ballgame) or *tlachtli* (the ballcourt) by the Mexica and other Nahuas, contests were presided over by Xochipilli, god of the ballgame. The game is still played today in northern Mexico, where it is called *ulama*. Cortés was so impressed by the Mexica game, he took a team of ballplayers back to Spain, where they played for Charles V.

The ballgame had profound ritual significance in Mesoamerica; it was as important as ball-playing sports are to modern societies. It was also a cosmic ceremony, with the two teams representing life's great dualities—male and female, night and day, sun and moon.

Players struck rubber balls with their hips and buttocks (and, less commonly, arms and elbows), wearing leather hip-guards; elite players wore more elaborate gear (as in the illustration above, from a classic Maya pot). Courts varied in shape but typically had two stone sides with a vertical hoop on each side (as at Copan, below).

Matthew Restall

Related to religious beliefs, but also to Mesoamerican understandings of agricultural cycles, was (9) a sophisticated knowledge of the celestial bodies and their movements. This formed the basis of a complex permutation calendar that featured a long-count (rather like our years, centuries, and millennia), a 365-day solar year (like our year), and an additional cycle of 260 days. Calendrical knowledge, religious beliefs, and—above all—political and historical records were all written down on materials ranging from fig-bark paper to bone to stone; Mesoamericans had developed (10) a complex hieroglyphic writing system—more accurately, the three related systems of the Aztecs, Mixtecs, and Mayas. These systems were partly pictographic and partly phonetic. The most complete system was that of the Mayas, meaning that the literate Maya minority could express anything they wanted in writing. The sophistication and cultural significance of writing also meant that in the sixteenth century **Nahuas**, Mixtecs, Mayas, and other Mesoamerican groups would easily make the transition to alphabetic writing.

For their part, Andean cities were also carefully planned and oriented, with (1) stone or adobe temples of great size, some of them pyramidal, but often U-shaped. As in Mesoamerica (and unlike ancient Egypt), these enormous monuments served as stages for religious-political drama rather than personal sepulchres for elites—though there were (2) no ball courts.

Andean cities were also (3) places of material exchange and craft specialization. Items traded over great distances included (4) *Spondylus* and other marine shells, salt, fine textiles, and a variety of utilitarian and decorative metal items. Feathers and gold dust from the Amazon were also prized. Andean metallurgy was far more advanced and widespread than that of Mesoamerica; long before the rise of the Inkas one finds arsenical bronze tools, copper currency, and even platinum jewelry.

The Andean diet varied considerably but generally consisted of (5) potatoes and other high-altitude tubers, maize, beans, squash, and capsicum peppers. At lower altitudes manioc, seafood, or freshwater fish were equally important. Guinea pigs, or **cuyes**, and llamas, the only domesticated animal of any size in the Americas, were eaten on special occasions; curiously, llamas were never milked. Tobacco was sometimes employed in ritual healing ceremonies, but from Colombia to Chile, mildly stimulating coca leaves and maize beer were the preferred stimulants. Intensive agriculture entailed complex terraces, long aqueducts, and extensive raised fields.

These human-constructed features in the landscape, along with many natural ones, were—like the ubiquitous ancestor mummies (see Image and Word 1.2)—regarded as deeply sacred. Unlike in Mesoamerica, the Andean worldview tended to conceive of the landscape in (6) radial, rather than strictly cardinal, terms. Surviving temples contain sculptures of fierce, semi-human feline and reptilian creatures, suggesting (7) religious themes still evident in lowland South American shamanism. Religion and politics were not separate concerns, however,

---

Nahua [NAH-wah], Mixtec [MEESH-tek], Maya [MY-ah]   native groups in Mesoamerica; the Mexica (Aztecs) were a Nahua people

Cuy [KWEE]   a guinea pig domesticated and eaten in the Andes

IMAGE AND WORD 1.2   Mountain Mummies

Above left: "First chapter, burial of the Inka Illapa Aia, deceased": the ruling Inka and his wife (standing on the left) make liquid offerings to the mummified corpses of a previous Inka king and queen (on the right, the dead king sitting on a stool, the queen kneeling). An open burial tower is in the background.

Above right: "Burial in Collasuyu": A nobleman and his wife in Collasuyu, part of the Inka Empire, drink corn beer while he also pours some of it as an offering to the mummified sitting corpse of an ancestor. In the background are the bones of older ancestors.

One of the great mysteries of Inka history and culture surrounds the ritual burial or sacrifice of children atop some of the Andes' highest peaks, including the highest mountain in the Western Hemisphere, Aconcagua. Several of these burials were happened upon by mountaineers in the late twentieth century in Argentina, Chile, and Peru. A few intrepid archeologists soon followed, hoping to beat looters to what were clearly some unusually well-preserved sites. What the archeologists found were scattered offerings of well-dressed boys and girls—usually adolescent girls, and usually solitary—interred in simple stone tombs linked to the surface by tubes and openings. The children apparently died of hypothermia or exposure after consuming maize beer, and all were naturally mummified by the extremely dry and cold, high-altitude environment.

Why would the Inkas select children for sacrifice rather than, say, warriors? And why bury them in such forbidding, high-altitude environments? In fact, warrior sacrifices somewhat similar to those found in Mesoamerica were practiced by ancient

(continued)

IMAGE AND WORD 1.2   Mountain Mummies (continued)

Andean peoples such as the Moche, who also built substantial pyramids. More common, however, was mummy worship, an ancient Andean tradition found in both lowlands and highlands. Mummified ancestors, rulers, and shamans were thought to inhabit an intermediary world between the here and the hereafter, and were thus revered for their alleged ability to act as intermediaries for the living in their communications with the spirit world. In Andean cosmology, then, mummified humans were not thought to be entirely dead but rather in a state of suspended animation.

In the case of the child mummies of the southern Andes, a few documentary fragments from just after the Spanish conquest suggest that regional lords subject to the Inkas occasionally gave up their most beloved children to serve as intermediaries between the world of the mountain spirits and the world of the Inka state. Priests from Cuzco oversaw the sequence of rituals that ended following a somber and no doubt exhausting mountain climb. The mountain burials have been linked to the Inkas' highly complex radial system of spatial organization as well as to the older tradition of venerating mummies linked to high-status families, as in the pictures above. Like the many Aztec human sacrifices, the Inkas' live burial of children remains difficult to understand.

---

since Andean temples from the earliest to latest times were clearly the site (like their counterparts in Mesoamerica) of (8) human sacrifice. It is likely, however, that human sacrifice (*ritual execution* or *the making of human offerings* are more accurate and neutral phrases) was practiced on a relatively small scale, with the singular exception of the Aztecs in the last century before the Spanish invasion.

Like Mesoamericans, Andeans gave considerable attention—and mythic weight—to (9) astronomical phenomena. However, Andean peoples appear not to have developed writing systems of the traditional kind, instead employing (10) knotted strings, called **khipus**, to record numbers, lineages, and perhaps historical events.

THE AZTEC AND INKA EMPIRES

As we shall see in the next chapter, the fifteenth century was an era when empires were born on the Iberian Peninsula, a birth that would soon bring Portuguese and Spanish invaders to the Americas. By coincidence, at the same time the two largest empires of the Americas were beginning their expansion. In 1428, the **Mexica** (better known to us as the Aztecs) took control of much of the Valley of Mexico, the key foundational event in the genesis of the Aztec Empire. And in 1438 a Quechua prince seized power and began to turn the Inka kingdom into an empire—the greatest that the Americas had ever seen.

Khipu [KEY-pooh]   knotted strings used by Andeans to record numbers, lineages, and possibly historical events

Mexica [me-SHEE-ka]   popularly called "Aztecs" in modern times; the native group that created the city of Mexico-Tenochtitlán [me-SHEE-ko tenoch-teet-LAHN] and the Aztec Empire

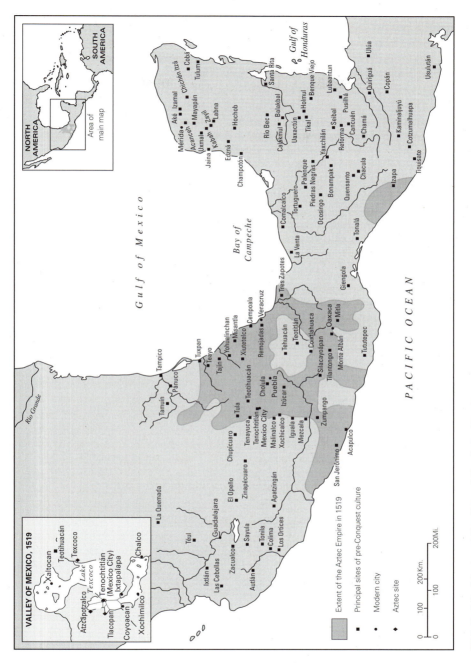

M A P 1.2 Mexico at the time of the Aztec Empire

Like many cultures, the Mexica had turned the history of their ancient semi-sedentary lifestyle and migration into an origin myth, according to which the original nomadic Mexica lived on the shores of a mythical Lake Aztlán (hence the modern name Aztec, which first came into vogue in the eighteenth century). Here they wandered until their patron god **Huitzilopochtli** told them to migrate south and to settle where they saw an eagle with a snake in its mouth alight on a prickly pear cactus (an image preserved today on the Mexican national flag). This omen was sighted in 1325 on an island in Lake Texcoco, where the Aztecs then founded the twin cities of Tlatelolco and Tenochtitlán.

This lake was in the center of the Valley of Mexico (the lake is now covered by Mexico City), where the Aztecs had been living as mercenaries on marginal marsh lands for about a century, according to their own history. After 1325 they continued to sell their military services and to pay tribute to the dominant city-state in the valley, Azcapotzalco, while also slowly building their own network of tribute-paying subject towns and pursuing an aggressive policy of marrying Mexica nobles into the ruling families of the valley.

The turning point in Mexica history came in 1427, when **Itzcoatl** became the fourth Aztec king. The following year he formed an alliance with two lakeside cities, Texcoco and Tlacopan, and led a successful war against **Azcapotzalco**. This was the birth of the Aztec Empire. For the next century, the Aztecs engaged in an aggressive imperial expansion across central Mexico and to its southeast. The Aztec method of imperial rule was not direct; local elites were confirmed in office, providing they were willing to accept client status within the empire. But the Aztecs did require significant tribute payments in the form of labor and a wide variety of goods—from bulk food products to luxury items.

The Aztec ideology of empire was profoundly interwoven with religious ideas and beliefs. The ritual execution of war captives and other carefully chosen victims had been practiced in Mesoamerican societies for thousands of years, but in the fifteenth century the Aztecs appear to have taken human sacrifice to new levels, both in terms of meaning and scale. Huitzilopochtli, the patron god of war and of the imperial capital, was the divine audience for the killing of war captives, who typically had their hearts removed and their heads placed on the skull rack in the plaza of Tenochtitlán. Children were sacrificed to Tlaloc, the rain god, who needed their tears. The temples of the war god and rain god dominated the skyline of the imperial capital (see Image and Word 1.3). The annual sacrifice to Tezcatlipoca was a specially chosen young man who led a life of luxury and privilege for a year before his execution. At some festivals, there was a single victim; at others, there may have been hundreds or even thousands.

Huitzilopochtli [weets-eel-op-OCH-tlee] and Tlaloc [TLAH-lok]   the gods of war and rain, patron gods of the Mexica and their capital city

Azcapotzalco [ass-kah-pot-ZAL-koh], Texcoco [tesh-KOH-koh], Tlacopan [tla-koh-PAN]   cities in the Valley of Mexico

Itzcoatl [eets-koh-ATL]   the Mexica ruler who effectively founded the Aztec Empire

IMAGE AND WORD 1.3 The Imperial Capital of Mexico-Tenochtitlán

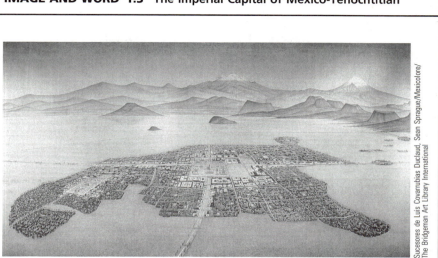

Sucesores de Luis Covarrubias Duclaud, Sean Sprague/Mexicolore/
The Bridgeman Art Library International

The first Europeans to set eyes on the Aztec capital were amazed at its size, setting, and beauty. The conquistador Bernal Díaz wrote that he and his fellow Spaniards were rendered speechless. The twin island cities of Tlatelolco and Tenochtitlán—with their grid of canals, busy streets, and two plazas bounded by pyramids and plazas—seemed to float on the shimmering lake. European cities were cramped and chaotic by comparison. Lake Texcoco, divided by a great dike to keep saltwater from the city and prevent flooding, was covered in canoes; its shores were studded with more cities, each with their own plazas and pyramids. There were about a quarter of a million people living in Tenochtitlán and several million in the whole valley (with the central Mexican population at an estimated 15 million or more).

To visit the city, you approached it either by canoe or along one of the three great causeways that connected it to the lakeshore and held the aqueducts that brought in fresh water. You first passed some of the small raised cornfields called *chinampas* that bordered the lake and city. Then you entered the outer neighborhoods, or *calpulli*, of the capital, which was divided into four quarters, each with eight or more *calpulli*. Closer to the center you reached the palaces where the royal family lived and where imperial administrators worked; one of the palatial compounds included a large zoo. At the heart of the city was the great plaza, dominated by twin pyramids devoted to Huitzilopochtli and Tlaloc.

To a lesser extent, other Nahuas (Nahuatl-speaking peoples of central Mexico) also embraced this culture of ritualized violence. The Tlaxcallans, for example, who had always resisted the Aztec Empire that surrounded their city and its lands, likewise cut out the hearts of prisoners of war. In fact, Tlaxcala and Tenochtitlán had extended this ritual to the battlefield itself, where conventional warfare had been replaced by the Flowery Wars (*xochiyaoyotl*); red blossoms were scattered on the ground to represent the blood of warriors, and selected warriors were then exchanged as captives to be sacrificed. Tlaxcala remained independent, but its life was overshadowed in numerous ways by the existence of Aztec hegemony across central Mexico, breeding generations of resentment that would prove crucial to the outcome of the Spanish invasion.

Tlaxcala was not the only city-state to resist Aztec expansion. To the west of the Mexica imperial capital lay the city of Tzintzuntzan, the center of the Tarascan kingdom, a modest empire in its own right. Lesser kingdoms and cities also resisted the Aztecs, a couple of which became surrounded by the empire's clients, as **Tlaxcala** was. But more often than not, the campaigns of Itzcoatl and the five emperors who followed him further augmented Aztec control—from Moctezuma Ilhuicamina, who succeeded his uncle Itzcoatl in 1440, through three of the first Moctezuma's sons, Axayácatl, Tizoc, and Ahuitzotl. The rulers of tributary cities from throughout the empire, who attended Ahuitzotl's coronation in 1486, "saw that the Aztecs were masters of the world, their empire so wide and abundant that they had conquered all the nations and that all were their vassals. The guests, seeing such wealth and opulence and such authority and power, were filled with terror."

After the reigns of his three sons, the first Moctezuma's grandson and namesake, **Moctezuma Xocoyotl**, became emperor. From 1502 until his murder by Spanish invaders in 1520, he aggressively consolidated his authority and extended the empire of his ancestors. Long after his death, both Spaniards and natives unfairly blamed the second Moctezuma for the destruction of his empire; he became a convenient scapegoat and an easy way of explaining Aztec defeat. In fact, the arrival of Spaniards set loose a chain of events beyond Moctezuma's control, while for the previous 18 years the emperor had been very much in control, increasing the authority and influence of the empire more than any of his predecessors.

At around the same time that the Aztec Empire was being created by Itzcoatl, something similar was being achieved thousands of miles to the south. In 1438, Cusi Yupanqui, a secondary prince in the Inka kingdom, crushed an attempt by the neighboring Chanca kingdom to annex the Inka heartland centered on Cuzco. This victory prompted him to force his father into retirement and seize the throne, or rather, fringed crown, the *maskapaycha*, from its designated heir. Yupanqui also renamed himself **Pachacuti**, meaning Earthquake or World-Changer. The world he changed was the past, which was cast as preparation for Pachacuti's arrival (even the Chanca threat may have been manufactured by Pachacuti as a pretext for his power play); the present, in which his rule was legitimized and the Inka political system reorganized to accommodate the administrative demands of the empire that Pachacuti devoted his reign to building; and the future, which was conceived as a succession of campaigns to bring Inka civilization to all the other Andean peoples. The similarity between what were in effect the Aztec and Inka imperial charters is coincidence; the two empires developed independently and were not aware of each other's existence.

Tlaxcala [tlash-KAH-lah]   central Mexican city-state that resisted conquest by the Mexica

Moctezuma Xocoyotl [mock-teh-ZOO-mah shock-oy-OTL]   aka Moctezuma II or Montezuma, Aztec emperor at the time of the Spanish invasion

Pachacuti [pach-ah-COOT-ee]   Inka ruler who effectively founded the Inka Empire

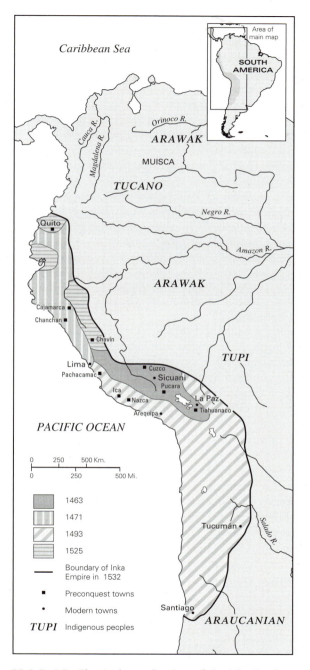

MAP 1.3 The Andes at the time of the Inka Empire

Whereas the Aztec Empire covered a relatively modest 100,000 square miles and included enclaves of unconquered city-states, the Inka Empire covered a vast contiguous region that stretched 2,600 miles from Ecuador to Chile, sandwiched between Amazonia and the Pacific. We call the empire after its ruler ("Inka" was the emperor's title), but it was Quechua peoples based in Cuzco who created the empire, which they called **Tawantinsuyu**, the Land of the Four Quarters.

Like the Aztecs, the Inkas expanded their empire though a combination of military conquest, threats of military action, and alliance building. But whereas the Aztecs emphasized indirect rule and tribute collection, the Inkas constructed a more centralized and direct system of imperial control—one that came closer in structure to the empires of the ancient Mediterranean. There were four characteristics of Inka rule that stand out, none of which have close parallels in the Aztec system. These were (1) the emphasis on extracting labor rather than tribute payment in goods, although both were important. Under the imperial labor system, called the *mit'a* (literally "turn," called this both in ancient and colonial times, for it was preserved under Spanish rule), local farmers worked lands appropriated by the Inka state as well as their own lands, while men took turns serving in the Inka armies and on urban construction sites. There was a labor rotation system in central Mexico, called *coatequitl* (literally "snake-work"), but it was not manipulated at an imperial state level.

The **mita** also provided labor for (2) the building of an extensive 14,000-mile network of royal roads. In form these ranged from wide highways to rope suspension bridges spanning mountain gorges, permitting royal llama herds and relay runners, armies and tribute goods to be moved up and down the empire. The road system, unique in all of the Americas, tied together a chain of warehouses that stored food, textiles, and other goods, all of which supplied armies, fed *mita* workers, and maintained the wealthy Inka elite.

Roads also facilitated (3) the forced migration of entire communities, sometimes temporarily and sometimes across great distances, to meet a particular labor demand or help pacify a frontier or rebellious region. While such communities were encouraged, even required, to maintain their original identities, the Inkas also imposed (4) their own language of **Quechua** throughout the empire as the tongue of imperial trade and administration. The Inkas also used *khipus* to store tribute information and convey messages. The two rulers who succeeded Pachacuti, his son Topa Inka and grandson Huayna Capac, continued the policy of nonstop conquest campaigns. As the empire spread, so did its system of roads, garrisons, warehouses, labor control, and rapid communication through runners and *khipus*.

Tawantinsuyu [tah-wahn-teen-SUE-yoo]   Land of the Four Quarters, the name the Inkas gave to their empire

Mita [MEE-tah] and coatequitl [kwa-tek-EETL]   rotational labor systems in the Andes and central Mexico, respectively

Quechua [KECH-wah]   native language of central Peru, made the language of the empire by the Inkas

IMAGE AND WORD 1.4 How Machu Picchu Became Possible

Dan Breckwoldt/Shutterstock.com

One of the wonders of the world, the ruined Inka city of **Machu Picchu**, sits perched upon a knife-edged ridge high in the Peruvian Andes. Despite crowds of visitors, the site retains a distinct aura of mystery. Machu Picchu was clearly built by the Inkas, as the numerous trapezoidal doors, windows, niches, and other features testify, but what was it for? And why was it built here, amid sheer granite cliffs and cloud forest? When archeologist Hiram Bingham was first led up the mountain from the banks of the Urubamba River in 1911, he surmised that Machu Picchu was actually Vilcabamba, the lost city of Manco Inka and other rebels against Spanish rule. Later excavations of what appeared to be mostly female skeletons suggested something else, a kind of Inka convent or isolated repository of *acllakuna*. These were sacred virgins, or "nuns of the sun." Other evidence seemed to suggest the city was a kind of strategic outpost: part fort, part lookout.

Today these theories have been largely discounted, but we still do not know for certain how or why Machu Picchu came to be. Nevertheless, after years of intensive research on the core features of Inka society, especially religious and political patterns, a more plausible set of explanations has been put forth. A number of early colonial documents have been critical to the project of deciphering the site. Machu Picchu may well have housed *acllakuna*, but it was likely built late in Inka times to commemorate a series of military victories by the emperor Pachacuti. The "city" of Machu Picchu was apparently one of a series of sumptuous and elaborate royal

(continued)

Machu Picchu [MAH-choo PEEK-choo]   royal palace and city built in the high Andes by Pachacuti and his successors

IMAGE AND WORD 1.4   How Machu Picchu Became Possible (continued)

estates, a number of which were built farther up the Urubamba and Vilcanota Rivers, toward the Inka capital of Cuzco, and in neighboring valleys.

Machu Picchu, despite its steep location, may have been planted with coca and maize as well. The site is heavily terraced, supplied with carved stone irrigation works, and is located in a lower, hotter, and wetter ecosystem than that of Cuzco. Production could not have been great, however, given the paucity of farmable surface area, and the estate was probably not even self-sufficient when fully staffed. Significantly, however, coca and maize were both closely linked to Inka religious ritual, and herein lies the key, it seems, to Machu Picchu.

As demonstrated by archeologist Johan Reinhard and others, Machu Picchu fits neatly into the Inkas' sacred Andean landscape. The site, located above a dramatic bend in the Urubamba River, is surrounded by lesser and greater peaks, including two snowcaps over 6,000 meters (c. 20,000 feet) high. The Inkas revered mountains, especially glaciated ones, since they were thought to be linked (as they are) to the seasonal hydrological cycle so critical to agriculture. Celestial patterns, including the path of the sun and movements of the stars, were also deeply imbedded in Inka religious thought. The Milky Way, for example, was conceived of as a sort of heavenly river. From Machu Picchu and adjacent hills, a number of celestial risings and settings could be associated with notches and peaks in the mountainous horizon.

There is other evidence to suggest that Machu Picchu was primarily a religious site. All over the saddle in which Machu Picchu sits and in surrounding hills the Inkas built massive stone temples, often incorporating native outcrops of rock. One temple was floored with sand, evidence of rituals tying the mountains to the sea, a common theme of Inka religion. Other stone outcrops, like the so-called Intihuatana, were carved into geometric shapes, suggesting sites of sacrifice—communication points with deities above and below the earth's surface. Some have interpreted these stones as markers for celestial observation. Caves, considered by many Andeans to be the birthplace of ancestor-deities, were also altered for ritual use, including mummy storage, in and around Machu Picchu.

Machu Picchu was clearly a sacred site, but why was it abandoned? We may never know for sure, but scholars have suggested that its maintenance probably became too costly or onerous following the death of Pachacuti Inka. Perhaps the estate fell into disuse during the succession crisis and civil war that broke out after the death of Huayna Capac. Whatever the case, we are extraordinarily fortunate that Machu Picchu was not looted or otherwise disturbed during colonial or early national times. Today it provides stark and indelible testimony of Inka aesthetics and ingenuity at their peak. From a more Andean point of view, it serves also to remind us that human societies once believed in sacred symbiosis, in living in synchronicity with the motions of earth, water, and sky.

In 1525 **Huayna Capac** was campaigning on the empire's frontier north of Quito—close to the present-day border between Colombia and Ecuador—when he received news of an epidemic sweeping through the empire from the south and

---

Huayna Capac [WHY-nah KAH-pahk]   grandson of Pachacuti; Inka emperor who expanded the empire into what is now Ecuador and died shortly before Spaniards invaded, perhaps from smallpox already ravaging the capital of Cuzco. This was probably the first wave of smallpox to pass across South America, deposited by Europeans as far away as the southern Atlantic coast. Sometime in the late 1520s, Huayna Capac died suddenly. Historians cannot be certain how the Inka died, but it was probably epidemic disease, perhaps smallpox, which claimed both him and shortly afterward his chosen heir—before a single Spaniard set foot in the Inka empire. The throne then fell to two brothers, Atawallpa and Huascar, who agreed to divide the empire between them, an arrangement that disintegrated into civil war within a couple of years. It was this divided empire that the Spaniards discovered in 1532.

One might imagine that the two great empires of the Americas in the early sixteenth century, the Aztecs and the Inkas, would prove to be formidable hurdles to Spanish invaders, while smaller states—from the kingdoms of the Mayas to the tribal bands of the Jívaros and the Tupis—would easily succumb to conquistadors, missionaries, and Iberian settlers. In fact, it was the opposite. While no native states succumbed easily to the invaders, empires fell within a matter of years, and smaller groups, including those that had resisted Aztec or Inka incursions, resisted incorporation into the Spanish or Portuguese empires for decades, if not centuries.

KEEP READING

A fine introduction to this chapter's topic is John E. Kicza, "The Peoples and Civilizations of the Americas Before Contact" (one of the American Historical Association's Essays on Global and Comparative History, 1998; reprinted in *Agricultural and Pastoral Societies in Ancient and Classical History,* edited by Michael Adas, 2001, and incorporated into Kicza's *Resilient Cultures: America's Native Peoples Confront European Civilization, 1500–1800,* 2003). Students may also find Charles C. Mann's *1491: New Revelations of the Americas Before Columbus* (2005) useful.

Scholarly but accessible textbooks on specific civilizations are Michael D. Coe, *Mexico* and *The Maya* (regularly updated with new editions); David Webster, *The Fall of the Ancient Maya: Solving the Mystery of the Maya Collapse* (2002); and for South America, Karen Olsen Bruhns, *Ancient South America* (1994), Michael Moseley, *The Incas and their Ancestors* (2003), and Terrence D'Altroy, *The Incas* (2002).

More basic, image-heavy textbooks are Serge Gruzinski, *The Aztecs: Rise and Fall of an Empire* (1992) and Carmen Bernand, *The Incas: People of the Sun* (1994).

2

✷

An Emerging Atlantic World

The Rise of Empires in West Africa

Atlantic Africans in the Age before Columbus

Portugal and Castile in the Age before Columbus

The Dawn of the Atlantic World

Disease, Demographic Disaster, and the Trade in African Slaves

H istorians estimate that the continent of Africa was home to over 100 million people around 1492, the year of Columbus's famous first voyage across the Atlantic. Some 50 million people inhabited West and West Central Africa, the primary regions from which slaves were taken to Europe and the Americas. Western, or "Atlantic" Africa thus had about the same population as that of the Americas or Europe in the late fifteenth century. Over 2,000 languages were spoken throughout the continent, most of them derived from four major roots (**Afroasiatic, Nilo-Saharan, Khoisan, and Niger-Congo**; almost all Africans brought to the Americas spoke a Niger-Congo language). In the three and a half centuries after 1492, more Africans would cross the Atlantic to colonize the Americas than Europeans by a factor of at least four to one. More than half of all those enslaved were transported to regions we now call Latin America.

The collision of cultures that created the Atlantic World is often character-ized as a meeting of Europeans and Native Americans, with Africans as an after-thought. But Iberians reached West Africa decades before they sailed to the Caribbean, and Africans played a central role in the emergence of a unified Atlantic system of production and trade. This chapter paints brief portraits of the peoples, states, and nascent empires of western Africa and of the Iberian

---

Afroasiatic, Nilo-Saharan, Khoisan, and Niger-Congo   Africa's four language families

25

TIMELINE	
650–1600	Era of sub-Saharan slave trade
seventh century	Islam begins its spread into sub-Saharan Africa
711	Muslims from North Africa invade Iberia
850–1250	Main Muslim-Christian wars of the Reconquista
1100–1500	West Africa's late medieval dry period; rise of Mali and Songhay empires
1179	Portugal becomes an independent Christian kingdom
1420s on	Portuguese explore and settle Madeira, the Azores, and other Atlantic islands and establish tradings posts on the West African coast
1479	Isabella, queen of Castile, marries Ferdinand, king of Aragon
1441–1870	Era of transatlantic slave trade
1488	Portuguese (led by Bartolomeu Dias) round the Cape of Good Hope at the foot of Africa
1492	Columbus reaches the Caribbean; Granada, the last Muslim kingdom in Iberia, is conquered; Jews expelled from Spain; Spain consolidates its control over the Canary Islands
1493–1498	First European settlement in the Caribbean, La Isabella on Hispaniola
1500	Portuguese discover Brazil
1506–1543	Reign of Afonso I, the first Kongo king to convert to Catholicism
1571 on	Increased Portuguese military presence and support of pro-Portuguese regimes in West Central African kingdoms
1591	Moroccan forces capture Songhay cities of Gao and Timbuktu

Peninsula in the centuries before Columbus—paying particular attention to the fifteenth century. We then turn to the tale of the early Atlantic crossings and the first efforts at Spanish colonization in the Caribbean. The chapter closes with a look at the birth of the Atlantic Slave Trade.

THE RISE OF EMPIRES IN WEST AFRICA

What geographers call West Africa (the northern portion of our "Atlantic Africa") counted a few imperial states, along with a vast number of settled agricultural and equestrian warrior chiefdoms around 1500. As in the Americas, and for that matter, Europe, conflict was common throughout western Africa prior to the arrival of Europeans. Far-flung tributary empires such as Ghana and Mali, for example, rose and fell independently of outside forces. Like their imperial contemporaries in the

Americas, the Mexica and the Inkas, both proved vulnerable to uprisings and intrigues instigated by conquered enemies. Also like their American counterparts, none of these states developed programs of overseas trade or expansion despite access to sailing technologies.

African states made war on each other for various reasons, but control of resources, riverine and overland trade routes, and people were the main causes. Despite the importance of Islam, the spread of religion appears not to have been a main driver of warfare in West Africa between 1500 and about 1800. The arrival of European traders on the Atlantic coast after 1440 tended to exacerbate internal conflicts over resources such as gold and copper, and the resulting increase in warfare produced a growing stream of captives to be traded away as slaves.

The dynamic kingdoms of Mali and Songhay emerged on the banks of the middle and upper Niger River between the thirteenth and sixteenth centuries. Both kingdoms relied on the Saharan caravan trade to link them to the Mediterranean world, initially focused on Mamluk Egypt. The rulers of Mali and Songhay were devout Muslims, and it is possible that their initial power derived from protection of long-distance Muslim traders. The emperors themselves, however, came from local chiefly dynasties – all of them renowned war heroes. One, **Mansa Musa** (*mansa* meaning "conqueror") of Mali, made the pilgrimage to Mecca in 1325. Musa's distribution of gold during a stop in Cairo was so generous that it became legendary (see Image and Word 2.1).

West African gold, collected from the sands and gravels of the headwaters of the Senegal, Gambia, and Niger Rivers soon drew the attention not only of Muslim traders and monarchs, but also Christian European ones. Traditionally, West Africa's scattered gold mines were worked by subordinate farming peoples in the off-season. Some miners had been enslaved due to regional wars, and beginning in the late fifteenth century, Portuguese traders in present-day Ghana traded slaves brought from elsewhere for West Africa's gold. Throughout West Africa, control of human beings was always more prestigious than control of land, livestock, or any other form of property.

West African states in this period were, loosely speaking, confederations—dozens of paramount chiefs or petty kings owed their power, wealth, and sustenance to numerous tributaries and captive laborers. In general, as in many parts of the precontact Americas, precolonial West African politics were dominated by charismatic and intelligent warrior-princes. There were few bureaucrats and judges. As in the cases of Mali and Songhay, a common means of extending authority, another practice found in the Americas, was by offering to protect vulnerable traders, as well as segmented or concentrated agricultural groups, from semi-sedentary or non-sedentary raiders.

From Western Sudan to Lower Guinea, a different political model predominated: fortified towns, plus some city-states, all headed by chiefs and petty kings. Archeologists are still deciphering traces of these often huge, walled enclosures,

---

Mansa Musa [MAN-sah MOO-sah]   emperor of Mali, made famous pilgrimage to Mecca in 1325

some of which housed thousands of inhabitants. Several of these walled cities were quite similar to their neighbors in terms of subsistence patterns, language, and culture, but most fought with each other as often as they cooperated. Enslavement of war captives was common. These features of competitiveness and chronic captive-taking would play a profound role in shaping relations with European traders. As in the case of Mesoamerica, it is not useful to refer to these units as tribes. They were simply too complex, and too stratified; the best analogy, though also inadequate, is late medieval European city-states.

IMAGE AND WORD 2.1   **Epic Scenes from an African Empire**

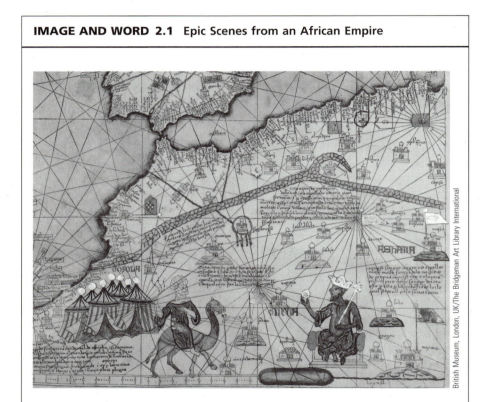

British Museum, London, UK/The Bridgeman Art Library International

In this 1375 Catalan map (above), an Arab merchant on a camel rides to meet Mansa Musa, emperor of Mali, who holds out a huge gold nugget, as if inviting traders to come and barter in his legendary capital city. Malinese emperors, such as Musa or Sunjata, received visitors on thrones such as the one pictured in the map—but beneath an arch of elephant tusks, surrounded by a vast retinue that included the official spokesman, executioner, cavalry officers, musicians, and women of the court.

Although Mali's rulers had coverted to Islam in the eleventh century, by Mansa Musa's day women were no longer veiled. Arab visitors were shocked by this and surprised by the prominent role played by high-ranking women in Malinese politics and society. This is also illustrated in the great epic Malinese tale, the *Sunjata*. In the scene quoted below, Sogolon, mother of the legendary emperor Sunjata, prepares for marriage to King Naré Maghan. Throughout the *Sunjata*, women, characterized as both good and evil, exert extraordinary influence over affairs of state, particularly matters of succession. Sogolon, a hunchback called derisively "Buffalo Woman," manages not only to marry a handsome king but also to outwit any number of scheming rivals. In the end it is she alone who ensures that her son, Sunjata, fulfills his destiny as supreme ruler of Mali. He would go on to conquer in her name.

> The royal drums of Nianiba announced the festivity at crack of dawn. The town awoke to the sound of tam-tams which answered each other from one district to another; from the midst of the crowds arose the voices of griots singing the praises of Naré Maghan.
> At the home of the king's old aunt, the hairdresser of Nianiba was plaiting Sogolon Kedjou's hair. As she lay on her mat, her head resting on the hairdresser's legs, she wept softly, while the king's sisters came to chaff her, as was the custom.
> "This is your last day of freedom; from now onwards you will be our woman."
> "Say farewell to your youth," added another.
> "You won't dance in the square any more and have yourself admired by the boys," added a third.
> Sogolon never uttered a word and from time to time the old hairdresser said, "There, there, stop crying. It's a new life beginning, you know, more beautiful than you think. You will be a mother and you will know the joy of being a queen surrounded by your children. Come now, daughter, don't listen to the gibes of your sisters-in-law." In front of the house the poetess who belonged to the king's sisters chanted the name of the young bride.

As Iberians were opening up the Atlantic, a new empire arose in West Africa. The Songhay Empire, centered at **Gao** (east of Timbuktu), won greatest renown under Sonni Ali (1464–1492). Like the *mansas* of Mali, or the Inka Pachacuti, Sonni Ali was a conqueror. He deployed highly trained companies of equestrian lancers, plus huge numbers of boatmen to dominate both the Niger River and vast swaths of inland territory. At his height, Sonni Ali claimed an unprecedented expanse of Sudanic West Africa. Had he had access to modern technologies, his empire would no doubt have grown larger.

Sonni Ali's successors did not share his ambitions or talent for conquest, and as the Aztecs and Inkas had learned, managing large empires was often much harder than winning them. Eventually, also like the Aztecs and Inkas, Songhay fell quickly and unexpectedly to a small number of intrepid conquerors arriving from far away. Fresh from their defeat of the Portuguese king, Sebastian (who had made a foolish foray into northern Africa in hopes of boosting his crusader credentials), Moroccans under Sultan Mawlay Ahmad began raiding south across the vast Sahara in 1578. After an extraordinary crossing of the desert, the Moroccans, aided by a number of Spanish Moriscos trained to use state-of-the-art firearms, they captured the cities of Gao and Timbuktu in 1591. Songhay's conquistadors took home

Gao [GOW] and Timbuktu [tim-buck-TOO]   major cities of the Mali and Songhay empires

vast amounts of gold and a number of slaves, but the Sahara proved too formidable a barrier, and they ultimately failed to hold on to their new colony.

South of the equator lay the Congo, or Zaire, River basin, the world's largest freshwater catchment area after South America's Amazon. The coast grew steadily drier heading south to Angola, terminating in the formidable deserts of Namibia. Human settlement in the greater Congo region, mostly along riverbanks and coast, and around the margins of the rain forest, was ancient and highly diverse in terms of adaptation. Most West Central Africans spoke derivations of Western Bantu, and Islam was known but remained marginal. West Central Africans lived in kin-based villages, a small minority of them subordinate to paramount chiefs or petty kings. We know of no overarching empires comparable to those of West Africa, but it appears that the region stretching from modern Cameroon to southern Angola was characterized by a cultural coherence similar to that of Mesoamerica.

Of key importance for later Latin American history was the rise of Kongo, a modest kingdom misnamed by the Portuguese after the title of its warlords, the *manikongos*. The **manikongos** came to power in part by monopolizing copper deposits. By the time the Portuguese arrived in the 1480s, Kongo's kings ruled an area stretching from the right bank of the Zaire River south and east some 300 kilometers. They received tribute, and took slaves, from a large number of subordinate villages. Several outlying kingdoms located to the north and east resented Kongo's power, and began to challenge it in the sixteenth century. Some of these rivals had been victims of Kongo slave-raiding. Beginning in the 1480s, enslaved West Central Africans began to make up an increasing portion of all slaves traded by sea.

ATLANTIC AFRICANS IN THE AGE BEFORE COLUMBUS

West Africans and West Central Africans in the centuries before 1492 faced a variety of challenges and opportunities. Two major proponents of change in West Africa, particularly, were the expansion of Islam and a long dry period lasting from roughly 1100 to 1500. Even where Islam was dominant, local religious notions survived. Even non-Muslim West Africans believed in a creator-god, but this god was not easily appeased. Everyday ritual thus tended to emphasize communication with more accessible ancestor spirits. These spirits were thought to aid against a host of other, potentially evil forces. As in many Native American religions, animal and plant spirits were also considered potent. Snake spirits were sought by ironsmiths, for example.

West African *génies*, like Andean huacas, often included features in the landscape: boulders, springs, rivers, lakes, and groves. Peoples living along the southern margins of the savanna, or open grasslands, were especially reverent

---

Manikongo [mah-nee-KONG-go]   warlord and ruler in the Kongo kingdom

toward groves of sacred trees. They frequently built villages alongside patches of old-growth forest. Tree spirits were encouraged through animal sacrifice.

Over time, agricultural communities adopted wandering craft specialists and bards. The presence of these "strangers" caused local patterns of behavior and language to change. The dry period (ca. 1100–1500) prodded Mande-speaking smiths and others to migrate southward, where they introduced secret societies and other special groupings that scholars call "power associations." When men and women joined such power associations, they were expected to undergo complex, multistage initiation rites. Once in, they were required to follow strict rules. One function of these secret societies, most of them governed by masked (i.e., symbolically anonymous) elders, was to diffuse clan rivalries.

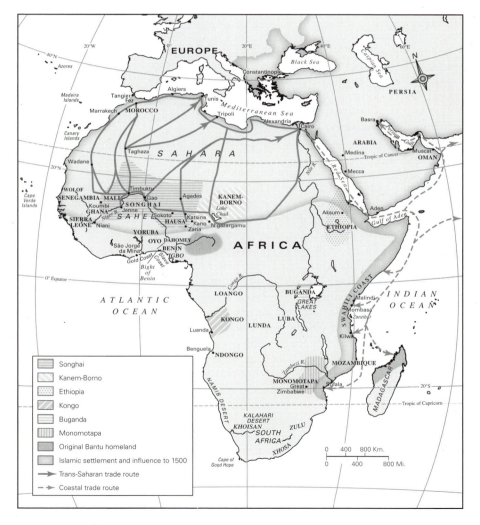

M A P 2.1 Africa in 1492

Long-distance traders and warriors introduced Islam to many parts of Africa after the seventh century AD. The religion became dominant mostly in the north, from about 10° N latitude northward, and along the rim of the Indian Ocean where Swahili traders engaged in overseas trade. Small Christian and Jewish communities carried on in isolated pockets in the northeastern Horn and Maghreb, or Mediterranean coast, but they did not engage in wars of expansion. One factor motivating Portuguese exploration was the belief in a lost Christian king known as Prester John, whom they imagined would serve as a key ally against Islam throughout Africa. Ethiopian Christians did not choose to play this role.

In the arid north where Islam predominated, African beasts of burden included dromedaries, donkeys, and horses. Cattle were also kept in the interior highlands and far south, but in most of tropical Africa, large livestock were impossible to raise due to the deadly tsetse fly. The tsetse fly severely limited horse breeding south of the Sahara, and partly as a result, Arabian, or Barbary, war horses were greatly prized by chiefs and kings hoping to expand their realms. One of the most popular and lucrative items imported by the early Portuguese in Africa were horses. Other domestic animals included goats, swine, guinea fowl, sheep, and dogs. In general, **animal husbandry**, as in Europe, was far more developed in precolonial Africa than in the Americas.

Sub-Saharan Africa differed from the Americas, and indeed from the rest of the world, in terms of its highly challenging human disease environment. A variety of infections and parasites afflicted Atlantic Africans due in part to the lowland tropical environment. Chief among these was malaria. Malaria is believed to have originated in Africa in part because of human co-evolution with the tsetse fly. Lacking domesticated livestock hosts in regions where the fly was common, malaria-carrying mosquitoes turned instead to humans for their blood meals. Repeatedly infected, over time, most sub-Saharan Africans developed total immunity to the *vivax* form of malaria, but only partial immunity to the more deadly, *falciparum* variety. The falciparum variety remained a major killer of African children. Though unwittingly introduced by the slave trade, malaria was not as quick to take root in the tropical Americas as smallpox, measles, and other Old World ailments. Once it did, however, densely populated lowland regions proved deadly to all but the most immune Africans and their descendants.

African mining and metalsmithing were also quite advanced by most pre-Columbian American standards. In West and West Central Africa, copper metallurgy was highly developed by 1500, and many fine works in copper, bronze, and brass have survived as testament to this technical sophistication. Goldsmithing was similarly sophisticated, though less widespread. Unlike the more common but still highly prized copper, Africa's gold was steadily drawn away into long-distance trade networks, first linking the continent to the Mediterranean Sea and Indian Ocean and later to the Atlantic world.

Animal husbandry   farming of domesticated animals

The major technical contrast between Atlantic Africa and the Americas was in the use of iron. Whereas no known native American culture harnessed iron technology prior to European arrival, in western Africa, whether in Mali or Angola (a name derived from *ngola*, or "smith"), iron workers abounded. Blacksmiths were not simply artisans but also semi-religious figures and even kings. In fact, throughout sub-Saharan Africa, metal forging was a secretive and mystical process similar to alchemy. Despite their secrecy, African metalsmiths produced extraordinary quantities of tools, ornaments, and lasting works of art.

Craft specialization in part spurred Africa's internal trade, some of it carried out over vast distances, but most commerce consisted of bartering for basic commodities. The salt trade, for example, as in the Andes and Amazon before 1492, in most places consisted of trading goods in kind directly for a dietary necessity rather than a formal, commercial business. Tools were similarly traded directly for food, textiles, and livestock, but bits of gold, copper, and iron sometimes served as currency. In some areas cowry and other seashells, rather like Mesoamerica's cacao beans, functioned similarly as money. As the slave trade grew, so did the monetization of Atlantic Africa, partly in gold, but mostly in shell, copper, and bronze currencies not valued by Europeans.

Trade ties between African societies sometimes led to political ties, and in a few cases the desire to expand or protect trade stimulated chiefs and kings to form lasting confederations. Yet competition usually prevailed over cooperation; alliances were usually a product of necessity. Ecological stresses such as droughts most often spurred new confederations—along with outbreaks of war. Many captives drawn into the transatlantic slave trade were double or even triple victims—first of droughts or floods, then of war, and finally of the dehumanizing machinery of the slave trade itself.

In the absence of large livestock, most Atlantic Africans were **hoe-agriculturalists**. Key crops were millet, rice, and sorghum, plus yams and bananas in certain areas. Where rainfall was too high to grow staple crops, Africans hunted game, collected medicinal plants, and harvested other products. Wherever they lived, Atlantic Africans, like Europeans and Asians, embraced a host of Native American crops after 1492. Maize became critical throughout Central Africa, in particular, along with cassava (manioc), peanuts, chili peppers, beans, squash, and tobacco. Although well suited to much of Atlantic Africa's lowland tropical environment, manioc was difficult to prepare and added tremendously to women's daily workloads.

PORTUGAL AND CASTILE IN THE AGE
BEFORE COLUMBUS

In 1492, the year of the death of the great Songhay emperor Sonni Ali, there was as yet no Spanish Empire. As a political entity, Spain barely existed. The

---

Hoe-agriculturalists   farmers dependent on metal-tipped hoes for tilling the soil

Iberian Peninsula had not been under the control of a single political authority since Roman times (218 BC to the 470s), having been invaded a millennium before Isabella and Ferdinand's day by Visigoths from northern Europe. An unstable Visigothic kingdom was overrun by Muslims (specifically Arabs and Berbers) crossing from North Africa in 711 AD, but the Islamic invaders did not long remain united or able to control the whole peninsula. For the next eight centuries, the political map of Iberia was an ever-shifting patchwork of Christian and Muslim kingdoms. Iberians of both religions mostly lived and traded in peace with each other and with the substantial Jewish community, but warfare periodically broke out, and between 850 and 1250 those wars saw the gradual southward push of a Christian-Muslim border. By 1250 Portugal had more or less assumed its present-day limits, having come into existence as an independent Christian kingdom in 1179. Castile's acquisition of Seville just before 1250 left Granada as the sole Islamic kingdom in Iberia.

Once a small landlocked kingdom in the center of the peninsula, Castile emerged in the medieval period as a militaristic new Iberian state. Kingdoms

M A P 2.2   Iberia in the Age of the Reconquista, 711–1492

with long Atlantic or Mediterranean coastlines, such as Portugal, Granada, and Aragon, looked outward; Aragon had a modest empire in the Mediterranean, and Portuguese interest in Africa and the Atlantic led in part to Columbus's voyages. Meanwhile, Castile was developing an aggressive political attitude of intolerance and expansion—one that would eventually evolve into a philosophy of imperialism. Castile's rise was a violent one marked by a pattern common to empires small and large: Castilians who entered into the service of the king and fought for him with success were rewarded with seized territories and booty, lordship over—or even ownership of—conquered peoples, and social elevation. These new lands then became the staging ground for further expansion, as other Castilians sought to march down the only real avenue of social and economic opportunity. The religious dimension of increased intolerance was symbolized by the Holy Office, or the Inquisition, directed against Jews and Muslims in Iberia and later used as an instrument of religious and social control in the Americas.

The process, as just described, does not sound noble. But Castilians and other Christian Iberians developed a framework for this expansion that gave it the most noble purpose imaginable; they viewed it as a Christian crusade to rid Iberian lands of infidels, a crusade they dubbed the Reconquest—**la Reconquista**. The Reconquest, as a way of looking at Iberian history, allowed the past to be reconstructed as a crusade led by Christian heroes and featuring Muslim villains. The best known of these heroes was **El Cid**. Rodrigo Díaz fought for both Muslim and Christian kings, winning the nickname *al-sayyid*, Arabic for "the master." El Cid's modest origins and mercenary career were disguised by his popular image as a bold and romantic nobleman of epic military prowess. Sixteenth-century conquistadors would consciously seek to emulate him, and Cortés's official biographer drew the inevitable comparison, just as Spanish kings would for centuries be the El Cids of their own eulogies.

That the El Cid remembered in the fifteenth century and later was as much a mythical as a historical figure matters less than the fact that Castile had created his legend—and put it to the service of an expansionism that made it by far the largest Iberian kingdom by 1479. In that year Isabella took control of Castile, and Ferdinand, whom she had married a decade earlier, became king of Aragon. The two kingdoms remained separate partners, but Castile was the dominant one, especially after the conquest of the last Muslim kingdom, Granada, in 1492. With the acquisition of Granada's half a million people (thousands of whom were immediately enslaved), Castile's population leapt to five million, in contrast to the roughly one million each in Aragon and Portugal (the 200,000 inhabitants of the remaining northern kingdom of Navarre would fall under Castilian control in 1512).

Thus in 1492 Iberia primarily consisted of two kingdoms, the larger Castile and the smaller Portugal. With Castile an increasingly powerful kingdom across the mountains to its east, Portugal had by the fifteenth century become an Atlantic

---

la Reconquista [reh-kon–KEY-stah]   the Reconquest; the sporadic conflicts between Christian and Muslim kingdoms in Iberia, 711–1492

El Cid   Castilian hero of the Reconquest celebrated in epic poetry

state; it spent that century developing an oceanic trade that ran from the Baltic through Lisbon and down into the Mediterranean and along the Atlantic shores of Africa. Portuguese expeditions had traveled 1,500 miles down the African coast by the death in 1460 of Prince Henry the Navigator (b. 1394), whose patronage of research and development in shipping and exploration was matched only by his crusading zeal (he was also titled Grand Master of the Order of Christ)—and later rivaled only by that of John II. In John's reign (1481–1495) the Cape of Good Hope was rounded and a sea route to Asia pioneered.

Castile became involved too in Atlantic expansion, even going to war with Portugal over islands west of Morocco, but the Castilians continued to play a catch-up game during the fifteenth century—as symbolized by Isabella's willingness to support the desperate and misguided Columbus. Castile's recent experience was thus more with territorial expansion and consolidation, Portugal's more with exploration and economic expansion at sea.

Yet despite these differences, the two kingdoms had much in common. Although Castile is usually seen as the principal moving force behind the breakdown of relative religious tolerance, sometimes called **convivencia**, Portugal was a Reconquista kingdom, too, and also participated in Iberia's great anti-Semitic century that began with the massacres of Jews in 1391 and culminated in the final expulsion of all Jews from both kingdoms in the 1490s. John II of Portugal permitted tens of thousands of Jews expelled from Castile in 1492 to migrate to his kingdom, on payment of a special tax, but five years later King Manuel I (John's successor) forced all Jews in the kingdom to convert or leave. That same year Manuel expelled all Muslims that were not slaves, and in 1502 Isabella and Ferdinand followed suit, imposing the choice of conversion to Christianity or exile and loss of property.

Roman Catholicism took on a nationalistic character toward the end of the Reconquest, and as such it required a symbol more venerable than El Cid. The choice was St. James, or Santiago, known as the Moor-slayer. The apostle James was allegedly buried in the Galician town of Santiago de Compostela, and in the medieval period the town grew to be one of Europe's most visited pilgrimage sites. "Santiago!" was to be the battle cry of the conquistadors in the Americas, and many churches would be adorned with paintings and carvings in wood and stone of the mounted saint, beneath his rearing horse a half-dozen decapitated, turbaned heads. Castilian religious jingoism was never subtle.

The Reconquista and the expulsion of the Jews have fed an Iberian stereotype that make it hard to imagine that Castile and Portugal also participated in the Renaissance, but humanist ideas did indeed spread to both kingdoms in the fifteenth century and helped to stimulate a florescence in the written and visual arts. Although the Renaissance in Iberia was rooted in local culture and history, the legacy of *convivencia* connected Iberians to ancient Rome and Greece in unique ways. For example, Christian and Muslim scholars worked together to translate and interpret ancient Greek texts that had been preserved in Arabic.

Convivencia [kon-vee-VEN-see-ah]   religious tolerance or the peaceful coexistence of Christians, Muslims, and Jews in medieval Iberia

King Alfonso X of Castile created a school of translators in Toledo; the epitaph on the tomb of his father, Ferdinand II, who died in 1252, was written in Castilian Spanish, Latin, Hebrew, and Arabic.

Iberians placed great emphasis on city living. One of the first things Hernando Cortés did on landing on the shores of the Gulf of Mexico was to found a city. This was typical of sixteenth-century Iberian practice. Castilians in particular, who had lived through many centuries of sporadic warfare and whose original territories were the driest in the peninsula, valued urban residence over living in the villages and hamlets that dotted the countryside. Spanish historian Juan Pablo Mártir Rizo (1593–1642) wrote in the seventeenth century that Castile was "a kingdom made of cities," a remark equally applicable to late medieval times.

Iberian cities were not large—only four, Lisbon, Toledo, Seville, and Granada, had over 30,000 inhabitants by 1492—but their identity as cities was firmly established. Barcelona, though modest in size, had many of the characteristics of a city-state, sending its own ambassador, with entourage, to the court. Burgos, a town rich in merchants, had fewer than 5,000 people at the end of the fifteenth century. Most towns held between 1,000 and 2,000 inhabitants.

But as small as such cities and towns were, they viewed themselves in distinctly urban terms and contained most of the Iberian population—even those whose lives tied them to the land. Aristocrats with great estates and rural day laborers alike tended to maintain their homes in town. Formal municipal status was jealously guarded; it meant a certain amount of political independence and the right to farm regional taxes. The monarchy often sought to limit such rights, often by playing town councils and local nobles against each other (as in the cases of Burgos and Segovia). The strategy worked well for the monarchy, especially prior to 1500, although Castile and Portugal were not entirely spared the kinds of major conflicts with the nobility that tested monarchs elsewhere in Europe.

Alliances between nobility and monarchy were less beneficial to the Iberian masses. In 1500, less than 3% of the population owned 95% of the land. Castilian and Portuguese peasants, who comprised 80% of the population, were no longer serfs in the strict sense of being forced to live and work in a particular district. But Castile and Portugal suffered from a scarcity of arable land. Burdened by rents, church tithes, and taxes, Iberian peasants also had to contend with the **Mesta**, the sheep raisers' guild that enjoyed extraordinary territorial privileges and royal support due to the tax revenues from sheep farming and wool exports. By the time of Ferdinand and Isabella's marriage in 1469, the Mesta's flocks had grown to over 3 million head of sheep.

Better off were another 10% of Iberians who were also commoners but who worked as artisans or professionals of some kind. Vibrant medieval port cities such as Lisbon, Bilbao, Valencia, and Barcelona supported a wide range of craftsmen, many of whom organized themselves into powerful guilds. As was typical of all Iberians, but especially of those who enjoyed some kind of opportunity, commoner professionals sought to live and work in the city. Craft shops initially relied on young, uncompensated apprentices and hired journeymen—or

---

La Mesta   the Castilian sheep farmers' guild

day-workers—for labor, but with the economic revival that followed the Black Death, some master craftsmen grew wealthy enough to purchase slaves.

Slave trade growth in the fifteenth century meant that Iberian city-dwellers became part of an increasingly multiracial society. For even as Muslims and Jews were being persecuted and religious homogeneity imposed by force, the age-old Iberian practice of enslaving one's enemies was taking on a new dimension. Beginning in 1441, the Portuguese imported black slaves directly from West Africa—more than 35,000 of them by century's end, when black slaves had become a modest presence in numerous Castilian cities, too, and Seville and Valencia had thriving slave markets and significant African populations. In subsequent centuries Iberians would thus take with them to the New World the idea that an elite urban household was made complete by African slaves, and a fully developed city featured an enslaved black underclass.

The growing participation of Africans in Iberian societies was important not only to urban development in Spain and Portugal in the fifteenth century; it provided a crucial impetus for Iberian expansion into the Atlantic. Arguably, the quest for direct access to West African slaves led directly to the Iberian discovery of the Americas.

THE DAWN OF THE ATLANTIC WORLD

The kingdoms of the Iberian Peninsula underwent a gradual but profound transformation in the fifteenth century, at the same time bringing changes to an ever-widening Atlantic world. If Iberian expansion seemed destined to reach the Americas by the end of the fifteenth century, it was by no means predictable that Columbus would lead the first voyage that crossed the Atlantic in 1492, returning to Spain in 1493. Because Columbus made all four of his trans-Atlantic voyages under license from the Spanish monarchs, we might expect him to have been from one of the Spanish kingdoms. In fact, his real name was Cristofero Colombo, from the Italian city-state of Genoa, and he spent most of his early career as a navigator in Lisbon.

During the half-century or so before Columbus's voyages, Lisbon became the launch board of Atlantic exploration. The Portuguese explored and settled islands in the Atlantic Ocean and founded fortified trading posts or **feitorias** on the West African coast. By the 1420s, hundreds of settlers were farming the uninhabited Azores and **Madeira** islands. Portuguese peasants migrated to the Azores to grow wheat for the mother country, while slaves taken on the nearby Canary Islands and parts of northwest Africa worked the early plantations of Madeira. By 1450, Madeira's slave-produced sugar was sold in London and other northern European markets at great profit.

Feitoria [fay-toh-REE-ah]   Portuguese permanent trading post

Madeira [ma-DEER-ah], Azores [ah-SORE-eesh]   Atlantic islands conquered by the Portuguese

By the time of Prince Henry the Navigator's death, the Portuguese had colonized the Cape Verde Islands off West Africa and were actively trading for gold and slaves in Senegambia. By 1471 the Portuguese reached what they called the Gold Coast, and in 1482 a *feitoria* was established in present-day Ghana. São Jorge da Mina, or "St. George's mine," would serve for over a century as Portugal's major West African gold and slaving fort. The Portuguese also claimed equatorial islands such as Príncipe and São Tomé, where captives brought from the African mainland grew sugar. By 1478, Madeira and the Canaries were producing more sugar than any other plantation site in the Western world, but tropical São Tomé soon replaced them, and served as the model for later plantation development in the Americas. By 1485, the Portuguese had reached Congo. In 1487 the Pope issued an "expansion bull" sanctioning the Portuguese initiative in the Atlantic and the genesis of the Portuguese Empire. The next year the Cape of Good Hope was rounded and the discovery of a sea route to the lucrative spice islands of Southeast Asia seemed inevitable.

Given its limited resources, rugged terrain, and small population (a million in Henry the Navigator's day), Portugal's extraordinary rise to prominence in the fifteenth century appears almost miraculous. How was it achieved? To borrow the real-estate agent's mantra: location. Most capital was accumulated in trade rather than feudal estates, with exports of wine, salt, and olive oil to northern Europe serving as the base of the kingdom's economy. Wheat and other grains were the primary import, followed by textiles and other consumer goods. In other words, the Portuguese benefited from their location midway between the vibrant Mediterranean and northeast Atlantic trade circuits. As they ventured abroad, the Portuguese would continue to supply these two markets with goods, increasingly high-value, exotic items such as gold, sugar, and spices. At the same time, they pioneered one of the most lucrative and infamous businesses of all time: the Atlantic slave trade.

Portugal's location made it the ideal departure point for Atlantic voyages. The ocean's wind system had for millennia discouraged Europeans from sailing far west. But by sailing down the African coast, ships could catch the Canary Current, which in addition to prevailing winds blew them across to the Americas. There was therefore nothing special about Western civilization that allowed Europeans to "discover" the Americas (Asians and Polynesians had been sailing long distances for centuries before 1492); it was rather the century-long development of Iberian-African trade that led to that accidental discovery.

As a result of Portuguese activity, Lisbon attracted not only Genoese but also Venetian, Florentine, Catalan, and Castilian cartographers, navigators, sailors, merchants, slave traders, and bankers' agents. It was a piece of the Portuguese pie that Columbus sought with increasing desperation during the 1470s and 1480s, failing to find adequate financial backing or royal license either in Portugal, where he concentrated his efforts, or Castile or England, where he pitched his ideas in the 1480s. His failure can be explained partly in terms of his connections, which in a world governed by patronage were not as good as they might have been, and partly by his poor grasp of world geography. Only in Columbus's mind was he a great visionary suffering the derision of a society not yet ready to accept his forward-thinking dream—although this image of the Genoese loner as the persecuted genius was central to the mythical Columbus that was constructed in the nineteenth century. The educated classes of the day knew the earth to be round and they knew its circumference, more or less; Columbus, on the other hand, believed the world was smaller than it actually is, and thus for decades attempted to sell to potential backers the misguided notion that one could sail west across the Atlantic to Asia.

Columbus was not alone in feeling frustrated and excluded by Portuguese successes. The Castilians had made increasing efforts during the fifteenth century to be part of the process of Atlantic expansion, even going to war with Portugal over the Canary Islands. However, much of Castile's expansionist energies had gone into forging the network of kingdoms that would become Spain. A milestone year in that process was 1492—when Isabella rode in triumph through the gates of Granada, Castilians consolidated control over the Canary Islands, and a century of anti-Semitism climaxed in the expulsion of the Jews. Columbus's journey to Granada in April 1492 to seek another audience with Queen Isabella was therefore lucky timing for him and for Spain; the meeting led to royal sponsorship, the crossing of the Atlantic, and the discovery of the Caribbean islands—their discovery by a Genoese holding a Spanish license to explore and settle.

The first European town in the Americas was founded by Columbus at the end of 1493. He named it La Isabella, after his patron (see Image and Word 2.2). It flourished briefly but collapsed after five years. Although La Isabella was settled by Spaniards—the 1,500 who accompanied Columbus in 17 ships on his 1493 voyage—the town was conceived in the Portuguese tradition in which Columbus was steeped. The fifteenth-century Portuguese exploration of the West African coast was characterized by the creation of trading posts. Columbus saw La Isabella as a royal trading settlement—in Spanish, *factoría*—along these lines. It was to generate wealth through trade with Hispaniola's native population, act as a stepping stone to further exploration, and be the foundation of a regional governorship that Columbus could pass on to his sons.

IMAGE AND WORD 2.2 The "First" House

Christopher Columbus "anchored in a large river port where there was an Indian village," wrote fray (Brother) Bartolomé de Las Casas, describing the first European settlement in the Caribbean. Columbus "thanked God for the amenity of the land and rightly so, too, for the location is rich in stones, tiles, and good earth for the making of bricks, besides being very fertile and beautiful." That settlement was the town of La Isabella, on the island of Hispaniola. The site, and Columbus's residence, have both recently been excavated by archaeologists. These paintings reconstruct the town and the Columbus House as they would have appeared ca. 1494. Today the site is one of the Dominican Republic's national parks.

© National Geographic Images

© National Geographic Images

But neither Columbus nor the Spaniards who came with him realized that the Caribbean could not support the mercantile model of colonization upon which La Isabella was built. The fifteenth-century Portuguese model was based on trade with local people, which in West Africa meant gold and slaves. Hispaniola was already inhabited, by the Taínos, but there was no comparable tradition on the island of slaving or gold-mining. Furthermore, West Africans were organized into fully sedentary societies and complex kingdoms, whereas the **Taínos** were politically fragmented and semi-sedentary, living as much from hunting and fishing as from agriculture.

It is possible that the trading model might eventually have been adapted to Caribbean realities, but the Spanish authorities were quick to take advantage of Columbus's failure. In 1496 the capital was moved to a new Spanish town, Santo Domingo, and four years later Columbus was arrested and removed from the island (he would make two more voyages between Spain and the Americas, but never again hold a governorship). During the first decade of the sixteenth century, a Spaniard, Nicolás de Ovando, took over the governorship of Hispaniola, while other Spaniards began to conquer and occupy the other major Caribbean islands—Cuba, Jamaica, and Puerto Rico.

This model failed even more dramatically than La Isabella had, for the same reasons; it was not well suited to the region and its native peoples. The Taínos were not accustomed to living under a harsh labor system and a strict religious and political regime. This, combined with the model's brutal imposition and the impact of disease, ensured failure. Frustrated, Spaniards resorted to greater violence and to the mass enslaving of native groups throughout the islands and the circum-Caribbean mainland—methods that soon proved to be counter-productive.

DISEASE, DEMOGRAPHIC DISASTER, AND THE TRADE IN AFRICAN SLAVES

The Dominican friar Bartolomé de Las Casas offered estimates ranging from 1 to 4 million for the size of the Taíno population on Hispaniola at the time of Columbus's first voyage (see Image and Word 2.3). In fact, Las Casas's lowest estimate was probably about right, meaning his claim that the island's native population declined by some 90% during his lifetime (1484–1566) was more or less accurate. But how accurate was the friar's assertion that this decline resulted from the "egregious wickedness" of Spanish colonists?

Certainly, conquest violence and the brutal imposition of systems of colonial exploitation on Hispaniola and other Caribbean islands played an important role in this demographic catastrophe. But the crucial factor that Las Casas ignored was that of epidemic disease. The friar can hardly be blamed, as Spaniards were only just beginning to grasp the devastating degree to which diseases such as smallpox

---

Taíno [tah-EE-no]   native peoples of Hispaniola [hiss-pan-YO-lah] and neighboring islands; sometimes also called Arawaks

IMAGE AND WORD 2.3   Las Casas and the Black Legend

Archivo de Indias, Seville, Spain/Mithra-Index/The Bridgeman Art Library International

Bartolomé de las Casas first arrived in the Americas in 1502, at the age of 18, as one of the Spaniards accompanying the new governor of Hispaniola. Bartolomé's father, a merchant from Seville, had come to the island with Columbus the previous decade. At first, Bartolomé helped his father in the business of supplying the conquistadors who had begun invading other Caribbean islands. But he was more interested in learning Taíno and in the priesthood.

Ordained in Rome in 1507, Las Casas returned to the Caribbean a few years later, joining conquistadors in Cuba as a priest. This experience convinced him that Spanish methods of colonization were ineffective and immoral. Las Casas had received *encomiendas*, or grants of native labor and tribute, on both Hispaniola and Cuba. He now renounced these benefits and began a lifelong campaign to convince the crown to abolish the institution and to permit priests, not conquistador-settlers, to create and govern the colonies.

Attempting to practice what he preached, he experimented with model settlements in Venezuela and Guatemala, with little success. Having joined the Dominican Order, and serving briefly in the 1540s as Bishop of Chiapas (in today's southern Mexico), Las Casas was uncompromising and increasingly militant in his denunciation of Spanish mistreatment of native peoples. He was hated by settlers, denounced by the viceroy of New Spain, and recalled back to Spain.

These were signs, however, that his persistence was paying off. The New Laws of 1542, which protected natives from enslavement and other abuses, reflected Las Casas's arguments. His *Brief Account of the Destruction of the Indies* and other such treatises were published and widely read. A skilled propagandist and court politician, Las Casas enjoyed royal patronage and the right to make his case against colonial abuses until his death in 1566.

(continued)

IMAGE AND WORD 2.3   Las Casas and the Black Legend (continued)

Las Casas's reputation has continued to grow over the centuries, in particular in two ways that can mislead the modern reader. First, his books were translated into other European languages and read widely, some during his lifetime but most of them in subsequent centuries. Used as anti-Spanish propaganda, especially by the English, Las Casas's works underpinned the Black Legend—the depiction of Spanish imperialism as excessively brutal and immoral, a negative stereotype that survives today in many Protestant countries. The Black Legend's implication that the Spanish were cruel because they were Catholic is ironic in view of Las Casas's insistence that the colonies should be run by priests.

The second way in which Las Casas's posthumous reputation can be misleading is his modern status as an icon of humanitarianism. His passionate denunciations of native suffering have often blinded modern readers to the fact that Las Casas was not a modern figure. He was slow to condemn the African slave trade, and never questioned the idea that native Americans should be made Christians. He questioned Spanish methods of conquest and colonization but not the existence of the Spanish Empire.

---

and measles affected Native Americans. Isolated for thousands of years from the Old World pool of bacteria, viruses, and parasites, native peoples had far less immunity than did Europeans and Africans to the diseases carried across the Atlantic. Largely as a result of high mortality rates during the regular epidemic outbreaks of the sixteenth century, Native Americans had fallen in number from an estimated 65 million in 1492 to as few as 5 million a century later.

Spaniards were dismayed at how quickly native numbers fell in the Caribbean. Las Casas's arguments as to the cause of the disaster were taken seriously because crown and settlers alike sought explanations in the hope of preventing such demographic disasters in the future (see Image and Word 2.3).

Despite these concerns, the Castilian model of colonization survived and became central to Spanish settlement on the American mainland: (1) Spanish invaders sought sedentary native populations upon which to construct colonies, which they settled and ruled, with each province part of a new kingdom (the first in the Americas was New Spain), made possible through (2) formal alliances with native nobility; (3) the conquered local peoples were converted to Christianity and (4) required to pay tribute (a basic head tax) to the Spanish crown and through the **encomienda** (allocation of the labor and tribute of native towns, but *not* a grant of land or slaves); if necessary, (5) native peoples were resettled into concentrated towns (**congregación**); and (6) slavery was legal.

Encomienda   a grant to a Spanish settler of the tribute and labor from a native village or region

Congregación [kon-greg-ass-YOHN]   the congregation or resettlement of native peoples into concentrated, centrally located towns

The model was thus altered with respect to slavery. Mainland conquest campaigns of the 1520s and 1530s were not slave raids, and in 1542 the crown decreed that native subjects of the empire could not be enslaved except as temporary punishment for rebellion. Instead the category of permanent, "chattel" slave was restricted to black Africans. Slaves from Africa's west coast had been a part of Spanish colonization in the Americas from the start, but they played an increasingly important role as the sixteenth century wore on—replacing the native population in the Caribbean and supplementing native workers on the mainland. As a result, an earlier colonial model, one pioneered by the Portuguese, came to claim an important place in the Americas—the sugar plantation worked by African slaves. The sugar–slave system would come to dominate Portuguese colonization in Brazil and European colonization in the Caribbean.

Although its scale and form were profoundly altered as a result of the transatlantic trade, the concept of chattel slavery was not introduced to Africa by Europeans. Like virtually all so-called traditional societies, including most native groups of the Americas, the chiefdoms and kingdoms of Africa made routine use of the labor of war captives and their descendants. In some cases surplus slaves were traded over long distances for commodities, such as salt or iron tools; in others they were retained to augment the households of chiefs and kings. Throughout western Africa, whole colonies of enslaved peoples were forced to grow food, fish, hunt, or tend livestock for the benefit of their owners and also to mine gold, iron ore, and copper. When Portuguese traders arrived along the coast of West and West Central Africa in the fifteenth century, they encountered mostly slave-based societies. After some ill-advised raids on coastal villages, Portuguese slavers shifted to exchanging foreign commodities for captives.

Especially after 1480, the Portuguese blended trade, military alliances, and missionary endeavors in their efforts to establish a lasting presence in both West and West Central Africa. By 1491 Portuguese priests had converted much of the Kongo aristocracy to Roman Catholicism. The key convert was the son of the *manikongo*, Nzinga Mbemba, who later ruled as Afonso I (1506–1543). Afonso's conversion was genuine; he learned to read, studied theology, and renamed Mbanza, the capital city, São Salvador ("Holy Savior"). One of the king's sons joined the priesthood in Lisbon and returned to Kongo following consecration in Rome. Ultimately, however, Christianity, came to be monopolized by Kongo's elites and Portuguese missionaries opposed the expansion of an African priesthood. Portuguese military aid, meanwhile, buttressed Kongo politically and fueled slave raiding and the slave trade. Early slaves were sent to the sugar plantations of São Tomé.

IMAGE AND WORD 2.4   Statistical Shock: Numbers from the Slave Trade

The drawing on the next page depicts captured West Africans, yoked in pairs and being transported to be sold as slaves. As the drawing illustrates, whole families were often sold into slavery. Note also that the overseer is himself a West African, for it was primarily Africans, not Europeans, who made the initial captures; Europeans

---

(continued)

**IMAGE AND WORD 2.4   Statistical Shock: Numbers from
the Slave Trade (continued)**

then purchased slaves along the Mediterranean or West African coasts. As the table
below shows, from the seventh to fifteenth centuries, slaves were transported across
the Sahara to Europe and the Middle East. While that trade continued for a couple
of centuries, it was dwarfed after 1450 by the new transatlantic trade.

Estimated millions of slaves	transported from West & West Central Africa to	via	in the period
4	Europe & the Middle East	Sahara	ca. 650–1450
1	Europe & the Middle East	Sahara	1450–1600
(5 million subtotal)			
0.3	Europe	Atlantic	1451–1870
0.5	British North America	Atlantic	1451–1870
1.7	Spanish America	Atlantic	1451–1870
4.7	Caribbean	Atlantic	1451–1870
4.2	Brazil	Atlantic	1451–1870
(11.4 million subtotal)			
(16.4 million total)			

The Kingdom of Kongo was overrun by angry neighbors in 1569, but Portuguese gunners led a counter-attack and restored the Christianized monarchy five years later. In return for continued support, Kongo's leaders supplied the Portuguese with many thousands of slaves well into the next century. As the market for enslaved Africans grew in the Americas, the Portuguese sought new trading posts farther south. In the 1570s slavers established a permanent military colony in Angola. Beginning on the island of Luanda, this colony became one of the largest and longest-lived clearinghouses for the transatlantic slave trade. Soon after, a post was established still farther south at Benguela.

Overall, West Central Africa would supply some 5 million, or nearly half of all recorded slaves (approximately 11 million) sent to the Americas between 1519 and 1867 (see Image and Word 2.4). Most landed in Brazil, but others were sent as far afield as Jamestown, Virginia, and Potosí, Bolivia. Wherever they came from, African slaves, whom the Portuguese called **peças**, or "pieces," were overwhelmingly peasants, poor millet, rice, and sorghum farmers struggling to eke out a living at the drought-prone, war-scarred margins. A few were nobles and warriors. At least two thirds of the captives were men.

Why, we might ask, were so many Africans ultimately sent along this transatlantic "way of death," as some described it, by fellow Africans? Like the riddle of the Spanish conquests in the Americas (see Chapter 3), the answer lies in native perspectives. Just as the category of "Indians" had no local meaning before Spaniards arrived in the Americas, so was there no such category as "Africans," much less "blacks," before the arrival of the Portuguese. These racialized macro-identities made no sense among ethnically, religiously, and politically diverse native peoples engaged in their own internal and regional endeavors, peaceful and otherwise.

Three trends therefore led to the presence of African slaves in the Americas: (1) the existence of the slave trade in Africa and Iberian entry in the fifteenth; (2) the Iberian discovery of the Americas as an accidental by-product of Iberian overseas trade; and (3) the demand for African slaves in the Caribbean in the wake of native demographic collapse in the sixteenth century.

The crucial year that determined how the narrative of Iberian expansion into the Atlantic would lead into the Americas was 1492. But shortly thereafter, the narrative splits: Spanish energies were directed to the mainland, where they encountered great native empires; while the Portuguese found profit not only in Brazilian sugar but also in supplying the Spanish Empire with African slaves. The new world that was being created contained some elements of Columbus's vision (symbolized by La Isabella as a *feitoria* and base for exploring Asia) and some elements of Las Casas's vision (of colonization based on conversion, not conquest). But it reflected far more the expansive ambition of Queen Isabella (whose grandson, the emperor Charles V, would rule the most wide-ranging empire the world had yet seen) and the entrepreneurial spirit of conquistadors such as Cortés. Above all, the new world of colonial Latin America would

---

Peças [PEH-sahs]   Portuguese term for slaves, literally "pieces" or "units"

feature more profound contributions by Native American and African peoples than anyone in the late fifteenth century could have imagined.

KEEP READING

On Africa and the Slave Trade, we suggest George E. Brooks, *Landlords and Strangers: Ecology, Society, and Trade in Western Africa, 1000–1630* (1993); Linda M. Heywood, ed., *Central Africans and Cultural Transformations in the American Diaspora* (2002); Joseph Miller, *Kings and Kinsmen: Early Mbundu States in Angola* (1976); Walter Rodney, *A History of the Upper Guinea Coast, 1545 to 1800* (1970); Paul Lovejoy, *Transformations in Slavery: A History of Slavery in Africa*, 2nd ed. (2000); Patrick Manning, *Slavery and African Life: Occidental, Oriental, and African Slave Trades* (1990); and John Thornton, *Africa and Africans in the Making of the Atlantic World, 1400–1680*, 2nd ed. (1999).

On Spain and Portugal, we recommend *Spain: A History*, edited by Raymond Carr (2000); Blackwell's series of textbooks on Spain, including *The Spain of the Catholic Monarchs, 1474–1520*, by John Edwards (2001); C. R. Boxer's classic *The Portuguese Seaborne Empire, 1415–1825* (1969); A. J .R. Russell-Wood, *The Portuguese Empire, 1415–1808 : A World on the Move* (1998); Stanley G. Payne, *A History of Spain and Portugal*, 2 vols. (1973); and Anthony Disney, *A History of Portugal and the Portuguese Empire*, 2 vols. (2009).

On other topics in this chapter: Felipe Fernández-Armesto, *Columbus* (1991); Chapter 1 of Matthew Restall, *Seven Myths of the Spanish Conquest* (2003); Suzanne Austin Alchon, *A Pest in the Land: New World Epidemics in a Global Perspective* (2003); and Noble David Cook, *Born To Die: Disease and the New World Conquest, 1492–1650* (1998).

3

✳

The Riddle of Conquest

From Cuba to Mesoamerica

From Panama to Peru

Who Were the Conquistadors?

The Other Side of the Conquest

Solving the Riddle

Francisco de Jérez, the first conquistador of Peru to publish an account of the Spanish invasion of the Inka Empire, asked, "When in ancient or modern times have such huge enterprises of so few succeeded against so many?" For centuries it was believed by many in the West that the European discovery and colonization of the Americas was the most momentous event in history, and thus its explanation was considered of great importance. The perception of the Conquest as a riddle—How did so few conquer so many?—has persisted from Francisco de Jérez's day to the present.

This chapter explores the various aspects of the Spanish Conquest, along the way solving the Conquest riddle. We explain how and why Iberians reached most corners of the Americas, who these conquerors and settlers were, what they did and how. The chapter's focus is the half-century from 1500 to about 1550.

FROM CUBA TO MESOAMERICA

The Spaniards did not leap quickly from the discovery of the Caribbean islands to the defeat of the Aztec Empire. There was a full generation between the first Columbus voyages of the early 1490s and the discovery of the Mexican coastline in the late 1510s. This was enough time for hundreds of Spaniards to acquire considerable experience exploring new coasts, invading new lands, subduing

TIMELINE

1493–1519	Spanish exploration and colonization of the Caribbean
1519–1521	The Spanish-Mexica war, culminating in the Cortés-led Spaniards and their Tlaxcallan allies destroying the Mexica (Aztec) imperial capital of Mexico-Tenochtitlán
1520s	Spanish consolidate control over central Mexico, make initial invasions of Guatemala and Yucatan, and explore northern Pacific coast of South America
1524–1529	Spanish invasions of highland Guatemala under Pedro and Jorge de Alvarado, with major role played by native warriors from Mexico and Oaxaca
1527–1542	Spaniards under the three Franciscos de Montejo invade Yucatan three times, establishing a colony in the 1540s
1532	The Inka Atawallpa captured by Pizarro at Cajamarca in northern Peru, executed in 1533
1534	Inka capital of Cuzco captured; Spaniards found a new capital at Lima in 1535
1536	Revolt by the Inka Manco Capac who besieges Cuzco before retreating to Vilcabamba (which is not conquered until 1572)
1537–1548	Civil war between Spaniards in Peru
1540s–1880s	Almost continuous failure of Spanish colonial (and then Chilean national) authorities to subdue the Mapuche
1572	Execution of rebel Inka emperor, Tupac Amaru Inka, in Cuzco, Peru
1684–1687	Native rebellion in the Chocó (in today's Colombia) forces Spaniards to reconquer the region; resistance continues through the eighteenth century
1697	Spanish conquest of the Maya kingdom of Petén Itzá (in today's northern Guatemala); Itzá resistance continues through the eighteenth century

native peoples, and setting up the institutions of colonial rule. Those who imagined peaceful relations between Europeans and Native Americans found their idealism overshadowed by the widespread enslavement and brutal treatment of Caribbean natives. The collapse of island populations led to a ban on the enslaving of natives; Spaniards headed to the American mainland looking not for slaves but for wealthy kingdoms upon which to construct colonies of free tribute-paying Christianized "Indian" subjects of the king.

Cuba became the staging ground for the conquest of Mesoamerica. Voyages of 1517 and 1518 explored the coasts of the Yucatan peninsula and the Gulf of Mexico. These voyages were sponsored by the governor of Cuba, Diego

Velázquez, who commissioned one of the **encomenderos**, or fief-holders, on the island to lead a third expedition in 1519. This encomendero's name was Hernando Cortés. Velázquez held the **adelantado** or official invader's license, so Cortés was only supposed to explore, not invade. The Spanish system of conquest created a chain that linked each new settlement to the next one—Hispaniola to Cuba to Mexico, for example. But the apparent stability of the system was undermined by the tendency of each conqueror to look back up the chain to the king in Spain, to go around or even betray their patron and acquire direct royal patronage. Velázquez correctly suspected Cortés would do just this and attempted at the last minute, in vain, to stop him sailing from Cuba. Once Cortés's 500 men had landed on the Mexican mainland, Cortés grounded most of his 11 ships and formally declared direct allegiance to the king. He founded a city (a ritual act only), creating a town council whose votes of support lent a veneer of legality to his actions. It would be six years before Cortés would receive royal approval, in person in Spain, for his revolt against Velázquez and his war against the Mexica.

Spaniards who explored—and then invaded—the mainland of Mesoamerica tended to encounter immediate resistance from natives defending their communities. This was Cortés's experience as the Spaniards moved slowly inland toward the Mexica capital city. Two factors prevented the Spaniards from being wiped out during these early months of their invasion. One was the advantage of their steel swords, which allowed them to kill large numbers of native warriors while only receiving superficial wounds from the brittle, obsidian-bladed daggers and clubs that were the primary weapons of Mesoamerican fighters. This led to the second factor: When native rulers could not destroy Spanish forces, and keeping them at bay (as the kingdom of Tlaxcala was able to do) was costly, they sought to accommodate the invaders in some kind of alliance.

Cortés and native rulers thus found common ground. The Spaniards wanted to move on to the Valley of Mexico to confront the Mexica emperor with as many native allies as possible. Native rulers were keen to see the Spaniards leave their communities and were willing to hedge their bets on the possibility of the collapse of the Aztec/Mexica Empire. Some, like the Totonacs, were subject to the Mexicas and quick to rebel against them. Others, like the Tlaxcallans, had resisted Mexica expansion and were eventually persuaded to take a chance on destroying their old enemies.

The Spanish advanced toward the Mexica capital of Tenochtitlán and in November 1519 entered the city as guests of the Mexica emperor, Moctezuma Xocoyotl. Conversing through Cortés's Nahua interpreter, **Malinche** (see Image and Word 3.1), Moctezuma delivered a welcoming speech to Cortés that he

---

Encomendero [en-kom-en-DARE-oh]   holder of an *encomienda* or grant of native labor and tribute

Adelantado [a-del-an-TAHD-oh]   "invader" or holder of a royal license to invade and conquer

Malinche [mal-EEN-chay]   Nahua noblewoman who acted as Cortés's interpreter during the Spanish invasion of the Aztec/Mexica Empire

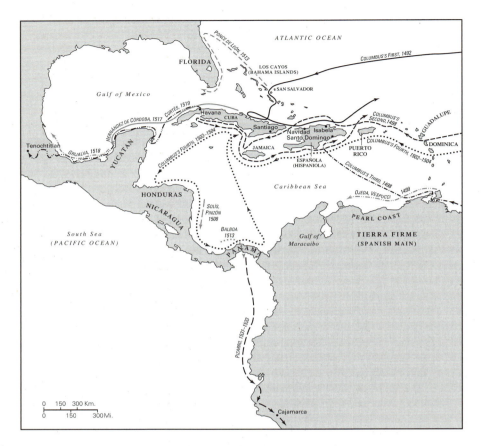

M A P 3.1 Mexico and the Caribbean in the Conquest Period

interpreted (in a letter to the king) as a speech of surrender. Intrigued by these foreigners who had disrupted a corner of his empire, Moctezuma sought to display his majesty through hospitality. But the Spaniards, outnumbered and fearful, soon resorted to treachery and terror; Cortés seized and imprisoned Moctezuma and ordered that anyone who so much as raised a hand against the Spanish and their allies be publicly cut to pieces and fed to the dogs. These were stock tactics developed by conquistadors in their decades of Caribbean slave raiding, tactics that proved even more effective against mainland imperial peoples who depended on their divinely sanctioned kings.

Over the next eight months the Spanish–Tlaxcallan invaders, partially contained within the center of the city, engaged in periodic looting and guerilla-style warfare. Meanwhile, disease, the third great Spanish advantage (along with steel weapons and native allies), struck the Mexica; a smallpox epidemic caused massive mortality in the city and across central Mexico. Ironically, the people who would give the world maize, tomatoes, chocolate, vanilla, and a thousand

IMAGE AND WORD 3.1 Go-Betweens

Pocahontas and Malinche are the best known interpreters of the age of European discoveries and conquests in the Americas. But they were by no means the only such go-betweens. Malinche (aka Malintzin or doña Marina) was a Nahua noblewoman enslaved by Mayas when Cortés reached Mexico. When her skills as a diplomat and interpreter made her indispensable to the Spanish leader, her status rose dramatically. In modern Mexican mythology she is regarded as a traitor, a collaborator, even a harlot. But Malinche was not seen as a traitor in her own day, even by the Mexica. Instead, her reversal of fortune from exiled slave to woman of great power and status was interpreted as but another trick of the fickle gods. Her transformation was cause for awe, not derision. In their numerous and often graphic paintings of the conquest, Nahua artists working shortly after the arrival of the Spanish often placed Malinche at the center, poised and confident, speech scrolls emanating from her mouth (see below, left). For a culture that called its kings *tlatoque*, or "speakers," this was significant.

An Andean christened Felipe likewise played an important role as a *lengua* (see below, right, where he is shown interpreting for Pizarro and Atawallpa). In Yucatan, a Maya nobleman named Gaspar Antonio Chi became the senior interpreter for Spaniards and Mayas in the colony, mediating between them for over half a century. Native interpreters were also crucial in Brazil; one historian has argued that only through the agency of interpreters and other go-betweens were the Portuguese able to establish a colony there.

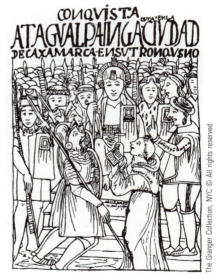

other life-sustaining and pleasurable foods were now receiving only the most deadly ingredients of the **Columbian Exchange**: viruses and bacteria. Amid this bloody stalemate, Cortés ordered that images of the Virgin Mary be placed atop Aztec temples to assert the power of the invaders' god. He also took a contingent of Spaniards and native allies back to the Gulf Coast to confront a company of Velázquez supporters that had sailed from Cuba to challenge Cortés; they were defeated, and most joined Cortés, who returned to Tenochtitlán to find that the stalemate had shifted in favor of the Mexica. Led by Pedro de Alvarado, the Spaniards were under siege.

The desperate Spaniards murdered Moctezuma (claiming that he was stoned to death by his own people) and on the night of June 30, 1520, attempted to flee the city undetected. But Mexica warriors were waiting and killed about half the Spaniards and thousands of Tlaxcallan and other native allies. Cortés and his bedraggled Spanish forces eventually regrouped with Tlaxcallan assistance, but it would be over a year before Tenochtitlán and its twin city of Tlatelolco fell. Cut off from the mainland, the Mexica faced disease and starvation, then attack by land and water. Brigantines were built on the shores of Lake Texcoco. Armed with cannon, these small boats helped pound remaining Aztec warrior contingents in canoes. The city was taken and pillaged, block by block, by the Spanish and their allies. Finding not gold but piles of bodies, victims of smallpox and siege warfare, the invaders razed the city. It would be years before Mexico City would rise from the rubble of Tenochtitlán.

In 1521 the Mexica Empire was destroyed, but its framework of trade routes, tribute lists, and diplomatic relations between ruling families remained in place. Spaniards immediately sought to make use of that framework and convert it into an elemental part of the structure of their empire in Mesoamerica—which they renamed the Kingdom of New Spain. The Mexica had employed their own chain of conquest in the region, and so in the 1520s the Spaniards used that chain—and even used Mexica warriors, survivors of the war who joined other Nahua allies—to expand the frontiers of New Spain.

Conquistadors invaded highland Guatemala in the 1520s, and Cortés himself led an expedition down to Honduras, which was eventually conquered in the 1530s; a small colony was founded in Yucatan in the 1540s. The chain of conquest led Spaniards quickly into most corners of Mesoamerica—and, soon after, north into what is today the U.S. Southwest, and west across the Pacific to what would be renamed the Philippines. But the founding of colonies would prove to be a protracted and highly contested process. The core challenge was to win the hearts and minds of millions of former Mexica subjects and other native groups who were officially subjects of the king of Spain. This would be the long story of colonial Mesoamerica, a "New Spain" so unlike its Iberian namesake.

Columbian Exchange   the exchange of plants, animals, viruses and bacteria between Old and New Worlds that followed Columbus's voyages

FROM PANAMA TO PERU

Just as one chain of conquest ran from Hispaniola to Cuba to Mexico, another ran from Hispaniola to the Isthmus of Panama—and from there down the Pacific side of South America. The conquest and settlement of a small colony on the Atlantic side of the isthmus began in 1508, and five years later Panama received the first Spanish bishop appointed to the mainland of the Americas. That same year (1513) the Pacific side of the isthmus was discovered by Vasco Núñez de Balboa and a black slave of his—the first recorded sighting of the Pacific Ocean by Europeans and Africans.

Over the next decade, Spaniards established a settlement at Panama City and began to explore the coast and ocean to its south (which Spaniards called the South Sea). Among the early settlers on the isthmus were the Pizarro brothers, who came from Extremadura, the same region of Spain as Cortés (see Image and Word 3.2). When one of the brothers, Francisco, sailed from Panama in 1522 in

IMAGE AND WORD 3.2 Conquistador Cousins

This portrait of the "invincible" Cortés as a 63-year-old conquistador was first published in 1588 as the frontispiece to Gabriel Lasso de la Vega's flattering *Valiant Cortés* (left), and these depictions of Diego de Almagro and Francisco Pizarro were included in Felipe Guaman Poma de Ayala's 1615 *Nueva corónica y buen gobierno* (right).

(continued)

IMAGE AND WORD 3.2   Conquistador Cousins (continued)

Hernando Cortés was born in the early 1480s in Medellín, Extremadura, a dry, poor region of western Spain. He was the son of an illegitimate lesser nobleman, Martín Cortés. He read law at the university in Salamanca for a couple of years, later working as a notary. He went to Valencia with the intention of seeking his fortune with the Spanish forces fighting in Italy, but he changed his mind and went to the Caribbean instead—arriving in his early 20s. He thus had more than a dozen years of experience as a conquistador-settler on Hispaniola and Cuba before invading Mexico. After a decade of exploration and conquest in Mesoamerica, he returned to Spain; in 1529, not long after meeting with the king in Toledo, Cortés ran into Francisco Pizarro, who was there seeking a license from the king to invade Peru.

Cortés's mother was a Pizarro, and he was therefore a distant relation of the Pizarro brothers—Francisco, Gonzalo, Hernando, and Juan, all of whom participated in the Spanish invasion of the Inka Empire. Like Cortés, the Pizarros were from Extremadura—from the town of Trujillo. Their father was a lesser nobleman and a veteran of the wars in Italy. Francisco was an illegitimate son by a local farmer's daughter. Francisco was never legitimated; he remained all his life illiterate, a consummate gambler, and a man more at home fighting or working with his hands than governing or discussing matters of law (in this respect he was different from Cortés, whose letters to the king are artfully composed). Pizarro briefly visited Italy and may have come close to following in his father's footsteps there. But, like Cortés, he chose "the Indies" over Italy—and instead sailed with an uncle to the Caribbean. Just as Cortés won *encomiendas* in Cuba, so did Pizarro win them in Panama. It is not clear how close Francisco was to his brothers in childhood, but they were ready to follow him after 1529—including Hernando, the eldest and only legitimate brother. In that year, Francisco added to his two and a half decades of conquest experience in the Americas a royal license to invade Peru.

That license gave Pizarro the right to be governor of whatever he conquered in South America; it excluded his junior partner for the second half of his years in Panama, Diego de Almagro. Pizarro never accepted Almagro as an equal, and Almagro never forgave Pizarro, claiming all southern Peru for himself in 1537, in defiance of Pizarro's authority. The Pizarros organized an army against Almagro, defeating and executing him. His son took revenge, assassinating Francisco Pizarro in 1541 in Lima. In the subsequent conflicts, Almagro's son and Gonzalo Pizarro were executed. Juan Pizarro had died earlier, during the siege of Cuzco. Of the four Pizarro brothers, only Hernando would die like Cortés—as a wealthy old man, back in Spain.

---

search of a mythical chieftain called "Pirú," he had no idea that events high in the Andes Mountains to the south would conspire to favor his dream of repeating the success of Cortés. Many Spaniards hoped to find another empire like that of the Aztec/Mexica. But there was only one other, that of the Inkas, and it was Pizarro's to find. Yet he was to discover—as had Cortés and the other Spaniards that had invaded Mesoamerican kingdoms—that while native emperors might be seized with relative ease, their empires did not fall overnight.

In the end, it was only after nearly ten years of fruitless searching and humiliating failure before Pizarro, his brothers, and their partner Diego de Almagro marched at last into Peru, the heartland of the Inka Empire. In the meantime

Pizarro had acquired Quechua translators steeped for several years in Castilian Spanish; a small army of men with horses, armor, and state-of-the-art weapons; and also a license from Charles V. By late 1532, when Pizarro's forces began their inland march across a coastal desert so unlike the jungles they had left behind, the myth of "Pirú" (today's "Peru") at last seemed like a tangible reality.

Tawantinsuyu, as the Inkas called their empire, was in the midst of a civil war in 1532. The Inka Huayna Capac had died of symptoms characteristic of smallpox, and his heirs, Atawallpa and Huascar, had spent the subsequent five years battling for supremacy. When Pizarro and his 168 men climbed into the northern Andes to meet the emperor in the sacred city of **Cajamarca**, Atawallpa was celebrating a victory over his brother. Atawallpa hoped, like Moctezuma in Mexico, to draft the well-armed foreigners into his service. Despite the wonder provoked by their horses, firearms, and steel swords, the Inkas did not mistake the Spanish for gods. Eyewitness evidence from the first moment of contact suggests that Andeans and Mesoamericans saw the Spaniards and their African slaves as foreign men to be examined and turned away, accommodated, or used, as circumstances allowed.

Spanish conquest procedure, however, was to initiate a diplomatic encounter that would then treacherously turn into a violent taking of hostages—preferably the seizure of the king. Thus in November 1532, Pizarro and his men captured Atawallpa in a surprise attack. Having supplied the foreigners with food and lodging, the Inka had no reason to suspect that they would seek to kidnap and ransom him, much less murder him. Humiliated, Atawallpa was held hostage for nearly a year as his subjects scrambled to gather up gold and silver to free him. The Inkas possessed far more gold and silver than the Aztecs, and the hoard of metals offered to free their leader, whom most Andeans regarded as a divine being, was staggering, so much so that the word *Peru* became instantly synonymous with great wealth among Europeans. The association would soon be reinforced with the discovery of immensely rich silver mines in Inka territory. Despite the ransom, however, the Inka Atawallpa was executed in 1533 on Pizarro's orders. The treachery was complete. And yet the true military conquest of Tawantinsuyu was yet to come.

Pizarro and his lieutenants went on to capture **Cuzco**, then **Quito**, the empire's two capitals. Both were subdued by 1534, but an heir of the Inkas once friendly to the Spanish, Manco Capac, nearly managed a reconquest of Cuzco in 1536. The siege killed one of Francisco Pizarro's younger brothers and several other Spaniards, but Manco was ultimately forced to retreat down the Urubamba River, past Pachacuti's palace complex at Machu Picchu. There in the wet lowlands, at a site called Vilcabamba, he and a series of successors would maintain an alternative Inka state. It would survive until 1572.

With so much wealth and territory at stake, Spanish conquistadors began battling one another, and eventually the crown, for control of Peru. Once Pizarro

---

Cajamarca [ka-ha-MAR-kah], Cuzco [KOOZ-koh], and Quito [KEY-toh]   the principal cities of the Inka Empire

and his followers had achieved military conquest in much of the Andean highlands, representatives of Charles V intervened in hopes of establishing order and collecting taxes in precious metals. Among the new proclamations was one limiting conquistador access to *encomiendas*. Another was a law that banned the enslavement of native peoples in the Americas. Bartolomé de las Casas had won his day at court.

WHO WERE THE CONQUISTADORS?

The narratives above have focused on Cortés and Pizarro more than other Spanish conquerors, but those two men stand out from the thousands of other conquistadors only by their good fortune and ability to do well what other company captains also did. In other words, in most respects Cortés and Pizarro were typical conquistadors—meaning what?

The identities, experiences, and life stories of the Spaniards who participated in the conquests in the Americas were varied. But a typical conquistador was a young man in his late 20s, semiliterate, from southwestern Spain, trained in a particular trade or profession, seeking opportunity through patronage networks based on family and hometown ties. Armed as well as he could afford, and with some experience already of exploration and conquest in the Americas, he would be ready to invest what he had and risk his life if absolutely necessary to be a member of the first company to conquer somewhere wealthy and well-populated.

This archetypal conquistador would not in any sense be a soldier in the armies of the king of Spain. Although the conquistadors are often misleadingly referred to as soldiers—and they were certainly armed, organized, and experienced in military matters—they acquired their martial skills not from formal training but from conflict situations in the Americas. Expedition members tended to be recruited in recently founded colonies—the chain of conquest discussed above meant that most participants already had some experience in the New World. For example, among the Spaniards who participated in the famous capture of Atawallpa at Cajamarca, at least two thirds had prior conquest experience and more than half had spent at least five years in the Americas.

Conquistadors were motivated by a search for economic and social opportunity. The letters Cortés wrote to the king, published in the conquistador's lifetime and still in print today in many languages, give the impression that Spaniards were driven by a sense of loyalty to crown and church. This image of the conquistadors was constructed for the benefit of the king, who was well aware of the personal ambitions and motives of the conquerors. Nor should the Spaniards be seen as pathological gold-seekers; they sought gold and silver because precious metals were the only nonperishable easy-to-ship item of value that could pay the merchants and creditors who funded conquest campaigns.

In the words of Francisco de Jérez, conquistadors "were neither paid nor forced but went of their own will and at their own cost." They joined conquest expeditions in the hope of acquiring wealth and status. Spaniards called these ventures "companies." While powerful patrons played important investment roles, it was the captains who primarily funded companies and expected to reap the greatest rewards. The spirit of commercialism infused conquest expeditions from start to finish, with participants selling services and trading goods with each other throughout the endeavor. The conquerors were, in other words, armed entrepreneurs. The members of a successful conquest company hoped to be granted an *encomienda*, which would afford them high status and often a superior lifestyle among fellow colonists. As there were never enough *encomiendas* to go around, the most lucrative grants went to those who had invested the most in the expedition— and survived to see it succeed. Lesser investors received lesser grants (a few dozen, instead of thousands, of indigenous "vassals") or simply a share of the spoils of war.

Conquest companies also lacked formal ranking; they were headed by captains, the sole named rank and one that varied in number. The record of the division of spoils at Cajamarca listed the men in two categories only, *gente de a caballo* (men on horseback) and *gente de a pie* (men on foot). A man could move from one category to the other by buying a horse (or losing one).

Conquistadors were overwhelmingly middle-ranking men, from occupations and backgrounds below the high nobility but above the commoner masses (as was true of Cortés and Pizarro; see Image and Word 3.2). Following the founding of the city of Panama in 1519, the 98 Spanish conquistador-settlers were asked to state who they were in detail. Seventy-five responded. Only two of them claimed to be professional soldiers. Sixty percent claimed to be professional men and artisans, occupations from the middle ranks of society. A similar analysis of the conquerors of the New Kingdom of Granada (today's Colombia) is less precise as to occupations and probably exaggerates the numbers of middle-ranking men. Nevertheless, the data clearly show that men of some means or property, professionals, and entrepreneurs of some kind predominated. Likewise those Spaniards at Cajamarca in 1533 who recorded their occupations were not career soldiers but professionals and artisans who had acquired various battle experience and martial skills. A third of those who stated their occupation were artisans: tailors, farriers, carpenters, trumpeters, a cooper, a swordsmith, a stone-mason, a barber, and a piper/crier. The same kinds of artisans had also accompanied Francisco de Montejo on his first expedition into Yucatan in 1527, along with the usual professional men—merchants, physicians, a couple of priests, and a pair of Flemish artillery engineers. An unspecified number of the artisans and professionals invested in the company were confident enough of its outcome to bring their wives.

We also know the age and birthplace of over 1,200 conquistadors who participated in the original invasions of Panama, Mexico, Peru, and Colombia. The make-up of each expedition was similar, with an average of 30% from the southern Spanish kingdom of Andalusia, 19% from neighboring Extremadura, 24% from the core kingdoms of Old and New Castile, and the remainder from other regions of the Iberian Peninsula. Other Europeans were rare, restricted to the odd Portuguese, Genoese, Flemish, or Greek man. In age, the conquerors ranged from teenagers to the occasional 60-year-old; the average age of the men who went to both Peru and Colombia was 27, with the vast majority in their 20s or early 30s.

In terms of education, again the range was broad, from men who were completely illiterate and uneducated to the occasional man of considerable learning.

Despite the impression given by conquistador chronicles, the fully literate were in the minority in conquest companies—although the paucity of farmers among conquistadors meant that literacy rates were slightly higher than back in Spain. Eyewitness narratives such as those by Bernal Díaz and Cortés on Mexico, and Francisco de Jérez on Peru, are classics partly because they are rare. Most conquistadors wrote or dictated "merit" reports in a formulaic style. Despite the common misconception that literacy gave Spaniards an advantage over Native Americans, members of conquistador companies could probably read and write no better than the most literate Native American societies, such as the Mayas.

Nor was the correlation between social status and literacy among conquistadors as close as might be expected; the colonial chronicler Juan Rodríguez Freyle, a Bogotá native, claimed that some city council members of the New Granada settlements used branding irons to sign documents. Among the 10 leaders of the famous 1532–1534 invasion of Peru, including the four Pizarro brothers, four were literate, three were semiliterate (they could sign their names), and three were illiterate (including Francisco Pizarro).

Spanish men were not the only people who fought with invading companies. A small number of Spanish women accompanied the conquistadors; of the thousand-odd Spaniards who entered Mexico with Cortés in 1519 or with other companies in the 1520s, 19 Spanish women participated to the degree that we might call them *conquistadoras*, and there is evidence of at least five of them actually fighting. Spaniards also brought with them African slaves and servants, their numbers increasing from less than a dozen in each company to many hundreds per expedition after 1521. Black conquistadors tended to be ignored in Spanish histories of the conquests, yet they were not only ubiquitous but also much valued as fierce fighters. The title of *conquistador* was also appropriated soon after the conquest by Maya, Zapotec, and other indigenous elites that had allied with Spanish invaders and won certain privileges in the new colonial system—as we shall see below. Finally, in the decades after their discovery of Brazil in 1500, the Portuguese gradually established small settlements along the Atlantic coast of their fledgling colony. They did not call themselves conquistadors, but, like their Spanish counterparts, they engaged local native peoples (the Tupi and others) with a combination of violence and accommodation.

THE OTHER SIDE OF THE CONQUEST

The spectacular collapse of the Mexica and Inka empires in the 1520s and 1530s has led to the notion that the Spanish Conquest was a dramatically rapid affair, and that subsequent campaigns by Spaniards and Portuguese allowed the Iberian kingdoms to soon absorb all but the most obscure corners of Latin America into their empires. But the Conquest was in fact highly protracted in two ways: (1) in terms of consolidation (it took the Spaniards and the Portuguese decades in some areas, centuries in others, to consolidate their control over local native peoples); and (2) in terms of geography (some regions were not invaded until decades or even centuries after Cortés attacked Moctezuma's empire). Furthermore, while some indigenous leaders continued to resist colonial rule, others were able to accommodate Spanish demands in a way that inverted the Conquest or muted their subordinate status within the new colonies.

Native peoples were not as quick to accept Spanish definitions of pacification as conquistadors claimed. The 1524–1529 invasion of highland Guatemala is a good example. Led by Pedro de Alvarado, a veteran of the 1519–1521 war against the Mexica, the first campaign allegedly resulted in the Spanish conquest of the highland Mayas and the foundation of a new Spanish colony—with subsequent violence the result of rebellions by Cakchiquel and Quiché Mayas. This was Alvarado's version, and it prevailed for centuries. We now know, however, three other sides to this story. One is the perspective of Pedro's brother, Jorge, who led a second invasion force into Guatemala in 1527–1529. In the words of one Spaniard who fought in these wars, "when the captain Jorge de Alvarado came to conquer this land … the country was at war and was unconquered, for there were few people [i.e., Spaniards]." When Pedro left for Spain in 1526, he left behind devastated Maya kingdoms, ongoing hostilities, and the mere semblance of a new colony. From this angle, Pedro's invasion was a failure; Jorge was the real conqueror. The second side to the story comes from the Nahuas and other Mesoamerican warriors who accompanied both Alvarado campaigns. Pedro's few hundred Spaniards were outnumbered by some 6,000 Mexica, Tlaxcalteca, Zapotec, Mixtec, and other allies. Jorge brought somewhere between 6,000 and 10,000 native warriors from central Mexico. They not only fought side by side with Spaniards but also engaged in their own battles against Mayas. They told accounts of the invasion in which they made far greater sacrifices than their Spanish allies—who then reneged on agreements and failed to honor promises. The third side to the story comes from the Mayas themselves. Contrary to Spanish claims, Maya leaders insisted they did not surrender and then revolt, but attempted to negotiate with and accommodate the invaders—whose greed and violence forced Mayas to defend their homes and families any way they could.

To the north of highland Guatemala, other Maya peoples resisted Spanish incursion, too. Beginning in 1527, a series of three invasions of Yucatan led by the Montejo family produced two decades of warfare and resulted in a small Spanish colony in the peninsula's northwest corner. Spanish maps marked the rest of the peninsula as *despoblado* ("uninhabited"), when in fact most of the Maya area was settled and unconquered. The Maya kingdom of the Itzá (in today's northern Guatemala) was not conquered until 1697, and while Yucatan's colonial frontier slowly moved south and east over the centuries, there remained independent unconquered Maya communities through to the twentieth century.

There were also South American examples of native refusals to accept the Spanish version of conquest history. In the **Chocó** region (of today's Colombia), the **Citará** and other native groups were first decimated by disease, and then

---

Chocó [cho-KOH], Citará [see-tah-RAH]   the name still used for the gold-rich northwest Pacific lowlands of Colombia and one of the native groups of the region who resisted Spanish rule through most of the colonial period

faced bloody warfare, enslavement, and forced relocation by missionaries. Yet they refused to be subdued, for centuries resisting relocation, labor demands, and attempts to change marriage and burial practices. In 1684–1687 an organized native rebellion in the Chocó killed 126 Spaniards and their African slaves and drove out the rest. The Spanish soon returned, and eventually some natives in the Chocó became converted. Spanish culture had a long-term impact in other ways, as natives adopted new material goods and farm animals and learned to use the Spanish legal system to defend themselves. Yet it is still fair to characterize the "pacification" of the Chocó as a violent conflict that lasted for most of the colonial period—the definition of a protracted conquest.

A final example comes from the foot of South America—the rugged coastline, gently rolling hills, and dense temperate rainforests that are the homeland of the Mapuche, one of the Americas' most resilient native cultures. Across nearly five centuries, they successfully resisted attempted conquests by the Inkas, the Spanish, and the Chilean nation-state. Several factors explain their success: (1) Mapuche culture (divided into many sub-groups) stressed a fierce independence and military tradition, with boys reared for a life of warfare; (2) the Spanish lost their technological advantage when Mapuche warriors adopted horses, guns, knives, and steel swords, while at the same time perfecting what the Spaniards called *guerrilla* ("little war") tactics; and (3) whereas native allies made Spanish conquests possible elsewhere in the Americas, the Mapuche appropriated this strategy from their enemies in 1599, forging a long-lasting confederacy with indigenous neighbors. The Spanish never conquered the Mapuche, and not until the 1880s did Chilean armed forces manage to partially subdue the Mapuche using modern weapons and threats of annihilation, a process similar to that used against native peoples of western North America and the Argentine *pampas* (plains) in the same era. Yet there remain a half million Mapuche today, and they are still proclaiming their independence.

When it became clear that the Spanish invaders had come to stay, native rulers and noblemen sought to accommodate, modify, or resist Spanish demands in various ways. Whatever their response, they all made decisions based on their evaluation of the best interests of their dynastic family and the community they ruled—not the interests of native peoples as a whole (as neither "Indians" nor Andeans, nor even Mayas, shared a sense of common identity). For example, the rulers of the Nahua town of Quauhquechollan formed an alliance with Cortés in 1520, negotiating their incorporation into the new Spanish colony in Mexico. In return for agreeing to Spanish tribute and labor demands, the town's ruling nobility were confirmed in office and participated in subsequent wars as conquistadors themselves—helping to defeat the Mexica in 1521 and playing a major role in the conquest of highland Guatemala in 1527–1529.

In the Maya lowlands, local leaders adopted comparable strategies. When Cortés passed through the small Chontal Maya kingdom of Acalan in 1525, the captive Mexica emperor, Cuauhtémoc, tried to convince the Chontal king to join him in a revolt against Cortés. The Chontal king, Paxbolonacha, declined the offer and instead told Cortés of the plot. When the Spanish immediately executed Cuauhtémoc and a few days later left the kingdom with their African slaves and Nahua allies, Paxbolonacha's decision must have seemed the wisest. In Yucatan, a Maya dynasty named Pech adopted a different appeasement strategy, permitting the Spaniards to settle in their corner of the peninsula. In 1542 the Pech town of Tiho became Mérida, the capital of a new Spanish colony. Pech lords were baptized, confirmed as noblemen and rulers of the surrounding towns, and participated in campaigns in other regions of the peninsula. They subsequently identified themselves as conquistadors; for example, Nakuk Pech and Macan Pech both styled themselves in Maya-language accounts of the Conquest as *yax hidalgos concixtador en*, combining Maya words with Spanish terms for "nobleman" and "conqueror" to mean "I, the first of the noble conquistadors."

For other Maya lords, allegiance to family and faction triumphed over other considerations. In the Itzá kingdom, not far to the east of Acalan, increasing pressure from the Spanish in the 1690s intensified factional tensions among the ruling elite. The response of the Itzá king was to send his nephew, Ah Chan, to Mérida in 1695 as an ambassador of peace and submission. The king hoped that a nominal recognition of colonial control might save his seat on the throne—a strategy that had worked for Paxbolonacha and his descendants in Acalan throughout the sixteenth century. Ah Chan was baptized Martín Chan, after his new godfather don Martín de Ursúa, the governor of Yucatan and soon-to-be conqueror of the Itzás. Ah Chan remained loyal to this strategy of appeasement through the Spanish invasion of the Itzá kingdom, only abandoning the Spaniards six months after the kingdom's conquest. Concluding, with good reason, that Spanish colonial rule was a disaster in the region, he became a leader of the Itzá resistance, ruling an independent kingdom of Itzá, Chol, and Mopan Mayas in the forests of what is now northern Guatemala and Belize until at least 1757.

Accommodation, followed by resistance, was a common pattern among native elites—in the Andes as well as in Mesoamerica. The rugged hill country and wet lowlands to the east of the Andes remained a conquest frontier throughout colonial times, much like the Maya Petén, and a place of periodic accommodation and rebellion. East of Quito, in a lowland jungle region populated by Quechua speakers called the province of Quijós, the indigenous leader Jumandy initially aided Spanish settlers and missionaries rich in trade goods. Once it became clear that settlers wanted only to force the lowland Quechua to mine gold in the Napo and other Amazon tributaries, however, Jumandy rebelled, driving the Spanish out in 1579. Only a trickle of missionaries eventually returned once Jumandy's revolt was put down.

Numerous Inka refugees also fled to the eastern lowlands following the Spanish conquest of the coast and central highlands, establishing an autonomous kingdom called Vilcabamba north of Cuzco. This "neo-Inka state," as some historians have called it, survived until 1572, when its hereditary leader, Túpac Amaru I, was captured and executed. Túpac and several predecessors had long accommodated Spanish missionaries and traders, so much so that the swift change in crown policy under Viceroy Toledo that led to the last Inka's capture and gruesome death came as a great surprise.

With the benefit of hindsight, many of these indigenous changes of heart with regard to the Spanish presence appear perplexing and even self-defeating. It is thus essential to search for native sources that can help explain them. Accounts of conquest events in native languages sometimes confirm Spanish sources. But more often they change our understanding of such events dramatically. For example, we would know nothing of Paxbolonacha's role in the death of Cuauhtémoc were it not for the Chontal Maya account of the affair, as Spanish sources make no mention of the Maya king's involvement.

SOLVING THE RIDDLE

In this chapter we have seen how the solution to the riddle of the Spanish Conquest—How did so few conquer so many?—lies in understanding who first viewed the Conquest in this way: the conquistadors themselves.

During the centuries of colonial rule, Spaniards believed that their conquests in the Americas were not just remarkable, but miraculous—made possible by their moral superiority. The conquest was providential; God had ordained it, using Spaniards as his agents to bring the true faith and the benefits of civilization to the pagan barbarians of the New World. As a result, in Spanish eyes there was something miraculous about military triumphs over great empires such as those of the Aztecs and Inkas. One conquistador, Gaspar de Marquina, in a letter to his father, remarked of the capture of Atawallpa that "God gave us the victory miraculously over him and his forces."

But divine intervention did not detract from the credit due to the conquistadors, for, in the words of Cortés, "Spaniards dare face the greatest peril, consider fighting their glory, and have the habit of winning." Santiago, the patron saint of the Reconquest, and the Virgin Mary may have been seen coming to the aid of the Spaniards during crucial conquest battles, but Spaniards still insisted that the skill and confidence with which they wielded their swords and other weapons made all the difference. These two factors—military superiority and unwavering self-confidence—have been dominant explanations of the Conquest for much of the past five centuries.

But while technological disparities clearly played an important role in military encounters, the Conquest is better understood and explained if the military factor is placed within the context of a group of five factors. The deadly impact of (1) disease on the Native American population, especially epidemics such as smallpox and measles, was massive. While germs traveled faster than Spaniards did, killing Native Americans before they ever saw a European face, the conquistadors were nevertheless greatly outnumbered among sedentary societies such as the Aztecs and other Nahuas, the Mayas, and the Andeans. This numerical imbalance was largely offset by (2) native allies. The highly localized nature of Native American identities fostered native disunity. This made possible the Spanish recruitment of large numbers of native warriors under their own leaders, the acquisition of native interpreters, and the collaboration of indigenous élites in conquest campaigns and colony building.

Combined with the impact of these two factors, the (3) advantages of Spanish weaponry were significant. The weapon that was most useful to the conquistadors, the one that killed more native warriors and saved invaders more often than any other, was the steel sword. Of secondary importance were guns, horses, and war dogs or mastiffs; these were not available to all Spaniards and were only useful under particular circumstances, although Spaniards greatly prized horses. Yet despite the benefit to Spaniards of epidemic disease, native allies, and the steel blade, there remained moments in the history of the Conquest when the invaders perished anyway—and moments when they would have perished were it not for a fourth factor.

This factor was (4) the circumstances of the Spanish invasion. Spanish invaders risked nothing beyond their own skins. Pressing on held the promise of great wealth and social prestige; turning back assured debt, ignominy, and perhaps the retribution of a betrayed patron. Native leaders, in contrast, were defending more than their lives. At stake were the lives of their families, the future status of their descendants, the welfare of whole communities. Symbolic of these concerns was the Mesoamerican view of war as a seasonal activity; they waged it when it was not time to plant or harvest. Native peoples were thus motivated to seek compromise and accommodation with an invader willing—and often able—to keep fighting until such an accommodation was reached. Indigenous leaders could not possibly have known that such compromises would result in three centuries of Spanish colonial rule.

But there was a fifth and final factor to solving the Conquest riddle. It is also important to remember that Spanish rule did not destroy Native America; like native rulers, (5) Spaniards themselves also compromised. Much as they hoped to transplant Iberian civilization to the Americas, and often seemed to believe they had succeeded, the colonists were obliged from the start to accommodate to native civilizations. They thereby fostered the genesis of hybrid cultures, which over the centuries came to comprise something new—Latin American civilization.

At the start of Part I we suggested that the riddle of the encounter of worlds was why it happened when it did, and how; and why has it been seen for so long as a discovery and conquest? In the previous chapters, we saw how in the centuries before 1492 western Africans and Native Americans developed great civilizations that did not motivate them to cross the Atlantic. In contrast, developments in Europe, especially in Iberia and parts of Italy, motivated exploration of the ocean. The resulting collision of Iberians, Africans, and native peoples in the Americas was violent partly because neither Africans nor Native Americans had sought the encounter. Iberians, who had not expected to find a new world, sought to dominate it in ways that provoked resistance. They did violence to black slaves and native peoples deliberately, in acts of war; accidentally, through the introduction of new diseases; and symbolically, by writing histories of the encounter that privileged European discovery and conquest and marginalized non-European roles. But none of the peoples that met in the Americas in the sixteenth century was willing to play a marginal role. As we shall see in Part II, all contributed to colonial Latin America's unique brew of cultures.

KEEP READING

This chapter is written to work with Matthew Restall's *Seven Myths of the Spanish Conquest* (2003), but we also recommend the following as additional (or alternative) texts: Stuart B. Schwartz, ed., *Victors and Vanquished: Spanish and Nahua Views of the Conquest of Mexico* (2000), which neatly juxtaposes Spanish accounts, chiefly that of Bernal Díaz, with Nahua and other native accounts; and Matthew Restall, *Maya Conquistador* (1998), which presents Maya accounts of the Conquest of Yucatan. Matthew Restall and Florine G. L. Asselbergs, *Invading Guatemala: Spanish, Nahua, and Maya Accounts of the Conquest Wars* (Latin American Originals 2) (2007) is designed for classroom usage.

For those seeking fuller access to primary Spanish sources in translation, we suggest the following editions: Bartolomé de Las Casas, *The Devastation of the Indies* (1992); Hernán Cortés, *Letters from Mexico*, Anthony Pagden, ed. (1986 edition); Bernal Díaz, *The Conquest of New Spain* (either the classic Penguin edition or, preferably, the 2009 edition by David Carrasco); Pedro de Cieza de León, *The Discovery and Conquest of Peru*, Alexandra Parma Cook and Noble David Cook, eds. (1998); James Lockhart and Enrique Otte, *Letters and People of the Spanish Indies* (1976), especially Part I; and J. Michael Francis, *Invading Colombia: Spanish Accounts of the Gonzalo Jiménez de Quesada Expedition of Conquest* (Latin American Originals 1) (2007).

Accessible secondary works on aspects of the Spanish conquest include Inga Clendinnen's *Ambivalent Conquests: Maya and Spaniard in Yucatan, 1517–1570* (2nd ed., 2003), which pairs well with *Maya Conquistador*; Anna Lanyon's books, *Malinche's Conquest* and *The New World of Martin Cortes* (2000 and 2004); and on the Andes, *Quito 1599: City and Colony in Transition* by Kris Lane (2002); and John Hemming's *The Conquest of the Incas*, originally published in 1970 but still a gripping read. Instructors using Matthew Restall, Lisa Sousa, and Kevin Terraciano, *Mesoamerican Voices: Native-Language Writings from Colonial Mexico, Oaxaca, Yucatan, and Guatemala* (2005) might assign Chapters 1–3 here.

The definitive books on the Quauhquechollan map and the Spanish Conquest of the Itzás, suitable for more advanced undergraduates, are, respectively, *Conquered Conquistadors: The Lienzo de Quauhquechollan, a Nahua Vision of the Conquest of Guatemala*, by Florine G. L. Asselbergs (2004), and Grant D. Jones's *The Conquest of the Last Maya Kingdom* (1998).

On the Chocó, see Caroline A. Williams, *Between Resistance and Adaptation: Indigenous Peoples and the Colonization of the Chocó, 1510–1753* (2005). On Guaman Poma, see Rolena Adorno, *Writing and Resistance in Colonial Peru*, 2nd ed. (2000). The full text of Guaman Poma's *El primer nueva corónica y buen gobierno* has also been placed online by the Royal Library of Denmark, where the original text is housed (www.kb.dk/elib/mss/poma/).

PART II

✴

Colonial Compromises
(1550–1740)

The colonial middle period, sometimes called the Baroque, witnessed the consolidation and evolution of Latin American societies. Indeed, it is only here that the term "Latin America," though not applied until the mid-1800s, gains meaning.

Although vast areas remained in the hands of native peoples and runaway slaves throughout this era, in former core Native American regions such as highland Mexico and the Andes, the Spanish created a string of hierarchical, urban, Catholic societies. Radiating out from colonial cities was a more populous rural, village-oriented world of indigenous tribute-payers, enslaved African plantation workers, and mine laborers of varying heritage. Most Portuguese settlers clung to Brazil's long and fertile coast, where they established port cities and plantations staffed with a mix of enslaved Native Americans and Africans.

Soon after conquest Spanish America came to rely on silver mines for foreign exchange and Portuguese Brazil on sugar. Gold, found in many parts of Spanish America, was discovered in Brazil just before 1700. Funded by these and other sources of income, priests and missionaries sought to impose orthodox Catholicism on all of Latin America's subject peoples. Despite harsh punishments by the Inquisition and other Church institutions, conversion was only a partial success. As people mixed, moved, and intermarried, colonial Latin America grew more socially complex and distinct from either Europe or Africa. It also grew more politically independent.

The Spanish and Portuguese colonies faced numerous challenges in the middle period: slave revolts and the problem of maroons, or runaways; the prolonged conquest of native peoples on the colonial frontiers; the challenges of exploiting native labor and tribute payments without provoking violent resistance; the threat of northern European pirates and the states that sponsored them; the difficulty of imposing Catholic orthodoxy on a population that was culturally diverse and dynamic; and the inevitable mixing of peoples that Iberian administrators had hoped to control by keeping apart. Thus the riddle of this period was how, in the face of all these challenges, did the colonies persist? The answer lies in the intricacies of the colonial compromise—in the many ways in which Spaniards and Portuguese combined violence (or its threat) with concessions to non-Iberian subjects, and the many ways in the non-Iberian majority continued to help create and shape the colonies.

4

✳

Plunder and Production

Portuguese Ships, African Slaves, American Colonies

Slavery in the Early Colonies

What Was the "Republic of Indians"?

Land and Labor

Frontiers

The Pirate Challenge

For all their emphasis on military conquest, the Spanish and Portuguese had no desire to eliminate Native American populations. Quite the contrary; from the time of Columbus and Cabral, native peoples were seen as the Americas' main source of wealth. Spaniards in particular sought to acquire the tribute networks of the native empires and kingdoms they conquered and to build their colonies upon native communities. Their agricultural surpluses were to be collected and redistributed by Iberian landlords in a way resembling European feudalism, and the Indians' surplus labor would be used to construct cities, tend livestock, harvest European crops, and mine for gold and silver. In both Brazil and Spanish America, Native American labor was the base upon which the colonial economy was built.

However, from the start of European exploration, conquest, and settlement in the Americas, enslaved Africans were brought along to do various kinds of work, from hard labor to highly skilled tasks. Black slaves and free servants fought for Spanish masters against native warriors defending their lands; they worked as household domestics and auxiliaries in small businesses; and where the native population was sparse or declined the most, Africans labored in large numbers as plantation or mine slaves.

In the first half of this chapter, we shall see how Africans and their mixed-race descendants sought to improve their lives in numerous ways; to resist the subordinate, involuntary circumstances of their passage to the New World; and to forge the bonds of family. In the second half of the chapter, we explain how indigenous peoples at the colonial core were transformed into Spanish and

TIMELINE

1441	The Portuguese begin the Atlantic trade in African slaves, dominating it until about 1640
1482	The Portuguese establish a trading post at São Jorge da Mina, on the coast of present-day Ghana
1495–1510	First American gold boom-and-bust cycle takes place on Hispaniola
1505–1540	Rise and fall of pearl beds off the Venezuelan coast
1534	Donatary captaincies created in Brazil. Only those of São Vicente and Pernambuco succeed by devoting resources to sugar production for export.
1542–1543	Implementation of New Laws restricting *encomienda* system
1545	Discovery of silver in Potosí (soon followed by Zacatecas and Guanajuato in Mexico)
1549	Jesuits arrive in Brazil and begin creating aldeias, or indigenous mission communities
1572–1575	Creation of mita labor draft in Potosí silver mines
1580	Philip II of Spain annexes Portugal, thus gaining effective control of Brazil and Portugal's slaving posts in western Africa
1580–1640	Portuguese hold asiento, or monopoly contract, to supply Spanish America with African slaves
1592	Potosí reaches peak production
1622 and 1628	Spanish lose part of the silver fleet in a hurricane, and then all of it to Dutch pirates led by Piet Heyn
1630–1654	The Dutch occupy much of northeastern Brazil, from the mouth of the Amazon to Pernambuco
1640	Portugal rebels against Spanish rule, interrupting the supply of slaves to Spanish America
1655	English take Jamaica from the Spanish
1697	French possession of the western end of Hispaniola is formally recognized by the Spanish as the colony of Saint Domingue

Portuguese subjects as defined by their conquerors. We then look at how within the bounds of colonialism indigenous peoples carved out spaces and challenged or used the colonial regime to meet their own needs. On the colonial fringes, indigenous life was different; many of the patterns of the core regions were sharply altered or simply did not apply. Finally, the chapter looks at the threat that the northern European powers, primarily the Dutch and English, posed to the Spanish Empire in the period we call "the colonial middle."

PORTUGUESE SHIPS, AFRICAN SLAVES, AMERICAN COLONIES

As we saw in the previous chapter, Portuguese traders began to ship African slaves to Iberia in the 1440s. Thus before the Americas were reached, the basic structure of the slave trade was established: Portuguese ship captains purchased slaves from African rulers and merchants on the coasts of West Africa and West Central Africa; these slaves were then sold in urban markets to the Iberian elite, who put them to work either as domestic servants or on large-scale tropical plantation or gold-mining operations.

These two broad categories can also be applied to slaves in the Americas: (1) auxiliary slaves, ranging from black conquistadors fighting alongside their owners, to slave men assisting merchants, to female wet nurses and domestic servants; and (2) mass slaves, meaning slaves who worked in large groups on sugar plantations, in gold diggings, and similar enterprises. The first Africans crossed the Atlantic with Columbus—from then until the trade finally ended in the late nineteenth century, some 11 million Africans were forced to cross the Atlantic on a grueling journey known as the Middle Passage (see Image and Word 4.1). Many died during the voyage, and others died before even making the journey.

Enslaved Africans did not end up evenly spread throughout the Americas. Most were taken to the Caribbean islands (a reasonable estimate is 4.7 million) and to Brazil (4.2 million). This was because sugar plantations dominated the economies of the Portuguese colony of Brazil, and of the English, French, and other European colonies in the Caribbean; it was in those places that the greatest demand for slave labor developed in response to soaring overseas consumer demand for sugar. Another half-million Africans ended up in British North America, many to work on the tobacco, rice, and later cotton plantations that developed there in the eighteenth and nineteenth centuries; British North America was unique in that the enslaved population grew naturally, with substantial encouragement from slave owners, whereas the tropical colonies relied on constant imports, mostly of young men. The majority of Africans brought to the Americas had the misfortune of being mass slaves, mostly plantation workers. Of the estimated 1.7 million Africans who were sold to Spanish owners in the Americas, most fell into the category of auxiliary slaves. Although many worked in mines, on plantations and ranches, and even in textile mills, the demand for African slaves was staunched in most Spanish colonies by the ready availability of Native American workers.

Although it was Spaniards, not Portuguese, who carved out colonies throughout much of the Americas in the sixteenth century, the Portuguese continued to dominate the slave trade well into the seventeenth century—aided by

---

IMAGE AND WORD 4.1 The Middle Passage

It is difficult to imagine the suffering endured by the more than 11 million African captives forced to cross the Atlantic Ocean in early modern times. The ordeal itself has come to be known as the Middle Passage, an oddly benign-sounding name for the excruciating months that slaves spent huddled in floating wooden prisons. Some Africans imagined the slavers' ships to be floating slaughterhouses crossing a great lake or river to satisfy white cannibals inhabiting a distant, sterile land. Portuguese sailors unambiguously dubbed them "death ships" or "floating tombs." Perhaps troubled by this sense of damnation, Portuguese priests in Luanda, Benguela, and elsewhere in Portuguese Africa baptized as many slaves as they could before departure. Portuguese ships, like Spanish gold and silver mines, were virtually all named for saints.

Northern Europeans, increasingly in charge of the slave trade after 1640, took a more dispassionate approach. For them, slaves were more like highly valued livestock requiring efficient but impersonal handling. In other words, the care and feeding of slaves were treated as matters of health, not faith. Rations were the subsistence minimum of maize, rice, or millet gruel, with a bit of fish or dried meat added from time to time. Men, women, and children were assigned separate quarters. Women were given a cotton cloth to wrap around their bodies, whereas men were often kept naked to add to their already abject humiliation. Exercise was required on deck in the form of dancing to drums during daylight hours. As if cattle, slaves were showered with sea water before the nighttime lock-down. The hold, ventilated on most ships after initial experiences with mass suffocation and heat stroke, was periodically splashed with vinegar.

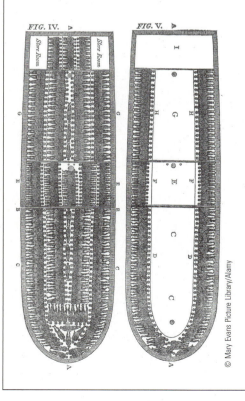

FIG. IV.   FIG. V.

© Mary Evans Picture Library/Alamy

Despite these measures, slave mortality on the 1–3 month voyage across the Atlantic was high. On average, between 10% and 20% of slaves did not survive the cramped conditions, physical abuse, and generally unsanitary environment aboard ship. This high mortality rate is all the more alarming in that these slaves had been selected for their relative good health in the first place, leaving countless others behind to perish in makeshift barracks, dungeons, and coastal agricultural plots. Many more died soon after landing in the Americas, often from dysentery and other intestinal ailments. Some who were emotionally overwhelmed committed suicide along the way by hurling themselves into the ocean or strangling themselves in their chains. A few enraged men managed to kill a crewmember or even a captain before being summarily executed. Successful slave mutinies, in which women as well as men participated, were rare but not unknown.

Although there were some minor protests of the horrors of this crossing by Iberian clergymen going back to the sixteenth century, it took the extraordinary eighteenth-century deterioration of conditions aboard slave ships to awaken the conscience of participating nations. In earlier centuries, 30–40 sailors oversaw 200–300 slaves, but as ships became more congested, the number of slaves onboard rose closer to 400. (The image on the previous page, a detail from the plans of the English slave ship *Brookes*, shows how "tight packing" was designed to squeeze in as many slaves as possible.) In England, most importantly, African survivors of the Middle Passage such as Olaudah Equiano were called to testify before Parliament in the late eighteenth century. Their testimonies, backed by the impassioned pleas of prominent Quakers and other religious figures, were finally heard. In 1808 the Atlantic slave trade was abolished by the British, who imposed the ban on other nations; gradually, the Middle Passage ceased to exist. Slavery itself, however, would persist in the Americas for 80 more years.

the effective union (through royal marriages plus an invasion of Lisbon by Philip II) of Spain and Portugal from 1580 to 1640. In fact, we can divide the era of the slave trade to the Americas into two halves: the Portuguese half, from 1492 to 1640; and the English half, from 1640 to the nineteenth century. During the later decades of the Portuguese period, some 7,000–8,000 slaves were brought across the Atlantic every year; by 1640, some quarter of a million Africans had been forced to come to Spanish America, and a similar number to Brazil. Many Europeans were involved in the Atlantic slave trade to some extent or another, but the English dominated the trade in later centuries, bringing far more slaves to American colonies than even the Portuguese did.

Given the rudimentary technology, poor communication, and lack of medical understanding characteristic of the era, the overseas trade in enslaved African captives proved lucrative because European investors cut costs at every turn and because the inhabitants of tropical western Africa were a highly resilient people. Recognizing their physical weakness vis-à-vis malaria, yellow fever, and other tropical maladies typical of this region, Portuguese slavers planted few settlement colonies, preferring instead to establish only a small number of secure posts between Upper Guinea and Angola. The slave trade within Africa was mostly in local hands. In many places mixed, Afro-Portuguese communities developed, serving as intermediaries who shared the faith and language of the slavers.

On the African side of this cruel commerce, few commodities produced by Europeans except guns and gunpowder were attractive enough to stimulate trade, although as we have seen, war horses were an early favorite. Portuguese slavers eventually found substantial African markets for plain and print cotton cloth from South Asia, cowry shells from the Indian Ocean's Maldive Islands chain, and iron and copper from parts of Europe, particularly Spain and Sweden. In terms of both volume and value, cloth was most significant throughout the period of the slave trade. By the later seventeenth century, if not before, Brazilian and other American commodities such as rum and tobacco were being exchanged for slaves in significant quantities. Thus, however immoral and disruptive of African life it appears in retrospect, the slave trade probably seemed at the time to be mutually beneficial for European buyers and African sellers. Only the slaves themselves felt otherwise.

SLAVERY IN THE EARLY COLONIES

Africans quickly found their way into virtually every sector of colonial society. Most were enslaved, some were freed or managed to purchase their own freedom, others settled in native communities. Many enslaved African men worked as overseers on indigenous-staffed ranches and farms. Others served as squires and footmen for Spanish, Portuguese, and occasionally high-ranking indigenous lords. Enslaved African women engaged in a wide variety of household auxiliary work, staffing convents as well as private homes. Most African women worked alongside indigenous women and girls.

Where there was quick wealth to be had, however, a different type of slavery arose. Gold, sugar, pearls, and other prized commodities were thought to warrant intense exploitation, and such work was often as deadly as it was demanding, especially to immune-deficient Native Americans. From an early date in both Spanish America and Brazil, African laborers were preferred over natives in labor-intensive industries due to their greater resistance to a wide range of diseases.

There were several export-oriented sectors in which large numbers of African slaves labored in the first years after conquest, particularly in the lowland gold mines of Hispaniola, Mexico, Honduras, Panama, Peru, and New Granada. As gold deposits played out by the mid- to late sixteenth century, however, slave labor in Spanish America's mines faded, to be revived in some places later in the next century. Following models already established in the east Atlantic, the sugar plantations of northeastern Brazil were the next frontier for large-scale African slavery.

Slaves were considered a form of capital. They could be a source of both rents and credit (they could even be mortgaged), yet they were also recognized as human beings with certain rights and potential for self-improvement, including self-purchase and spiritual salvation. Spanish and Portuguese laws dating to medieval times required that slaves be indoctrinated and made to receive Catholic sacraments, and that they be allowed to purchase their own or their spouses' or children's freedom with monies earned beyond daily quotas. A slave had the right to initiate a legal action called a **coartación**, in which two assessors (one

---

Coartación [koh-ar-tah-SYOAN]   legal action of self-purchase initiated by a slave in the Spanish Empire

picked by the slave, one by the owner) evaluated the slave in court; a price was set, the slave made a down payment, and as a *coartado* took the first step toward freedom. Not all masters complied with these requirements, but enough did to have some impact on the nature of African slavery in the Iberian colonies. Access to freedom and incorporation into the Catholic fold were core features of the slave system in Latin America.

Those enslaved Africans who were most willing to acculturate to Iberian ways, and most especially to the Catholic religion, were chosen as intermediaries and work-gang bosses. Slave captains negotiated with the ruling class for better living conditions, reduced production quotas during droughts and other crises, and other concessions. Some, on the other hand, bargained mostly for themselves—for personal or family gain rather than the good of the larger slave community. But work gangs were stratified, too, and there were many examples of slaves struggling for a degree of autonomy and respect within this early, preindustrial system. Certain tasks, such as tool sharpening, for example, were often entrusted to already skilled African blacksmiths. Others brought knowledge of rice cultivation, gold prospecting, weaving, and pottery making. Critical medical knowledge, such as the curing of snakebites and dressing of postpartum wounds, was left in the hands of African curers and midwives. Slaves who built and sailed ships, or carved and paddled or poled canoes, were similarly prized for their accumulated or inherited skills. Slavery, in short, was as ubiquitous as it was complex.

Auxiliary slaves were quite common in the early colonial period, particularly in Spanish America. African men and women served as cooks, grooms, laundresses, and majordomos, often overseeing large households and ranches whose main workforce was indigenous. Africans in auxiliary roles tended to identify more with Hispanic culture than with indigenous ones, although many slaves were accused of continuing to practice their African religions. In rare cases this might include Islam. There were even a few African auxiliary slaves accused of practicing Judaism, the faith of their secretly practicing Portuguese-Jewish masters. Acculturation could work in the other direction, too. Slaves in overseeing roles, for example, had to learn indigenous languages such as Quechua, Maya, and Nahuatl, making them more knowledgeable in many cases than their European masters of indigenous ways and concerns. These auxiliary slaves' positions of relative power brought them a certain amount of respect from indigenous tributaries and other native subjects, and occasionally also from Spaniards. Some African overseers were well-hated, however, and more than a few were killed in the course of uprisings, as they were more vulnerable to physical attack than their Spanish masters. Some indigenous workers regarded African auxiliaries as symbols of collaboration and oppression while others saw them as allies.

Brazilian plantation slavery followed a different path, in that in most regions Africans gradually came to replace enslaved indigenous workers in the fields and mills. From as early as the 1540s, Portuguese mill and plantation owners did not distinguish between Native Americans and Africans in the same way as their Spanish counterparts. Throughout Brazil, native peoples were referred to as

negros da terra, or "blacks of the land," a suggestion that both Africans and native Americans were imagined by these European outsiders to be "natural slaves." This Aristotelian mode of thinking fit well with the interests of colonial merchant-capitalists by offering a justification for enslavement of even peaceful peoples, whether African or Native American. In the fields and mills, this indiscriminate approach to forced labor had a partial flattening effect in terms of the formation of racial hierarchies, although prices for native slaves always remained low in comparison to those of Africans. African slaves were more resistant to disease, more likely to acculturate to Portuguese ways, and less likely to run away permanently.

To prevent widespread rebellions among the mass, enslaved population, Portuguese masters soon employed a variety of clever, socially divisive mechanisms. One was to heighten the distinction between newly arrived and creolized, or acculturated, African slaves. Newly arrived Africans were publicly ridiculed for their distinct speech patterns, hairstyles, and ritual scarifications, or "country marks." Their incorporation into the slave regime entailed complex rites of passage intended to have a socially "erasing" effect. Those slaves born in the colonies were distinguished even further from those born in Africa, and slaves of mixed heritage were treated in yet other, separate categories. Light-colored mulattoes, for example, were often promoted to high-ranking auxiliary roles in both household and mill. Enslaved natives, despite the initial confluence of "racial" terms (the word *raza* was not yet current, although color was constantly noted), were similarly distinguished from their fellows, as were their mixed, Afro-indigenous offspring. Color and culture, in short, were the key markers used by Portuguese planters to divide and rule a large enslaved population. This pragmatic early strategy of control formed the foundation of Brazilian racism.

WHAT WAS THE "REPUBLIC OF INDIANS"?

Families of African descent lived in what we might call "attached subordination" to Europeans in the Americas. In Spanish America, this attachment had a formal political structure. In the new colonial settlements, officially dubbed *villas* (towns) or *ciudades* (cities), Spaniards governed themselves through a town council, called a *cabildo*; the Spanish *cabildo* and local Spanish residents constituted the *República de Españoles* in that town. African slaves and their descendants did not have their own república; they were in theory attached to the Spanish one, as dependents of Spanish owners or employers.

Native peoples, however, were assigned equivalent political status, living in the *República de Indios*. These were not "republics" in any sense of our understanding of the word, but rather referred to the fact that Spaniards and "Indians"

Negros da terra   literally "blacks of the land," a sixteenth-century Portuguese term for enslaveable native Brazilians

governed themselves—albeit on different levels, as beyond the village level, all political authority was in the hands of Spanish colonial administrators.

Few Native American communities were granted villa or ciudad status; they were almost all *pueblos* (literally, "villages," but the term applied to communities ranging in size from less than a hundred to thousands of inhabitants). Every native pueblo had its own cabildo, a town council modeled on the Spanish institution but interpreted differently by native peoples. The cabildo system may look like an institution imposed on indigenous communities by the colonists—and that was indeed how Spaniards viewed it—but in practice it was merely a new veneer over an ancient system of government by village elders. Native cabildo officers tended to be senior male representatives of elite families in the pueblo, usually the same families that had dominated the area before the Conquest. The numbers, titles, and terms of office of cabildo officers varied according to local custom.

Every cabildo had a notary or scribe, a position of far greater importance in the native cabildo than in its Spanish equivalent; Spaniards often commented on, and complained about, how litigious "the Indians" were and how well their cabildos engaged the colonial legal system. Above the cabildo was the governor— sometimes called *gobernador*, sometimes given native titles of rule (such as *kuraka* in Peru or *batab* in Yucatan), sometimes a **cacique** or dynastic lord descended from precolonial kings or rulers. In some places, such as in the Mixtec region of southern Mexico and in parts of the northern Andes, *cacicas* or elite women ruled their communities (see Image and Word 4.2).

The *República de Indios* in any given native community was thus its governor and cabildo, its official pueblo status, and its residents. Some places, where Spaniards had settled on the site of old native towns, had two cabildos, representing both repúblicas; the most obvious example is Mexico City, where there was both a Spanish cabildo and a Nahua cabildo—the latter to govern the native residents of Tenochtitlán, as Nahuas continued to call the city throughout the colonial period.

Native peoples themselves did not refer to their community as a pueblo or República de Indios—they used the indigenous name of the place, to which a saint's name was usually prefixed, and they continued to use native terms for community. In Mesoamerica, for example, the Nahua municipal community was the **altepetl**, the Mixtec one was the **ñuu**, and the Yucatec Maya equivalent was the **cah**. These terms applied to the smallest village as much as to the most impressive town or city, and they encompassed not just the cluster of homes centered on the local church but also the lands pertaining to the place, its people, and its history—that is, a deeply-rooted sense of identity and belonging.

Cacique [kah–SEE–kay]   Arawak (Taíno) word for ruler, adopted by Spaniards to refer to hereditary lords throughout the Americas (female equivalent, cacica)

Altepetl [al–te–PET], ñuu [new], and cah [kah]   examples of Mesoamerican terms for the city-state or municipal community (in Nahuatl, Mixtec, and Yucatec Maya, respectively)

IMAGE AND WORD 4.2   The Cacica

In the image below, the cacica of a native village outside Bogotá is memorialized in a fresco painted on the wall of the local church. The privilege of being painted for posterity, combined with the depiction of her as piously praying, holding a rosary and wrapped in a mantle of office, all reflect her high status in the community. Her elaborately patterned garment shows how indigenous craftsmanship was still highly valued and proudly displayed long after the Spanish Conquest.

Another cacica from the northern Andes ordered in her will, filed in Quito in 1606, that a chapel be built for her family and that numerous masses be said for her soul and for those of her relatives. She also named a female heir, cleverly side-stepping the standard Spanish policy favoring male caciques.

The northern Andes was not the only region of the Spanish America where noblewomen from old dynasties wielded local power. Among the Mixtecs of Oaxaca, in southern Mexico, cacicas ruled and laid claim to privileges of nobility. One such woman, doña Catalina de Peralta, was (despite her Spanish-sounding name) the Mixtec heiress to the rulership of the town of Yucundaa (called Teposcolula by Nahuas and Spaniards) in the 1560s. She presented ancient painted manuscripts and early colonial wills to prove her case, and in 1569 took ritual possession of the palace (still called *La Casa de la Cacica*, and open to visitors today). The ritual, described in the written record of the proceedings, featured both Spanish practices (symbolic door-slamming and stone-throwing) and traditional Mixtec ones (the noblewoman and her husband sitting on reed mats to mark their assumption of rulership).

Courtesy of Kris Lane

At the level of altepetl and cah, old traditions of micropatriotism, or local allegiance, persisted through the colonial centuries. Highly localized clothing styles, speech patterns, and religious affiliations, usually through the Catholic cult of saints, distinguished one community from another. Indigenous food ways persisted virtually everywhere, although with the addition of certain introduced items, including barley, sugar, plantains, and meat and cheese derived from European domestic animals. A major point of contention with the Spanish was in the realm of religion, where Christianity was adopted and adapted in local and often unorthodox ways (sometimes leading to disagreements that turned violent).

Continuity of rule and community survival were not always possible. Some communities disappeared entirely due to the early colonial population decline (see Image and Word 4.3), combined with Spanish attempts to concentrate

IMAGE AND WORD 4.3 The Columbian Exchange

In a landmark 1972 book, historian Alfred Crosby argued that the most significant consequences of 1492 were not political or even commercial, but biological. What Crosby called the "Columbian Exchange" referred to the massive transatlantic transfer of animals (including humans), plants, and diseases that followed in Columbus's wake. Many such transfers—such as the introduction of rats and smallpox to the Americas—were unintentional. Yet all had profound consequences. Northern European populations, for example, grew rapidly following the introduction of Andean potatoes, which thrived in cool, wet climates. Tomatoes, chocolate, and tobacco were gradually but profoundly absorbed into European cultures of cuisine and consumption. South Asian cooking was forever changed after the introduction of American capsicum peppers, which thrived in the eastern tropics.

In the Americas, European cattle, sheep, pigs, goats, horses, and other large domestic mammals rapidly altered whatever terrain they were let loose on, sometimes with catastrophic consequences. Although indigenous cuisines, farming practices, and transportation modes were often changed for the better, large animals had the drawback (like modern automobiles) of needing lots of fuel. In the worst case, the highlands of central Mexico were quickly denuded and reduced to deserts following the introduction of sheep in the sixteenth century. Lacking predators and

Stapleton Collection/Corbis

(continued)

IMAGE AND WORD 4.3   The Columbian Exchange (continued)

---

having access to vast new pastures, their populations exploded. Thus a kind of slow environmental and cultural conquest was achieved by the spread of Old World plants and animals.

Even more tragically, Native American populations were devastated by Old World pathogens such as smallpox, measles, and influenza. The image on the previous page, from Jean de Léry's 1588 *Histoire d'un voyage fait en la terre du Bresil*, is a highly stylized depiction of a Brazilian shaman, or native healer, with Tupis dying from epidemic disease. Since Africa and Eurasia had long been linked by waves of trade, warfare, migration, and pilgrimage, diseases such as smallpox, measles, and mumps had become endemic. That is, the repeated epidemic spread of these and other pathogens helped create a substantial and frequently replenished pool of people with acquired immunity, or helpful antibodies, often gained in early childhood. Epidemics of influenza and plague could be devastating in Africa and Eurasia, but never to the extent that they would be in long-isolated regions overseas.

In the early modern Americas, poor hygiene and medical care, chronic warfare, forced labor, and malnutrition all accompanied European conquest, rendering new disease agents all the more destructive. Throughout the Americas and Pacific Islands, indigenous populations declined by almost 90% within a century. Recovery, and with it acquired immunity, did not come for centuries.

---

surviving villagers into central settlements (the flawed and largely unsuccessful policy called *congregación*). In the 1570s, Viceroy Toledo congregated the remnants of some 900 villages in what is now Bolivia into 44 settlements. Many Andeans drifted back to their old homes and lands, just as thousands of Mayas did in the wake of congregación efforts in seventeenth-century Yucatan; but much of the damage done to local life was irreversible. Other places were profoundly altered by developments such as changes in the local economy, by the settlement in the area of outsiders (such as mixed-race migrants or natives from elsewhere), or by the village's location on one of the colonial trunk-lines (the arteries of trade and communication).

Still, for other pueblos the colonial middle was a period of relative calm and stability—cultural, economic, and political. Underpinning this mid-colonial florescence of Mesoamerican and Andean communities was the role played by the local native elite. Spaniards sought out indigenous leaders who, in exchange for certain labor and tax exemptions, would act as intermediaries. This became increasingly important as the *encomienda* disappeared in core areas, and the crown began to collect indigenous surplus production in the form of tribute, first in products of the land, then in cash. Local headmen (and occasionally headwomen) were responsible for collecting tribute twice a year and for assembling workers for labor drafts. In some cases village leaders protected their subjects from Spanish exploitation, and in other cases they profited from it.

The role of the native elite was crucial, therefore, to both the survival of the native community and the functioning of the Spanish colonies. The colonial system permitted—and depended on—the persistence of native elites in three ways: (1) the institutionalization of village identity and corporate integrity, in the form of the *República de Indios* and *cabildo* government, as described above; (2) the redirection of ancient tribute systems in Mesoamerica and the Andes, so that tribute—in the form of labor, goods, and, eventually, primarily cash—became the essential material link between the crown and its native subjects; and (3) the need for middlemen to govern native pueblos and mediate the tribute relationship between natives and the crown. Spaniards saw class differences, or socioeconomic hierarchy, as part of the natural order of things, with the maintenance of a nobility as a sign of a civilized society. They therefore never questioned the confirmation of local status and position by native elites. Only in the late colonial period did native elites find their position under siege.

LAND AND LABOR

Toward the end of the seventeenth century, the Mexican village of Sula, a Nahuatl-speaking altepetl not far from Mexico City, put its local history to paper. In one episode, Mexica (Aztec) forces came down to conquer Sula—led by a Spanish woman. The village was successfully defended by two brothers, whose weapons included the ability to turn into quail-serpents and the wielding of colonial-type land titles.

The story is an evocative example of how native communities absorbed outside influences and the changes brought by Spanish colonialism, without losing their own cultural traditions and sense of micropatriotic identity. From the Sula perspective, Mexico was divided less between Spaniards and Nahuas than it was between locals and outsiders (be they Spaniards or fellow Nahuas from Tenochtitlán-Mexico City). The telescoping of Mexica and Spanish conquests of the area reflected the fact that narrative chronology mattered less than Sula's historical ability to defend its territory. The tale also illustrates the importance of land ownership to community identity. This folk history was written down as part of a land dispute between Sula and a Spanish estate owner, and the local cabildo was thus concerned to demonstrate that it had title to the lands—a title that was both ancient and verifiable within the colonial legal system.

Indigenous lands in Spanish America were communally held and legally inalienable, although in some places predatory Spaniards cleverly advanced their own claims. Everywhere the introduction of European livestock proved a mixed blessing, at best. In a world without such animals, there had been no need for fences, but as soon as they multiplied their desire to graze in indigenous maize fields created headaches and in some cases full-blown subsistence crises. One of several colonial legacies, communal indigenous land-holdings (commonly called *ejidos*), continues to be a source of contention in Latin America today.

Over time, Spanish estate owners acquired communal lands from native villages and private plots from native farmers. The general long-term trend was for land to pass from native to Spanish hands, often with no or inadequate compensation. However, it is important to emphasize that most such transfers appear to have been legal sales, and that this was a gradual development. While Spanish colonial rule was undoubtedly exploitative, the basis of that exploitation was the acquisition by Spaniards of the product of native labor. It would have been counterproductive for colonists to destroy native villages or seize the land that sustained native villagers. Controlling native labor was always more important than acquiring native land.

The first institution used by Spaniards to control indigenous labor was the *encomienda*. Applied in the early years of Caribbean colonization, the *encomienda* was an "entrusting" of indigenous villagers to prominent Spanish men, often in reward for military service. Holders of *encomiendas*, called *encomenderos*, had rights to indigenous surpluses in the form of foodstuffs, cloth, and other products, which they could trade or barter in the Spanish marketplace. They also had rights to surplus adult male labor, which they applied to a variety of enterprises, most importantly gold mining. In exchange, the *encomendero* was to protect his subjects from bellicose neighbors and pay a priest to provide instruction in the Catholic faith. Villagers were not to be moved from their traditional landholdings, and their subsistence was not to be disturbed.

Encomenderos were more concerned with the exploitation of their native subjects than their long-term well-being. Abuses by *encomenderos*, and crown concerns over *encomendero* power, led to efforts to abolish the institution. The Spanish elite resisted, the crown compromised, but by 1600 the *encomienda* had faded away in all but the poorer provinces and frontier districts.

In central Mexico, where the *encomienda* was first phased out, the crown established a kind of labor roundup called the *repartimiento*. Non-noble native men between the ages of 18 and 50 were subject to periodic service in a variety of projects in the agricultural off-season, including church construction, public works, and mining. Workers were supposed to be paid and cared for, but many were lucky to receive food and a bit of coarse cloth. It was through the repartimiento that many of Mexico's first silver mines, most of them located in the desert north, were staffed. The most important of these were located in the hills around Zacatecas and Guanajuato, many days' journey from Mexico City. When indigenous hands became scarce with population decline around 1600, African slaves were brought to work alongside the survivors. Mostly uncompensated indigenous labor had thus enabled mine owners to accumulate enough money and credit to purchase slaves. Also as a result of increasing scarcity, however, wage labor appeared. Spanish mine owners hated paying wages and withheld them whenever possible. But, despite their complaints, many native men became professional, salaried miners.

In much of Spanish South America, even beyond the limits of the old Inka Empire, the *encomienda* was replaced by an institution resembling the Mexican repartimiento but deriving from native practice. Patterned on the Inka *mit'a*, or "turn," system, the Spanish **mita** demanded adult indigenous men to work for extended periods in about the same range of activities found in Mexico. Most important for central Peru and Bolivia were the silver mines of **Potosí**, staffed with mita labor by 1575. Workers from hundreds of miles away were required to travel to Potosí for one out of every seven years. The trip was so disruptive, and the work so dangerous, that many *mitayos*, or mita workers, did not survive. To keep them working, native miners were given coca leaves to chew; by the 1570s some 90% of Spanish-controlled coca production went to Potosí. Even worse were the mercury mines of **Huancavelica**, Peru, where draft laborers not injured in cave-ins developed debilitating nervous disorders. As in Mexico, draft labor in the Andes only exacerbated population decline, stimulating a turn to African slavery in many profitable enterprises and inadvertently stimulating the appearance of wage labor.

Natives in both Brazil and Spanish America were exploited in other roles, as cowboys, farmers, canoe paddlers, fishermen, porters, and construction workers. In the Valley of Mexico, a massive drainage project consumed the lives of thousands of indigenous men. Nearly all the great churches of Spanish America, the region's most tangible and often admired colonial heritage, were built by native carpenters, stonemasons, plasterers, and painters. It is critically important to remember that the entire colonial Latin American edifice was built with the blood and sweat of indigenous and African workers.

FRONTIERS

Beyond the limits of the old Mesoamerican and Andean empires, where indigenous populations tended to be smaller and more dispersed, the Spanish tended to re-create conquest patterns of settlement and exploitation. In places where precious metals or other prized commodities were to be had, the *encomienda* was revived, often followed by a turn to African slavery as indigenous populations declined due to overwork, displacement, and disease. As seen above, this pattern was followed throughout the gold fields of New Granada, for example, and also in the cacao groves of Venezuela. Where mineral and other resources were less evident, as in parts of Amazonia and what is today the southern and southwestern United States, missions and forts predominated. Here indigenous labor was

---

Mita   literally "turn" in Quechua, the Inca language, but used by the Spanish to draft male workers from all over the Andean highlands to participate in mining, road construction, and many other types of projects

Potosí   A city in south-central Bolivia founded in 1545 and home of the richest silver deposits in history

Huancavelica   A city in highland Peru founded in 1564 and home of the Americas' largest mercury deposits

mostly exploited to support small numbers of Spanish settlers, soldiers, and priests. Wherever Native Americans were congregated into villages, as happened in the missions of Florida, Texas, California, and southern Arizona, they tended to suffer the effects of epidemic disease more acutely. Surrounding indigenous groups, many of them hostile to the Spanish, made life on any frontier extremely tenuous.

Intermediate regions such as Paraguay, home to large numbers of sedentary **Guaraní** and also non-sedentary Guaycuruans upon Spanish arrival, followed a different path. Early Spanish settlers in and around the future capital of Asunción created a hybrid institution called the *encomienda-mitaya*. Here the Guaraní, who vastly outnumbered the foreign intruders, essentially saturated the agricultural and livestock-raising economy and even married into the elite, settler class. *Mestizaje*, or race-mixing, was so profound here that Guaraní, rather than Spanish, was soon the dominant language. Farther up the Paraguay and Paraná Rivers, Franciscans, and then Jesuits, established large missions, most of them funded by collection and sale of a local tea called *yerba maté* (the latter term referring to the gourd in which the tea was consumed). Although it never became popular in Europe like chocolate and other American products, mission-produced yerba was consumed throughout Spanish South America and southern Brazil by the turn of the eighteenth century. Some charged that the Jesuits were profiting too handsomely from the labors of their native parishioners. Catholic Guaraní, along with the missionaries and settlers, contrasted themselves with the feared Guaycuruans, who, like the plains Indians of North America, adopted Spanish horses and occasionally preyed on their settlements and livestock herds.

In Brazil, by contrast, Native American slavery persisted for many years despite repeated prohibitions. By the mid-sixteenth century, Portuguese settlers were transforming Brazil's northeast coast into the world's most productive sugar region, a transformation that demanded many able hands. Before long, African slaves became the dominant workforce in Brazil, but even as late as the early seventeenth century, a large number of cane cutters, canoe paddlers, cowboys, and porters were enslaved Native Americans. On some plantations and ranches, native workers were still the majority when the Dutch captured Pernambuco in 1630.

As in Africa, the demands of the cane fields and mills, in particular, stimulated a complex slave-trading network reaching far into the backcountry. Similarly, the Native American slave trade gave rise to a number of intermediaries, often multicultural go-betweens versed in several indigenous languages along with Portuguese. In the case of Brazil, the slave traders of the interior, many of them mestizo men from the São Paulo region, came to be known as **bandeirantes**, a name derived from the banners they hoisted in their campaigns.

Guaraní   Indigenous people of Paraguay and neighboring territories who came under control of Jesuit missions over the course of the colonial period

Bandeirantes   literally "flag-bearers," but used in colonial Brazil to refer to participants in slave-hunting expeditions

After the crown officially outlawed native slavery in 1611, Paulistas persuaded the Brazilian authorities to permit an *encomienda*-type system of personal service. Called *administração* ("administration"), the system treated native servants as slaves in all but name—bartering them, leaving them to heirs in wills, and even giving them as dowry gifts. Native slaves and bandeirantes would continue to be found in backcountry Brazil until the late eighteenth century, when the Portuguese crown finally cracked down on the institution.

THE PIRATE CHALLENGE

In 1628 the Spaniards suffered a devastating loss when the entire silver fleet fell into the hands of the Dutch. If the loss of revenue was not bad enough (and it was alleged to be five times greater than the gold and silver won from Atawallpa in 1533), the details of the incident dealt a major blow to the prestige and confidence of the Spanish crown. Shockingly, the general and admiral in charge of the fleet had fled Dutch corsairs, whom they greatly outnumbered, without offering any resistance. The entire fleet was caught stranded among reefs and sandbars in the Bay of Matanzas, just east of Havana, Cuba.

The Spanish general and the admiral were arrested on charges of desertion and dereliction of duty. The great Lima-born Spanish jurist Juan de Solórzano Pereira composed a 540-page condemnation of the officers, arguing that their crime justified the punishment considered the most ignominious (for Christians, anyway) in the Spanish empire—death by hanging. Although Spanish lives were not lost, among Solórzano's 500 points of argument was the claim that "kingdoms and states have nothing more important than their reputations" and "honor and good reputation are worth more than life and property."

As for the Dutch "pirates" (they represented Dutch state interests as much as the Spanish general and admiral represented those of the Spanish crown), their captain, Piet Heyn, became a national hero still cheered by Dutch soccer fans today. Meanwhile, the Dutch West India Company, which had funded Heyn's expedition, paid 50% dividends to shareholders that year and financed a related company enterprise against Brazil that resulted in the seizure of the lucrative sugar district of Pernambuco in 1630. The Dutch were not driven from Brazil until 1654.

Although Solórzano claimed that the 1628 loss "was the first treasure of the Indies to fall into enemy hands," he also argued that "pirate invasions and depredations at sea were very common." Unfortunately for Spain, the massive problem of defense against pirates and other foreign enemies would only grow in the late seventeenth and eighteenth centuries. Not only Spanish ships but also Spanish and Portuguese port towns remained extremely vulnerable to Dutch, French, and English assaults. Before long, piratical raids turned to territorial annexations. The French occupied one end of Santo Domingo, which was formally recognized by the Spanish in 1697 as the French colony of Saint Domingue. By the mid-eighteenth century Saint Domingue was the most profitable sugar colony in the Americas (until it dissolved into war in 1791, emerging as Haiti in 1804). Meanwhile, in 1655, the English permanently acquired Jamaica, going on to claim and then consolidate their hold over key Atlantic waterways.

Thus the Iberian empires faced a crisis in the seventeenth century, brought on in part by the rise of three new European seaborne empires—those of the English, Dutch, and French. Foreign interlopers were corsairs and privateers (state-sponsored pirates), bona fide pirates, or freelance criminals of varying nationality and ethnicity interested only in booty. The pirates of the late-seventeenth-century Caribbean were especially legendary (see Image and Word 4.4). They sacked Spanish port towns throughout the middle period, sometimes forcing territorial concessions. Equally damaging was the pernicious and persistent role played by pirates of all stripes in contraband trade along the thousands of miles of Spanish American coastlines.

The relative weakness of the Baroque state and the culture of corruption among colonial officials meant that the colonists themselves often participated in smuggling. The crown also became highly concerned with another type of alleged internal enemy. During Spain's 1580–1640 control of Portugal, Portuguese merchants continued to supply both Brazil and Spanish America with African slaves, and Portugal's Far Eastern holdings continued to yield luxuries such as spices, silk, and fine porcelain. Portuguese merchants, always interested in returns in precious metals, managed to penetrate Spanish American markets in the period of unification. Among these were many so-called New Christians, or descendants of forced converts from Judaism to Catholicism. As Portuguese subjects (i.e., potential spies and traitors) and as potentially secret Jews (even worse, according to Baroque Catholic thought), these merchants

---

IMAGE AND WORD 4.4 Pirates of the Caribbean

For the diverse inhabitants of the Latin American colonies, the rise of contraband trade with foreigners was as dangerous as it was lucrative. Given the risks entailed by capture—including summary execution—few colonists or outsiders got involved unless they had ready access to state-of-the-art weapons, swift sailing vessels, and some safe haven such as an offshore island or patch of inaccessible forest or desert. Many contraband traders who felt persecuted by Spanish or Portuguese officials, including some renegade colonists, soon turned to piracy. In theory, piracy entailed preying on established commerce for personal gain, yet in practice it was less about accumulating fortunes in pieces of eight and doubloons—as legend would have it—and more about redirecting saleable stolen goods to established contraband markets. Legitimate trade, contraband, and piracy were but points along a commercial spectrum in the Habsburg era.

This is not to say that pirates did not overstep the bounds of accepted commercial practice from time to time. With the growth of French, Dutch, and English populations in the Caribbean after 1650—most of them rootless young men bound to plantation owners, ship captains, and military officers—violent pirate attacks grew in frequency and intensity, mostly in the Caribbean, and with the Spanish as the main victims. Bases in Haiti, Jamaica, Belize, Honduras, and Tortuga gave men like Henry Morgan (depicted below), Laurens de Graaf, and Francois L'Ollonais room and means to roam.

Rather like the early Spanish conquistadors, the pirates of the colonial middle assembled and pooled assets, forming ad hoc companies with the promise of so many shares of booty when all was said and done. The usual targets of pirate raids were small coastwise trading vessels, the ships of the fleet being too large and well-armed to be vulnerable. Next were small coastal towns, whose inhabitants could be kidnapped and forced to pay a ransom in coin, church ornaments, slaves, or tobacco. By the late seventeenth century, the so-called buccaneers of the Caribbean were so numerous they attacked regional Spanish American capitals, laying waste to old Panama, Maracaibo, Campeche, Veracruz, and Cartagena. Veterans of this theater of war found their way to the Pacific by the 1680s, where they attacked the many secondary ports of Mexico and Peru, camping out on the Galápagos Islands and sacking such important trade centers as Sonsonate, Guayaquil, and Paita. Due to the cumulative effect of attacks on small coastal settlements here and in the Caribbean, the Spanish withdrew from many zones, with notable effects on long-term development.

Photo by Rischgitz/Getty Images

The scene changed after 1700, but this was little comfort to the Spanish. The seventeenth century saw the northern European empires torment the Iberian powers by sponsoring pirate rampages in the Caribbean, Atlantic, and Pacific, and by seizing some of their colonies. In the eighteenth century northern Europeans focused on consolidating, expanding, and profiting by their American possessions. This did not bring peace—indeed, there were imperial wars throughout the century—but it did gradually bring the golden age of piracy to an end.

and their families were harshly persecuted by the Inquisition tribunals of Lima, Cartagena, and Mexico City in the years surrounding Portuguese independence in 1640.

Meanwhile, the Dutch, many of whom were Protestants, had been engaged in an independence struggle with Spain since the late 1560s. Having secured their homeland, the Dutch proved increasingly hostile and effective on the high seas. By virtue of crown unification after 1580, the traditionally more neutral Portuguese inherited Spain's many enemies. Of these, the Dutch would hurt them most. Dutch ascendancy was capped by the creation of the East (1602) and West India Companies (1624), both of which sponsored large-scale naval and infantry attacks on Spanish and Portuguese overseas holdings, including Piet Heyn's "piratical" 1628 seizure of the silver fleet.

In the Americas, the West India Company's largest project was the 1630 acquisition of Pernambuco. An attempt to seize the Brazilian capital of Salvador was repulsed by a combined Spanish-Portuguese fleet, the largest to cross the Atlantic to date. What followed were a little over two decades of skirmishing, with the Dutch occupiers increasingly on the defensive. Under the brief but enlightened administration of Count Maurice of Nassau, Dutch Brazil enjoyed a degree of religious tolerance not seen before or after, and Dutch artists and naturalists created a substantial scientific and painterly legacy. For some, at least, Brazil was a kind of paradise. Due in large part to a declining interest among Amsterdam-based company investors, the Dutch colony in Brazil was ultimately confined to the port of Recife and its near hinterland by 1650. In 1654 a mostly Brazilian force—made up of Native Americans, Africans, and creole Portuguese—drove out the Dutch for good.

Meanwhile, the Portuguese endured increasing competition from sugar-producing colonies in the Caribbean, where English, Dutch, and French planters copied Iberian models with growing success. Spanish and Portuguese colonists continued to benefit from the labor of African slaves and their descendants, and also from the toil of indigenous workers in the "Republic of Indians." But on the margins of their colonies were semi-subdued or unconquered native peoples, and as the period of the colonial middle wore on, Iberians faced increasing challenges from other Europeans in the Americas—be they pirates or planters.

KEEP READING

On the topic of sugar and slavery in the American colonies, we recommend Sidney W. Mintz, *Sweetness and Power* (1985), and Stuart B. Schwartz, ed., *Tropical Babylons: Sugar and the Making of the Atlantic World, 1450–1680* (2004). On the early slave trade, see John Thornton, *Africa and Africans in the Making of the Atlantic World*, 2nd ed. (2000). On relations between Africans and natives in the Americas, see Matthew Restall, ed., *Beyond Black and Red: African-Native Relations in Colonial Latin America* (2005). A collection of essays on the black experience in Colonial Latin America is Jane G. Landers and Barry M. Robinson, eds., *Slaves, Subjects, and Subversives* (2006).

An example of the *coartación* proceedings mentioned above is Chapter 20 in Richard Boyer and Geoffrey Spurling, *Colonial Lives: Documents on Latin American History, 1550–1850* (2000); also of some relevance here are Chapters 1–3, 6, 8–9, 11, 13, 17, 19, 21, and 22.

Also relevant are many of the documents presented in *Mesoamerican Voices*, edited by Matthew Restall, Lisa Sousa, and Kevin Terraciano (2005). There is no comparable corpus of Andean documents, but Guaman Poma's great commentary is available as *The First New Chronicle and Good Government*, ed. and trans. David Frye (2006). The full original text has also been made available by the Danish Royal Library at http://www.kb.dk/elib/mss/poma/.

For students writing research papers, there are many relevant monographs that study native communities and experiences in particular regions of Latin

America. Among these are James Lockhart, *The Nahuas after the Conquest* (1992), Stephanie Wood, *Transcending Conquest* (2003), Matthew Restall, *The Maya World: Yucatec Culture and Society, 1550–1850* (1997), Kenneth J. Andrien, *Andean Worlds: Indigenous History, Culture, and Consciousness under Spanish Rule, 1532–1825* (2001), David T. Garrett, *Shadows of Empire: The Indian Nobility of Cusco, 1750–1825* (2005), and Barbara Ganson, *The Guaraní Under Spanish Rule in the Río de la Plata* (2003).

For further reading on the topic of piracy and imperial defense in the Caribbean, we suggest Kris Lane, *Pillaging the Empire: Piracy in the Americas, 1500–1750* (1998); Carla Rahn Phillips, *Six Galleons for the King of Spain: Imperial Defense in the Early Seventeenth Century* (1986); and John Lynch, *The Hispanic World in Crisis and Change, 1598–1700* (1992).

5

The Battle for Orthodoxy

The persistence and pervasiveness of Roman Catholicism is perhaps the most obvious legacy of the colonial period in Latin America. Yet just below an apparently homogeneous surface, a wide variety of local beliefs and practices can be discerned—many of them not approved by high church officials even today. Indeed, the nature of Latin American Catholicism has been contested since the beginning of colonial times between a variety of folk and orthodox camps. Many of the most persistent of these disputes can be traced to the period following the Iberian invasion, when the Catholic Church was itself embattled in Europe, sharply challenged by Protestants, internal critics, and the powerful Islamic empire of the Ottomans.

In the Americas, the missionary friars who entered Mexico in the 1520s and other regions of Mesoamerica and the Andes in the decades that followed were full of optimism. They conducted mass baptisms of hundreds, occasionally thousands, of native converts, convinced that they were rapidly routing the devil—who they believed lay behind native religions. However, that optimism had faded by mid-century, leading to harsher approaches to conversion and a generalized suspicion of indigenous backsliding and outright heresy. As will be seen, people of African and Jewish descent were also singled out and persecuted.

However, one result of these efforts—at first optimistic, later more stoic—was an extensive body of writings by Franciscans and others on Native American

TIMELINE

1478	Spanish Inquisition founded; informally at work in Spanish America until 1569–1571, when it is formally established in the colonies; spreads to Portugal in 1547 and informally operating in Brazil throughout colonial period
1524	The first 12 Franciscan friars arrive in Mexico to begin converting the Nahuas to Christianity
1536	Don Carlos Ometochtzin, Nahua ruler of Texcoco, burned at the stake
1545–1563	Council of Trent redefines deviancy in the Roman Catholic world
1560s	Taqui Onkoy rebellion in Peru
1562	Violent summer campaign against idolatry among the Mayas of Yucatan, led by Diego de Landa
1569, 1570, and 1610	Founding of Inquisition headquarters in Lima, Mexico City, and Cartagena
1571	Founding of a separate inquisitorial body, sometimes called the Indian Inquisition, to police native peoples
1590s–1690s	Century of greatest Inquisition interest in witchcraft in Spanish America, more or less coinciding with the witch craze in Europe and North America
1610s	Santidade movement in Brazil destroyed by colonial Portuguese authorities
1640s	Main campaign of torture, execution, and property confiscation against New Christians, accused of covert Judaism, in Spanish America

religion and culture, and on the challenges of the **Spiritual Conquest**. At the same time, native rulers brought up as Christians often embraced the faith; they contributed to the building of elaborate local churches and to the growth of local saint cults and religious brotherhoods (or **cofradías**). Enslaved and free Africans and their descendants did likewise throughout Brazil (where brotherhoods were called **irmandades**). During the colonial middle (late sixteenth to early eighteenth centuries), a general turn to piety spurred the foundation and expansion not only of brotherhoods of all types (Iberian settlers, native peoples, and African slaves)

Spiritual Conquest   a blanket term for all Spanish and Portuguese efforts to convert Native Americans to Christianity

Cofradía [coh-frah-DEE-ah] and Irmandade [ear-mahn-DODGE-ee]   Spanish and Portuguese for religious brotherhood or confraternity, whose members were usually restricted to one ethnic or racial group, and whose officers maintained a treasury and the cult of a patron saint

but also of male and female religious orders and the secular church. The recently formed Jesuit order was another institution that sought to aggressively defend, spread, and, in some senses, modernize Roman Catholicism.

This chapter explores how Spanish authorities—primarily church officials—attempted to impose and maintain orthodoxy. We begin with the Spiritual Conquest and early efforts to establish orthodoxy (conforming to norms of belief and behavior), then turn to deviancy (behaving differently from the norm) in colonial society, especially heresy and witchcraft, bigamy and forbidden sex. We end with a brief look at crime and punishment, summarizing how church and crown authorities used public punishments to dissuade crimes. The colonies contained a hugely varied population, from semi-converted Jews to semi-pagan native parishioners to African-born slaves. Preventing that population from doing, saying, or believing the "wrong" things was a massive—and often uphill and losing—battle.

THE SPIRITUAL CONQUEST

Don Carlos Ometochtzin was a Christian convert. He was also the native ruler of Texcoco, an important Nahua city-state (or *altepetl*) that sat on the edge of Lake Texcoco and had been one of the three city-states that made up the so-called Triple Alliance that had underpinned the Mexica Empire. In the early years after the fall of that empire, the Franciscans placed great emphasis on the conversion of native lords and nobles, reasoning that their subjects would thereby more readily follow their leaders into the new faith. It was therefore momentous—and shocking to almost everyone in colonial Mexico—when don Carlos was arrested in 1536 by the Spanish Inquisition.

Don Carlos Ometochtzin was charged with idolatry and **apostasy**, meaning that he was accused of clinging to his preconquest or pagan religion. Particularly damning from the Franciscan viewpoint was the fact that don Carlos had secretly kept, and worshipped, a large collection of images of the old gods (or idols, as Spaniards classified them). He was swiftly tried by Inquisition officials and then burned at the stake.

The execution of don Carlos—a supposed model of the Christian native ruler who turned out to be a hidden pagan—sent ripples throughout the Spanish Empire in the Americas. Early confidence faded, but the church's resolve to root out paganism and idolatry hardened. The Franciscans were soon joined by Dominicans and Augustinians, and by 1560 there were over 800 friars in Mesoamerica. Because Spaniards invaded the Andes later than they did Mesoamerica, and then fought among themselves for a decade, the Spiritual Conquest in Spanish Peru was more protracted than it was in Mesoamerica. But by 1580 there were friars at work in almost every corner of what had once been the Inka Empire.

Apostasy   in the context of colonial Latin America, the renunciation of Christianity by a convert and the return to pagan religion

Meanwhile, popular protests in Mexico over the public burning of the Nahua ruler don Carlos Ometochtzin contributed to a prolonged debate over Inquisition methods, including discussion over possibly removing Native Americans from Inquisition jurisdiction. When, in 1562, Diego de Landa, the head of the Franciscans in Yucatan, tortured over 4,000 Mayas (hundreds to death) during a summer-long campaign against idolatry, the debate moved more quickly; in 1571 a separate body, often referred to as the Indian Inquisition, took over responsibility for the religious policing of native Christians.

However, the creation of the Indian Inquisition did not mean the abandonment of coercion or violence as a method of conversion. The death penalty was no longer to be used on native idolaters, but torture was used as an investigative tool from the sixteenth through the eighteenth centuries, as were various types of corporal punishment. Priests whose livelihood revolved around the indoctrination of indigenous parishioners reacted to this prohibition of Inquisitorial interference by taking on many of the Holy Office's functions, and even torture mechanisms, themselves.

The result—from northern Mexico to Chile—was an inconsistent, yet occasionally quite violent, application of Inquisition-style investigations into charges of idolatry. In virtually all indigenous cultures, idolatry was a term without meaning. Stones, graven images, and other material manifestations of the sacred were omnipresent. From the perspective of many natives, they did not seem entirely distinct from Baroque Catholic images, which were widely understood to be sanctified representations and even containers of holiness. Many priests did make sharp distinctions between native and Catholic approaches to the material world, however, and in sixteenth-century Peru a full-blown indigenous conspiracy to revert to the old faith was feared. To root out what became known as the Taqui Onkoy rebellion, Andean villagers were called in to testify against their neighbors, and those named were tortured, exiled, and otherwise punished. Although consistent with the temper of the times, Peru's so-called **Extirpation of Idolatry**, which flared up in the hinterland of Lima several times in the seventeenth century, was mostly the pet project of a small number of ambitious priests and bishops.

In Yucatan too there were sporadic campaigns of extirpation throughout the mid-colonial period. As in Peru, these campaigns were dependent on the zeal of particular senior priests. Unlike Andeans, the Mayas had maintained a vibrant writing tradition before the Spanish Conquest, and thus extirpators in Yucatan focused as much on codices or hieroglyphic books as they did on idols. Although Diego de Landa had publicly burned a great number of codices in his campaign of 1562, priests continued to find and destroy Maya books for over a century after this. As a result, only a handful of pre-Conquest codices survive today.

In both Yucatan and Peru, extirpation campaigns claimed to emphasize the positive messages of Christian teaching and indoctrination. These aspects of

---

Extirpation of Idolatry   campaign to uproot and destroy native religious beliefs and practices (including the worship of pre-Christian images or "idols")

church efforts were usually overshadowed by the violent methods of coercion, correction, and punishment. The efficacy of these methods—the degree to which they resulted in a profound embrace of the Christian faith by native peoples—was the subject of much debate by priests in colonial Latin America and continues to be debated by historians today.

BOOKS AND BUILDINGS

One of the friars involved in the trial of don Carlos Ometochtzin was Bernardino de Sahagún. He concluded from the trial, and from his experience traveling around New Spain preaching to Nahua villagers, that Spanish missionaries and priests needed to be better informed. Only by truly understanding native religion and culture could Spaniards hope to fully convert native peoples. Sahagún became one of the leading figures in the literary manifestation of the religious renaissance in New Spain. Beginning in the mid-sixteenth century, Sahagún, along with other Franciscans and Dominicans, produced a great series of written guides. These included grammars and dictionaries of native languages, detailed accounts of native religions, and conversion tools such as confessional manuals, catechisms, and sermons in native languages. These methods were a renaissance of Christian ideas in ways that the friars did not always intend, for they turned the process of conversion into a conversation—a two-way exchange of concepts and practices that forced Christianity to adapt to local native ways of thinking and doing things.

Thus although Mesoamericans found it harder and harder to produce traditional literary works, and saw hieroglyphic and pictographic books burned or marginalized, they contributed to many church-sponsored books as informants, ghost writers, and artists. At the same time, new genres of books written alphabetically but in native languages developed in Spanish colonies. The most notable of these are the primordial titles (or *títulos*). These were land titles that were turned by native scribes throughout Mesoamerica into community histories, drawing on since-lost codices and local oral traditions. Pre-Conquest and pre-Christian literary roots are even more in evidence in the Books of Chilam Balam (or Books of the Jaguar Priest). These Maya-language volumes were maintained in dozens of villages across Yucatan by local scribes throughout the colonial period. The books recorded a wide variety of information—from local history to calendrical knowledge to herbal cures—often presented in the form of riddles and fables. Both primordial titles and Chilam Balam books reflected the impact of the Spiritual Conquest, as the arrival of Christianity is more often presented in a matter-of-fact way than in a critical one. In both examples, native authors sought to reconcile traditional knowledge with Christianity, and to adapt old ways of recording knowledge to new technologies and political realities.

The Franciscans and other friars thus significantly affected the cultural landscape with their vigorous literary activities. But they also made a literal impact on the landscape by tapping into native traditions of monumental architecture and encouraging the construction of church buildings. New churches were typically built on the same site as pre-Christian temples, often using the same foundations, pyramidal platforms, and many of the same stones. By the end of the sixteenth century, hundreds of churches had been constructed in Mesoamerican parishes; church construction in Peru was slower but equally extensive by the middle of the colonial period. In the countryside, friars had to begin with modest structures. But the pride that Mesoamerican towns had invested in local pyramids and temples was soon transferred to churches, producing oversized and highly varied church buildings throughout the region.

In cities, the transition from old temples to new churches was faster and more spectacular, even if it took decades to actually finish many buildings. One of the more beautiful Inka temples in Cuzco, the Coricancha, was converted into the Church of Santo Domingo, preserving most of the ancient masonry. An impressive cathedral was begun in Mexico City in 1563, adjacent to the ruins of the great pyramid and temple of the Aztecs, and the building continually expanded through to 1700. The dominant architectural style of church buildings throughout the seventeenth century was the Baroque, which featured highly detailed exteriors and elaborate interiors centered on gold-drenched altarpieces. The style extended from Mexico City and Lima all the way to modest parish churches in Ecuador and Guatemala, where, while parishioners might not be able to afford much in the way of gold decorations, exteriors were brightly and distinctively painted.

THE HOLY OFFICE

In the so-called Baroque period—our "colonial middle"—Iberians developed a number of institutions to defend, enforce, and spread the faith. We have already seen how the Spiritual Conquest was led by friars from various religious orders and taken up by friars and secular clergy under the auspices of the Indian Inquisition. However, the regular Inquisition—the Holy Office—remained the most important religious institution in the colonies, with far-reaching political and social influence. Inquisition officers were charged with rooting out heresy, policing public morality, and preventing the spread of allegedly dangerous books.

True believers, like gemstones, were difficult to judge. Everyone had their opinions, and all Baroque Catholics, regardless of wealth, education, sex, or color, were deemed fallible sinners. Thus, in ascertaining the depth of an individual subject's faith, Church leaders chose to emphasize visible evidence of belief, such as ritual practices and daily comportment, rather than an ability to articulate doctrine. Heretics and apostates were to be identified by their deviant practices. Such practices included bigamy, homosexuality, failure to attend mass, improper observance of feasts, use of blasphemous language, and hiring a witch to cast love-magic spells. It was believed that if they were not caught, punished, and reformed or rooted out, followers of unorthodox practices and beliefs would "infect" the larger body of believers. This stern view was heavily reinforced by the Habsburg monarchs, beginning with Philip II (who reigned from 1556 to 1598). In Baroque times, church and state were essentially two sides of the same coin.

The Holy Office of the Inquisition predated Habsburg rule. First established in Italy, the Holy Office was imported to Spain in the era of Ferdinand and

Isabella (in 1478). As Columbus set sail for the Americas, the fledgling Spanish Inquisition busied itself persecuting, and often sentencing to death, the peninsula's remaining Jews and Muslims. Unable to do harm even to the bodies of heretics according to the rules of the Church, inquisitors handed their victims off to secular authorities for torture and execution (see Image and Word 5.1). The Inquisition was established in Portugal in 1536, touching off another wave of anti-Semitic hysteria and mass emigration. Following the Council of Trent, Inquisition offices were established in Lima (1569), Mexico City (1570), and Cartagena de Indias (1610). No permanent office was ever established in Brazil, although periodic visits by Portuguese inquisitors in the late sixteenth and early seventeenth centuries led to some startling discoveries and gruesome punishments.

IMAGE AND WORD 5.1   The Rack

The most common colonial-era torture device was known as the *burro*, or "rack," here displayed in the Inquisition museum in Cartagena, Colombia. The suspect or victim was laid on the burro's table face up, his or her wrists and upper arms tied to one end, ankles and thighs to the other (the objective was to inflict pain both by stretching joints and squeezing large muscles). Inquisitors then asked questions while assistants, usually native servants or African slaves, turned the large handles. As each ratchet clicked, the pain mounted, and the interrogation continued. Victims were repeatedly ordered to "tell the truth." A notary recorded the entire business, including the number of times the rack was turned and the cries of pain and agonized facial expressions made by the victim. It was not uncommon for victims to end the sequence of torture *vueltas*, or "rounds," permanently disabled.

Alex Segre/Alamy

Although there is still considerable debate as to whether the Inquisition was a medieval survival or a modern innovation, it was in any case a fairly efficient promoter of conformity in the places where it was most powerful. As with any bureaucracy, few wished to fall into its clutches. Still, documentary evidence suggests that even in the major capitals and trade centers of Lima, Mexico City, and Cartagena, where the Holy Office was headquartered, heretics never seemed to be in short supply. As in its earliest campaigns in Spain, the Inquisition in Baroque Spanish America focused mostly on rooting out alleged practitioners of Judaism. "Hidden Jews," usually so-called New Christians, or forced converts and their descendants of Portuguese or Andalusian descent, were most avidly sought and most harshly punished. Even still, there were marked waves of tolerance and intolerance, which tended to coincide with the political and military calms and crises experienced in Spain. A series of terror-inspiring autos-de-fe, or public humiliations and executions of alleged Jews and other nonconformists, took place in Mexico City and Lima between 1639 and 1651. This wave of persecution, the deadliest in colonial Latin American history, coincided with the rebellion of Portugal against Spanish rule and with the unhappy settlement of a long conflict with the Dutch.

Other victims of the Inquisition included alleged bigamists, blasphemers, homosexuals, witches, and even a few unlucky Protestant pirates. Bigamy—or "the crime of double marriage"—was not uncommon because divorce in the modern sense did not exist. Irreconcilable couples thus tended to seek their own solutions and ran the risk of paying a high price. Whatever the charge, the Inquisition relied on voluntary denunciations and carefully gathered witness testimonies. An individual under investigation was arrested but not presented with any charge. Instead, the person in question was calmly asked if there was anything he or she might like to confess. Under this subtle and insidious form of pressure, and faced with an apparently open-ended inquiry, many defendants gave Inquisition authorities more information than they were after. Other defendants knew precisely what was expected of them and what the consequences of confession or denunciations of others might be, so they clammed up. Inquisitors then decided whether or not to apply a variety of torture mechanisms to lubricate the process, including the rack, simulated drowning, and cords tightened around various fleshy and bony parts of the body. Torture in the course of interrogation was standard throughout Europe in the Baroque era, but the Inquisition's highly methodical and documented application of it set it apart—and made it infamous.

It is difficult to know if or how much ordinary Baroque Catholics in Spanish and Portuguese America feared the Inquisition, but its ability to ruin lives and tear apart friends and family was certainly known. In addition to the focus on alleged Jews, Inquisition records indicate an inordinate tendency to punish people of African descent for alleged deviancy. African and African descended women were frequently tried in all of the Inquisition's Spanish American tribunals, usually for witchcraft, and many men of African heritage, often long-distance mule-drivers and others of limited status and means, were charged with bigamy. This tendency to focus on the so-called New Christian and Afro-American minority populations has led some historians to view the Inquisition as an institutional precursor to the modern terror mechanisms employed by fascist states. However we may wish to categorize it today, the Inquisition's long, Baroque shadow certainly appears to have reinforced the notion of an embattled Iberian Catholicism. To belong socially in Baroque Latin America was to participate, actively or passively, in the scapegoating of potential traitors.

ORTHODOXY AND DEVIANCY

One may imagine that in the colonial middle, when torture was standard practice and the Baroque Catholic church seemed all-powerful, that few individuals, much less organized groups, might have questioned authority. Certainly conformity was the aim of both church and state in the Iberian colonies, but on close examination it appears that neither Spain nor Portugal, nor for that matter the missionary orders or the Inquisition, were anywhere near as powerful or all-knowing as some observers have claimed. There was much room, in other words, for alternative beliefs and behaviors—what officialdom regarded as deviancy. That said, if one did get caught, the consequences could be dire.

In the middle period, deviancy was defined according to cumbersome sets of secular and religious rules, most notably the Compiled Laws of the Indies (or Philippine Code, as these laws were called in Brazil) and the Edicts of the Council of Trent. The Laws of the Indies covered everything from flag design to the size and shape of mining claims. They also contained a number of criminal statutes. Some laws derived from Greek and Roman precedent; others had grown out of Spanish or Portuguese, and later American colonial, experience. Laws regarding slavery derived mostly from late medieval experience, in the wake of the Reconquest, whereas those regarding native peoples grew out of the colonial one.

The Edicts of the Council of Trent were published after a series of meetings among Church elders in northern Italy that lasted from 1545 to 1563. These edicts did not entirely replace existing canon or Church law but rather clarified key points of belief and practice in the aftermath of the Protestant challenge presented by former priests Martin Luther and John Calvin. The Tridentine Code, as historians sometimes call the edicts, strongly reiterated the importance of eliminating heresy in all forms. It also mandated prosecution and punishment of baptized Catholics allegedly engaged in superstitious practices such as witchcraft, fortune telling, and astrology. These popular tendencies proved far more difficult to monitor and punish than heresy. Finally, the Edicts of Trent reinforced the Church's focus on core life-stage rituals called sacraments, especially marriage. Codifying marriage meant codifying sex. Sex outside marriage was strictly forbidden by Church elders, and sex within it sharply circumscribed. In essence, sex was defined as an inherently sinful and filthy act that happened to be essential for human reproduction.

Defining deviancy in a far-flung, multicultural world like that of colonial Latin America was a daunting task. Effective communication of rules and edicts was stymied by vast distances, interruptions in the fleet system, gaping language barriers, and wildly varying levels of religious and civic literacy and acculturation.

Fornication, for example, or premarital sex, was technically both a sin and a crime in Baroque times. Yet even among cloistered, closely monitored Spanish nuns, it happened with alarming frequency. Men, and most notably priests, found their way over convent walls. But the laws and edicts kept coming, and some individuals do appear to have been singled out for public trials and exemplary punishment. It seems that in their frustration, state and church authorities sometimes resorted to terror to induce conformity. As in countries where capital punishment is still practiced, gauging how well people learned the lessons of state terror was difficult.

The forms of criminal deviancy in the colonial middle would be relatively familiar to modern observers, with crimes ranging from petty theft or plagiarism to rape and murder. Some misdeeds not often taken up by criminal courts today but of great concern to colonists included slander, or public name-calling meant to besmirch another's honor. Honor claims were often settled outside the courts by men of high rank in the form of duels. Resulting deaths and injuries were then taken to court and presented as willful murders or attempted ones. Colonial Latin America's courts were always busy thanks to a culture that promoted litigiousness as a standard form of social interaction and status assertion. The colonial legal system also differed from modern ones (at least in terms of the letter, if not execution, of sentences) in that identical crimes were punished differently according to the rank of the offender. A slave convicted of theft, for example, might be punished with 50 lashes on the public pillory, whereas the son of a wealthy landowner convicted of the same deed might expect to pay a fine of 50 pesos. There could be even starker differences in sentencing, as we shall see below.

Far removed from today's legal guarantees of religious freedom, the early modern Iberian states sought to sharply control the beliefs and practices of subject peoples. Patrolling this more subjective realm of deviancy was the Holy Office of the Inquisition. In indigenous communities, a range of parish priests and members of regular orders such as the Franciscans and Jesuits policed belief and behavior, although as few priests lived in native communities for any length of time, attention to native activities was intermittent. Whether in a native village or a Spanish city, officials viewed heresy—the rejection of orthodox Catholicism in favor of some other religion or sect of Christianity—as most threatening. Use of magic or witchcraft to achieve some specific, short-term goal (usually one not admissible by prayer) was somewhat less challenging to the core faith but still highly punishable. Priests were always concerned with the sexual behavior of parishioners, indigenous and otherwise (and if the documents are to be believed, priests were almost as consistently accused of sexual transgressions themselves). Idolatry, as we have seen, was considered the peculiar vice of Native Americans virtually everywhere in the Spanish colonies. The Portuguese in Brazil, notably, seemed less interested in labeling native religious deviancy as idolatry. The Church's view of heresy, idolatry, backsliding, witchcraft, and other "thought crimes" would shift according to place and time, but the intensity of punishments was most profound in the middle period.

HERETICS AND WITCHES

People labeled heretics by the Roman Catholic Church—particularly Jews, but also Muslims, Protestants, "Illuminists," and others—were thought to be a grave danger to the larger body of believers. As such, they had to be discovered and eliminated from every corner of the empire. Non-Catholics were not simply seen as a potential source of intellectual challenges to core beliefs and patterns of behavior. Their ability to persuade was not at issue. Much more than this, heretics were regarded as an insidious and evil source of pollution or infection. Their deviant, devil-inspired beliefs would corrupt the Church from within and prevent the salvation of its faithful members. Since beliefs were difficult to articulate or fathom, Church elders focused on more visible outward practices, signs by which one might determine a person's faith. By treating heresy as if it were a kind of disease or poison—yet seeking out its devotees according to apparently heterodox practices such as fasting or lighting candles outside designated days— the Church set the stage for scapegoating, or the periodic sacrifice of innocents. Some scholars have argued that scapegoating, however unjust, serves the social function of discharging accumulated anxieties. In the colonial middle, the main victims of such scapegoating episodes would be alleged Jews, female slaves of African descent, and indigenous shamans.

In both Old World and New, the Inquisition was most interested in rooting out heretics, yet as we have seen, relatively few were found, and even fewer were publicly executed. A small number of foreigners from northern Europe were unlucky enough to fall into inquisitors' hands, but most of the Inquisition's victims were otherwise legal Portuguese New Christians living in key ports and administrative capitals after about 1590. Based on Inquisition records, it appears that only a few of those prosecuted were aware that their beliefs or ritual practices were of any significance beyond the realm of the household. Some appear to have been, at least in their minds, sincere Catholics. Still, at the core of many New Christian merchant clans persecuted in the early seventeenth century were ardent believers in Judaism, usually matriarchs or patriarchs who had a keen understanding of what inquisitors called "the Law of Moses." The serial torture, executions, and losses of property suffered by New Christians in New Spain, Peru, and New Granada in the years around 1640 were nothing short of horrific.

Witchcraft, or the use of potions, powders, spells, and herbs for the control of others—or to do harm to others—was a far more widespread phenomenon than heresy in colonial Latin America. The practice of witchcraft was not restricted to women, although women were more often singled out than men by Church authorities. However, the witch craze that swept the Atlantic world in the late sixteenth and seventeenth centuries, resulting in the execution of tens of thousands of women (mostly single, older women in Protestant countries), had an indirect impact on Latin America. The vast majority of Inquisition investigations into witchcraft and related crimes during colonial times took place in the mid-colonial period—precisely the Protestant witch craze era. But in an interesting contrast to northern Europe and New England in the same period, the witches of seventeenth-century Latin America were only rarely tried and punished as devil worshipers. Almost none were executed. Commonly called **brujos** or **hechizeras** in Spanish America, and **feiticeiros** or **curandeiras** in Brazil, they were sometimes dismissed as either suffering the superstitions of the ignorant or as fraudulently claiming to heal wounds and transform love lives. According to the Church, the crimes of these "witch doctors" and shamans more often bordered on charlatanism, or the exploitation of common peoples' gullibility. It was not that priests doubted the efficacy of spells and potions—all inhabitants of the colonies, from African slaves to Spanish priests to native corn-farmers, believed that such things could work. But they often doubted the skills of those accused of practicing the craft. Only if they directly invoked the devil were witches treated as potential heretics.

Witchcraft was used for many purposes in colonial times. Most surviving documents in the Inquisition files detail cases of women procuring potions and spells to ensure the fidelity of their mates—or acquire new affections. Others sought witches to help them divine some future occurrence or locate some lost person or item. Still others sought revenge, paying for spells and herbs that might include poison. Most disturbing for elites were servants and slaves who used witchcraft as a form of class revenge. As such, a slave's lingering gaze was not just a look, it was the "evil eye." However Church authorities viewed it, witchcraft was generally believed to be effective in the colonial middle. Its practice was secretly perfected by male and female specialists, almost always of African or indigenous descent. Cases of witchcraft, found virtually everywhere in the colonies, hint at the existence of a significant underworld of beliefs and rituals that deviated sharply from the ideal Catholic world described by the Edicts of Trent.

BAROQUE CATHOLICISM

Much of the stimulus for the Catholic renaissance in both Iberia and the colonies derived from the same edicts of the Council of Trent that defined heresy. In what amounted to a conservative defense of medieval Catholicism, the edicts reemphasized the central importance of the sacraments, most importantly marriage, the celibacy of the priesthood, and the existence of Purgatory. The various local cults of Mary and the saints were also reinforced, along with the central role of relics, or holy objects, and their importance in sustaining pilgrimage sites. The foundations were laid for the mid-colonial growth of saint cults such as that of the Virgin of Guadalupe (see Image and Word 5.2). Most scandalously for Protestants, indulgences, or payments to the church in exchange for a guarantee of a shortened stay in Purgatory, were not only retained but also expanded.

Brujo [BREW-hoh] and hechizera [etch-eess-ER-ah]   Spanish terms for witch

Feiticeiro [fay-tee-SAY-roh] and curandeira [koo-rahn-DAY-rah]   Portuguese terms for witch

IMAGE AND WORD 5.2   Sister and Saint

Museo Nacional de Historia, Castillo de Chapultepec, Mexico/Jean-Pierre Courau/The Bridgeman Art Library International

Photo by Susana Gonzalez/Getty Images

Sor (Sister) Juana Inés de la Cruz (1648–1695) is widely considered today to be Colonial Latin America's greatest poet. A nun in convents in Mexico City from the age of 19, Sor Juana was a prolific author whose defense of a woman's right to education, and the secular nature of some of her plays and poetry, eventually provoked the ire of the archbishop. In the final years of her life she was pressured to stop writing and forced to sell her library of 4,000 books. In the centuries since her death, she has become a literary, nationalist, feminist, and even lesbian icon.

During Sor Juana's lifetime the story of the apparition of the Virgin of Guadalupe became well-known in Mexico. According to the tale, first recorded in the 1640s, the Virgin appeared to a Nahua villager named Juan Diego in 1531. Although there is no historical evidence to support the story, its importance to the development of a distinct Mexican Catholic tradition is indisputable. The Virgin of Guadalupe's popularity grew in late colonial times and by the twentieth century she was viewed by many as the patron of all Latin America. Juan Diego was canonized in 2002, becoming the first Native American saint.

The image of Sor Juana above was painted by Miguel Cabrera (1695–1768) in 1750. He was a native of Oaxaca in southern Mexico, of Zapotec and Spanish descent, and in his lifetime recognized as the most accomplished painter in Mexico. He also painted the image above of Juan Diego, one of the first portraits of the future Nahua saint. Cabrera produced many portraits, as well as paintings of Mexico's castas or racial types (see Image and Word 6.3 and 7.2). But most of his work was religious in content, including famous paintings of the Virgin of Guadalupe.

What this meant for the Spanish and Portuguese, blessed (or burdened) as they were with the world's most lucrative overseas empires, was a self-ascribed responsibility to defend and spread Catholicism worldwide, in Europe, the colonies, and beyond. As believers in the core regions of Spanish and Portuguese settlement hunkered down and devoted more of their time and income to church-related activities, missionaries set out to transform more and more distant frontiers. This was the age of the church militant. We have seen how this was manifested in the core colonies in Mesoamerica and the Andes; we shall shortly turn to the topic of missionary activity in the colonial hinterlands and on the frontiers.

The Baroque period was also marked by an exponential growth in the power and social influence of religiously devout Catholic women, particularly those who entered convents. The women of the Habsburg court set the tone for one form of solemn, matriarchal piety by founding and funding whole new reclusive female orders such as that of the Encarnación, while lone, visionary figures such as Teresa of Ávila set another. This was an era in which a poet nun such as Sor Juana Inés de la Cruz could become a celebrated literary giant, known not just for religious writings but also for secular—even sensual and erotic— poetry, but still end up censored by an archbishop (see Image and Word 5.2). Women in Baroque Iberia were not simply followers of priests' and other men's orders, but builders of the faith in their own right, and more radically, exponents of its deepest mysteries.

In the colonies, this trend toward female religious exuberance was far more notable in Spanish America than in Brazil. Convents, initially created to house the orphaned mestiza daughters of the conquistadors, ballooned into virtual cities within cities after 1600. Regional capitals had half a dozen of them or more by the later seventeenth century, each technically overseen by male priests and religious orders. There were different convents, and states of profession, for all classes and tastes. Women from the lowest social classes, like the freed slave and visionary of Lima, Úrsula de Jesús, could not become nuns, but rather only **beatas**. Latin America's only female saint, Rose of Lima, was also a beata. Widowed elite women sometimes entered convents in a similar role (having sacrificed their precious chastity to the vile but necessary tasks of marriage and childrearing). They were often accompanied in their reclusion by indigenous or enslaved African house servants, who toiled away in the convent's kitchens and washrooms much as before. Suffering inside the convent walls, in other words, was not limited to those who, like the anorexic Santa Rosa, dedicated themselves to enlightenment through mortification. Few nuns were able to convince themselves that, like Sor María de Agreda, they could leave their bodies and preach to "the Indians" in Mexico.

Since nuns entered convents as symbolic "brides of Christ," they often brought with them substantial dowries. Without a spendthrift husband to waste

---

Beata [beh-AHT-ah]   a woman who has devoted herself to a life of piety and chastity but has not taken the full vows of a nun

these precious funds on cockfights or reckless business ventures, nuns' dowries were pooled and invested in various, mostly conservative ways. Abbesses and wealthy widows sometimes directed these investments, but most were legally in the hands of male priests. Some convents owned rural haciendas, urban rental properties, and even gold mines, all of them administered by salaried men. Convents also loaned cash to large landowners at a church-mandated rate of 5% a year in exchange for a lien on some piece of urban or rural property. Many such borrowers, never able to repay the principal, paid interest on these loans (called *censos*) for multiple generations, leaving the convents in effect owners of the pledged estates. Convents served, like other church institutions, as colonial banks, and with the steady addition of new sisters, they were increasingly wealthy ones.

The period of the colonial middle corresponded with two major historic trends: the decline of Iberian political power in Europe and the so-called counter-reformation of the Catholic Church. The result, both in Iberia and the colonies, was the emergence of what one historian has called a "Baroque culture of crisis." A general turn to religious reflection, self-punishment, and increased church building was notable throughout Spanish and Portuguese America. The proliferation of convents was but one of many manifestations of the trend. Baroque ideas, practices, and institutions would only subside following the slow penetration of Enlightenment thinking in the middle of the eighteenth century. With the Baroque's heightened sensitivity to public displays of faith came an interest in identifying alleged unbelievers who might "pollute" the faithful corps. Finally, the church militant went also to the untamed fringes, to "reduce" semi-sedentary and non-sedentary native peoples to both church and state authority. Unbelievers could be found on every front.

One way to maintain the optimism of the early years of Spiritual Conquest, then, was to carry the gospel to new peoples beyond the conquest frontier. Both Spanish and Portuguese authorities sponsored members of the regular religious orders, primarily Franciscans and Jesuits, to open new mission fields in the rugged backcountry. The main areas of expansion in the Baroque era were northern Mexico and Amazonia. In these regions missionaries penetrated deeply, although their attempts at conversion were no more satisfying than they had been in the old colonial core. After a series of dramatic martyrdoms, the missionaries settled in for a long stay.

Because native groups in colonial hinterlands such as Amazonia were semi-sedentary or non-sedentary, the missionaries' insistence that new converts settle in central settlements or mission towns was highly disruptive to traditional lifestyles. During the seventeenth century the Franciscans established hundreds of missions across the far Mexican north and what is now the southern United States—from the Chesapeake to Florida to Arizona. Almost none resulted in permanent settlements, and the most successful of them, among the Pueblo peoples of New Mexico, erupted in a violent revolt in 1680 (not until 1700 did the Spanish regain control of the region). In Brazil, Jesuits and Franciscans resorted to the tactics used by slave-raiding Portuguese settlers, rounding up Tupi natives and forcing them to live in mission villages called ***aldeias***. The practice made

Tupis more susceptible to disease (a third of aldeia residents died in the smallpox epidemic of 1559–1562, for example) and more vulnerable to slave raiders. Although missionaries denounced the enslaving of natives in Brazil, they did not shy from renting out their aldeia Tupis to work for Portuguese settlers.

Many Tupis fled aldeias to join maroons or communities of escaped African slaves in the interior of Brazil. In some of these settlements, a religious movement developed called **santidade**; the movement was an open revolt against Portuguese colonialism and was messianic in its promotion of the idea that a golden age was approaching when Brazil would be free of Europeans. By the turn of the seventeenth century up to 20,000 Afro-Brazilians and Tupis lived in santidade villages, where they appointed their own pope and bishops, sent missionaries to other villages, and built their own idols. In the 1610s this fascinating political-religious experiment was destroyed by a Portuguese military expedition.

FORBIDDEN SEX

The Inquisition was also deeply interested in the sex lives of colonists. As in so many other aspects of Baroque life, one's comportment in the bedroom was tied to salvation. The basic rules put forth by Church elders forbade incest, bestiality, sodomy, masturbation, fornication, adultery, and polygamy. To be safe, in short, sexual intercourse required two married partners of the opposite sex. Even then, sex was not to be enjoyed, and could only be engaged in using the so-called missionary position. To engage in foreplay of any kind was to flirt with sin, and to perform oral sex or enter other "mistaken" orifices was to commit sodomy.

Despite, or perhaps because of, the Church's many rigid rules, colonists of all social classes found sexual satisfaction in one way or another. Fornication was impossible to prevent whether in city or countryside. Priests and nuns, according to many documents, were on closer terms than the rules of chastity demanded, and sailors of the fleet often found that they preferred one another's company to that of landlubbers. As is true today, the Church tended to deal (or not deal) with its own members privately. For its part, the Inquisition managed to try and convict a number of bigamists, usually twice-married men of modest status, and so-called sodomites, usually homosexual men.

Examples of sodomy cases, however, reveal that social attitudes toward homosexuality were more complex than the fact of its illegality might suggest. In 1595 in Charcas (in modern Bolivia), a senior priest named Dr. Gaspar González was prosecuted for sodomy; his lover, a young apothecary's assistant, was publicly executed, but González went on to hold the prestigious post of *visita* inspector in

---

Aldeia [al-DAY-ah]   village (Portuguese); mission settlements in colonial Brazil

Santidade [san-tee-DAH-gee]   messianic religious and political movement of Tupis and maroons in late sixteenth century Brazil

the diocese of La Plata. There he lived openly with a young man named Diego Mexía; the priest was publicly affectionate toward Diego, took him on parish inspections, and bought a seat for him on the La Plata town council. Eventually the church court in the city arrested, tried, and convicted both men for sodomy. But whereas Diego was tortured so badly that he remained disabled in both arms, and then sentenced (with cruel irony) to six-year service on the royal galleys, Dr. González escaped torture, had his conviction overturned in a Lima court, and remained a priest. Clearly status, as mentioned above (and importantly, office-holding, senior male status), trumped "guilt."

In Mexico sodomy prosecutions (and executions in general) were far less common throughout the colonial period than they were in mid-colonial Peru and Bolivia. Cases suggest that men might enjoy lifestyles and relationships that were technically deviant, provided they did so discreetly and under the protection of position and status. Homosexuality was a luxurious risk that only the elite could afford to take. The few sodomy cases prosecuted by the Portuguese Inquisition in Brazil in the middle period suggest a pattern similar to Mexico's, where tolerance was closely tied to the status of the alleged offenders.

Only a few women were brought before the Inquisition for alleged sex crimes, among them the famed Basque cross-dresser Catalina de Erauso (ca. 1585–1650). In 1600 Erauso was on the verge of taking her vows as a young teenager in a Spanish convent. Instead she escaped, cut her hair, and redesigned her clothes. She then lived as a man, eventually crossing to Peru, where she led a hell-raising, picaresque life, seducing women, getting into fights, even committing murder. As a reminder of the strange twists that could result from the colonial period's rigid sexual politics, Erauso was set free by inquisitors once witnesses confirmed her virginity. In 1626, she was given a special dispensation from the pope to continue wearing men's clothing; notorious throughout the Spanish world, she lived the rest of her life as a muleteer and businessman in Mexico.

CRIME AND PUNISHMENT

Vast bundles of records from the middle period suggest that thieves, confidence artists, murderers, and other criminals were not much deterred by Iberia's ponderous bodies of laws and gruesome public punishments. All cities, and many towns, had jails, but these were only temporary holding places; prisons and penitentiaries did not yet exist. Convicted criminals were instead whipped, fined, executed, or exiled. Some were sent to serve in forts on dangerous frontiers or in Caribbean and South Sea galleys. It was hoped they would never return, and indeed, they rarely did. Penal colonies per se did not exist in colonial Latin America, although many of Brazil's first Portuguese settlers were exiled criminals who had been dropped off among potential indigenous trading partners. Detention implied guilt, and spontaneous confessions were strongly encouraged. The process of extracting information from unwilling defendants was closely regulated by law, but, as with Inquisition processes, it often included painful physical, not to mention psychological, torture (see Image and Word 5.1). Just to be on the safe side, defendants were read a sort of liability waiver saying that any broken bones or other injuries (including death) sustained during torture were their own fault.

Torture for the purpose of extracting confessions was not considered punishment. That came later. Those convicted of heinous crimes such as cold-blooded murder, insurrection, or treasonous intercourse with foreigners were usually drawn and quartered, or torn apart limb from limb by horses. Remaining body parts were then distributed on pikes for display along the roadside as a warning to others. More often, capital punishment was carried out in the town or city plaza by garrote (strangling against a post) or hanging. Beheading, which could present technical difficulties, was less common. Public whipping and other forms of humiliation were frequent but tended overwhelmingly to be applied only to people of the lower strata, such as Indians, African slaves, and people of mixed ancestry. In Brazilian towns the **pelourinho**, or public pillory, was a constant reminder of crown justice through public punishment.

Despite the grim drama of public executions, fodder for the fears and imaginations of colonial inhabitants as much as for our own, few of those unfortunate enough to be arrested by the Inquisition were sentenced to die (estimates range from 1% to 5% of those prosecuted). Many more died in jail awaiting trial, as jail conditions were appalling. Others died from the wounds inflicted during public whippings or from the brutal regime of hard labor in the royal galleys or forts.

In the second century of colonial occupation, the Spanish and Portuguese attempted to promulgate and enforce a host of secular and religious laws in the Americas. Given the communication difficulties typical of the times, they were surprisingly effective. By the end of the colonial middle, at least, Spanish subjects living in places as distant from one another (and from Madrid) as Arizona, Puerto Rico, and Bolivia had the same basic understanding of state and church laws and regulations. To judge from their litigiousness and open devotion to Catholicism, Brazilians from Amazonia to Santa Catarina were equally astute and indoctrinated. This tendency to conform to the laws of the realm, a general feature of nearly all societies, was nevertheless counterbalanced by a similar human tendency to rebel or persist in more localized or tried-and-true beliefs and practices.

With righteousness so narrowly defined, deviancy was understandably common in the colonies, particularly at the more petty levels and among the barely educated rural masses. Even with a general idea of right and wrong in mind, one could not help but stray. Spectacular punishments of alleged heretics and hard-core criminals were rare but undoubtedly memorable—a marker of the outer limits of secular and religious behavior. On a more day-to-day level, one had to be careful around priests and magistrates; in an instant they could turn your life upside down. Most people probably learned to steer clear of authorities of any kind, or to bow deeply in their presence.

Pelourinho [pell-oo-REEN-yoo]   public pillory in Brazil

KEEP READING

Students and instructors might consider the following primary sources: Of particular relevance here is Chapter 8 of Matthew Restall, Lisa Sousa, and Kevin Terraciano, *Mesoamerican Voices: Native-Language Writings from Colonial Mexico, Oaxaca, Yucatan, and Guatemala* (2005); and Chapters 7–9, 13–14, 26–27, and 29–36 of *Colonial Latin American: A Documentary History*, edited by Kenneth Mills, William B. Taylor, and Sandra Lauderdale Graham (2002). Also relevant are several chapters in Restall's *Maya Conquistador* (1998), specifically Chapters 7 (which presents examples of the Chilam Balam literature mentioned above), 8 (on a Christianized Maya nobleman), and 9 (on Landa's anti-idolatry campaign of 1562 and Yucatec Maya responses to it); Catalina de Erauso, *Lieutenant Nun: Memoir of a Basque Transvestite in the New World* (1996) and Chapters 3, 6–7, 9–10, and 12–13 of *Colonial Lives: Documents on Latin American History, 1550–1850*, edited by Richard Boyer and Geoffrey Spurling (2000). Sor Juana's complete works are available online at http://www.dartmouth.edu/~sorjuana/.

With respect to secondary sources, students writing research papers might consider any of the following monographs: Richard Boyer, *Lives of the Bigamists: Marriage, Family, and Community in Colonial Mexico* (1995); Louise Burkhart, *The Slippery Earth* (1989); Fernando Cervantes, *The Devil in the New World*; Martha Few, *Women Who Live Evil Lives* (2003); Nicholas Griffiths and Fernando Cervantes, eds., *Spiritual Encounters: Interactions between Christianity and Native Religions in Colonial America* (1999); Laura A. Lewis, *Hall of Mirrors: Power, Witchcraft, and Caste in Colonial Mexico* (2003); Kenneth Mills, *Idolatry and Its Enemies* (1996); Nicholas Griffiths, *The Cross and the Serpent: Religious Repression and Resurgence in Colonial Peru* (1996); Martin A. Nesvig, ed., *Local Religion in Colonial Mexico* (2006); Susan Schroeder and Stafford Poole, eds., *Religion in New Spain* (2007); Stuart B. Schwartz, *All Can Be Saved: Religious Tolerance and Salvation in the Iberian Atlantic World* (2008); Pete Sigal, ed., *Infamous Desire: Male Homosexuality in Colonial Latin America* (2004); Irene Silverblatt, *Modern Inquisitions: Peru and the Colonial Origins of the Civilized World* (2004); Javier Villa-Flores, *Blasphemy in Colonial Mexico* (2005); and Stephanie Wood, *Transcending Conquest* (2003).

6

✳

Daily Life in City and Country

Cities and Towns

Pursuits of the Privileged

Mines and Mining Camps

The Changing Countryside

Plantations

Maroon Communities

Diet and Disease

Identities

Captain don Josephe de Mugaburu was a prominent Spaniard in Lima in the seventeenth century. As an officer in the viceroy's palace guard, stationed on the main plaza of the city, Mugaburu was witness to many of the public events and activities of his time. Fortunately, he kept a diary.

"Saturday, the 28th of September of this year," wrote Mugaburu in 1686, "eight men were sentenced in the chapel of the Inquisition for being married two, three, four, and five times; and others for other offenses they had committed." He added, "Of these eight, only three were flogged through the streets." Four days later, don Tomás Paravisino, general of the armada or official fleet that had left Lima's port of Callao the previous May, returned "from Panama with many ships loaded with dry goods"—an event that inspired "much rejoicing for his arrival." A month later, to celebrate the king's birthday, "bulls were run in the plaza of Lima," following a procession by General Paravisino and other crown officials, who "rode around the plaza three times on the footboard of a carriage. It was a very happy afternoon."

Mugaburu's diary presents a bustling metropolis with a varied and dramatic public life. People of all ranks and races participated in public events, while the colonial authorities seemed ever present. Official spectacle, law and order, seem to triumph over crisis and dissent; there were pirate threats and native rebellions, but the violence that took place within the city was typically the judicious violence of hangings and burnings at the stake. Mugaburu's Lima raises some of the subjects examined in this chapter: We begin in colonial capitals such as Lima,

111

TIMELINE	
1533–1544	Decade when most of the important Spanish American regional capitals were founded
1540s	Start of the expansion of African slavery in the sugar fields of Brazil
1550–1640	First gold cycle in New Granada
1571	Maroons of Panama aid Elizabethan corsair Francis Drake
1599	Treaty between maroons of Esmeraldas, Ecuador, and Spanish crown
1600–1694	Maroon complex of Palmares flourishes in the Brazilian interior
1693	Discovery of gold in Minas Gerais, Brazil
1700–1725	Founding of major mining towns in Brazil's south-central highlands
1746	Earthquake destroys Lima and its port of Callao

moving out to towns, mining camps, plantations, native villages, and remote maroon (runaway slave) communities, before returning briefly to Lima. The chapter compares urban life to rural life, treating such topics as disease and diet, working conditions, and leisure opportunities.

Mugaburu makes passing mention of black slaves and mulattoes in Lima; as was typical of Spanish accounts of the time, Africans and their descendants are barely recognized for their contributions to the locally evolving culture and economy. However, as we saw in Chapter 4, slavery quickly took root throughout Latin America in early colonial times. African slaves in the Americas fell into two broad categories—mass slaves and auxiliary slaves. Most slaves were forced to labor on sugar plantations or in gold mines (mass slaves), although many were incorporated into the service sector, often acting as intermediaries between Spaniards and native workers (auxiliary slaves). Whether in mining towns, port cities, or viceregal capitals, displaced Africans and their descendants established vibrant and durable communities and created new, blended cultural forms. As the colonial middle wore on, high levels of miscegenation (race-mixing) swelled black communities with free coloreds (free people of mixed African descent). Thus the free-colored presence slowly extended into every region of Latin America. Consequently, in this chapter we pay as much attention to black and colored inhabitants of city and country as we do to other colonial subjects.

CITIES AND TOWNS

The Spanish American capitals of Lima and Mexico City, and even the mining metropolis of Potosí, were highly cosmopolitan by 1600—even the most sophisticated snob was challenged to keep up with changes in fashion. Brazil's capitals of Salvador, Rio de Janeiro, and Ouro Prêto matured somewhat later, but by the mid-eighteenth century all three gave the great, old Spanish American cities a run for their money. Certain streets and **barrios** (city neighborhoods) were already famous for their craft specializations, others for their gambling and prostitution houses, and still others for their transient populations and mixed cultural flair. Whole city blocks were dedicated to female enclosure in the form of convents—virtual cities within cities. Here, in the centers of colonial city life, were schools and universities, monumental churches and monasteries, courts of justice, palatial homes, and exclusive shops. In the capital one rubbed elbows with the colonies' most powerful people. The capitals in particular—but the provincial cities, too—were labyrinths of intrigue.

For the Spanish especially, the colonial city was a kind of theater space for the display of civic and religious virtue. It was also a carefully orchestrated cluster of symbols of power, a planned monument to a particular vision of civilized life. For the Spanish elite, the countryside was uncouth, illiterate, pagan, and earthy, whereas the city was (at least ideally) a paragon of rectilinear order, education, Catholic religious devotion, and refinement. The city was a place of permanence, of stone, while the countryside was thatch and mud, transient and dirty. The city was also a place of concentrated authority, of governmental, religious, and commercial power.

For a variety of reasons, including an interest in public health, the Spanish established a rigid, gridiron plan for their overseas cities (see Image and Word 6.1). Spanish cities in America looked much the same in layout, whether in Chile or New Mexico. Wealthy and important people, the self-styled Spaniards of increasingly variable colors lived in thick-walled, two-storey houses as close to the plaza as possible—within the **traza**, or central grid of blocks. Cities had rules that governed everything from the supply of water, meat, and grain to the sorts of garments market women were allowed to wear in public. Some cities established night patrols to snare citizens engaged in naughty after-hours behavior. Church and state were never separate in the Iberian world; urban moral order, such as clean gutters or a properly located slaughterhouse, was thought to be a reflection of godliness.

Although dominated by elites, such as the encomendero class and their descendants, and later in some cases by merchants and government officials, the city was from the start a place of great diversity. Indigenous, African, and mixed-heritage servants, salespeople, artisans, porters, and builders made up the mass of urban dwellers; their movements were constant, difficult to monitor, and, in times of rebellion, profoundly subversive.

In most Spanish American cities, the urban lower classes tended to be predominantly indigenous in the middle period, although coastal cities such as Cartagena and Lima achieved African and African-descended majorities by the

---

Barrio   Urban, non-elite neighborhood

Traza [TRAH-sah]   central grid of city blocks, where important buildings and elite homes were located

IMAGE AND WORD 6.1   The Best-Planned Cities

"Since the city was founded in our own time, there was opportunity to plan the whole thing from the start," wrote royal chronicler Gonzalo Fernández de Oviedo in 1535, describing the capital of the island of Hispaniola. "Thus it was laid out with ruler and compass, with all the streets being carefully measured, and as a result, Santo Domingo is better planned than any city I have seen."

Spaniards arrived in the Caribbean with early Renaissance ideas on city planning, loosely consisting of the notion that cities should be well-ordered, with streets running in straight lines. But Spanish American cities had indigenous roots, as well as European ones. A crucial, under-recognized influence on sixteenth-century Spanish city planning was the Mexica capital of Tenochtitlán, whose central plaza and grid of canals and streets had so impressed Spaniards. Other well-ordered native cities, such as the Inka capital of Cuzco, were similarly influential. Although the process of turning Tenochtitlán into Mexico City (pictured below) began in the 1520s, the most important Spanish American cities were established and planned in the decade of 1533–1544. These included Bogotá, Buenos Aires, Cartagena, Lima, Quito, Santiago de Guatemala, and La Plata. The layout of these new cities also crossed the ocean back to Spain, reflected in the new Spanish capital of Madrid (founded in 1561) and in the new laws of 1573 requiring cities to be laid out with grids and central plazas. This idea of what a city should look like spread through the capitals of Europe, where it eventually became seen as an entirely Renaissance invention, although its origins may be as much Native American as European.

second quarter of the seventeenth century. Brazilian cities followed this latter pattern, such that by the late eighteenth century, Rio de Janeiro had the largest black population—free and enslaved—of any city in the Atlantic world. Merchant-dominated cities such as Buenos Aires and Havana, which grew in importance mostly in the late eighteenth century, also had significant slave populations.

Ports such as Santo Domingo, Veracruz, Panama, Cartagena, Lima-Callao, and Buenos Aires soon came to rely exclusively on slaves as stevedores, sailors, and construction workers. In Havana and Guayaquil, enslaved Africans built and repaired the ships of the line. Lima, with its nearby port of Callao, was a mostly black city by 1640 and was home to the Americas' only black saint, the former slave Martín de Porres. Nuns throughout Spanish America were served by enslaved black women within the walls of the convent, and one, Ursula de Jesús of Lima, became an esteemed beata, or holy woman, herself. Enslaved black men and women were also found in virtually every elite urban household, and their relations with other slaves in the city—and with their masters—were intimate and a frequent topic of dispute. Black slavery infused Spanish American urban life.

Salvador da Bahia, the early capital of the Portuguese colony, developed the deepest and most complex Afro-Brazilian urban culture, but the later capital of Rio de Janeiro was not far behind. By the end of the colonial period, Rio had the largest enslaved black population of any city in the Atlantic world. Slavery was so ingrained in everyday life in Brazil that freed slaves often considered slave ownership a natural avenue to social and economic gain. Brazil's most famous colonial architect and sculptor, Francisco Antonio Lisboa, known popularly as Aleijadinho, was the son of a Portuguese immigrant and an enslaved African woman.

Black culture in urban colonial Spanish America was marked by music and religious ritual. Black confraternities sponsored elaborate parades on their patron saints' days and for larger celebrations such as Corpus Christi. Black celebrants developed a musical style sometimes called the **negrillo**, which fused African rhythms, lyrics in an Afro-Spanish dialect, and traditional Spanish themes. African drumming was widely noted for its complexity and, per many pious priests, for its tendency to inspire "sinful" body movements. In some places African instruments such as the marimba and banjo were added to the Spanish repertoire of the guitar, violin, clarinet, sackbut, harp, and other instruments. Many of Spanish America's most notable modern musical styles, including salsa, merengue, and tango, grew out of this colonial fusion. Likewise, Afro-Brazilian religious traditions such as candomblé, and musical styles such as the samba emerged from colonial milieux of cities such as Salvador and Rio.

Negrillo [neg-REE-yoh]   musical fusion of African rhythms, Afro-Spanish lyrics, and traditional Spanish themes

By modern standards, none of these cities were large. Even at their height in the middle period, the Spanish American metropolises of Lima and Mexico City did not top 100,000 inhabitants. These numbers were nevertheless comparable to the populations of Europe's biggest cities of the time. More modest cities such as Guadalajara, Santiago de Guatemala, Bogotá, Quito, Cuzco, Arequipa, and Salvador da Bahia only reached 50,000 inhabitants when their rural hinterlands were included in the total. Cities such as Caracas, La Paz, Asunción, Santiago de Chile, and Mérida (Yucatan) were smaller still—more like large towns until the eighteenth century, when they rapidly gained in size and importance. Still other cities, such as Recife and Santo Domingo, faded from importance and shrunk in size in the middle period, their age of splendor having passed.

Throughout colonial Latin America, towns of a few hundred to perhaps a few thousand inhabitants proliferated in the hinterland of the great cities, some of them centers of agricultural or livestock raising enterprises in their own right. Others sprang up around trading and provisioning points or crossroads along the mule and ox-cart tracks that tied colonies together. Still others were associated with missionary and military frontier outposts. Whatever their initial reason for being founded, most towns were miniature versions of the great cities, complete with town squares (in the Spanish case) and centrally located pillories (in the Portuguese one). Towns that aspired to city status might be blessed with the royal assignation of **villa** or *vila*, a title that was more often a reflection of the status of certain inhabitants than overall size. *Villas* sometimes differed from towns in that they possessed stone churches and other more permanent buildings. Many, such as Ibarra, Ecuador, and Ouro Prêto, Brazil, grew into important regional capitals.

Other towns grew and prospered because of their location along the **trunklines** of the colonial economy—the routes that brought in new settlers, African slaves, native workers, and imported goods, while simultaneously bringing out export goods such as Bolivian silver, Ecuadorian textiles, or wax from Yucatan (see Map 6.1). La Paz and Oruro (both in modern Bolivia) owed their growth to being on the trade routes that linked the Peruvian coast and eastern lowlands to silver-rich Potosí (South America's largest city in the middle period). Campeche, for example, remained a *villa* and was politically subordinate to Mérida, the capital and only city in Yucatan, but the port-town was just as important to the colony's economy. Puebla de los Ángeles benefited from its location on the Mexico City–Veracruz highway; Puebla was the size of Lima in late-colonial times, with cathedral bell towers deliberately built a tad taller than those of Mexico City.

Villa [VEE-yah]   Spanish town (vila [VEE-lah] in Portuguese)

Trunkline   main economic arteries or trade routes that linked colonial mines, ports, towns, and cities

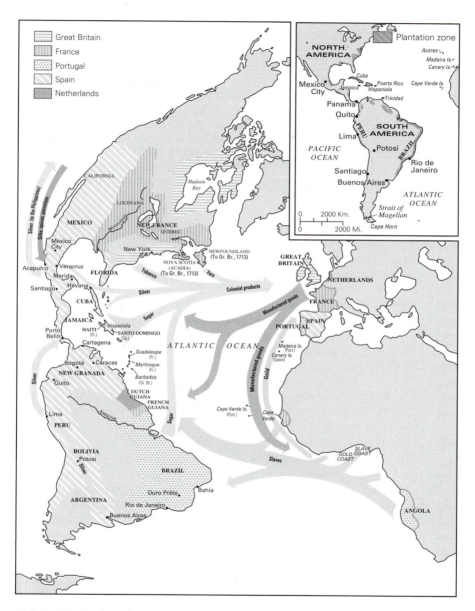

M A P   6.1   Trade and City in the Colonial Atlantic World

PURSUITS OF THE PRIVILEGED

Although deeply devout in their Catholic beliefs, wealthy Latin Americans constituted a genuine leisure class, and their lives consisted of more than prayer and con-
templation. Elites sought diversion in various forms—from card games and music

recitals to poetry and theater, from bullfights to massive fireworks displays. Even the Inquisition's autos-de-fé were viewed as a form of public entertainment; the floggings and hangings that don Josephe de Mugaburu witnessed in seventeenth-century Lima were events that brought the elite, as well as the plebeian classes, onto balconies, rooftops, and streets to enjoy the spectacle.

The colonial middle coincided with Spain's Golden Age of literature. Colonial elites proved avid consumers of this boom in secular literary production. Some of the great works of the period, especially poetic and historical ones, were written by elite colonists themselves, although most printing was done in Spain. The printing presses of Mexico City and Lima were mostly devoted to production of religious works, including some in indigenous languages. Ships' manifests and sale records from the Baroque period show that wealthy urbanites from New Mexico to Chile were reading the picaresque novels of Cervantes and Alemán within a year of their printing in Spain. Such works were sold in colonial cities, but it was not uncommon for elite Spaniards to make business trips to Spain—typically a two-year affair—and to return with a few of the latest publications. Spanish Americans also purchased and even staged the plays of Lope de Vega and Calderón de la Barca, and some colonial authors were inspired to write plays treating local themes. Others enjoyed the epic poetry of colonial authors Ercilla and Castellanos. The historical works of mestizo writer Garcilaso "El Inca" de la Vega were also wildly popular.

In addition to these Spanish and colonial works, elite readers were avid consumers of the classics. Aristotle was considered the prime authority in many things, but Greek and Roman authors such as Herodotus, Thucydides, Cicero, and Marcus Aeneus Lucan were also widely available. The Inquisition maintained a list, or index, of prohibited books, but surviving colonial libraries and other references show that allegedly forbidden works were not difficult to find. Most of these books were not expensive for elites, although an average title cost as much as a year's tribute for most Native Americans. Literacy outside elite circles was not widespread.

Elite colonial music, like much literature, was overwhelmingly religious. Some colonists purchased songbooks that included romantic and military ballads, but most music was intended to accompany religious services. Polyphonic choir music was common everywhere, accompanied by pipe organs and a variety of wind and string instruments. Both European choral and instrumental traditions were picked up by African, indigenous, and mixed-heritage musicians, and soon new forms and rhythms emerged. The Guaraní of Paraguay produced a massive corpus of religious music to be sung in Guaraní and following Guaraní forms, and Africans and their descendants developed an extraordinary range of blended musical styles that formed the base of most modern Latin American popular music—the complexity and variety of which reflects the centuries of cultural interaction between Iberians, Africans, and native peoples in the colonies.

Mugaburu noted that in 1686 the authorities in Lima chose to celebrate the king's birthday by running bulls in the city plaza, a decision that symbolizes the enduring popularity of bull baiting in Spanish America, beginning with its introduction from Spain in the sixteenth century. Most colonial bullfights were not as finely choreographed as modern ones, but the essential contest between man and beast was still at the core. Lancers on horseback and matadors with capes and swords were standard in some places, while in others the "fight" was a more informal, country affair oriented toward teasing and dodging the bulls amid much drinking and clowning.

The cockfight was even more popular than the bullfight, in part because it was easily appropriated by the popular classes. Raising fighting cocks was not an expensive hobby. Still, cockfights were staged at official times in the colonial period and were administered by elites who held special licenses. In the same way that alcohol and playing cards were supposed to be sold only by licensed officials, the cockfight was seen as a source of state revenue. The administrator purchased the right to stage cockfights for several years in a row from crown officials, then recouped his costs by gathering a portion of the wagers made by participants and spectators. Like the bullfight, the cockfight was as much a ritual of machismo as it was a bloody spectacle.

MINES AND MINING CAMPS

Occupying a space somewhere between town and country were the many mining camps of middle period Spanish America and Brazil. Mines tended to be located in rugged backcountry regions, often in places not otherwise amenable to urban development. Still, as the extraordinary case of Potosí demonstrates, mining camps could grow to enormous size and sophistication despite their geographical isolation. In Spanish America and later Brazil, mining camps, in part because of their general isolation from agricultural and manufacturing centers, stimulated a quick linking of city and countryside. Some camps became towns, and some of these, such as Guanajuato and São João del-Rei, became regional capitals. Most mining towns settled down and became more orderly with time, but all had a deserved reputation for crime, prostitution, filth, contraband trade, and corruption. The prospect of easy money drew a variety of hustlers, charlatans, and thieves.

The silver mines of Mexico and Peru were mostly staffed by indigenous draft laborers and later free wage earners. Only very wealthy mine owners and refiners in these regions purchased Africans, and given the dangers of underground work, most chose to employ slaves in refineries and mints. In these highly specialized environments slaves gained a variety of technical skills that would have been wasted on temporary workers. Thus, Spanish access to the indigenous mita and repartimiento for unskilled workers meant that Africans and their descendants in the silver towns enjoyed a somewhat higher status. They were skilled artisans, many even possessing the legal credentials of master craftsmen. With this came a higher monetary value, which in turn made self-purchase more difficult.

Many Africans and their descendants lived and worked among the thousands of scattered gold mines and washings of Spanish America and Brazil. In New Granada (present-day Colombia), slavery and gold mining became most closely intertwined. Whole regions, such as the Pacific coast, are still populated by descendants of enslaved African miners. Here, slave communities formed with relative speed, as mine owners rapidly shifted away from Native American labor (mostly based on the encomienda rather than mita or repartimiento)—financing their purchase of Africans with gold.

Absentee mine owners living in distant highland towns and cities thus became the rule, leaving huge numbers of enslaved, largely African-born miners to the oversight of temporary administrators and, more often, trusted slave "captains." As contact with Spaniards was minimal, slaves and their descendants blended African and select indigenous cultural forms all along the Pacific coast, the survivals of which are still notable today. Slaves also had ready access to gold, which allowed some to purchase their freedom or that of loved ones. By the later colonial period, large numbers of free black gold panners scoured New Granada's many rivers in search of subsistence. Among slaves, work stoppages in exchange for better rations and other concessions were common, especially along Colombia's wet and gold-rich Pacific coast. Given the many dangers of life in such a demanding, rainforest environment, African curers emerged as a special, elite class among slaves. Economy and ecology, in short, combined in this region of colonial Latin America to create a genuine neo-African enclave.

The great gold and diamond mines of Brazil, meanwhile, discovered in the decades around 1700, were somewhat different. As in the case of sugar, Portuguese entrepreneurs overwhelmingly sought to work their claims with large groups of young African men. In their greed, and with the relatively low cost of slaves brought from Portuguese slaving outposts in Africa, the idea of reproducing the workforce did not figure, particularly in the midst of the mad rush for profits that marked the first half of the eighteenth century. Over 300,000 African slaves were brought to the mining districts at this time, nearly all of the tens of thousands of slaves brought to the mines were men. Such overwhelming numbers of men concentrated in Brazil's southeastern high country soon led to disorder—including rebellion, flight, and rampant trade in contraband gold and gems. The few African women brought to the region were frequently treated as prostitutes and concubines by the similarly large population of Portuguese men, most of them recent immigrants. Such was life on the booming frontier. Still, some enslaved women managed to carve out relatively comfortable spaces for themselves, owning mines, slaves, and urban real estate. The former slave Francisca da Silva of Diamantina, for example, became one of the richest women in the Brazilian interior.

THE CHANGING COUNTRYSIDE

In the vast Latin American backcountry, everyday life could seem to outsiders to be stuck in a pre-Columbian time warp. The majority of indigenous peoples carried on farming maize, potatoes, manioc, and other crops much as they had done for millennia. In the Andes, others herded llamas and alpacas. Most paid tribute to imperial authorities twice a year in goods or cash. Many worshiped the old fertility gods, too, though sometimes behind the guise of Catholic saints. Most native peoples continued to live in self-governing villages. There the pace of life was slow, the year marked by the seasonal cycles of agriculture and the calendar of saints' days. The influence of the outside world was gradual, and the absorption of native villagers into the exploitative economic systems of the Atlantic world was not yet so blatant and disruptive as to produce the kinds of village rebellions that were to mark the late eighteenth century. There were exceptions—in the 1660s whole villages of Mayas fled into the unconquered forests from southwestern Yucatan to escape colonial demands, and in 1680 the Pueblo peoples of New Mexico rose up violently to throw off colonial rule—but such exceptions showed how relatively stable most colonies were.

Indigenous languages survived everywhere but especially in the countryside. European missionaries learned to preach in local tongues if they wished to be understood; if their language skills were inadequate, they ran the risk of being denounced as ineffectual by native parishioners. Only in certain commercial enclaves, most of them urban, were native languages beginning to be displaced by Spanish and Portuguese in the seventeenth century. With their large and densely settled indigenous populations, the two core colonial regions of Mesoamerica and Upper Peru were perhaps most notable for the persistence and everyday character of native languages (and, more broadly, cultures). In these regions, even elite Spanish speakers tended to be raised by Nahuatl-, Maya-, or Quechua-speaking wet-nurses and house servants. Rural life, considered by educated Spaniards and Portuguese as generally coarse and beneath contempt, was overwhelmingly associated with "Indianness."

Looks could be deceiving, however. In truth, native men and women in larger rural communities were often as cosmopolitan as their European overlords. Some traveled great distances to find employment (or just as often, to avoid forced work stints in mines and other projects), to transport goods by sea and land, and to participate in the market. Some native noblemen even traveled to Spain to seek an audience with the king. In Spanish colonial cities, indigenous women were a fixture in the marketplace, constantly hustling alongside mestizas, mulattas, and other women of color to carve out a space for profit-making against the wishes of male Spanish merchants and wholesalers.

Beyond the realm of tastes and travels, town and country in colonial Latin America were closely linked. Cattle—introduced early into the colonies and outnumbering the declining native population by 1600—were a major link between town and country. Livestock raising lands, or ranches, were tied to all Spanish American and Brazilian cities, towns, and mining camps. These provided the cities and towns with steady supplies of meat, hides, tallow, and dairy products. Substantial numbers of raw cowhides were also exported to European markets. Only in the case of highland Peru and Bolivia were the native herd animals (llamas and alpacas) significant, mostly for indigenous use in transport and textile manufacture. Some ranch lands or pastures were carefully measured by surveyors and even divided by trenches and stone or adobe walls. This was especially true of agriculturally rich and densely populated savannas, where keeping grazing animals out of neighboring agricultural fields was a constant battle.

Far more often, ranches were extensive, vaguely delineated territories, as in the semiarid expanses of northern Mexico and northeastern Brazil. The only way to keep track of animals in the land of the open range was by branding and through periodic roundups, or rodeos. Ranchlands were dominated by small numbers of black, indigenous, or mixed-race men who developed distinctive cowboy cultures. The Mexican **charro**, Andean **chagra**, Brazilian **vaqueiro**, Venezuelan *llanero*, and Argentine **gaucho** were all products of the colonial ranch economy. These hard-bitten, hard-drinking, leather-clad men came periodically to the city with their herds. Their visits, marked by whoring, drinking binges, and violence, were not soon forgotten.

Connected to many of the ranches of backcountry Latin America were large agricultural estates built around the mass production of wheat, maize, sugar, and other foods. Some estates in Guatemala produced indigo dye, derived from plants that were sown and harvested several times a year. The great estates, called **haciendas** in Spanish America and *fazendas* (or **engenhos**, in the case of sugar) in Brazil, tended to be owned by urban elites and church organizations, such as the Jesuit order.

The great estates of Latin America were economically dynamic, fairly sophisticated agricultural businesses. But they depended overwhelmingly on the labor of neighboring native villagers and resident black slaves. When these labor systems were absent, estate owners tried to ensnare free workers, often peasants driven to desperation by drought or other contingencies, through advances of merchandise and other forms of indebtedness. The great estate was, for the most part, a place of bondage and discipline.

Large estates were of two basic types: (1) those oriented toward overseas export, such as the slave-staffed sugar engenhos of northeastern Brazil and the cacao, or chocolate, estates of Venezuela; and (2) those oriented toward internal, urban markets, such as the hundreds of wheat, maize, brandy, and cattle haciendas of the Spanish American interior. Ranchers on the islands of Cuba and Hispaniola helped supply the great annual fleets with salt meat and hides. In all cases, elite owners only rarely visited their landholdings, preferring instead to reside in what they regarded as the more civilized city. Overseers and majordomos—who tended to be Spaniards on the larger estates, but more often mestizos, mulattoes, or blacks on the smaller ones—were left in charge of everyday production on both export and internal market-oriented estates.

Small farms, called **fincas**, **chacaras**, or **estancias** in Spanish America, were another feature of the mid-colonial rural landscape. Like the great estates, some were

---

Charro, chagra, gaucho, and vaqueiro [va-KAY-roo]   the cowboy in Mexico, the Andes, Argentina, and Brazil, respectively

Hacienda [ass-YEN-dah]   great agricultural estate in Spanish America (fazenda in Portuguese)

Engenho [en-ZHEN-you]   sugar mill, or estate, in Brazil

Finca, chacara, or estancia   small agricultural estates, or farms

oriented toward urban markets and others toward transatlantic ones. In Brazil, some small landholders, called *lavradores de cana*, or "cane farmers," produced sugarcane for neighboring *senhores de engenho*, or mill lords. They paid the mill lords for use of the expensive machinery needed to squeeze and distill sugar in portions of cane or juice. Refined sugar was then traded to merchants for slaves, tools, and luxury commodities. Although few managed to do so, many cane farmers in the middle period hoped to accumulate slaves and money and someday build a mill of their own. As in Spanish America, other rural farmers in Brazil tapped into the export market by growing tobacco, a product that required little capital investment but that could yield some cash return. In later years, tobacco would become a significant alternative to sugar for small farmers in Cuba, coastal Mexico, and New Granada.

PLANTATIONS

The ultimate fate of most Africans forced to cross the Atlantic was a life of labor on a sugar plantation. The largest portion were absorbed into the Brazilian plantation system, but Spanish America was also a highly significant destination, receiving more than three times the number of Africans sent to the future United States. The first Spanish American plantations were established on Hispaniola shortly after Columbus's time, and the model soon spread to Mexico, Peru, and other mainland districts. By 1519, sugar mills and plantations were found all over the island of Hispaniola, some staffed by as many as 300 African slaves. Plantations on Cuba and Puerto Rico soon followed. On the mainland, none other than Hernando Cortés invested a substantial portion of the wealth accumulated through conquest in a large sugar plantation staffed by African slaves. Similar plantations and mills, most of them tended and run by black Africans, could soon be found from Venezuela to coastal Peru. For the Spanish, like their Portuguese neighbors, African slavery and sugar plantations seemed a natural combination. The pattern was soon expanded in Brazil and later, after about 1640, in the non-Spanish Caribbean.

In the early years, black community formation was nothing short of miraculous. African slaves were often relatively few in number, mostly male, born in many unrelated and distant parts of western Africa, and isolated by the nature of their work. Still, Africans soon blended traditional cultural practices, languages, and beliefs with those thrust on them by the Spanish and Portuguese. Sexual relations with both Europeans and Native Americans quickly led to the appearance of mixed-heritage children whose status was legally ambiguous. The result—often noted within one or two generations of arrival—was a hybrid plantation culture, more often than not influenced by a heavy dose of Native American practices, life-ways (including cuisine, house construction methods, and so on), and languages. Particularly in the early years, many African men found mates among Native American women, in some cases guaranteeing freedom from slavery to their children. Uncomfortable with the idea of a new population that could not easily be enslaved or drafted to serve like those defined as "pure Indians," the Spanish forbade (but never prevented) such unions.

Where groups of slaves living on one plantation reached the hundreds, as happened in several Spanish American regions as early as the sixteenth century, local identities and marriages prevailed. Spanish American plantation owners encouraged family formation, and hence natural reproduction, among their slaves. African women were avidly sought by Spanish buyers. Families made slave communities stronger, but encouraging natural reproduction had the adverse consequence of allowing owners to exploit the considerable labor power of women and children. In areas where plantations bordered substantial indigenous communities, as in parts of Ecuador and Peru, ties of god-parentage linked enslaved Africans and their descendants with Native Americans.

The plantation regime in Brazil was generally harsher, with many slaves literally worked to death within a few years of their arrival on American shores. Cutting sugar cane was back-breaking work, and many of the tasks in the sugar mill were dangerous; all in all, Brazilian sugar plantations were lethal destinations for African slaves (see Image and Word 6.2). Opportunities for forging family life were restricted by working conditions and the planters' emphasis on what they considered men's work; African women were relatively few in Brazil, virtually throughout the nearly three and a half centuries of the slave trade.

Nevertheless, despite the gender imbalance among Afro-Brazilian slaves, black communities formed early in all of Brazil's sugar zones, especially in Pernambuco and Bahia. Plantation slaves were expected to grow their own food between cane planting and harvest cycles, and some managed to produce a surplus that they then exchanged at market for clothing and other material comforts that rendered slave life less demeaning. Others managed to trade items such as tobacco and fish caught on feast days for cash, which was often used to purchase freedom for oneself or for loved ones. As in Spanish America, religious brotherhoods in Brazil often played the role of savings and loan institutions, holding money safely until the needed sum was accumulated. Brazil's black brotherhoods grew most prominent in the mining districts opened by the early eighteenth century.

MAROON COMMUNITIES

Slave resistance was manifold, but most threatening of all to European masters were the communities formed in the backcountry by fugitive slaves. Runaway slaves (called **cimarrones** by the Spanish, "maroons" by the English) were a constant problem to Europeans from the beginning of the slave trade. As early as 1503, Africans escaped the plantations, mines, and cities of Hispaniola to live

---

Cimarrón   Spanish term for runaway slaves, or "maroons"

IMAGE AND WORD 6.2 The Sweet and the Bitter

It may be hard to believe today, but sugar was once a scarce commodity. When Muslim traders first brought it to the Mediterranean in the eighth or ninth century, sugar served as a medicine and rich person's condiment. European confectioners began to experiment with sugar in late medieval times, but demand only exploded in the sixteenth century with the Iberian push into the Atlantic. Almost overnight, sugar became a significant source of calories in many European diets. Though in time it came to be associated almost exclusively with slave labor, sugar was initially produced by mixed gangs of slaves and free workers.

Cutting the tough cane stalks was an exhausting task, and workers were assigned daily quotas of several tons of cane (the image above depicts black slaves hacking and hauling in the cane fields). Sugarcane is also woody, and difficult to squeeze to remove its precious juice; complex mills were needed. Animals powered some mills, but those powered by waterwheels were much more efficient, making them more profitable. Access to water was usually limited, and sugar mills were expensive to build and maintain, so most sugar growers cultivated small plots and only dreamed of owning mills. Mill workers had it the worst, by far, however, especially the enslaved women who fed canes into the rollers. Mills ran all night in harvest season, leaving workers exhausted and accident-prone. An English visitor to Brazil around 1600 described how hatchets hung next to mill rollers for emergency amputations, an all-too frequent occurrence. (The image below is a somewhat sanitized nineteenth-century depiction of sugar mill activity on a plantation in Latin America.)

Making white crystal sugar from raw cane juice was also a difficult and exhausting process. Workers tended fires and stirred the boiling juice in huge copper vats. They then reduced it in a series of smaller vats into a concentrated syrup, which was poured into molds to crystallize as brown sugar. Women were usually assigned

(continued)

IMAGE AND WORD 6.2   The Sweet and the Bitter (continued)

the task of whitening the sugar loaves and preparing them for shipment. They used wet clay to bleach the sugar, then removed the loaves from their molds and carefully packed them in crates. All phases of sugar production demanded skill and attention, giving rise to many task-specific positions, for example, purger, or purifier, mold-maker, and crating supervisor. Since sugar making was so complex, capitalized, and time sensitive, some historians regard it as a precursor of industrial production. However we may classify it, sugar making proved a demanding and even deadly business for millions of enslaved Africans and their descendants.

At the other end of the chain were sugar consumers. In the Mediterranean and Europe, Muslim, then Jewish and Christian, chefs embraced the versatile new sweetener (much easier to handle than honey) to create pastries, preserves, and candies. By 1600, sugar had become a standard ingredient in many foods and was not much more expensive than salt. Sugar's increasing availability and dropping price were the direct result of the expansion of Atlantic slavery, first in the East Atlantic islands (Madeira, the Canaries, and São Tomé), and then in the Americas, primarily the Spanish Caribbean and Brazil.

The rise of sugar as a product that more and more people craved, one that made European elites on both sides of the Atlantic rich and powerful, sealed the fate of millions of Africans. Without sugar, the Atlantic slave trade would have looked very different and might have barely existed at all.

in freedom, often among Indians. Panama was another early site of maroon community formation, and there maroons aided English pirates such as Francis Drake as they attacked Spanish mule trains loaded with the silver of Peru. Substantial maroon communities soon formed in Mesoamerica and the Andes, usually in remote sites that still allowed for preying on Spanish commerce, livestock herds, and agriculture.

In Mexico and Ecuador around the turn of the seventeenth century, several maroon groups became so strong that district authorities were forced to cede them legal autonomy. In exchange for promising not to aid foreign intruders or raid plantations for more fugitives, the maroons were granted autonomy and peace. Maroons in New Granada were still more numerous, given that region's many gold mines, plantations, and other slave-based activities. One community in the hilly interior beyond Cartagena, San Basilio, remained outside Spanish domination for so long that its inhabitants developed a separate dialect and festival culture still evident today.

The largest runaway community of all was the **quilombo** (maroon town) of Palmares in the Alagoas hills of Brazil's Pernambuco sugar district. Founded shortly after 1600, Palmares grew into a confederation of maroon settlements with an estimated total population of 20,000. As in most maroon settlements, Palmares was also home to indigenous fugitives. Like the maroons of Orizaba, Mexico, and eastern Panama in the sixteenth century, those of Palmares respected a monarch. In the late seventeenth century, amid attacks led by Portuguese planters, King Ganga Zumba organized defenses and negotiations. When these proved futile, a more militaristic leader, Zumbi, assumed control. Even his astute leadership was insufficient in the end, and Palmares was destroyed in 1694. The discovery of gold and diamonds soon led to another wave of maroon community formation in Brazil, but none approached the size and sophistication of Palmares.

In some regions, slaves on the run were able to find refuge in remote rural communities. This was often harder to do in urban settings; despite their larger populations, towns and cities offered little chance for anonymity, what with colonial officials, watchful priests, and market-place busybodies. But in the countryside, where there were few Spaniards, native communities steadily absorbed black migrants—occasionally maroons but more typically free black or colored men who settled down with indigenous wives and became members of the local community. In the Maya villages of Guatemala and Yucatan, and the Totonac villages in the Veracruz region, such men spoke native languages, dressed as natives, and farmed corn with their native in-laws. In other areas, such as the coasts of Colombia and Venezuela and the Mexican Costa Chica, such villages developed near the sites of tobacco or cacao (chocolate) farms or free-colored militia garrisons—and thus became heavily or entirely black.

DIET AND DISEASE

As was true in most of the world at the time, the sciences of medicine and nutrition were not well understood in colonial Latin America. The Columbian Exchange greatly enriched the variety of foods and medicines available to all colonial inhabitants, but for much of the period the kinds of foods one ate and the types of cures one sought were highly restricted by cultural affinity and class.

Quilombo   Portuguese term (of Angolan origin) for runaway slave communities (the Spanish term was "palenque")

Rich Spaniards, for example, declined to eat what they regarded as "Indian food," and natives were often unimpressed with the foods, such as olives and wheat bread, that Spaniards considered essential to civilized living. Traditional medicinal practices were equally suspect in the eyes of many, although with time some important exchanges occurred. Enslaved Africans, on the other hand, found their nutritional and medical needs closely watched since they were so valuable, but, in the end, poorly handled.

From their first contacts with the American tropics, Iberians were stunned by the variety of unfamiliar foods and herbs they encountered. For their part, they brought a wide variety of domestic animals, along with the food crops they hoped to transplant. Spaniards eventually found ecological niches for virtually everything they brought, including vine and olive cuttings. Elites were slow to appreciate indigenous foods, especially the staples of maize and manioc. Still, foods such as the tomato, chili pepper, and potato were soon taken overseas, where they became essential ingredients of many world cuisines. Chocolate, like vanilla and other Mesoamerican luxury foods, eventually took hold among Europeans (see Image and Word 6.3)—as did the Andean stimulant coca.

Lowland indigenous peoples, meanwhile, adopted imported food crops such as plantains and sugarcane, and natives everywhere avidly consumed pork, chicken, and other Old World domestic animals and their byproducts. African slaves were generally given a high-calorie but nutrition-poor diet based on salt beef plus a ration of starchy carbohydrate such as maize or plantains. Enslaved women did their own cooking, often adding vitamins and minerals as well as flavor to this monotonous diet by raising a variety of mostly indigenous fruits, herbs, and vegetables. In some places African vegetables such as okra and even the imported luxury of cola nuts were consumed. Rice cultivation developed throughout Spanish America and Brazil from an early date, and it is likely that this labor-intensive food tradition blended Iberian and West African techniques of planting and preparation.

Poor diet in the cities, combined with unhealthy sanitation practices and hygiene habits, helped maintain the presence of disease and high mortality rates. Streets were open sewers, considered appropriate places to leave excrement and animal corpses. Only the elite owned manufactured soap, although bathing among Europeans appears to have been infrequent. Not until modern medicine began to emerge toward the end of the colonial period were physicians sufficiently knowledgeable or trained to do more good than harm; even by the low medical standards of the day, many practitioners were quacks. Studying medicine lacked the prestige of theology or the law (most universities in Spanish America were religious institutions, and the relative weakness of the church in Brazil meant the colony had no universities at all). Even less prestigious was surgery; many surgeons were just barbers who had acquired a certain skill with the saw and lancet. Barbers also doubled as dentists, as the standard remedy for toothaches was extraction.

In the countryside, especially in native villages, age-old folk medicine and habits of personal hygiene often created more sanitary living conditions than those found in the city. Most Mesoamericans, for example, benefited from a

---

IMAGE AND WORD 6.3 The 11 O'clock Shot

As with foods, the variety and quantity of alcoholic beverages steadily increased in the Americas during the colonial period. New drinks such as wine, brandy, and rum became popular alongside, not instead of, traditional native beverages (such as Mexico's maguey-based *pulque* and the Andean corn beer called *chicha*). Wine was being produced in Peru in the sixteenth century and in Chile and Argentina not long after that. Wine was soon distilled into brandy, which was more potent and kept longer. Rum—and its cheaper, stronger sibling, *aguardiente de caña*—was made wherever sugarcane grew and was popular throughout the colonies. A Spaniard was more likely to drink brandy, an Afro-Brazilian aguardiente (popularly called *cachaça*, or "booze," by the eighteenth century), and a Nahua pulque, but such divisions of consumption were by no means absolute. For example, during a party on a hacienda in Ecuador in 1768, one that led to a murder trial, Spaniards drank large amounts of wine, aguardiente, and a local intoxicant called *punche*.

The following is from a 1758 English edition of *A Voyage to South-America*, the published account of the travels through the colonies of two Spaniards, Antonio de Ulloa and Jorge Juan. The passage refers to what they witnessed in Cartagena, but it reflects patterns of consumption that were widespread throughout Latin America.

> The use of brandy is so common, that the most regular and sober persons, never omit drinking a glass of it every morning about eleven o'clock; alledging that this spirit strengthens the stomach, weakened by copious, and constant perspiration, and sharpens the appetite. Hacer las once, *that is to drink a glass*

Gianni Dagli Orti/Rodolfo Gonzalez Garza Collection Monterrey/The Art Archive

(continued)

IMAGE AND WORD 6.3   The 11 O'clock Shot (continued)

---

of brandy, is the common invitation. This custom, not esteemed pernicious by these people when used with moderation, has degenerated into vice; many being so fond of it, that during the whole day, they do nothing but hacer las once. *Persons of distinction use Spanish brandy, but the lower class and Negroes, very contentedly take up with that of the country, extracted from the juice of the sugar cane, and thence called cane brandy, of which sort the consumption is much the greatest.*

CHOCOLATE, here known only by the name of cacao, is so common, that there is not a Negro slave but constantly allows himself a regale of it after breakfast; and the Negro women sell it ready made about the streets, at the rate of a quarter of a real (about five farthings sterling) for a dish. This is however so far from being all cacao, that the principal ingredient is maize; but that used by the better sort is neat, and worked as in Spain. This they constantly repeat an hour after dinner, but never use it fasting, or without eating something with it.

In precolonial times, chocolate had been a luxury drink of the Mesoamerican elite, who mixed the ground cacao beans with water, hot chili pepper, and maize flour. During the sixteenth century the popularity of the drink spread first to all natives in Mesoamerica, as well as Spaniards and Africans, and then into South America. The spicy recipe was gradually supplanted by a sweet one, using vanilla, cinnamon, and sugar. Cacao production spread to Ecuador and Venezuela, while the market for chocolate drinks began to develop in Europe. In the image above—a detail from a painting of the 1770s by the Mexican artist José de Páez— a black servant is frothing a hot chocolate drink in the kitchen of a Spanish household. Her son by the Spanish master of the house is identified by the painter as mulatto.

---

deeply rooted tradition of herbal remedies, many of which they wrote down alphabetically after Spanish priests destroyed and banned hieroglyphic books. Franciscans noted, with some bemusement, how often Mayas bathed and how the women prided themselves on their clean hair and clothes. Other indigenous peoples, along with many enslaved Africans, bathed with aromatic and cleansing herbs in streams and rivers.

Nevertheless, no native medicines could meet the challenge of the new epidemic diseases that arrived with Europeans and Africans. As we have seen, the Columbian Exchange killed tens of millions of indigenous people who lacked acquired immunity to Old World pathogens. Dealing with disease, deadly and otherwise, was more art than science in the middle colonial period, and in many cases alleged cures proved deadly. For those suffering from viral infections such as smallpox, influenza, or measles, there was little to be done in the era before vaccinations beyond keeping the patient sheltered, fed, and hydrated. Such diseases were often treated with the traditional therapies of bloodletting and purging, both of which probably worsened the patient's condition. Bloodletting, considered a vile but necessary step in the road to recovery by all European colonists, soon became a Native American specialty. Indigenous phlebotomists were always in high demand, treating elites, fellow natives, and slaves alike. Even horses and other animals thought to be ill were bled. Purges were mostly made from bitter herbs and powdered tree bark. Caustic ointments made from mercury were used to treat syphilis, one of the few diseases thought to originate in the Americas. Like modern chemotherapy, the selective application of such toxins did work to staunch disease, but often with unpleasant side effects.

Colonial subjects of all rank and status suffered from diseases and wounds at some time or another in their lives, but most deadly for Europeans were the mosquito-borne ills of yellow fever and malaria. No treatment was developed for the former prior to modern times, but the latter was fought—and fairly successfully—with an infusion derived from the bark of a South American bush called *quina quina* (hence "quinine"). Its use was first noted by Europeans in the early seventeenth century. In this case, it appears that Native Americans in what is today southern Ecuador had adapted a local fever-reducing remedy to a new disease. By the early eighteenth century in the jungle mining zones of coastal Colombia, African snake-bite curers, usually elder men, were highly valued by their white masters. As in the case of quinine bark, they appear to have been adapting known curative techniques to a new environment. Common wounds were treated with a variety of astringents, or mineral salts, but infections such as tetanus still killed many colonial field and mine workers.

IDENTITIES

As colonial communities became more socially varied in every part of Latin America—from the viceregal capitals of Mexico City and Lima to the maroon towns of San Basilio and Palmares—so did racial and ethnic identities become more complex. Modern concepts of race did not exist until the end of the colonial period, but Spaniards used notions of ethnicity and class to create two related socioracial concepts: a person's *calidad* or socioracial "qualities" (ancestry, skin color and physical features, occupation, wealth, degree of Hispanization, public reputation and honor) determined his or her *casta* identity (such as *negra libre*, "free black woman," *mestizo*, "man of mixed Spanish-native parentage," and so on). But despite Spanish attempts to maintain a rigid "caste system," identities were increasingly flexible. This was because all the determinants of calidad were plastic or changeable—wealth and honor could be won and lost, occupation changed, ancestry rewritten, and although skin color was immutable its perception by others could be altered. Brazil differed primarily in that socioracial preoccupations centered mostly on African rather than indigenous heritage. Many people of part African ancestry rose to positions of wealth and prominence.

The political and economic hierarchy was likewise different in practice than it was in theory. Spaniards saw people in the colonies as ideally fitting into two "republics," consisting of Spaniards and "Indians"—with Africans denied their own "republic" and instead living in attached subordination to Spaniards. Theoretically, because in mid- and late colonial times only Africans (not natives) could be slaves, the social hierarchy placed Spaniards at the top, followed by mestizos and "Indians," with mulattoes and then Africans at the bottom. However, political and economic reality often placed people of African descent above natives. Free mulattoes acquired political bargaining power through militia service, and some passed sufficiently as Spaniards to enter the priesthood or hold political office. Black slaves and free colored employees acted as intermediaries between Spanish encomenderos, estate owners, and businessmen on the one hand, and native community leaders and workers on the other hand. In Brazil, a different sort of color hierarchy emerged as people of whole or part African ancestry filled virtually every possible role, from estate owner to field hand. As a general rule, Native Americans were far more marginalized than in Spanish America.

Despite considerable fluidity, colonial Latin America was not a racial democracy; on the contrary, it was rife with ethnocentrism, prejudice, and discrimination of all kinds. But the fact that identities were flexible meant that individuals could improve their status and use the legal system to protect it—even if such efforts only served to reinforce social prejudices.

Mugaburu's Lima of the late seventeenth century had become notoriously mixed, racially and culturally, by 1746—when the city was largely destroyed by a massive earthquake and its port of Callao completely wrecked by the accompanying tsunami. The disorder that ensued, and elite attempts to rebuild the city as a more ordered and segregated capital, fomented a crime wave blamed on Afro-Peruvians, a native Andean uprising, and fearful class- and race-based elite entrenchment. The Lima earthquake highlighted the complex fluidity of colonial identities but also the anxiety and antagonism that often surrounded them. The tensions and conflicts that followed the disaster of 1746 anticipated the turmoil of colonial Latin America's final half-century. During the two centuries of the middle period, compromises had held the colonies together, permitting them to prosper and expand. But after the 1740s, these colonial compromises faced new challenges and would eventually unravel.

KEEP READING

The Mugaburu diary, quoted at the start of this chapter, is available as Robert Ryal Miller, trans. and ed., *Chronicle of Colonial Lima: The Diary of Josephe and Francisco Mugaburu, 1640–1697* (1975). Witness testimony on the Ecuadorian drinking party mentioned in Image and Word 6.3 is in Chapter 15 of *Colonial Lives: Documents on Latin American History, 1550–1850*, edited by Richard Boyer and Geoffrey Spurling (2000); Chapter 14 is also relevant. Suitable as assigned course books would be Susan Migden Socolow and Louisa Schell Hoberman's *Cities and Society in Colonial Latin America* (1986) and *The Countryside in Colonial Latin America* (1996), both *Diálogos* books from the University of New Mexico Press. Also accessible is R. Douglas Cope, *The Limits of Racial Domination: Plebeian Society in Colonial Mexico City, 1660–1720* (1994). Also of relevance are Irving Leonard's classic study, *Books of the Brave* (1949; second edition 1992) and Geoffrey Baker, *Imposing Harmony: Music and Society in Colonial Cuzco* (2008).

Supplemental texts that relate to the African Diaspora element to this chapter are Matthew Restall, ed., *Beyond Black and Red: African-Native Relations in Colonial Latin America* (2005); Jane Landers, ed., *Slaves, Subjects, and Subversives: Blacks in Colonial Latin America* (2006); and Ben Vinson III and Matthew Restall, eds., *Black Mexico* (2009). An excellent textbook is Herbert S. Klein and Ben Vinson III, *African Slavery in Latin America and the Caribbean* (rev. ed., 2008). There are also many fine monographs on the African experience in Latin America; see the bibliography to Klein and Vinson's book. For Brazil's diamond district, see Júnia Furtado, *Chica da Silva: A Brazilian Slave of the Eighteenth Century* (2008). A fine new book on the Lima earthquake is Charles F. Walker, *Shaky Colonialism: The 1746 Earthquake-Tsunami in Lima, Peru, and Its Long Aftermath* (2008).

PART III

✳

Breaking Away (1740–1850)

In these three chapters we span the long century that took Latin America from a network of Spanish, Portuguese, and French colonies to a troubled, warring collection of young republics. Chapter 7 covers the eighteenth century, looking at how Spain defended its empire against the growing empires of the northern European powers, and at how Spain and Portugal faced the challenges of making their colonies more profitable and better governed. Despite such efforts, unrest and civil war swept the colonies in the half-century between 1780 and 1830, leading to the independence of almost all the colonies; this story is told in Chapter 8. The first-generation struggles of the new nations and the nature of their new governments are outlined in Chapter 9.

The riddle of this period is a simple question with a complex answer: How did Spain and Portugal lose their mainland American empires? The answer lies in the interplay between events in Europe and events in the Americas. It also lies in understanding the whole century surrounding Independence, not just the core Independence decades of the 1810s and 1820s. Finally, it should be remembered that Independence was not a foregone conclusion; developments after 1740 help explain why Independence occurred when it did, but they did not make it inevitable. Cuba and Puerto Rico, for example, remained "faithful islands" until the Spanish-American War at the turn of the twentieth century.

7

✳

War and Peace
in the Late Colonies

The Imperial Triangle

The Problem of Defense

The Pombaline and Bourbon Reforms

Silver and Gold Revived

Late Colonial Society

In much of the Atlantic world, the eighteenth century came with a bang. A new royal family, the House of Bourbon, was battling for the throne of Spain by 1701, and the discovery of major gold mines in the Brazilian interior beginning in the 1690s promised to revive the long-embattled fortunes of Portugal. As a result of these changes, both of which coincided with the eclipse of the Netherlands and the rise of French–British rivalry, the Spanish and Portuguese hoped to return to their past glory. More than ever, Iberian monarchs would depend on their American colonies to finance imperial recovery. Comeback was not easy. Recovery entailed at the least profound administrative and jurisdictional reforms, coupled with and intended to finance expansion and professionalization of the military. Most importantly, imperial recovery in late colonial times relied on improved collection of taxes, tributes, and other colonial duties, preferably in gold or silver. American treasure would once again constitute the sinews of war.

In the colonies, meanwhile, a number of more or less unrelated changes were also underway. Populations were growing everywhere, in both town and country, spurring the expansion of agricultural and livestock raising enterprises. Deadly epidemics still cut through the colonies from time to time, and lowland disease regimes remained permanently deadly, yet the general trend was toward growth and adaptation. In Spanish America, powerful hacienda and ranch owners

TIMELINE	
1693	Discovery of gold in south-central Brazil
1700–1815	Series of global, imperial wars between the Spanish, French, and British
1701–1713	War of the Spanish Succession
1739–1748	War of Jenkins' Ear and War of Austrian Succession, including 1740–1741 British siege of Cartagena
1739 and 1776	New viceroyalties of New Granada and Río de la Plata created
1750	Pombal begins reforms in Brazil and the rest of the Portuguese Empire
1755	Lisbon earthquake
1756–1763	Seven Years' War
1759 and 1767	Jesuits expelled from Brazil and Spanish America
1775–1783	Wars of the American Revolution
1789 and 1791	Beginning of the French and Haitian Revolutions
1803 and 1804	Defeat of Napoleonic forces in St. Domingue leads to sale of Louisiana to the United States and Haitian independence
1815	Napoleon defeated in Europe

increasingly bumped against and fought with indigenous subsistence farmers, who in turn increasingly struggled to meet the basic needs of their growing communities. In the language of Thomas Malthus (the effective founder of modern population studies in 1798), land pressures pushed and labor demands pulled; many rural folk who found subsistence farming difficult or impossible migrated to cities, mining camps, and, more often, haciendas and ranches in search of a living. Migration in such hard times often entailed indebtedness, and it always entailed the search for a patron. Population growth in Brazil, meanwhile, was mostly in the form of immigrants from Portugal and the east Atlantic islands, and from African slaves brought to mine gold. What Brazil needed most were women.

This chapter outlines the reforms implemented during the eighteenth century by the Portuguese and Spanish colonial authorities; the revival in gold and silver production and other economic developments; and the changes in late colonial society—including the evolution of regional American or "creole" identities.

THE IMPERIAL TRIANGLE

Contemporary observers liked to link Spain's supposed seventeenth-century decline with the compounding misfortunes of its royal house, the increasingly inbred and feeble Habsburgs. It was easy to exaggerate the connection, especially in the era of the impotent and sickly Charles II, aka "The Bewitched." After ruling for 35 undistinguished years over an empire whose wealth, population, and reputation were allegedly still in decline, Charles II died without an heir in 1700.

Charles had named a distant relative, Duke Philippe of Anjou, to succeed to the Spanish throne, but Philippe was a Bourbon, the grandson of French King Louis XIV. This left the many enemies of Spain and France, including England and Portugal, aghast at the thought of a unified French-Spanish empire, a genuine possibility should Philippe of Anjou inherit his grandfather's throne. A Habsburg alternative was proposed by English, German, and other conspirators, and soon Europe was at war to decide Spanish succession. The conflict lasted until 1713.

In the end, the Bourbon Philippe won his throne and ruled as Philip V of Spain until 1746 (the Bourbons still reign in Spain today). But Philip's throne was acquired at a price, as Spanish and French forces actually lost the war. In exchange for Philip's crowning, the English were granted the slave trade monopoly (or **asiento**) of Spanish America, along with limited access to the massive Spanish American trade in dry goods. Philip, in return, renounced all claims to the French throne. Portugal, in return for its role as Britain's ally in the war, received Colônia do Sacramento on the La Plata river estuary (in present-day Uruguay); British merchants and Brazilian ranchers used the settlement to illegally import goods into Spanish American colonies throughout the eighteenth century.

With the Dutch and Portuguese reduced powers in the Atlantic—relative both to their past glories and to the other European empires—the War of the Spanish Succession initiated a long series of wars between the three great global powers. These three—we have called them "the Imperial Triangle" of Britain, France, and Spain—battled it out on European, American, and Asian soil from 1700 until Napoleon's defeat in 1815. Alliances continually shifted, but the dominant battle lines were between France and Britain, with Spain often siding with France and Portugal usually allied with Britain. This century of intermittent world war helped bring about four great revolts and ultimately huge colonial losses for France and Britain, followed by Spain's and Portugal's loss of almost all their American colonies; these revolts were the War of American Independence among Britain's 13 northern colonies, the French Revolution, the St. Domingue slave revolt that led to Haitian Independence, and the Wars of Independence on the Spanish American mainland.

Although Britain held the *asiento* until 1748, this trade agreement with the Spanish crown was used as a pretext for extensive illegal trade with the Spanish colonies, leading to open conflict in 1739. The War of Jenkins' Ear (so named as the catalyst was a struggle between Spanish officials and an English smuggler named Robert Jenkins, who lost an ear to a Spanish blade) evolved into the War of Austrian Succession. This ended in 1748, but six years later the British and French began fighting in North America, leading to the Seven Years' War

---

Asiento   monopoly contract, granted by the crown, to sell African slaves in Spanish America

M A P 7.1 North America and the Caribbean in the Seven Years' War

(1756–1763). This war was a disaster for France and resulted in decisive British victories in Canada, the Caribbean, and India. Spain's decision to join the war in 1762 was equally disastrous—British forces occupied Cuba, Puerto Rico, and Manila (as the United States would do in 1898), and the British navy was left in complete control of the Caribbean.

By the 1740s, British naval superiority had become a serious threat to Spain's empire in the Americas. As early as 1741 (when only the sweep of epidemic disease through British forces prevented them from taking Cartagena), the British were confidently predicting that they had the might to take Cuba. Indeed, in 1762, the British successfully besieged Havana and seized all of Cuba. This was a loss that was only reversed through the Spanish surrender of Florida to Britain in 1763 and one that was even more traumatic to Spanish confidence than the loss of the silver fleet to Piet Heyn in the previous century. The irony of Britain's 11-month rule of Cuba is that their rapid and extensive reform of its economy transformed the island into a lucrative sugar plantation colony, worked by African slaves; rather than reverse these changes in 1763, Spaniards profited by them for over a century.

The Seven Years' War led indirectly in several ways to the conflict of 1775–1783 in North America. For example, Britain's efforts to pay off debts accumulated during the Seven Years' War exacerbated anti-tax sentiments in its American colonies—sentiments that contributed to the development of an independence movement. Then France saw an opportunity to exact revenge for its earlier defeats by joining the rebellious Anglo–American colonists in 1778, convincing Spain to join for similar reasons the following year. The independence of the 13 colonies was made possible by French and Spanish involvement; for its efforts, Spain not only saw Britain humiliated, but regained Florida.

The wars of the American Revolution had only been over six years when a conflict broke out in Europe that would have profound repercussions in the Americas. This was the revolution that consumed France, beginning in 1789. When, four years later, the revolutionary government executed the king and queen at the guillotine, Britain and Spain declared war on France. The war in Europe lasted for much of the next two decades, spreading as far as Russia and Egypt and including the French conquests of Portugal in 1807 and Spain in 1808. The French emperor, Napoleon Bonaparte, placed his brother Joseph on the Spanish throne, which led indirectly to the independence of most Spanish American colonies. Brazil hosted the exiled Prince Regent and later king, John VI, who only returned to Portugal in 1821. The Bourbon king of Spain did not regain his throne until 1814, and the war in Europe did not end until Napoleon's final defeat in 1815.

Meanwhile, revolutionary ideas had spread to France's most lucrative American possession, the sugar colony of St. Domingue. There an uprising by free people of African descent triggered a full-scale revolt by the slaves who made up 90% of the colony's population. War then consumed almost the whole island of Hispaniola until 1804. Both Spain and Britain sent armies but were defeated as a result of a brilliant and tenacious campaign by the main leader of the former slaves, Toussaint L'Ouverture, who also acquired the neighboring Spanish colony of Santo Domingo (today's Dominican Republic). Napoleon also sent a large force, but, despite the capture of L'Ouverture, the French could not prevent Haiti's birth as an independent nation. Napoleon had hoped to use St. Domingue as a base to consolidate and expand French Louisiana; defeat in the Caribbean convinced him instead to sell Louisiana to the United States in 1803.

THE PROBLEM OF DEFENSE

Spain and Portugal therefore faced enormous difficulties in defending their empires at the start of the eighteenth century. The problem was both an internal and external one. Externally, the mid-colonial problem of pirates gave way to a late colonial crisis of foreign power in the Americas, especially British control of the high seas. Internally, there remained the challenges of controlling the frontiers. This challenge took the form of unconquered or rebellious native peoples, maroon communities, the spread of foreign settlements, and in the late eighteenth century an explosion in local discontent, manifested in riots, revolts, and even full-scale rebellion. The Spanish and Portuguese crown and their colonial representatives adopted a variety of strategies to tackle the defense problem, some more successful than others.

One of the lessons of the War of the Spanish Succession was that Spanish land and sea defenses were terribly weak and outdated; they had been neglected too long. Only massive spending on shipbuilding, fortifications, armaments, and officer salaries would bring Spain up to par with its more powerful, upstart neighbors. The Portuguese would learn similar lessons following the loss of Rio de Janeiro to French forces in 1710–1711. The problem was not only an Atlantic and Caribbean one; Spain's defense ministers realized that the growing naval strength of England translated into greater vulnerability of both the Atlantic treasure fleets and formerly hard-to-reach targets in the Pacific Ocean. English voyages to the so-called South Sea (the Pacific) were not all successes during the War of the Spanish Succession, in part thanks to French help and English incompetence, but one privateer captain, Woodes Rogers, managed to seize an outbound Manila Galleon near Acapulco. Rogers also seized and sacked Guayaquil. As a result of these and other losses and humiliations, the Spanish called on local citizens to subsidize the expansion of fortresses and garrisons from St. Augustine, Florida, to Valdivia, Chile. The largest expenditures, taken from colonial pockets, would go toward fortifying the already castle-like Caribbean ports of Cartagena, Veracruz, and Havana; Cartagena's massive ramparts would hold up against the English attack of Admiral Vernon in 1741. The defenses of Acapulco, Panama City, Lima, and Manila, not to mention Cádiz and other Spanish ports, were also greatly improved after 1713.

Shipbuilding, armament manufacture, and officer training were other areas demanding attention. The venerable yards of Havana, Guayaquil, and Manila were modernized, as were those of San Sebastián in the Spanish Basque Country. Improvements in naval architecture were copied from the French and English, as were navigational instruments and eventually shipboard clocks precise enough to calculate longitude. The cannon foundries of Seville, meanwhile, vastly expanded and improved the quality of their production, sending big guns to all the forts and ships of the realm. In the colonies, most handguns, including muskets, pistols, and shotguns, were still made by local artisans. Quality, as a result, was highly variable. Royal gunpowder factories, meanwhile, were modernized and expanded in Mexico, New Granada, Ecuador, and Peru. They still relied mostly on forced labor, however, usually of indigenous draftees. Finally, Spanish military academies were formed in Madrid, Cádiz, and other cities to train an elite class of salaried officers.

Officers trained in Spain would eventually oversee the many colonial militias who had long borne the brunt of foreign attacks. Before 1767, there was no standing army in the colonies. Defense was instead the responsibility of local militias, divided into companies of Spanish settlers (who were often militiamen in name only) and companies of black and free colored soldiers, who tended to man frontier garrisons and coastal defenses. The heyday of the black and mulatto militias was the period from the early seventeenth to late eighteenth centuries, when such units received privileges such as tax exemption and were led by their own officers—for whom service was an avenue of upward mobility. But the reforms that followed the British capture of Havana in 1762 and other Spanish losses in the Seven Years' War led to an expansion and professionalization of colonial forces. Soldiers of many colors now learned to march in step, wear uniforms, and fire on demand. But colored companies also fell under command of white officers and were disbanded completely in the 1790s.

Another Spanish defense strategy was the extension of the mission frontier, especially in North America. San Antonio was founded in 1718 as the hub for a series of missions and garrisons designed to consolidate Spanish control over Texas—and ward off French encroachments from Louisiana. At the same time, the Franciscans built a chain of mission settlements from San Diego to San Francisco, aimed at securing Spanish possession of California. The colonial authorities worked hard to recruit settlers from Mexico to come to both Texas and California. After the Jesuits were expelled from the colonies in 1767, Franciscans took over and extended their missions in Baja California and Arizona.

All these efforts at defending the empire and expanding its frontiers were part of a larger crown effort to reform how the colonies were run. These efforts— known as the Bourbon Reforms (after the dynasty that ruled the Spanish Empire after 1700)—were rooted in issues of defense and in the early eighteenth century revolved around defensive strategies. In the second half of the century, however, the reforms expanded and evolved to become as much about administration, exploitation, and the economic health and profitability of the colonies. The reforms also spread to the Portuguese Empire (known as the Pombaline Reforms, after the Marquês de Pombal, the Portuguese minister who initiated the changes in 1750).

The Spanish and Portuguese had wasted no time lamenting their decline as imperial powers; already in the late-sixteenth-century poetry of Camoens and the early-seventeenth-century prose of Cervantes one sees the disillusioned colonial subject in full form. That Spain's Golden Age of literature and art should have coincided with Spain's political and economic decline should not be surprising, if we are to listen to historians such as José Maravall. In a culture of chronic crisis, loss was the inexhaustible vein one mined in both art and life. Yet, ironically, the enemies of Spain and Portugal doubted these laments as much as they believed them. Though weak in many ways, the Spanish and Portuguese empires proved more resilient, loyal, and effective than their colonial motherlands imagined. Colonial economies, too, increasingly dominated—like everything else—by local elites, also proved their worth. Just as Iberians met the challenge of imperial defense, so did they rise to the challenge of administrative reform and managed a variety of economic and social developments in late colonial times.

THE POMBALINE AND BOURBON REFORMS

During the eighteenth century, the Portuguese and Spanish Crowns set out to overhaul their strategies of colonial governance. This was a conscious effort to recover the national wealth and power that many Iberian officials believed had been in decline for nearly 200 years. They took their inspiration from the Enlightenment, a broad intellectual movement that stressed scientific principles of rationality and practicality while reducing the power of the Catholic Church in public life. These major administrative changes have become known as the Pombaline Reforms in Brazil and the Bourbon Reforms in Spanish America. They shared a similar mercantilist vision based in a belief that colonies existed solely for the benefit of the mother country. Growing out of this fundamental assumption, both the Pombaline and Bourbon Reforms attempted to centralize power in European institutions and to make the colonies more profitable.

In many ways, they were successful. At the same time, the reforms were so clearly intended to benefit the Portuguese and Spanish Crowns that they had the effect of angering and alienating their overseas populations. After decades of benign neglect, American creole elites, merchants, lower-level bureaucrats, and parish clergy suddenly found themselves excluded from civil and religious governance. They were more heavily taxed and government monopolies were crushing their local livelihoods. Furthermore, their beliefs were being monitored more closely by Inquisition spies, their precarious social hierarchy was threatened by a simplification of the complex racial classifications, and they were being held financially responsible for their own defense. Added to this powder keg of colonial resentment was the spark of the new philosophical ideas of liberty, fraternity, equality, democracy, republicanism, and self-government that emerged from the American and French Revolutions.

Sebastião José Carvalho e Melo, better known as the Marquis of Pombal (1699–1782), became prime minister of Portugal in 1750 and quickly made it clear that he intended to use his strength and charisma to force major changes on an inefficient and unwieldy system. Portugal was a small, relatively poor country with an expensive overseas empire that stretched around the globe to include outposts in Africa, India, and Asia. As if to complicate matters, Lisbon was devastated by an earthquake in 1755, the Portuguese government was engaged in a series of ill-conceived continental wars that had drained the treasury, and the out-of-touch royal court was lavishing untold sums of Brazilian gold on its own palaces and entertainment. Clearly the colonial economy could not sustain such largesse indefinitely. Pombal adopted a classic mercantilist strategy to modernize the Portuguese empire and make it run more efficiently. According to his plan, Portugal would industrialize and diversify its economy to produce finished, manufactured goods while Brazil (and Portuguese colonies in Africa and India) would provide raw materials, slaves, and captive markets.

Pombal redesigned the Brazilian colony's administrative structure. First, he asserted state control over the few donatary captaincies that remained in private hands and subdivided the territory into smaller and more effective administrative units run by government-appointed officials. Second, in 1763 he relocated the capital to the fast-growing southern city of Rio de Janeiro, reflecting the dramatic shift of the colony's economic power from the northeastern sugar regions to the southeastern gold mines and commercial trading ports (see Map 7.2).

To supervise the colonial economy more closely, Pombal formed a centralized *Junta do Comércio* (Board of Trade) in Lisbon in 1755. In 1767, he extended the system to the provincial level, creating a *Junta da Fazenda* (Board of Treasury) for each region that would collect tax data to report back to the central Board of Trade. Each junta also would be responsible for producing a specified amount of revenue for the Crown. Pombal also created three monopoly trading companies to extract resources

MAP 7.2 Latin America in the Age of Reform

from the Amazon region, Pernambuco, and Brazil's various coastal whaling villages. He then pushed for the introduction of profitable new export crops such as wheat, rice, and indigo to offset the declining sugar industry, and he set up boards of inspection for the tobacco and sugar depots in Rio de Janeiro, Bahia, and Maranhão. Quite clearly, Pombal was intent on extracting every bit of tax and customs revenue from Portugal's overseas empire, and in particular from Brazil.

The Pombaline reforms extended to other facets of Brazilian life and society. Pombal wanted to shore up Brazil's defenses against incursions from other European nations and therefore ordered that each captaincy maintain a census of all potential male recruits for a civic militia and bear the expense of defending itself. Pombal wanted to reduce the power and autonomy of the Catholic Church, which had always been weaker in Brazil than Spanish America but nevertheless was a major crown rival with great influence over the indigenous population in particular. He suspended the Jesuit missions near the Paraguayan border and eventually exiled the entire Jesuit order from Brazil in 1759. He took the responsibility for education from the Church and placed it under state direction, and he encouraged the study of more scientific and practical subjects rather than theology. Finally, Pombal eliminated another major source of Church influence when he instituted a new justice system that was based not in Church or canon law but rather on a secular, state-designed code. Under his guidance, the Portuguese government reasserted strong centralized control over its empire and started to reverse decades of decline.

In Spain, meanwhile, the Bourbon kings had begun a similar series of reforms in the second quarter of the century. Military reforms and other new defensive strategies were accompanied by administrative changes. To make their empire run more efficiently, the Bourbons decided to create smaller and more manageable units and to staff the positions with professional political administrators rather than cronies and incompetent sons of wealthy families. In 1739, they divided up the extensive Viceroyalty of Peru to create the Viceroyalty of New Granada, which encompassed the northern part of the continent. In 1776, they removed the southern regions from Lima's jurisdiction as well and created the Viceroyalty of the Río de la Plata with its capital in Buenos Aires. That same year, they created a *Comandancia General* (High Command) for the northern frontier of New Spain, a vast territory called the *Provincias Internas* (Interior Provinces) that included the Californias, New Mexico, Texas, Sinaloa, Sonora, Coahuila and Nueva Vizcaya. Some regions—such as Caracas, Chile, and Guatemala—were turned into Captaincies-General and given a greater degree of local autonomy. Within the viceroyalties themselves, the Bourbons adapted the French bureaucratic system and created a new position known as an intendant (**intendente**). First named in Cuba after the Seven Years War, intendants were given responsibility for military and financial affairs of a smaller geographic area. They were supposed to make sure that the Crown received its full share of the tax revenue and that any potential political discontent was kept under control.

The intendants became extremely unpopular figures among indigenous communities who found that ever-greater demands were being placed on them, and they often clashed with the governors of their districts who resented the loss of two major areas of authority. Bourbons tended to appoint European

Intendente   a new office created under the Bourbon Reforms; the "intendant" was responsible for military and financial affairs in a designated colonial region

Spaniards as royal officials, which frustrated and alienated American-born creoles who were shut out of lucrative employment in their own countries. Furthermore, while creoles were pleased to be involved in their own defense and their economies received a definite boost from the expanded military presence in their coastal towns and major cities, at the same time their taxes went up to pay for defense and the forts' demand for cheap labor drove up local wages. As a result, resentment grew. Creoles began to ask themselves why, if they were paying for their own defense and staffing it themselves, did they need to be part of the Spanish Empire at all? When a British adventurer invaded Buenos Aires in 1806, local Creole militias drove out the aggressor with no help from the Spanish viceroy. Their success only fueled talk of political independence.

As part of the Bourbons' effort to make the empire more profitable, they also set out to centralize, streamline, and professionalize a commercial system that had been characterized by a cumbersome bureaucracy and monopolistic trade practices. In theory, no colonial trade with foreign nations was permitted, exchange between the colonies themselves was banned, and all legal trade was required to pass through the central *Casa de Contratación* (House of Trade) in Spain where it would be taxed and sent on to its eventual destination. In an effort to reduce smuggling, increase customs and tax revenue, and energize new industries, the Bourbons slowly widened the scope of permissible trade activity. In 1765, they passed their first major Free Trade Act, which opened nine Spanish ports to direct trade with the colonies and no longer required them to pass their goods through the Casa de Contratación, although they did still have to apply for permits and keep full records. After 1774, the colonies were allowed to trade with each other. In 1778, a second, more comprehensive Free Trade Act identified 24 American ports that would be permitted to receive Spanish goods. The Bourbons abolished the complicated tax structure and replaced it with a single, flat tax of 6%, levied on all goods. Despite these significant measures to liberalize and energize the economy, the Spanish Crown nevertheless retained its fondness for commercial monopoly.

Trade with foreigners remained strictly prohibited. All ships used in the Atlantic trade had to be Spanish-built and their crews staffed with a majority of Spanish sailors. The Crown retained monopolies for itself on lucrative goods such as stamped paper, playing cards, olive oil, tobacco, gunpowder, and alcohol, and it strictly prohibited any colonial ventures that would compete with Spanish industries. Furthermore, the Crown chartered at least three major monopolistic trading companies with special privileges in specific geographic areas: the Caracas Company (1728); the Havana Company (1740); and the Barcelona Company (1755). Not surprisingly, among the most vocal supporters of independence were Creole merchants in major port cities such as Caracas and Buenos Aires whose ambitions had been frustrated by the preferential treatment that the Spanish crown showed to its European citizens.

The Bourbon reforms also targeted the institutional power and vast wealth of the Catholic Church. Influenced by trends in Enlightenment philosophy that sought to secularize government and public life, the Bourbons set out to limit the Church's influence. They aimed to reduce the clergy's size by passing legislation that required young men to attain the age of 25 before they were permitted to take their vows, obviously hoping that they would marry or enter another profession first.

In 1767, the Bourbons followed Pombal's lead by expelling the Jesuits, claiming that they were beholden to Rome and thus disloyal to the Spanish Crown. This action may have removed a wealthy and visible competitor, but it proved extremely unpopular among Creole Americans, many of whom had been educated by Jesuit priests. It also removed a significant intermediary group that had facilitated relations with indigenous communities in the frontier regions. The Bourbons also attacked the Church's financial base, confiscating all property that was not used for the immediate purpose of worship. Because there was no formal banking system in colonial Latin America, the Catholic Church often acted as lender and landlord, renting out its vast urban and rural properties and advancing sums to ambitious entrepreneurs and impoverished individuals alike. If the Bourbon state had managed to seize this vast source of capital successfully and called the loans due, the entire economic underpinning of colonial society would have been affected dramatically. In practice, although the confiscation of Church wealth remained a prized dream, the Bourbons were always too distracted by wars to implement their plan in full.

The Pombaline and Bourbon reforms represented a clear and concerted effort to modernize the Portuguese and Spanish empires in America after two centuries of slow decline. Ironically, their emphasis on rational, efficient administration and a more secular government that utilized principles of science and innovation was so successful that they alienated the very subjects on whom it was imposed. The reforms were so clearly intended to benefit European interests, in fact, that Brazilians and Spanish Americans started to resent their status as second-class citizens and began to suspect that their true interests lay with other Americans, those of different races and classes, and not those of their imperial administrators.

SILVER AND GOLD REVIVED

Imperial reorganization was expensive. Where would the money come from? As discussed above, the Spanish and Portuguese crowns improved income through a variety of ingenious and predatory means, and most especially through more rigorous tax collection. Amerindians were hounded for tributes, merchants for customs duties and sales taxes, and tobacco growers and distillers for their valuable, monopoly products. But the overall colonial money supply was itself a critical issue, and both the Spanish and Portuguese spent an overwhelming amount of their efforts in the eighteenth century trying to increase the output of their American colonies' many gold and silver mines. To an extent, they succeeded.

As it happened, a major reorientation of Spanish America's mining districts had taken place in the seventeenth century. The silver mines of Potosí had faded from their former glory, to be replaced by a number of dynamic silver districts in New Spain, including the namesake San Luis Potosí (see Image and Word 7.1).

Mexico's silver industry continued to grow throughout the eighteenth century, subsidized by mercury produced in Spain and mostly staffed with free laborers who shared in the mines' output. Hoping to encourage this trend, and to reverse the decline of Potosí and other Peruvian mines, the Spanish crown began to reduce taxes on mine production in the early Bourbon era, lowering mercury prices, and helping to guarantee mine owners' access to cheap labor and credit.

IMAGE AND WORD 7.1 The Two Potosís

© Sarah Meghan Lee/The Image Works

(continued)

IMAGE AND WORD 7.1   The Two Potosís (continued)

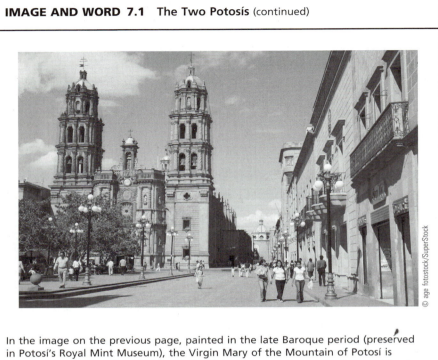

© age fotostock/SuperStock

In the image on the previous page, painted in the late Baroque period (preserved in Potosí's Royal Mint Museum), the Virgin Mary of the Mountain of Potosí is seen emblazoned on the hillside. By this date, however, her protection could not bring back Potosí's glory days of silver production; those had faded by the end of mid-colonial times, and in the eighteenth century it was the Mexican silver mines that made Spaniards millionaires. The Mexican mines included those at San Luis Potosí, named after the Bolivian site. Above are the Plaza de Armas and Cathedral Church, emblems of San Luis Potosí's wealth and importance in the Bourbon era.

In the case of Potosí and other South American mines, labor "reforms" entailed a revival of the much-hated mita system, which would eventually help spark the rebellions discussed in the next chapter.

Spanish America's gold mines, meanwhile, were expanded or revived in places such as New Granada and Chile. The mines of New Granada were mostly worked by enslaved Africans, and those of Chile by free mestizos and Amerindians. To stimulate investment, and hence production, the crown steadily reduced taxes on gold until they reached a low of 3% in 1777. New mints were established to buy and coin gold in hopes of stimulating commerce, and metallurgists and other European scientists were sent to help improve everything from prospecting to refining. All of these measures combined to yield an extraordinary increase in registered production, peaking just before the end of the eighteenth century. In both the silver and gold industries, the Spanish crown learned that government interference in the form of taxation on brute production was generally not helpful. It was more productive in the long run to tax trade.

Around 1693 a group of slave-hunters from São Paulo came across dark, lead-colored flakes of heavy metal near the headwaters of the São Francisco River, in the highlands of south-central Brazil. When melted down to remove the thin, discoloring outer layer, the flakes turned out to be gold. Within a few years a massive rush was on in Brazil, at its center a new town called the Vila Rica do Ouro Prêto, or the Rich Villa of Black Gold. In 1720 Ouro Prêto was named the capital of the new Captaincy of Minas Gerais, or "General Mines." Already there were at least 30,000 slaves in the goldfields of Minas Gerais, and almost as many young Portuguese men. The mines were lawless, chaotic, and incredibly rich. In trying to tap into the bonanza, the Portuguese crown would have its work cut out for it.

Following the Spanish example, and even Spanish mining law as contained in the Philippine Code, the Portuguese crown set a flat 20% tax on all gold production, the so-called **quinto real**. Twenty percent was a large cut, as the Spanish had discovered early on, so large that most Brazilian mine owners and merchants did what they could not to pay it. The Spanish had lowered gold mining taxes successively over the course of the colonial period to stimulate production and discourage fraud, but the Portuguese, with less experience in these matters, clung to the higher tax. They were soon forced to compromise, however, experimenting with head taxes on slaves, yearly quotas for different mining sub-districts, and so on. Still, the gold seemed to slip away.

One control was to make exchanges in gold dust illegal. Only bars melted down and stamped with a tax-paid seal in the regional capitals (along with imported coin) could circulate officially, according to law. As in Spanish America, even this proved impossible. Gold, even in its rawest form, was money; all one had to do was assay it and weigh it. Another control on gold flows was the Portuguese ban on the entry of the regular religious orders in the gold districts. This was a departure from Spanish practice, and it had the interesting consequence of strengthening religious brotherhoods, or irmandades, throughout Minas Gerais. Most of the outstanding architectural heritage of the region is associated with these devotees, the greatest donors among them lucky miners.

Brazil's gold rush had profound environmental consequences, too. The turning over of thousands of square miles of topsoil, along with massive deforestation to expose deposits and expand livestock fields and farms to support miners, left behind a deeply scarred landscape. Erosion, river sedimentation, and contaminated water supplies were but a few of the consequences of the gold rush. The discovery of diamonds in the drier and more delicate northern reaches of the

---

Quinto real   the "royal fifth" or twenty percent tax claimed by the Spanish and Portuguese crowns on gold and silver mined in the colonies

district around 1720 only exacerbated these problems. By the mid-eighteenth century, Brazil's mineral riches began to play out. Yet the colony was transformed. The linking of a gold-rich interior to numerous subsidiary agricultural and livestock-raising regions, as well as the export-oriented coast, made Brazil a whole colony for the first time. It now looked more like Spanish America.

LATE COLONIAL SOCIETY

The political and economic changes that swept through Latin America in the eighteenth century, particularly after 1750, were accompanied by a series of related social changes. One was demographic; for the first time since Iberians had arrived in the Americas, the total population grew. The number of Spanish and Portuguese settlers had steadily increased since the sixteenth century, but in the late colonial period other sectors of the population also expanded: There were many more slaves brought from Africa, while the free colored population exploded as a result of increased miscegenation with Iberians, mestizos, and natives; indigenous numbers began to rise, too, at first tentatively and haltingly in the seventeenth century but then steadily during the eighteenth; finally, the *casta* or mixed-race population of all kinds grew dramatically.

How did these demographic trends alter the colonies? First, the colonies looked more multiracial. Brazil's population doubled to two million during the eighteenth century, with the greatest increases among free people of African descent (by 1800 Brazil comprised well over a third African slaves, just under a third free coloreds, just under a third Portuguese and other whites, with a small indigenous minority). In the century before 1750, the population of New Spain grew by over 50%, a result more of casta than native Mesoamerican growth. By the turn of the nineteenth century there were over six million people in New Spain, some 140,000 of them in Mexico City (the largest city in the Iberian empires). The multiracial shift was especially visible in the cities, and not just the largest ones. For example, by 1750 Caracas had grown to some 30,000 inhabitants; Yucatan's capital of Mérida was about half that size but getting bigger every year; so was Buenos Aires, which grew so rapidly in the eighteenth century that it was as populous as Caracas by the 1780s. In all three cases, the mixed-race sector of mestizos and free coloreds grew proportionately far more than other sectors.

Second, the growth of these provincial cities illustrates the fact that areas that were marginal or peripheral in early and mid-colonial times saw late colonial booms. Frontiers became more settled, and new frontiers were created farther from the centers. Towns became small cities. Increases in the variety and quantity of trade attracted more people, who in turn drew more commerce. In Brazil, in the wake of the gold boom, the once sparsely settled south coast became as populous as the old sugar-oriented north coast. Settlers from Mexico migrated north into Texas, New Mexico, and California.

These demographic changes had a profound impact on social relations, especially in the cities and towns. The wealthy were richer than ever, especially in

Mexico, where the late colonial silver boom accounted in part for the presence of more than a hundred millionaire families (that is, families whose assets came to more than a million pesos, an astronomical sum). And the poor underclasses were larger in number and more underprivileged than ever, especially in Mexico City, where thousands lived in destitution. The middle sectors between the elite and the poor were increasingly varied and included less-privileged Spaniards as well as Hispanized natives and free coloreds. Spaniards could even be found among the poor. In other words, increasing socioracial complexity had slowly eliminated the original binary division of Spanish elite and indigenous subjects.

Alarmed by the pace of miscegenation, the Spanish elite sought to distance themselves more and more from the rest of the colonial population. One expression of the increased Spanish anxiety over race-mixing was the popularity of Casta Paintings (see Image and Word 7.2). Another was the response to the Royal Pragmatic, an edict that banned marriage between Spaniards and people of African descent; in the last decades of the eighteenth century, many took advantage of this edict to control the marriage choices of family members. The ability of parents to control the marriage choices of their children had declined since the early colonial period—with couples claiming, and the church supporting, the right to free choice based on romantic affection. The Royal Pragmatic thus allowed a father, for example, to prevent his daughter from marrying an unsuitable suitor by accusing the young man of being a mulatto. In many (perhaps most) lawsuits involving this edict, the real issue at stake was money; for example, two women who stopped their sister from marrying a man in a small town in Yucatan in the 1790s, on the grounds that he was a mulatto, admitted that they objected to his lack of means and feared he would spend the modest fortune the three sisters had inherited from their father. The irony of this, like many such cases, was that the ancestry of the sisters themselves was also probably mixed. Similar anxieties and contradictions abounded throughout late colonial Brazil. The more mixed the colonies became, the more the elite protested too much; by the late eighteenth century, trying to prevent mixed marriages was closing the barn door after the horse had bolted.

Despite constant attempts by priests, planters, and crown officials to control and monitor free and enslaved people of African and mixed descent, everywhere in colonial Latin America they carved out their own spaces and built communities. On the plantation, slaves created family and fictive kinship networks that formed a bulwark of dignity and group pride against an otherwise demeaning and harsh existence. In the gold mines, slaves found access to freedom in some of the Americas' harshest physical environments, negotiating constantly for more autonomy vis-à-vis the master class. In cities, castas and people of African descent asserted themselves in numerous ways, through group tasks, public events, and active participation in the market economy. The native majority in the countryside ensured through steady migration into town and city that all corners of Spanish America would retain an indigenous dimension. Black slaves and free coloreds also became Catholics, contributing to religious celebrations, developing their own confraternities and saint cults. Both black and native communities

IMAGE AND WORD 7.2   The Casta Paintings

Sets of paintings depicting the natural and racial life of Mexico became increasingly popular during the eighteenth century. Later dubbed "Casta Paintings," groups of 16 paintings on one panel (as in the anonymous example above) or in separate panels gave racial labels to the offspring of specific mixed-race couples. The labels and scenes chosen suggested that marrying down the socioracial hierarchy led to poverty and strife, whereas marrying "up" led to a redemption of the bloodline as African and Native roots became eclipsed by Spanish ones. One of the most accomplished Casta artists was Miguel Cabrera; see his work in Image and Word 5.2.

forged unique, regional interpretations of Christianity. Colonial Latin American life virtually always had a Native or African flavor.

Whether the Spanish and Portuguese elite liked it or not, Latin America's future was multiracial. It was not long before the colonies would become mestizo or mulatto nations. However, as the next chapter shows, the transition would not be an easy one.

KEEP READING

For students doing research on the period of the reforms, a fine biography is *Pombal: Paradox of the Enlightenment*, by Kenneth Maxwell (1995). Two books on late colonial Peru that are relevant here are Sarah Chambers, *From Subjects to Citizens: Honor, Gender and Politics in Arequipa, Peru, 1780–1854* (1999), and Charles Walker, *Smoldering Ashes: Cuzco and the Creation of Republican Peru, 1780–1840* (1999) and *Shaky Colonialism* (2008). Robert Patch's *Maya and Spaniard in Yucatan, 1648–1812* (1993) explores some of the larger economic and social issues of this chapter in the regional context of one province. Of relevance to the economic themes above are Charles Boxer, *The Golden Age of Brazil* (1962), David Brading, *Miners and Merchants in Bourbon Mexico* (1973), and Edith Couturier, *The Silver King* (2005). On the Casta Paintings, we recommend Magali Carrera's *Imagining Identity in New Spain* (2003) and the various publications of Ilona Katzew. Also see María Elena Martínez's *Genealogical Fictions* (2008).

8

※

The Wars of Independence

The Inka Strike Back

Long Live the People

**The Toothpuller and Tailor
Conspiracies**

The Cry of Dolores

Independence

When don Félix Calleja stepped down as viceroy of New Spain in 1816, he told his successor, don Juan Ruíz de Apodaca, that the rebellions that had swept across Mexico since 1810 were finally put down. Calleja styled himself a new Cortés; the turbulent kingdom had been reconquered and the colonial peace restored. Unfortunately for Viceroy Apodaca, this was far from true (see Image and Word 8.2). Within five years, New Spain would be lost to the Spanish crown forever.

The revolt of the British colonies in North America, beginning in 1776, initiated a period of resistance to European imperialism that would last over two centuries and result in the independence of almost every overseas colony by the end of the twentieth century. But that trend was not a simple one; it was marked in the middle by a dramatic expansion of the northern European empires in the nineteenth century, while the Iberian powers witnessed the collapse of their empires (by 1914 the British Empire controlled 21.5% of the world's land surface; France held 7.7%; the empires of Denmark, the Netherlands, Belgium, Italy, and Germany had gained a combined total of 7.9%; but Spain and Portugal only had 1% left each).

In this chapter we examine the uprisings against the colonial authorities that marked the second half of the eighteenth century in Latin America, and then the revolts and independence movements that spread across the continent between 1808 and 1830. The high point of those movements was 1821, when the original core colonies of New Spain and Peru declared independence from Spain. The questions we address are the following: Who led these revolts? What was their

TIMELINE	
1780–1784	Inka revivalists Túpac Amaru and Túpac Katari lead the Great Andean Rebellion
1781–1782	Comunero revolt in New Granada (Colombia)
1788–1789	Inconfidência Mineira plot in Minas Gerais (Brazil)
1791–1804	Slave revolt and independence wars in Haiti
1797	Two Spaniards, Gual and España, lead a revolt against royal government in Venezuela
1798	Conspiracy of the Tailors in Bahia (Brazil)
1807 and 1808	Napoleon's forces invade Portugal and Spain
1810–1811 and 1813–1815	Hidalgo and Morelos revolts in Mexico
1821	Independence declared in Mexico and Peru
1822	Pedro, prince regent of Brazil, declares the colony an independent empire
1822–1825	Independence movement spreads to the rest of Latin America, leaving only Cuba and Puerto Rico as Spanish colonies (until 1898)

goal? Were they civil wars or revolutions? And why did Brazil survive as a single state, whereas the Spanish American colonies broke up rapidly into many nations?

THE INKA STRIKE BACK

Theorists of revolution suggest that the gravest threats to colonial order come not during periods of neglect but rather when central authorities try to reassert their control and become more active in their overseas affairs. During the last decades of the eighteenth century, as the urban middling classes expanded in numbers, confidence, and economic power, and as indigenous peasants and enslaved Africans labored under increasing demands and brutal treatment, both the Portuguese and Spanish Crowns embarked on an ambitious overhaul of their colonial system. As we saw in the previous chapter, these reforms amounted to a large-scale and protracted campaign to make the Iberian empires better defended and more profitable.

But there was a price to pay in the provinces. The newly energized central administration tore apart the delicate fabric that had existed between European Spaniards and their American subjects, and it upset the already-tenuous socioracial balance within the colonies themselves. The pattern repeated itself throughout Latin America. Imperial arrogance alienated urban creoles, who then made common cause with people of lower classes and different racial groups to oppose the one thing they grew to despise: foreign domination.

We shall look at how this pattern was manifested in seven (of the many) revolts in Latin America, beginning with the Great Andean Rebellion in the 1780s (see Map 8.1), and returning at the end to the Andes and the birth of independent republics in the 1820s.

Throughout the colonial period, an excessive reliance on silver production in Mexico and Upper Peru (today's Bolivia) meant that other potential sources of wealth were left underdeveloped. There was little investment in agricultural or manufacturing sectors and entrepreneurial dynamism among the general population was not encouraged; in fact, the colonial administration's economic policies were restrictive and often outright destructive. For example, when the Bourbon reformers created the Viceroyalty of Río de la Plata in 1776, they reassigned the labor-rich region of Upper Peru to Buenos Aires' control; in retaliation, the jealous Lima authorities banned the importation of any goods that had passed through that rival port, thereby hurting their own local tradesmen as well. The Lima elite had vast fortunes based in silver mines and ferociously protected their privileged status by trying to hold any change at bay. Unlike the more dynamic outlying regions of the Spanish Empire, places such as Buenos Aires and Caracas where the Enlightenment ideals of personal liberty and freer trade had a tremendous practical appeal, in Lima they were viewed with suspicion or indifference. Any pressure for change that was felt in colonial Peru was generated

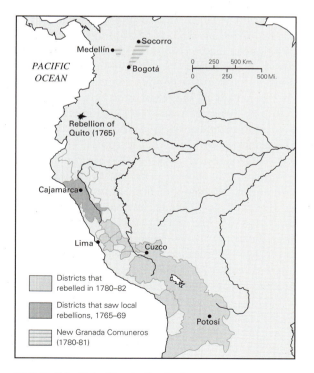

M A P 8.1 Rebellion in the Andes

by the real poverty of its indigenous population and the creole Americans' growing resentment at exploitation and bad local governance.

Although there had been intermittent revolts in rural areas throughout the colonial period, the first serious indication that the Spanish empire in America was facing a mortal crisis came through a series of loosely connected events known as the Great Andean Rebellion. The uprising lasted from 1780 until 1784 and spanned half a continent, stretching from the northern part of what is today Argentina, through Bolivia, Peru, Ecuador, and into Colombia. There were numerous lesser uprisings in the Andes and in New Spain in the late eighteenth century. But the Great Andean Rebellion was fundamentally different from these other revolts because its leaders represented a multiracial, multiethnic, and cross-class agenda and therefore the movement constituted a broader rejection of the imperial order than anything that had come before.

The Rebellion's most famous leader was José Gabriel Condorcanqui Túpac Amaru, a descendant of pre-Hispanic Inka royalty who held the prominent position of **kuraka** (cacique, or dynastic ruler) of Tinta, a small town in the hinterland of Cuzco. Túpac Amaru, whose name means "resplendent serpent," married a petite, feisty woman named Micaela Bastidas who became his passionate love and a shrewd political collaborator; together they had three sons and amassed a significant personal fortune in his mule-train business. Through his official public duties and his private business ventures, Túpac Amaru built up a vast network of connections that later he used to mobilize forces against the corrupt Spanish government in Peru. As cacique, Túpac Amaru initiated several complaints on behalf of his constituents, including a request to eliminate use of the *mita* to work the mines, an imposition on native communities that was explicitly forbidden in the King's own Laws of the Indies. He also protested against the ever-increasing taxes (which hurt not just native Andeans but all Americans) and against bad government in the person of the venal new **corregidor** (regional colonial administrator), Antonio Juan de Arriaga. His petitions met with stony silence. Enraged by the corruption and gross injustice that he had witnessed among the Crown's representatives in Lima, Túpac Amaru returned to his people intent on raising the banner of revolt.

At the same time as Túpac Amaru began to plot against the continuing presence of Spanish colonial administrators in his ancestors' domain, two other indigenous men raised the banner of revolt in separate but similar movements elsewhere in the Andes. Tomás Katari was the kuraka of Chayanta (in Upper Peru or Bolivia), and an Aymara commoner named Julián Apaza (who assumed the *nom-de-guerre* Túpac Katari) emerged as a leader in environs of La Paz. Like Túpac Amaru, both men protested both the burdensome tax structure and the arbitrary and cruel actions of their regions' corregidores. When corregidor

Kuraka [koo-RAH-kah]   native Andean lord of a town or province, usually from an old ruling dynasty (called a "cacique" by the Spaniards)

Corregidor   regional colonial Spanish administrator and frequent target of local grievances and revolts, in time replaced by intendants

Joaquín de Alos ordered Katari's arrest despite a royal order that had expressly forbidden it, Katari's two brothers held him captive until their rebel sibling was released. Túpac Amaru and Tomás Katari theoretically remained loyal to the Spanish Crown in the beginning but began their movements by criticizing the actions of its hated local representatives—the classic causes and strategies of late colonial revolts. Túpac Katari, however, was more radical from the start. Throughout the Andes and the rest of Spanish America, "Long Live the King, Down with Bad Government" was a popular cry that could rally supporters from many ethnic groups, regions, and economic classes without seeming unduly radical.

Events moved quickly. Túpac Amaru set his rebellion for November 4, 1780, a highly symbolic choice since that date also was King Charles III's birthday. On that Saturday, after sharing a sumptuous breakfast, the American cacique Túpac Amaru suddenly stood up and arrested the European corregidor Arriaga, symbolically reversing 250 years of colonial domination. Less than a week later, the unfortunate Spanish official was executed at Tungasuca in a spot the rebels called "the plaza of social justice." Acutely aware of the power of visual symbols, Túpac Amaru and Micaela Bastidas began to dress in clothing styled after pre-Hispanic royalty and demanded that the Inka Empire be restored to its legitimate leaders. On November 16, Túpac Amaru issued his famous Proclamation of Liberty, freeing the country's slaves. What had begun as an individual protest against localized political abuses quickly took on greater social, racial, and economic implications. A revolt, in other words, turned into a revolution.

Because of his enormous personal popularity and the responsive chord that his demands struck in the countryside, Túpac Amaru's movement spread quickly in all directions. It was as though an entire people had reawakened to its power after more than 250 years of brutal oppression. All racial groups in Peru could be found fighting under Túpac Amaru's standard—white creoles, native Andeans, mestizos, Afro-Andeans, and escaped slaves. He may have had as many as 10,000 natives and up to a thousand creoles under his command within a few days. Colonial officials were initially caught off guard by the magnitude of the Great Andean Rebellion, but they recovered quickly and sent out a hastily assembled "Army of Pacification" to deal with the problem. Militarily, at least, Spanish-led forces made quick gains. Recent Bourbon military reforms unwittingly paid off, in part by dividing indigenous and free-colored men into loyalists and rebels. Some of the older Cuzco Inka families also opposed the rebels as upstarts. Tomás Katari was recaptured and executed on January 9, 1781. Túpac Amaru, Micaela Bastidas, one of their sons, and several friends and family members were executed on May 18, 1781 (see Image and Word 8.1). But their reputation as freedom fighters, anti-imperialists, and redeemers of oppressed races everywhere has survived to the present day. In the highly charged political climate of the 1960s, Marxist urban guerrillas in Uruguay called themselves *Tupamaros* (and a future rap star was given the name Túpac Amaru Shakur by his African American activist mother). In twenty-first-century Peru, the *Movimiento Revolucionario Túpac Amaru* (Túpac Amaru Revolutionary Movement) has continued to foment a guerrilla insurgency in an effort to topple the central government and set up a socialist state.

IMAGE AND WORD 8.1 **A Baroque Postscript: The Distribution of Body Parts**

After the execution of Túpac Amaru, his family members, and fellow rebel leaders, their corpses were dismembered and the parts dispatched to be put on display in the Peruvian provinces. The order was titled: "Distribution of the Bodies, or parts thereof, of the Nine Offenders of the Rebellion, Brought to Justice in the Plaza of Cuzco, on the 18th of May 1781." The order listed the executed rebels and then detailed which body parts were to go to which provinces.

THE REBELS	José Gabriel Túpac Amaru
	Micaela Bastidas, his wife
	Hipólito Túpac Amaru, his son
	Francisco Túpac Amaru, his uncle
	Antonio Bastidas, his brother-in-law
	The Cacica de Acos
	Diego Verdejo, Commander
	Andrés Castelo, Colonel
	Antonio Oblitas, criminal follower
TINTA	José Gabriel Túpac Amaru's head
	José Gabriel Túpac Amaru's arm goes to Tungasuca
	The same for Micaela Bastidas
	Antonio Bastidas's arm to Pampamarca
	Hipólito Túpac Amaru's head to Tungasuca
	One of Castelo's arms to Surinama
	The other to Pampamarca
	The arm of Verdejo to Coporaque
	The other to Yauri
	The rest of his body to Tinta
	One arm to Tungasuca
	Francisco Túpac Amaru's head to Pilpinto
QUISPICANCHIS	Antonio Bastidas'arm to Urcos
	Hipólito Túpac Amaru's leg to Quiquijana
	Antonio Bastidas' leg to Sangarara
	The cacica of Acos' body to Sangarara
	Castelo's head to Acomayo
CUZCO	José Gabriel Túpac Amaru's body to Picchu
	His wife's body and head to Picchu as well
	Antonio Oblitas' arm on the road to San Sebastián

CARABAYA	José Gabriel Túpac Amaru's arm
	His wife's leg
	Francisco Túpac Amaru's arm
AZANGARO	Hipólito Túpac Amaru's leg
LAMPA	José Gabriel Túpac Amaru's leg to Santa Rosa
	His son's arm to Ayaviri
AREQUIPA	Micaela Bastidas' arm
CHUMBIVILCAS	José Gabriel Túpac Amaru's leg to Livitaca
	His son's arm to Santo Tomás
PAUCARTAMBO	Castelo's body to the capital
	Antonio Bastidas' head too
CHILQUES and MASQUEZ	Francisco Túpac Amaru's arm to Paruro
CONDESUYOS DE AREQUIPA	Antonio Verdejo's head to Chuquibamba
PUNO	Francisco Túpac Amaru's leg to the capital

© Georgios Kollidas/Alamy

Long after his brutal execution and dismemberment, Tupac Amaru II became a symbol of anticolonial struggle. No portrait from his lifetime survives, but he is here imagined as a kind of founding father on modern Peruvian currency.

Although royal officials in Lima hoped that they had decapitated the revolt by executing its main leaders, the Great Andean Rebellion had spread to the nearby Viceroyalty of New Granada (Colombia) and seeped into the cities. Beginning in 1780, over 60 *cabildos* (local town councils) lodged protests over recently raised taxes, the imposition of new Crown monopolies on tobacco and alcohol, and other intrusive aspects of the centralizing Bourbon reforms. Further-more, in an effort to disgorge more funds from its overseas colonies, Spanish royal officials increased the tribute requirements levied on native communities and demanded that the colonists pay for their own coastal protection. In this way, royal policies alienated all social and racial groups and their imperial policies had a detrimental effect on all economic classes. Creoles realized that this impe-rial arrogance revealed that Americans' true interests lay with other Americans; there could be no hope of fair treatment from Europeans.

On June 6, 1781, a group of creoles in Socorro (near modern Bucaramanga, Colombia) who called themselves the **Comuneros** (literally, "commoners") com-piled a list of 35 points that they wished to have addressed. Their local economy had been ravaged by Crown monopolies on tobacco, cane liquor, and aniseed. Like Túpac Amaru and Túpac Katari, they stressed their loyalty to the king and the Catholic religion but demanded to have some input into their own governance. Led by Juan Francisco de Berbeo, José Antonio Galán, and Manuela Beltrán, the Comuneros asked the Crown to repeal the unpopular taxes and monopolies that they found excessively burdensome and to reduce the unfair demand placed on Indian labor. Furthermore, they insisted that the Council of the Indies end its preferential treatment of European Spaniards when making government appoint-ments in the New World.

The Comuneros successfully expelled the Spanish authorities from Socorro and began to discuss further reforms as part of their broader agenda. There was significant pressure from Afro-Andeans who wished to abolish slavery and end tax-ation of free gold panners, and from indigenous peasants who wanted an end to tribute requirements and the restitution of their communal lands. These potentially divisive issues were already starting to cause serious disagreements among the Comuneros while the Crown regrouped and moved against them. Officials in New Granada initially acceded to the Comuneros' requests to buy some time, but they immediately reneged on their promises after military reinforcements arrived from Spain. Again, showing little creativity and proving that they had little perspective or foresight, colonial officials rounded up suspected conspirators and executed many of them, including ringleader Galán on January 30, 1782.

LONG LIVE THE PEOPLE

The 1790s were years of discontent and revolutionary ferment throughout Latin America, as middle classes started to resent the distant Bourbons' control of their lives and increasingly used the revolutionary rhetoric of freedom, liberty, and independence to give voice to their frustrations. Many began to call themselves

---

Comuneros   Mostly mestizo tobacco growers and tax rebels who marched on Bogotá in 1781, shouting "Long live the king and death to bad government!"

"Americanos." Furthermore, indigenous people and enslaved Africans did not need Enlightenment philosophers to explain to them what justice meant; they knew instinctively that a different social order was possible. In Venezuela, a region of the Spanish American empire that was settled late and sparsely, the merchant classes opposed the Caracas Company's monopolistic control and actively sought freer trade. There was a large enslaved population and an unusually high proportion of freed blacks and mixed-race residents who enjoyed greater social and economic mobility than elsewhere in the empire. Furthermore, Venezuela's strategic location at the intersection of the Caribbean Sea and Orinoco and Amazon deltas meant that it was at the center of key transportation and communication routes.

Beginning in December 1796, a retired military captain named Manuel Gual met secretly with a local lawyer named José María España to plot an overthrow of Spanish power in Venezuela and usher in a new age of democracy, republicanism, and egalitarianism. Their co-conspirators included a cross-section of the middle and professional classes: lawyers, soldiers, government functionaries, intellectuals, priests, artisans, *pardos* (free men of mixed African descent), and a few more radical upper-class types. Their movement was centered in the coastal town of La Guaira but quickly infiltrated the capital city, Caracas. Meeting clandestinely in safe houses and recruiting new members through word of mouth and secret messages sent in code, Gual and España spoke in impassioned patriotic terms of shedding blood for their homeland and creating a new, egalitarian society in which all races would be considered as brothers. Their new flag utilized the four colors white, blue, yellow, and red to symbolize the inclusion of the four main racial groups into the national body. On June 4, 1797, aided by jailhouse collaborators, they staged an attack on the prison at La Guaira and freed the three political prisoners who had been held there. One conspirator, Juan Bautista Picornell, printed 2,000 copies of a pamphlet titled *The Rights of Man and Citizen* and composed a song that included the lines "Long live the People/the Sovereign People/Death to the oppressors/Death to their cronies." Though Picornell fled to Trinidad, Gual and España set the date for a general uprising to be July 16, the feast day of the Virgin of Carmen.

The plot called for a revolt among the pardo militias on the appointed day, which was expected to set off a broader uprising among the general population. Unfortunately, authorities learned of their plans and moved in to arrest the more prominent leaders before the event got underway. Spanish officials placed a 500-peso bounty on the heads of any conspirators, and they raised this to 10,000 pesos for Gual and 5,000 pesos for España. Nevertheless, España managed to evade capture for nearly 18 months before being discovered and executed in Caracas' central plaza in May 1799. Gual died in exile in Trinidad in 1800, probably poisoned by a royalist agent. If there was any doubt about the true revolutionary nature of the Gual and España movement, papers found in their possession quickly proved how radical their vision for an independent Venezuela was. One document contained 44 clauses that would form the basis of the new state, including the abolition of slavery, the equality of all citizens regardless of race or ethnic background, full and free trade, freedom of the press, a republican and democratically elected form of government, and preferential treatment for American-born citizens.

The royalists' violent reaction may have pushed these ideas underground for the moment, but they could not be stamped out forever; many of the leaders of the 1810 independence movement had absorbed the message of the Gual and España revolt and were in a better position to put their words into effect.

THE TOOTHPULLER AND TAILOR CONSPIRACIES

The first three of the seven revolts discussed in this chapter were the Great Andean Rebellion, the revolt of the Comuneros, and the Gual and España uprising in Venezuela. For the next two examples, we turn to Brazil, where similar movements of discontent were developing—most notably the Inconfidência Mineira plot of 1788–1789 and the 1798 Conspiracy of the Tailors in Bahia.

In 1789, a group of 12 prominent citizens in the town of Vila Rica (today Ouro Prêto) in the province of Minas Gerais became inspired by the Enlightenment and the American Revolution and decided to stage a revolt against the Portuguese empire. It was an amorphous association with hazy and ill-defined goals and no coherent plan of action; they merely wanted to assassinate the governor and proclaim a United States–style of republican government. José Joaquim Maia e Barbalho, one of the more colorful leaders, was a former mathematics student who had made contact with Thomas Jefferson in Paris and used the code name Vendek. He was inspired by Enlightenment ideals but could not escape his upper-class origins and imagine a new social order. Vendek and his friends created a red and white flag, emblazoned with the not-too-catchy motto "Liberty, even if delayed," and spoke vaguely about setting up citizens' militias, diversifying the Minas economy to compensate for a declining gold industry, and reducing taxes on themselves. The plotters, or Inconfidenceiros, were privileged, white youths who wanted to free all Brazilian-born slaves but saw no inherent contradiction in importing new ones. They were playing at revolution, not realizing that once released, ideas cannot be easily contained. The only non-elite member of the Inconfidência Mineira was a disaffected petty officer named Joaquim José da Silva Xavier, better known as Tiradentes, the "Toothpuller," because he had served as an unofficial dentist to his troop. Not surprisingly, when the conspiracy was betrayed and the plotters rounded up and put on trial, the under-privileged (and possibly mixed-race) Tiradentes was sent to the gallows while many of the white youths received lesser sentences. On April 21, 1792, Tiradentes died in a hangman's noose, and his body was torn to pieces and dispersed throughout Brazil to send a clear message to other potential rebels; today, April 21 is celebrated as a national holiday and Tiradentes has become a symbol of Brazil's official identity as a mixed-race nation.

A little more than 10 years later, however, a different and more significant anti-colonial revolt took place in Salvador da Bahia, in the northeastern part of Brazil. The so-called *Conjuração dos Alfaiates* (Conspiracy of the Tailors) drew its support mainly from urban working-class mulatto men between the ages of 17 and 30 who were literate and had absorbed enough of the Enlightenment rhetoric of liberty and equality to understand that the Rights of Man also applied to them. In their outlook and demands, they went much further than the earlier Inconfidenceiros and advocated a full social revolution. In fact, the Bahian conspirators were radical republicans who were as opposed to racial discrimination and class hierarchies in Brazil itself as they were to continued Portuguese domination. Their fiery rhetoric called for political independence, religious tolerance, free trade, an end to aristocratic distinctions, and the abolition of slavery. One of their handbills set out the explosive idea that "Each soldier is a citizen, particularly the brown and black men who are abused and abandoned. All are equal. There is no difference. There will be only liberty, equality, and fraternity." A 23-year-old soldier named Lucas Dantas do Amorim Tôrres exclaimed, "We want a republic in order to breathe freely because we live subjugated and we cannot advance; if there was a republic there would be equality for everyone."

Of the 48 arrests made, 46 were male, 33 were mulatto, 11 were white, and 4 were black. Although there were four professionals (a surgeon, a Latin professor, and two commissioned military officers), the majority of the conspirators were working class (11 tailors plus assorted masons, carpenters, goldsmiths, shoemakers, sharecroppers, a folk healer, and enlisted soldiers). Significantly, nearly all were literate. The Conspiracy of the Tailors has been described as a "social revolution frustrated." Far more significant in its scope and its ambition than the Inconfidência Mineira, this plot included members from all sectors of Bahian society and reflected a greater class and race consciousness. The Pombaline reforms, and the shifting center of power from the north to the south within Brazil itself, had alienated an important region that found the words to express its discontent in the rhetoric of freedom, independence, and democracy.

THE CRY OF DOLORES

On September 16, 1810, a parish priest named Miguel Hidalgo y Costilla (1753–1811) in the north-central Mexican town of Dolores rang his church bell to call on his followers to rebel against royal authority. Although the exact words of this visionary man's *Grito de Dolores* (Cry of Dolores) went unrecorded, he undoubtedly whipped the crowd into a frenzy with such appeals as "Long live Mexico! Death to the Gachupines! Long live Ferdinand VII! Death to Bad Government!" Hidalgo's original complaints were typical of creole Americans throughout the continent: a desire for greater access to office, promotion of freer trade, and more political autonomy. He never advocated total independence from Spain but (like others in early stages of independence) said he merely wanted Mexicans of all races to be accorded equal status with European-born Spaniards. Hidalgo's followers, however, mainly natives and the rural poor, interpreted the Grito de Dolores to mean something quite different and began to attack European Spaniards and their property.

Hidalgo was a charismatic character who devoted more time to his secular pursuits than to his religious duties—unless, of course, religious duties can be understood more broadly to include bettering the social and economic lives of his flock rather than merely attending to their spiritual needs. He was posted to Dolores in 1803, a relatively prosperous parish near the mining town of Guanajuato with an annual income of 9,000 pesos. No less a person than European scientist and traveler Alexander Humboldt commented on the health-fulness of Dolores, noting approvingly that it had only 100 deaths for every 253 births. Hidalgo enjoyed dancing, gambling, women, and song. Over time, Hidalgo's understanding of his social reality became radicalized. He surrounded himself with a *tertulia* (discussion group) that was called *Chiquita Francia* (Little France), to which he invited not just the polite classes but also native men, the poor, and the mixed races. Padre Hidalgo recognized that the economic restrictions that Spanish imperial policies had placed on the colonies' activities had the effect of keeping them in permanent underdevelopment. To aid his parishioners, the priest introduced small industries into Dolores that would increase their skills and augment their income, too: beekeeping, pottery factories, silkworm farms, carpentry shops, and tanneries. His most audacious ventures, however, were the manufacture of wine and olive oil, openly flouting the Crown monopolies put in place to protect European industries. The rebel priest dared to think that New Spain ought to be run for the benefit of Americans.

Throughout 1810, Hidalgo had also begun another dangerous enterprise: stockpiling arms. He and his laborers started to make spears, machetes, slingshots, and other low-grade weapons. He had planned for an uprising to occur in Querétaro on October 2, 1810, but his plans were betrayed and he moved the date up to September 16. The call to revolt provoked a greater response than even Hidalgo himself could have anticipated: 25,000 indigenous rural folk joined his banner in less than a week. There was a bloody siege in Guanajuato on September 28 and, by the time Hidalgo's undisciplined mob reached the edge of Mexico City at the end of October, those numbers had swelled to 80,000. These were unimaginable numbers and the royalists only had 2,500 troops to oppose them. Nevertheless, the Spaniards' training and discipline prevailed; when he realized that he could not defeat their organized garrisons because of his lack of supplies and a coherent strategy, Hidalgo abandoned his people and fled northward toward the U.S. border. As Hidalgo's movement began to take on the character of a more radical social upheaval with a markedly indigenous and mestizo character, urban creoles who had initially supported his moderate stated goals became frightened and deserted to the royalist side. The memory of the Haitian revolution was still fresh in their minds and they did not wish to see it repeated on their own soil.

Miguel Hidalgo was caught in Chihuahua and transported back to the capital where he was first tried and excommunicated by the Inquisition, then handed over to a military court for further earthly judgment. He was found guilty of the implausible combination of charges that he was "a libertine, a heretic, a partisan of the French Revolution, a Judaizer, a Lutheran, a Calvinist, and a rebel schismatic suspected atheist." On July 30, 1811, Hidalgo and his co-conspirator Ignacio Allende were summarily executed, then drawn and quartered. Their bloody heads were removed to Guanajuato and left hanging in a prominent place for the next 10 years as a warning to other would-be rebels.

In the months that followed the Hidalgo Revolt, hundreds of thousands of natives and mixed-race people in the central provinces of Mexico were killed in a wave of royalist reprisals that did little to reconcile the disaffected classes to the presence of the Spanish Crown. New leaders took up Hidalgo's cause, most notably another parish priest, José María Morelos y Pavón. Unlike Hidalgo, Morelos organized and trained a disciplined army and called for Mexican independence and a representative government; where Hidalgo was a rebel, Morelos was a revolutionary. His program sought to preserve private property and the important role of the church in Mexican society, but slavery and the indigenous tribute burden were to be abolished. By late 1813, only months after Morelos came out in open revolt, royalist forces had him and the rebel congress on the defensive—although it was not until the end of 1815 that the Viceroy Calleja was able to capture and execute Morelos.

INDEPENDENCE

The deaths of Hidalgo and Morelos in 1811 and 1815 marked the ends of the sixth and seventh revolts summarized above. But, as Viceroy Apodaca lamented (see Image and Word 8.2), discontent and rebellion in Mexico persisted—culminating in Mexican independence in 1821. Shortly after, in January of 1822, the Central American provinces joined Agustín de Iturbide's Mexican empire. There had been no uprisings in Guatemala or neighboring provinces, nor much of an independence movement among the local Spanish elite (El Salvador even delayed joining independent Central America in 1822), but the authorities in Guatemala City preferred to join by choice rather than by force (as Iturbide threatened). When Iturbide fell from power in 1824 and Mexico became a republic, Central America broke away to become its own federal republic (later fragmenting into separate nations).

Events in Europe—the Napoleonic invasion of Portugal in 1807 and Spain in 1808 and the subsequent changes of Iberian regimes and constitutions—had much to do with the acceptance of independence in places such as Central America, where discontent had not boiled over into revolt. The same was true in Brazil, where independence came not because there was a popular uprising but because the local elite lost their faith in the mother country's ability to govern and protect them adequately. Whereas the Spanish king was deposed by

IMAGE AND WORD 8.2 Royalists and Rebels

Apodaca   Morelos

In October 1816, the new Viceroy of New Spain, don Juan Ruiz de Apodaca, Count of Venadito, submitted a report on the revolt; the rebels were disorganized but sympathy for them was widespread and seemingly indomitable. Hidalgo had been executed five years earlier, and Morelos the year before, yet the revolt persisted. At the rebellion's heart, and the source of greatest frustration to colonial officials, were **gavillas** or small bands of guerrillas. Wrote Apodaca:

> The gavillas that are disseminated throughout the kingdom generally are composed of the most perverse and audacious of the rebels, of army deserters, and of lost and abandoned peoples. Because of these evil qualities that they have lived with for a very long time, they are not attracted to any other occupation than robber, assassin, and libertine. The long time that they have carried on the rebellion has hardened them to the military campaign, and provided them with sufficient skill in the use of arms—especially regarding cavalry. With the help of some of our forces who have deserted to their ranks, and others who came from the United States, they have learned the art of making war and the means of fortifying advantageous positions.

Apodaca's reference to deserters anticipated the eventual collapse of the royalist effort to restore law and order to the Mexican countryside. This collapse culminated in the decision by Agustín de Iturbide, the royalist general promoted by Apodaca, to switch sides in 1821. Instead of continuing to battle the rebel leader,

Gavilla [ga–VEE–yah]   small band of guerilla rebels during the Independence wars

The Art Archive/Alamy

Iturbide

Vicente Guerrero (a future president of Mexico), Iturbide declared Mexico
independent from Spain (with himself as Emperor Agustín I). The viceroy's reference
to the United States also anticipated the North American invasion that 30 years later
would strip Mexico of its far northern provinces. A much later president, Porfirio
Díaz, would write that "if Morelos had lived to the year 1821, Iturbide would not
have been able to take control of the national insurrection; and the nation would
not have passed through a half century of shameful and bloody revolution which
caused it to lose half its territory."

(continued)

IMAGE AND WORD 8.2   Royalists and Rebels (continued)

Guerrero

The Art Archive/Alamy

Napoleon, the Portuguese prince regent (King John VI after 1816), fled to Brazil with a British escort and elevated the colony to a kingdom equal in status to Portugal. This encouraged the Brazilian elite to think of themselves as at the center of the empire, rather than a province of it. King John promoted this sentiment by remaining in Brazil until 1821 and addressing many of the political and economic grievances of the local ruling classes. When the king returned to Portugal, his son Pedro remained as regent in Brazil; by the fall of 1822, Pedro had given in to elite pressure to declare the colony an independent empire.

Meanwhile, an extensive independence movement had developed in South America (see Map 8.2). Although the Gual and España conspiracy in Caracas had radical intentions, the first effective South American independence struggles broke out in the Río de la Plata region, when local militia leaders—rather than Crown-appointed Spanish officials—defeated British forces after their capture of Buenos Aires in 1806 and Montevideo in 1807. Conflict between local elites and colonial officials spread into Upper Peru in 1809 and in 1810 resulted in creole leaders permanently acquiring political power in Buenos Aires. A disjointed independence movement, centered less on social or economic reforms and more on achieving local political independence from Spain and from other Latin American regions, spread during the 1810s from Buenos Aires across into Chile and up into what became Uruguay, Paraguay, and Bolivia.

At the same time, two creole Spaniards in Caracas began to develop a more coherent ideology of independence. Francisco de Miranda and Simón Bolívar were arguably the most radical and most influential leaders of Latin American

M A P 8.2 Independence in Latin America

independence. Miranda's career as a rebel had begun with a failed plot in 1806 and culminated in his role in the rebel government that ran Caracas from 1810–1812; Miranda was then arrested and sent to die in a Spanish prison, while royalists regained Venezuela and Bolívar fled to Colombia. Between 1813 and 1821 Bolívar led a rebel army back and forth across northern South America, eventually defeating royalist forces and imposing independence on Ecuador, Colombia, Venezuela, and Panama. Bolívar's vision was of a Gran Colombia, a single republic embracing these four regions.

For a brief time it seemed possible. Indeed, Bolívar's authority in South America extended even farther, as he and his gifted lieutenant, Antonio José de Sucre, led armies down into Peru, forcing independence on the Lima elites in 1824. The following year, Upper Peru, the last royalist holdout, fell to the rebel armies; the new republic was named after Bolívar, while its capital was named after Sucre, who became its first president. Bolívar continued to pursue his dream of a unified Spanish America, holding a unification conference in Panama in 1826, where delegates from Mexico, Central America, Peru, and Bolívar's own Gran Colombia signed treaties. But Bolívar's vision was no match for the momentum of fragmentation, and even Gran Colombia dissolved by the time of his death in 1830.

The Spanish American elite shared a common identity—they called themselves "Americans"—and Bolívar was not the only independence leader who hoped to forge a vast unified republic out of the colonies. But that ambition was offset by the desire among elites for local political power, by the regional cultures and identities that had developed over the preceding centuries, and by the fallout from the civil wars. Peru lost most of its traditional claims, as Chile and Bolivia espoused separate identities. Paraguay and Uruguay fought off control by Argentina and Brazil. Gran Colombia split into New Granada (Colombia plus Panama), Ecuador, and Venezuela. Central America dissolved into five separate nation-states. In the 1840s, Mexico lost Texas, then California; in all, the United States took half of Mexico.

Identities in the Americas had been micropatriotic before the Iberian invasions, and then remained largely so during the colonial period. Habsburg policies had actively encouraged such division and competition, and Bourbon redistricting only seemed to exacerbate regionalism. Even the revolts that had eventually led to the independence movement were rooted in local grievances and had local aims. Such localization of identity would present Latin America's new nations with considerable challenges in the centuries to come.

The revolts had started not as a revolution but as a protest in the mold of colonial uprisings—aimed not at independence or the overturning of the colonial regime but at righting local wrongs, replacing abusive local officials, and reducing taxes and other unpopular governmental demands. It ended up the other way around: a revolution took place that turned the great viceregal kingdoms of the Spanish American empire into a quarreling network of independent republics; but the local grievances of the rebels were addressed partially or not at all, and the few reforms and remedies that were attempted were undermined by the economic devastation of a generation of civil war. The new republics faced a grim future.

Border wars between the new Latin American nations persisted into the twentieth century. In addition to regional challenges, the new republics faced new threats from outside empires, especially Britain, France, and the United States. Internally, Latin American nations struggled to create stable political and economic institutions as well as their own unique cultural identities. Foremost among these issues was that of racial and ethnic diversity and the dual legacies of African slavery and an indigenous majority. It is to the great challenges of the nineteenth century that we now turn.

KEEP READING

A useful collection of primary documents on the Andean events discussed above is Ward Stavig's *The Túpac Amaru and Catarista Rebellions: An Anthology of Sources* (2008). The classic study of the Comuneros is John L. Phelan's *The People and the King* (1978). The most accessible, succinct book on independence movements (excluding Brazil) is Jay Kinsbruner's *Independence in Spanish America* (4th ed., 2004), but also see Jaime Rodríguez, *The Independence of Spanish America* (1988). An important scholarly work on Mexican independence is Eric Van Young, *The Other Rebellion* (2001). A useful collection of essays on Brazilian independence is A. J. R. Russell-Wood, ed., *From Colony to Nation: Essays on the Independence of Brazil* (1975). One of the best biographies of independence leaders is Karen Racine, *Francisco de Miranda: A Transatlantic Life in the Age of Revolution* (2002); we also recommend the biographical novel *The General in His Labyrinth*, by Gabriel García Márquez (2003), and John Lynch's biographies of Simón Bolívar (2006) and José de San Martín (2009).

9

※

Continuity and Change in the Early Republics

Political Challenges

The Rise of Caudillos

Economic Challenges

The Myth of Primordial Nations

"It is well known that the Spaniards conquered America, soaking its soil in blood, not to settle it but rather to seize the precious metals that it so abundantly produced." Thus argued the celebrated Chilean academic José Victorino Lastarria in an 1844 address before the newly founded University of Chile. He went on to say that Spanish imperial law, politics, and economic practices were all either repressive or stupid and ought to be abandoned. To realize its potential, Chile had to forget the past.

One of Lastarria's teachers, Venezuela-born Andrés Bello, responded to his student's claims. "Injustice, atrocity, treachery in war have not been committed by Spaniards alone but rather by all races in all times," he offered, adding, "American treasures inundated the world, while the treasury of the metropolis [i.e., Spain] was left exhausted and its industry embryonic." The Spanish, Bello argued, had groped and stumbled just as any other people might have in similar circumstances, and they suffered for it. Spain's greed and cruelty were not unique, and its empire, furthermore, was not an unmitigated disaster. Its laws and customs, developed over three centuries of trial and error, were no less instructive than Ancient Rome's. Chile, Bello concluded, should try to learn from its colonial past.

This early nineteenth-century Chilean debate highlights a core problem facing all of Latin America's fledgling nations. To what extent could they leave the colonial past behind? What ideas or lessons might they scavenge from its ruins? How would the transition from subjects to citizens be effected, and what

177

TIMELINE	
1820s–1860s	Spanish American nations ruled by dictators called caudillos
1823	United States declares Latin America to be in its sphere of influence, not Europe's, with Monroe Doctrine
1830	Death of Simón Bolívar
1836–1839	Union of Peru and Bolivia
1844	Dominican Republic freed from Haiti
1846–1848	United States–Mexico War, central conflict in 1835–1853, transfer of much of Mexico to the United States

roles should the nation-state or provinces have in education, public welfare, commerce, and industry? How big should the army or navy be? Models varied from the beginning. In the north, the United States embraced a secular, representative democracy that relied on broad civic engagement and a federal structure. At the other end of the spectrum, Brazil remained a highly centralized, officially Catholic monarchy ruled by a direct heir to the Portuguese throne.

Most Spanish American leaders sought a cleaner break with the colonial past than Brazil's but a less radical one than that of the United States. The problems they faced were manifold. Who could bear the weight of political authority in a largely illiterate Catholic society if not a divinely sanctioned king? How would revenues be raised if not by the Indian head tax of colonial times? Who would work plantations if not enslaved Africans? Who would educate the nation's youth, if not priests and nuns? In the face of such entrenched patterns of behavior, the liberal idealism of independence leaders such as Hidalgo and Bolívar quickly faded. Colonial traditions and institutions proved surprisingly resilient, and conservative defenders sprang up to revive them when liberal innovations failed. As if to add insult to injury, a host of economic woes converged to help discredit those arguing for change.

POLITICAL CHALLENGES

With the exception of Brazil and parts of Central America, the independence wars were economically devastating. Particularly in Peru, Venezuela, and Mexico, but also elsewhere, losses of people, livestock, buildings, and bridges were profound. The export economies of the colonial period, based on commercial agriculture, livestock breeding, and mining, all slumped. Desperate for income, many young Latin American governments sought British and French capital in the form of loans and investments in the formerly lucrative export sectors. It was far from enough to jumpstart revival.

Instead, defaulting on British loans or meddling in the affairs of French businesses quickly became pretexts for armed intervention, or "gunboat diplomacy."

The first attacks came, as if to spite the U.S. Monroe Doctrine of 1823, from Britain and France. Fortunately for the target countries, the Europeans were competing with each other. Efforts to stop French intervention in the 1830s, sometimes on behalf of the beleaguered Spanish, came as often from Britain as from within. For its part, the United States, not yet strong enough financially to be a major investor in Latin America, took advantage of Mexico's weakness and expropriated half the country by force in 1848 (see Map 9.1). Threats of foreign invasion, real and imagined, prompted costly military spending throughout the nineteenth century.

Other countries shared Mexico's internal turmoil, and some also had greedy neighbors. Internal divisions were the rule rather than the exception in the first decades after independence, and in many places they would persist much longer. Among the several destructive colonial legacies to haunt Latin America between independence and 1850 were: (1) *regionalism*, which spawned civil wars as well as international border disputes (see Map 9.2); (2) *underdeveloped economies* reliant on primary exports and forced labor, both of which stymied capital accumulation and the formation of a consumer base; (3) *weak financial institutions*, which kept capital scarce and expensive, all but prohibiting industrialization; and (4) intense

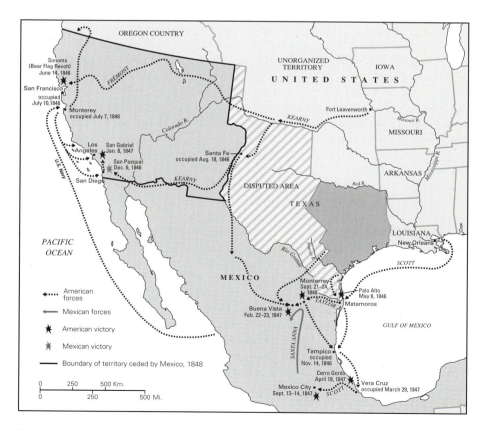

M A P 9.1 The Mexican-American War, or War of the North American Invasion

social stratification along lines of class, color, and ethnicity, all of which made national unity a challenge. Finally, machismo and (5) *patriarchal laws* made women's
lives in many countries even less free than under colonial rule. As these factors
combined with foreign scourges, many Latin Americans, especially the poorest
and most vulnerable, began to wonder if independence had been a mistake.

One significant change that came with Independence was the rise of party
politics. Two parties, the Liberals and Conservatives, quickly became dominant.
The Liberals, usually members of the educated urban merchant class, favored a
modest federal government, expanded suffrage, a weak Church, and free trade.
The Conservatives, many of them descended from traditional land-owning elites,
preferred a decentralized state that favored provincial interests, limited suffrage, a
strong Church, and many of the old colonial trade barriers and monopolies.
Liberals argued strongly against slavery and indigenous tribute; Conservatives
argued in favor of both. Perhaps surprisingly, many native Americans, especially
peasant villagers, sided with the Conservatives rather than the Liberals in times of
conflict, primarily because Liberals sought to break up communal landholdings
established under colonial rule. Enslaved Africans and free people of color usually
sided with the Liberals because of their antislavery stance.

Brazil proved relatively stable under its monarchy, but it was the exception
that proved the rule. (Even it faced the prospect of break-up when Emperor Pedro I
left for Portugal in 1831. Calm returned only after Pedro II took the throne in
1840.) Unfortunately for the majority of Spanish Americans, their early leaders,
including visionaries such as Simón Bolívar, were rarely adept at the business of
national government. Bolívar's mistake was arguably in thinking too big—he tried
to hold together a multinational confederation by force of personality. On the
other hand, most of his competitors thought too small. Liberal or Conservative,
early politicians routinely failed to see beyond their most immediate interests and
could not avoid the mistake of creating constitutions that did little more than
guarantee their hold on power. Indeed, one marker of political instability was
the frequent rewriting of constitutions, a common practice all over Spanish
America through the 1860s (and still going on in some of its countries today).

Partisan bickering soon gave way to violent coups and colonial-style cultures
of cronyism, all of which undermined the legitimacy of the state and encouraged
contempt for politicians as a group. Some able politicians such as Bolivia's Andrés
de Santa Cruz squandered their countries' futures by engaging in foreign adven-
tures rather than consolidating affairs at home. Others, such as Argentina's Juan
Manuel de Rosas, played off regional rivalries and even employed death squads
to squelch political opposition.

In response to this apparent chaos and illegitimacy of authority, the Brazilian
model struck some as a reasonable, if all-too-colonial, option. In Catholic societies long used to the notion of a divinely sanctioned king or queen as earthly
arbiter of justice, the idea of serving a secular figure, such as Chile's autocratic
(and part-Irish) independence leader Bernardo O'Higgins, was hard to accept.
In Mexico, Agustín de Iturbide sought to resolve the dilemma by having himself
crowned emperor, but the strategy backfired. Iturbide was ousted and then executed when he tried to return to power.

In Ecuador, the initially liberal Venezuelan independence leader Juan José Flores assumed a near monarchical role after breaking with Bolívar's Gran Colombia in 1830, putting on the trappings of a king and eliminating rivals until 1845. Others, such as Henri Christophe of Haiti, harbored similar monarchical desires, but most of these heroes of the Independence era held power by force rather than regal charisma. These mostly conservative regional strongmen were known as **caudillos**. They have often been seen as heirs to a tradition going back to the Spanish conquistadors. Whether that was true or not, after Independence, they graduated to the level of persistent national menace.

THE RISE OF CAUDILLOS

Though usually thought of as rough-hewn men on horseback, Latin America's early caudillos varied in personality and approach. Chilean kingmaker Diego Portales represented one type of autocratic figure and Venezuela's José Antonio Páez another. Portales was a businessman who sought to build a state unafraid to use force to protect the interests of entrepreneurs, and Páez was a traditional rural strongman who used his "plainsman," or cowboy, mystique to keep the country conservative—and under his thumb. Both of these examples harkened back to colonial times in that rule was dictated from above and was masculine, forceful, and uncontested—in a word, *patriarchal*. Caudillos seized and maintained power through highly personal networks of allies, friends, and family members—a system that was inherently unstable and hierarchical. *Dictator* was not yet a bad word, but it soon would be. Within a short time, centralized, executive authority won out over federalism from Mexico to Chile, and duties, not rights, defined the average citizen's political life.

Some caudillos were able to retain power for decades, becoming more and more eccentric with each passing year (a phenomenon also seen later in Latin America); Paraguay's Dr. Francia is perhaps the best example (see Image and Word 9.1). Others were in and out of power for decades, contributing more to their nation's instability than its progress; Páez was arguably such a figure (he was Venezuela's president in 1830–1835, 1839–1843, and 1861–1863), and Mexico's Santa Anna certainly was (again, see Image and Word 9.1).

Like Santa Anna, Haitian caudillo Jean-Pierre Boyer was also a great opportunist, similarly using the threat of foreign intervention to his own advantage. For him, threats from France and Great Britain justified formally annexing neighboring Santo Domingo in 1820. Despite his authoritarian streak, Boyer freed the last remaining slaves on the Spanish side of the island with annexation, an act that set a future course for Dominicans far different from those of neighboring Cubans and Puerto Ricans. Yet Boyer ruled with an increasingly heavy hand, attempting to restrict the free movement of peasants until he was deposed in 1843. The Dominican Republic was declared free the following year.

Caudillo   conservative, authoritarian, regional strongman

IMAGE AND WORD 9.1   Caudillo Extremes (and an Extremity)

© Georgios Kollidas/Alamy

Perhaps the strangest caudillo model emerged in Paraguay under Dr. José Gaspar Rodríguez de Francia. A bookish megalomaniac (see the stamp image above), Francia liked to be called "The Supreme." He carved a personal fiefdom out of what had been a poor province of Buenos Aires in 1814 and ruled it with an iron fist until 1840. Francia's dictatorship was so isolated and secretive that few outsiders knew what was happening in Paraguay. The pattern of rule by secret decree was followed by subsequent father-and-son caudillos Antonio Carlos López and Francisco Solano López, the second of whom sparked a disastrous war with Brazil and other neighbors that nearly destroyed Paraguay.

General Antonio López de Santa Anna, who ruled Mexico off and on from the 1820s to the 1850s, was a prime example of the caudillo as flexible opportunist. Santa Anna changed political affiliations numerous times in his long career, from royalist to rebel to liberal to conservative. Foreign invasions in 1829 and 1838 were opportunities to prove himself the nation's indispensable defender, and after he lost

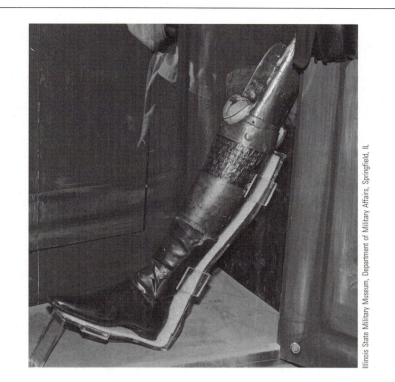

Illinois State Military Museum, Department of Military Affairs, Springfield, IL

a leg in the second invasion he had it publicly displayed and buried (the replacement is on display today at Camp Lincoln in Illinois; above). Crushing losses, he understood, could be turned into public relations gains. Even the disastrous U.S.–Mexican war of 1846–1848, which included a humiliating occupation of Mexico City and loss of half the national territory (see Map 9.1), was not enough to end Santa Anna's career, so good had he become at playing the victim.

ECONOMIC CHALLENGES

Independence, even for countries with minimal war damages, was costly. New nations began their existence with empty treasuries and often with massive indemnities to pay to the former motherland. Great Britain, self-proclaimed naval guarantor of independence, stepped in to offer loans of several million pounds sterling to almost any nation with enough raw materials to offer as collateral. As a result of this financial aid, most nations faced years of crippling debt, exchanging dependency on Spanish and Portuguese merchants for that on British banks.

The new dependency had other parallels to the old colonial arrangement. British diplomats secured special trading status for British merchants, special tariffs for British imports, and privileged access to Latin American mineral resources. Catholic Latin America even set aside British (i.e., Protestant) cemeteries. Among the first destinations of British investors and engineers were Latin America's fabled but moribund gold and silver mines, an echo of the greedy colonial aims denounced by Chile's José Lastarria.

There were other seeming continuities. In nations with substantial indigenous populations, such as Mexico and Peru, government income had long been reliant on the head tax, or tribute, paid by adult males identified by census takers as "Indian." As indigenous populations began to rebound in the eighteenth century after years of decline, this tax had become more critical as a source of government revenue. Ecuador was a classic case of a late colonial government that "mined" its Indians as if they were a natural resource. Most liberal independence leaders argued vehemently against the tribute, calling it an anachronism and an insult, but their conservative successors, faced with empty treasuries, were less enthusiastic. As a result, the tribute was simply renamed the "indigenous contribution" in Peru, Bolivia, and Ecuador, where it lasted until the early 1850s.

Conservative tides could flow in indigenous people's favor, however, and the Bolivian example is instructive. As in colonial times, mining was at the root of much evil in the form of physical suffering, state corruption, and environmental degradation, even as it brought in needed foreign exchange. Destruction of Bolivia's refineries and abandonment of mines during the independence struggles put this industry on hold despite early interest among British investors who dreamed of "pumping" Potosí. By coincidence, financial instability in London, combined with Bolivia's physical isolation, kept this from happening in the first decades after independence. Labor was the other limiting factor in Bolivia, since liberal president and independence leader Antonio José de Sucre had ended the *mita*, or forced indigenous draft.

For native Bolivians, independence meant a mix of things: The state's decision to end labor drafts but keep the head tax tended to reinforce indigenous identity and kept most native communities intact, supported by their communal lands. Modest agricultural growth resulted, and with it a growth in native populations. Keeping the head tax was a conservative measure, but as president from 1825–1828, the liberal Sucre tried hard to implement a wide range of reforms, including many reducing the power of the Church. Despite his efforts, nothing seemed to induce investment and growth of a reliable export sector. Sucre threw up his hands and returned to Venezuela.

General Andrés de Santa Cruz, a mestizo from La Paz, followed as Bolivia's president from 1829–1839, mostly as a liberal but not in the doctrinaire sense. Santa Cruz is best remembered for taking advantage of neighboring Peru in a moment of weakness, invading in 1836 (see Image and Word 9.2 and Map 9.2). Peruvian President Agustín Gamarra, a Cuzco caudillo and independence hero, had created the necessary chaos. Santa Cruz had served briefly as Peru's president after independence, but most Peruvians rejected his proposed "Peru-Bolivian Confederation," an echo, perhaps, of Bolívar's failed Gran Colombia. Even more vehement in their rejection of this union were neighboring Chileans, who felt a "super-Peru" would upset the regional balance of power. They invaded in 1839 and also supported Peruvian rebels.

IMAGE AND WORD 9.2   Constantly Erupting Wars

Flora Tristan (below) grew up in her mother's country, France (Tristan was Paul Gauguin's grandmother), but in 1833–1834 she visited the land of her father, Peru. In *Peregrinations of a Pariah* she wrote,

> The cities of Spanish America, separated one from another by vast tracts of wild and uninhabited territory, still have few common interests. One would have thought that their most urgent need was to be provided with a form of municipal government in keeping with the intellectual development of their respective populations; and to be united in a confederation based on the relations already existing between them. But in order to free themselves from Spain it had been necessary for them to raise armies, and as always happens the power of the sword prevailed. If there had been more contact between the peoples of the different republics, they would have discovered where their common interests lay, and Spanish America would not have been the scene of constantly erupting wars over the past twenty years. For Independence, that historic achievement, has not lived up to expectations.

Mᵐᵉ Flora TRISTAN .

Private Collection/Archives Charmet/The Bridgeman Art Library International

Tristan's words applied not just to the past but also to the future: for much of its first century, modern Latin America was beset by boundary conflicts and border wars (see map 9.2 on the next page). Tristan left Peru shortly before it was shaken by one such war—the War of the Confederation (or the Chilean-Confederation War) of 1836–1839, between the Peru-Bolivian Confederation created by its "Supreme Protector," Andrés de Santa Cruz, on the one side, and northern Peruvian rebels, Chile, and Argentina on the other.

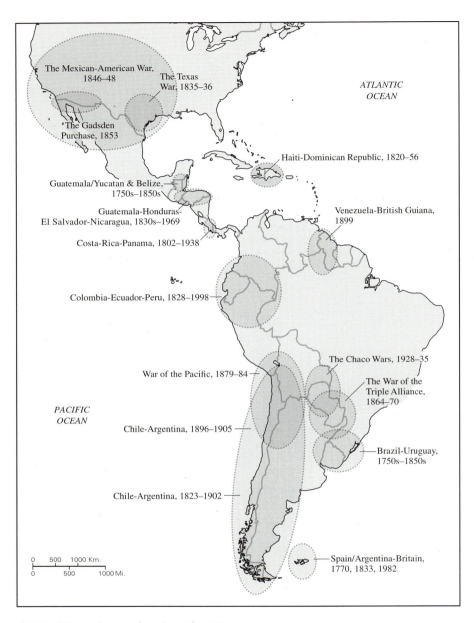

M A P 9.2 Latin American Boundary Wars

Santa Cruz was ousted and after a brief interlude was followed by General José Baillivián, who took office in 1841. General Baillivián governed more or less peacefully from 1841–1847. Under his rule the army was reduced in size, but military expenditures remained proportionally high. Tribute income still constituted a whopping 40% of state revenue, but duties on coca leaves and quinine bark were growing in importance.

An 1846 census, Bolivia's first, revealed a population of about 1.4 million, not counting an estimated 700,000 forest-dwelling indigenous people in the eastern lowlands. The population was about 90% rural, only 10% of school-aged children were in school, and overall literacy was barely 7%. Only 20% of Bolivians spoke Spanish. Quechua ranked just above Aymara as the first language of Bolivia's indigenous majority. Many mestizos spoke these languages, as well, some exclusively.

The census also revealed some 5,000 haciendas, few of them profitable, against 4,000 autonomous indigenous communities. Most of the country's population was clearly concentrated among the latter, which were becoming increasingly stratified internally. All these statistics, particularly with high indigenous fertility, pointed to a Malthusian land crunch. With mining still in a slump, the only vibrant sectors of the economy were the coca fields of the eastern piedmont and the national "breadbasket" of greater Cochabamba. Both relied almost entirely on the indigenous market.

Bolivia's situation in the 1840s was better for indigenous folks than for the white-mestizo elite, although fractures in indigenous rural life were widening. Things began to change in the 1850s, when technological improvements at last reached the mining sector. The surprise was that these were paid for mostly by Cochabamba hacienda owners, not foreigners. Steam engines were starting to drain old mines by mid-century thanks to merchant-consolidators. In Potosí, the Aramayo family bought up the Real Socavón Company and began to make it profitable. Bolivia's subsequent economic revival in the mineral export sector, in turn, made life hard again for the indigenous majority. They faced new demands on their labor and liberal attacks on communal landholding.

Economic fortunes were often unpredictable in the years of caudillo rule. Peru in the 1850s fell under the spell of Liberal caudillo Ramón Castilla. He was president from 1845–1851, and again from 1854–1862. Much of what buoyed Castilla's fortunes was fossil bird excrement, or **guano**, one of nature's best fertilizers. Thanks to a cold current streaming up from Antarctica, Peru had bountiful fish, and therefore fishing birds, plus a desert coast that fostered accumulation of bird droppings. In another fortunate conjunction it so happened that steamships made it economical for the first time in the 1850s to send tons of this material all the way around the tip of South America and across the Atlantic Ocean, where it nourished the exhausted soils of Europe.

Guano was found on a number of islands not far from Lima. It was easily extracted and shipped abroad without need of railways, steam shovels, or processing plants. Peru granted generous claims to a foreign enterprise, Anthony Gibbs & Co., but still reaped substantial tax revenues. Guano money soon allowed Peru, unlike virtually every other Latin American nation at the time, to pay off British lenders. The revenues also enabled President Castilla to carry out a number of liberal policies that might have been blocked by conservatives in other circumstances.

Guano   valuable phosphorous fertilizer made of seabird droppings, plentiful on Pacific islands near Peru

The hated indigenous tribute was abolished, along with African slavery, in 1854. The federal government had enough money on hand to pay an indemnity to slave owners of 300 pesos per person for 25,000 slaves, a total of 7.65 million pesos. The slaves themselves, as in so many places, got nothing. Other state funds were invested in attracting Chinese indentured workers to take the slaves' place in the cane and cotton fields of the coast, and to work in the guano pits and on new railroad projects. A total of 100,000 Chinese left the old Portuguese enclave of Macao for Peru between 1849 and 1874. An echo of the Middle Passage, between 10% and 30% of them did not make it. Guano, an unexpected gift of nature, had all but transformed Peruvian society in the space of a few decades.

Slavery was not so easily ended everywhere, and it indeed carried on as another core "colonial" institution in most of Latin America despite the shrill calls of liberal independence leaders. It ended only in 1886 in Cuba (still a Spanish colony at the time) and 1888 in Brazil (its last year as an empire; see Chapter 10). Where slavery ended earliest, as in Argentina, Chile, and Mexico, it had either ceased to be economically significant or it never had been. Only in Haiti was slavery ended by the enslaved themselves, serving as an inspiration to later, less successful rebels in Brazil and Cuba.

Colombia, or the Republic of New Granada as it was called, proved a different sort of battleground. Here Simón Bolívar had promised freedom to tens of thousands of enslaved Africans and their descendants during the struggle for independence, only to lose power to slave-holding conservatives from the gold and sugar zones of the southwest. It was not until Liberals took over again in 1851 that abolition was decreed. Still, as in Argentina and Mexico, freedom from slavery did not bring automatic political or economic benefits to former slaves. Suffrage in New Granada was hotly contested following abolition, and within a short time free people of color found themselves completely disenfranchised. To add insult, as in Peru and other countries it was their former masters, not they, who were indemnified for slavery.

THE MYTH OF PRIMORDIAL NATIONS

Institutions and patterns of colonial rule were not easy to shake off, as Andrés Bello understood. Nor was it necessarily wise to try to reject them all out of hand. Government structures and religious traditions, as well as social conventions in language, art, food, and material culture, bore numerous Iberian traces. Not all things Spanish or Portuguese were worthy of shame. The problem for Latin Americans was in deciding what to keep and what to jettison to form a viable national identity that distinguished, say, Peruvians from Bolivians. How could regions that had borne three centuries of socially and regionally divisive colonial rule forge a myth of primordial unity—that is, an identity and unity that had always been there waiting to be realized—and not something new, contrived, and artificial?

Indigenous antecedents proved a goldmine of national symbols. In some places they had provided the seed for regional creole identities since colonial times. Mexico and Peru were uniquely fortunate to have the great pre-Columbian empires of the Aztecs and Inkas to hold up as perfectly non-European precursors and cultural models. It was a double blessing. An imperial pre-Columbian heritage allowed Mexicans and Peruvians to claim that their nations were both "natural" and destined to greatness, and it also allowed them to gloat in relation to neighbors who lacked such a glorious pre-Columbian imperial past. Unfortunately for both countries, these ancient empires would not soon be rebuilt.

Chileans such as José Lastarria revived the fearless Mapuche Indian heroes of the conquest era, such as Chief Lautaro, and Colombians did likewise with their Muisca ancestors from the highlands around Bogotá. Ecuador traced its roots to the pre-Inka Kingdom of the Shyris, the creation of a late eighteenth-century Jesuit historian. In all these cases, including Mexico's and Peru's, past Indian greatness was just that—in the past. Current indigenous populations were universally seen by white and mestizo elites as obstacles to progress, and their cultural and linguistic diversity a threat to national unity. In some cases, shame turned to hatred. Many prominent nationalist intellectuals found highly autonomous Indians such as the Maya of Yucatan or Tehuelches of Argentina worthy of nothing less than extermination. Paraguay, with its large Guaraní population, was unique in embracing its indigenous heritage and bilingual society, but only within the context of a suffocating dictatorship.

Countries lacking a strong indigenous imprint, such as Costa Rica or Uruguay, could claim creole cuisine and music, at the least, and all counted some indigenous or African contributions to regional culture that could be singled out as unique or colorful. The celebrated **gauchos** of the Southern Cone pampas were an exemplary mix of African, indigenous, and European elements adapted to a unique, American environment; so were the **llaneros** of Venezuela and the **charros** of northern Mexico. Mixture, another colonial legacy, was not all bad. Still, for elites accustomed to copying European fashions in everything from law to opera, finding a native soul worthy of widespread emulation proved difficult. Despite the alleged romance of the range, not everyone wanted to be thought of as a cowboy.

Latin American independence movements and early national governments, though initially led by radical visionaries, were soon taken over by reactionary conservatives who feared social change and economic uncertainty. As a result, for the masses independence brought few tangible rewards. True citizenship remained a preserve of the wealthy, most of them white males. Landowning elites, often from the same families as in colonial times, shored up their fortunes while Africans continued to live in slavery, native Americans continued to labor in debt bondage and pay tribute, and people of mixed heritage continued to grapple for any rung on the social ladder where their color, poverty, or lack of education

---

Gauchos, llaneros, charros   regional variants on the cowboy, in the Southern Cone pampas, Venezuelan *llanos* (plains), and northern Mexico, respectively

might be ignored. The concept of divine kingship lived on in several places, too, while in others, caudillo-led patriarchy stood in for it.

Thus, despite great hopes, the newly independent nations of Latin America did not enjoy quick and progressive, much less revolutionary, change in their first 30 years of freedom. Whereas the colonial period had been marked by an unequal, dependent relationship with Spain or Portugal, the first half of the nineteenth century was marked by dependent, unequal relationships with Great Britain and France. The riddle of independence centered in large part on the link between the final decades of colonial rule and the collapse of empire in the decades surrounding 1820. Only in hindsight could the roots of independence be found in colonial developments; independence was not a carefully planned or inevitable event but largely a violent, chaotic, and protracted affair. This in turns helps to throw some light on the riddle of Latin America's early national period: How was so much promise and potential betrayed so quickly and thoroughly? Who, or what, was to blame?

KEEP READING

The following books explore many of the themes of this period: Jeremy Adelman, ed., *Colonial Legacies: The Problem of Persistence in Latin American History* (1999); Andrés Bello, *Selected Writings of Andrés Bello* (1997); Michael T. Ducey, *A Nation of Villages: Riot and Rebellion in the Mexican Huasteca, 1750–1850* (2004); Rebecca Earle, *The Return of the Native: Indians and Myth-making in Spanish America, 1810–1930* (2007); Peter Guardino, *The Time of Liberty: Popular Political Culture in Oaxaca, 1750–1850* (2005); Marixa Lasso, *Myths of Harmony* (2007); Florencia Mallon, *Peasant and Nation: The Making of Postcolonial Mexico and Peru* (1995); Cecilia Méndez, *The Plebeian Republic: The Huanta Rebellion and the Making of the Peruvian State, 1820–1850* (2005); James E. Sanders, *Contentious Republicans: Popular Politics, Race, and Class in Nineteenth-Century Colombia* (2004). On Francia, see Augusto Roa Bastos, *I the Supreme* (1986). On Brazil, Neil Macaulay, *Dom Pedro: The Struggle for Liberty in Brazil and Portugal, 1798–1834* (1986).

PART IV

✳

New Nations and Their Citizens (1850–1910)

In the three chapters of Part IV, we take the tale of modern Latin America into the twentieth century. Chapter 10 examines political developments, while Chapter 11 focuses more on economic affairs. Our discussion includes such key events as the abolition of slavery in Cuba and Brazil, the creation of Panama, the invasions of Mexico by the United States and France, the rise of coffee and bananas, and the start of the assault on the Amazon rainforest. In particular we explore what the heyday of *Liberalism* meant for the region—a term (not to be confused with today's liberalism) that defined a particular approach to political and economic progress; it promised expanding wealth for all, but it had the effect of exaggerating economic inequalities and promoting tight labor controls and limited freedoms for the majority of the population. The darker side of the Liberal project—its failure to bring a better life to Latin America's impoverished masses—is the subject of Chapter 12. Thus the unfolding riddle of late-nineteenth-century: "liberal" Latin America was the contrast between seemingly limitless natural bounty and widespread poverty and bondage.

10

✳

Liberals, Conservatives, and Capitalists

Liberal Ascendancy

Central America Divided

The End of Slavery in Brazil and Cuba

Colombia and the Struggle for Panama

"The war of the Argentine revolution has been double—first, war of the cities, initiated in European culture against the Spaniards, with the goal of giving greater expansion to that culture; second, war of the caudillos against the cities, with the goal of liberating themselves from all civil domination and developing their character and hatred of civilization." These are harsh words from Argentine writer and politician Domingo Sarmiento, in his 1845 classic *Facundo, or Civilization and Barbarism*. Sarmiento was a liberal reformer outraged by the opportunistic regime of caudillo Juan Manuel de Rosas, which had sent him and many others into exile. Rosas was not quite the uncultured barbarian Sarmiento made him out to be, and in many ways he was an early version of the "populist" leaders of the next century. Still, his regime was infamous for its brutal use of force to suppress dissent and its disinterest in institutionalizing national unity and progress. From his exile in Chile, Sarmiento felt he saw a liberal revival on the horizon for his homeland on the Río de la Plata, and with it a vast expansion in export-led capitalist growth. Little did he know that such a sea change would sweep across nearly all of Latin America at precisely this time.

The fall of caudillos such as Argentina's Rosas and Mexico's Santa Anna in the 1850s did not mark the end of strongman politics or conservatism. Both would return, or persist, albeit in changed form. Some conservative leaders

TIMELINE	
1852 and 1855	End of Rosas Era in Argentina and Santa Anna Era in Mexico
1864–1867	Maximilian rules Mexico as emperor
1864–1870	War of the Triple Alliance, with Brazil and Argentina occupying Paraguay 1870–1876 (see Map 10.1)
1871	Free Womb Law in Brazil
1879–1884	War of the Pacific (see Map 10.2)
1886 and 1888	Slavery abolished in Cuba and in Brazil
1889	End of the Brazilian Empire
1898	Spanish-American War
1899–1901	War of Thousand Days in Colombia
1903	Independence of Panama declared
1904–1914	Construction of Panama Canal

who staved off the liberal revival, such as Ecuador's Gabriel García Moreno, retooled and embraced railroads, steamships, and transoceanic telegraph cables even as they strengthened the church and stifled dissent. Brazil's Emperor Pedro II was another modernizing conservative who stayed in power until 1889. Yet in the half-century after 1850 it was Latin America's liberals who most promoted modernization of transport and communications, and who invited massive inputs of foreign capital in various export sectors. They believed this kind of change was long overdue.

LIBERAL ASCENDANCY

How did the liberal project measure up in the end? By the turn of the twentieth century it was clear that massive exports of minerals, hides, and tropical agricultural products had paid for many of the trappings of modernization in Latin America's urban centers and some of its ports. Still, this new income had not fostered industrialization or financial independence. If anything, exports had deepened dependency on foreign capital and manufactured goods. Only a tiny elite, many of them clever politicians, had become rich. Unfortunately for the mass of Latin Americans, export-led growth, whether under liberals or conservatives, often meant harder work for less pay. In Brazil and Cuba, it sustained slavery well beyond the end of the slave trade. Bounty vs. bondage: the riddle of the era.

Argentina, home of the archetypal conservative caudillo Juan Manuel de Rosas, was also home to some of liberalism's most accomplished spokesmen. Domingo Sarmiento, who eventually became president, represented one of several intellectual strains. Sarmiento's main interests were in improving Argentina

MAP 10.1 Latin America in the Age of Liberal Ascendancy

through education and immigration. As president after 1868, Sarmiento founded schools, libraries, and government institutions aimed at popularizing and improving literacy and technical instruction. One legacy of his regime was a country with one of the highest literacy rates in all of Latin America.

Not everything about nineteenth-century liberalism was admirable. Sarmiento's Argentina contributed to the near destruction of Paraguay in the 1860s (see Image and Word 10.1). And like many liberals of his time, Sarmiento embraced the era's

IMAGE AND WORD 10.1   The Immolation of Paraguay

WAR IN PARAGUAY—THE REV. FATHER ESMERATA, CHAPLAIN OF THE BRAZILIAN SQUADRON, EXHORTING THE PARAGUAYANS TO SURRENDER.

The War of the Triple Alliance, which broke out in 1864 when Paraguay went to war with its neighbors, Argentina, Uruguay, and Brazil, left Paraguay all but destroyed (or immolated, as one historian famously said). It was started by the land-locked nation's president, Francisco Solano López, who had succeeded his father in 1862. Solano López was in some ways a traditional caudillo—maintaining rule by taking the daughters of prominent families as his mistresses and using torture and murder to suppress opposition. But in other ways he was a progressive Liberal, turning the backward capital of Asunción into a European-style city. Yet his aggressive stance toward his neighbors brought on a brutal war that killed half of Paraguay's population of 450,000 people; battles of attrition anticipated the trench warfare that would devastate Europe half a century later (previous page, upper illustration), while the high death toll (previous page, lower illustration) meant that many women and children fought for Paraguay in the war's final years. In 1870 the country was finally overrun and Solano López was killed. Brazil and Argentina occupied Paraguay for six years, only permitting its continued existence as a harmless buffer between them.

dubious scientific claims about race, and he ardently hoped to see Argentina's mixed population replaced with immigrants of "pure" European stock. Far from embracing the gaucho as symbolic of Argentine identity, Sarmiento rejected the rugged, quarrelsome cowboy as something of a colonial ghost, an embarrassment he hoped would disappear with education and barbed wire fences. He cared even less for Argentina's Amerindian population. Although periodic warfare with indigenous nomads dated to the time of Rosas and before, policies of "removal" or extermination similar to those of the post–Civil War United States began under liberals such as Sarmiento.

Liberalism in Chile arose peacefully at the end of the 1850s, minus all the struggle and bloodshed typical of most other nations. Conservative presidents since independence had nurtured many of the institutions liberals favored, such as schools and universities, and they had also opened Chile to foreign investment. Liberal opposition had been more marked by matters of degree than irreconcilable differences, and thus the transition proved smooth. Like their Argentine neighbors, however, Chile's liberals saw their southern indigenous population as an obstacle to progress, and they began a systematic campaign against the Mapuche that set out to destroy them, either by force or persuasion, in 1881.

By contrast, Bolivia's large indigenous population, as we have seen, benefited somewhat from post-independence changes under both liberal and conservative-leaning caudillos. Political affairs grew chaotic after 1848 and failed to calm down with the 1857 election of Bolivia's first civilian president, José María Linares. Linares promoted free trade but proved more dictatorial than the generals who preceded him, and he was ousted in 1861. His ideas lived on in the form of a party called the Rojos, or "Reds." Bolivians, like their neighbors in Paraguay, resisted the standard Liberal-Conservative categories so common elsewhere, but Red policies tended to be liberal, especially when it came to the economy.

Money was at least as important as ideology in the liberal age, and in Bolivia's Atacama Desert potentially valuable nitrates were discovered around 1860. Mostly used as fertilizer, they would provide whoever controlled them with the sequel to the Peruvian guano boom. As it happened, the best nitrate fields were claimed by Chilean and British prospectors, who treated the Atacama region as their own and willfully disregarded Bolivian attempts to interfere in local disputes. Linares's successor discovered that he could not even raise an army to establish sovereignty in 1863. Bolivia's next president, General Mariano Melgarejo, lovingly remembered as the *caudillo bárbaro*, or "barbarian caudillo," was little different from his predecessors in failing to assert sovereignty. Melgarejo went so far in the opposite direction that some accused him of auctioning off the country's riches for a song. He was doing what the mining class wanted, as it was in their best interests to keep the British and Chileans happy. Opposition was countered with firing squads.

With mining taking off, other liberal reforms could be attempted, or so Melgarejo thought. In 1866 he tried to dissolve the indigenous **comunidades**, a move not unlike Mexico's 1857 Ley Lerdo, described below. Bolivians, particularly indigenous ones, were not ready to give in to the demands of the liberal state. Riots stopped the confiscation of communal landholdings, but not for long. Only the support of the mining sector, which had benefited so much from his policies, kept Melgarejo in office until 1870.

Bolivia's 1870s began with General Agustín Morales taking office just as massive silver deposits on the Pacific coast were being developed by (again) British and Chilean mining interests. A railroad built by U.S. entrepreneur Henry Meiggs linked these mines to the coast. Morales calmed tempers by returning confiscated indigenous lands, creating a Bolivian National Bank (1871), and putting strong silver currency back in circulation. Happy at his success, Morales won an 1872 election, only to be assassinated. An 1873 election brought back the Rojo party, but they discredited themselves by falling prey to corruption.

An 1876 coup brought General Hilarión Daza to power. Among his many mistakes, which included plundering the national treasury, Daza decided to impose a tax on production in the Atacama silver and nitrate fields. Representatives of the British-Chilean Nitrates & Railroad Co. balked and filed protest in Santiago (rather than the Bolivian capital of Sucre). Daza organized a punitive expedition, which provoked Chile to do what it had always wanted to do: annex the whole Atacama region.

The resulting War of the Pacific (1879–1884) (see Map 10.2) was Bolivia's undoing in a variety of ways, most importantly by cutting off its access to the Pacific Ocean. Still, mining did not suffer in the highlands as a result. Production of silver reached 1.1 million marks (a mark = 1/2 lb.) a year in the 1880s and 1.6 million marks a year in the 1890s. Output peaked in 1895 at 2.6 million marks, an echo of the colonial boom years of 1590s Potosí. Lima, meanwhile, was ruthlessly sacked and plundered by Chilean troops during the war, part of the high price Peru had to pay for siding with Bolivia. Chile also snatched a piece of Peruvian territory, including the colonial port of Arica.

Meanwhile, in faraway Mexico, internal Liberal-Conservative struggles took a far more violent turn than in Bolivia or the Southern Cone. Mexico had gotten off to a rocky start: The battle for Independence in the 1810s was

---

Comunidades   literally, communities; often refers to self-governing native villages or towns

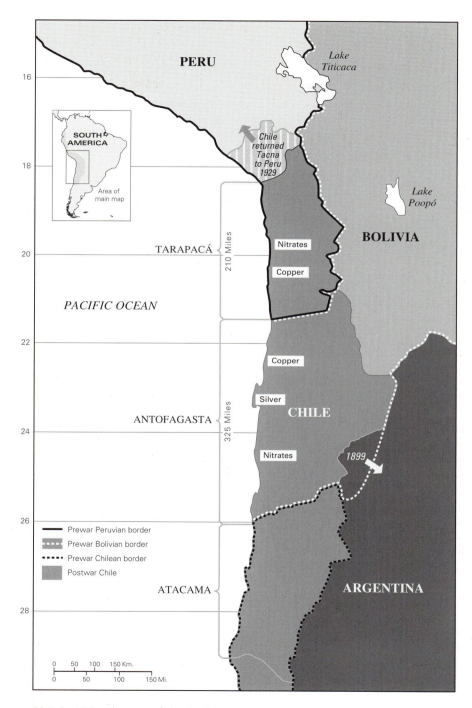

M A P 10.2 The War of the Pacific

especially destructive, and it was followed by 30 years of civil war, and a humiliating defeat at the hands of the United States which in 1847 robbed the republic of almost half its territory. Some sort of reform was clearly needed. The call was answered by reformers such as Melchor Ocampo, an advocate of French utopianism, and Benito Juárez, a native Zapotec-speaker from Oaxaca who became a legal advocate of indigenous communities, often against the clergy, and then governor of Oaxaca State. The Revolution of Ayutla, as Mexico's liberals called their rise to power after ousting Santa Anna in 1855, placed Juan Alvarez in the presidency, Ignacio Comonfort as vice president, and former exiles such as Juárez in the cabinet.

The Ley Juárez, or Juárez Law, abolished a number of clerical and military privileges and marked the start of what became known as La Reforma, "The Great Reform." Next came the Ley Lerdo, which called for forced auction of all nonessential church properties. Native villages were hurt by the clause enforcing the sale of common lands, or **ejidos**, but how many were sold remains unclear. Further laws took birth, death, and other registries out of the church's hands.

A new liberal constitution was framed in 1857. It resembled that of 1824 but called for a unicameral (one-house) rather than bicameral (two-house) legislature and a reining in of state powers. In short, it was centralist and anti-dictatorial in concept. The new constitution incorporated the anticlerical, antimilitary laws already in effect and included a bill of rights—a novelty in Mexico, where one could be jailed and even shot for publishing an antigovernment poem. Other liberal features included the abolition of slavery and other forms of forced labor, as well as noble titles. These aspects of the constitution were not particularly inflammatory—slavery had already been abolished in 1829.

What cut to the heart of Mexican society instead was the issue of the church. If North Americans fought their sectarian war over black slavery, Mexicans fought theirs over black robes. The War of the Reform was a bloody conflict lasting from 1858–1861, not as deadly as the U.S. Civil War but counting casualties in the tens of thousands. Against the Ayutla Revolution came the conservative Plan of Tacubaya. Well-armed and motivated, the conservatives drove out the liberal government, which reestablished itself first in the inland city of Querétaro, then on the coast at Veracruz. Mexico's large, rural indigenous population, recalling the liberal alienation of their *ejido* lands, fought on both sides.

The war went badly for the liberals until 1860, when a string of victories gave them Oaxaca, then Guadalajara, then Mexico City. The constitution and its most important supporter, Benito Juárez, returned to office in January 1861. Juárez's conciliatory stance toward the conquered conservatives nearly cost him the presidency, but other threats also loomed. State debts were so huge that Juárez declared a two-year moratorium on interest payments to foreign lenders. Spain, England, and France turned outrage into intervention with the London Convention, convened on Halloween 1861.

Ejidos   communal lands held by a rural community

The plan was to blockade Veracruz and collect Mexico's customs duties and apply them to the three nations' debts, a common "gunboat diplomacy" solution. But the expansionist plans of France's Louis Napoleon led him to believe an occupation would be successful; disgruntled conservatives were on hand to aid and abet. At Veracruz the Spanish and English discovered the Emperor's plans and withdrew. French troops began making their way to Puebla in early 1862, but an unfortunate encounter with liberal troops, some led by a young brigadier general named Porfirio Díaz, ended in a rout. The date was May 5, 1862, now celebrated as Cinco de Mayo. The French were back a year later with 30,000 soldiers; this time Puebla would fall.

Juárez lashed out at conservatives, especially clergymen, for supporting the invasion. Anticlerical legislation followed, but it did not stop the French. After the loss of Puebla, Juárez decided to abandon Mexico City. He exclaimed, "Adversity discourages none but contemptible peoples" (someone might have whispered, "but the prospect of a French bullet in the head discourages me"). The liberal government went north to San Luis Potosí while the French occupiers propped up a conservative junta; it was soon decided that Mexico needed a monarch, and one was found in the person of Austria's Archduke Ferdinand Maximilian of Habsburg (see Image and Word 10.2). With the Habsburg Emperor Maximilian came his Bourbon wife, Carlota. Colonial history seemed to be repeating itself as farce.

IMAGE AND WORD 10.2   The Ill-Fated Emperor and Empress

Apic/Getty Images

In 1863 Napoleon III of France persuaded the Archduke Ferdinand Maximilian to take the throne of Mexico. He and his wife (and second cousin), Princess Charlotte of Belgium, became the Emperor Maximiliano and Empress Carlota of Mexico (left). Carlota was descended from the French Bourbons, making their joint rule an odd reminder of colonial times. They were as progressive (i.e., liberal) as European monarchs got, but Mexico had not changed as much as the Juárez interlude might have suggested. For one thing, Mexico's creole elites were more conservative than any nineteenth-century European monarch. Maximilian's fault, aside from being a foreign interloper, was to try to remain independent of his conservative backers and bridge gaps between rich and poor. He won the hearts of neither.

(continued)

IMAGE AND WORD 10.2   The Ill-Fated Emperor and Empress (continued)

World History Archive/Alamy

When Maximilian's unpopular regime foundered, undone by a U.S.-backed resistance, French troops began to leave—as did Carlota, who in vain sought aid in Europe for her husband and ended up going mad in her palace on the Adriatic. The emperor was captured, tried, and shot in 1867; the painting above is Edouard Manet's famous (but somewhat fanciful) depiction of the execution.

The United States remained out of the picture due to its bloody Civil War, but Juárez still sent arms buyers and agents to court North American support. The Monroe Doctrine was in this case followed according to its original purpose—to protect a fledgling American republic from imperialistic Europeans. French foreign legionnaires forced Juárez and his followers north to El Paso del Norte (now called Ciudad Juárez), and a guerrilla war ensued. Juárez's followers received arms and active as well as tacit support from the north, and the French hold grew tenuous.

France sensed trouble in its newfound colony but was more concerned with European problems, such as the rise of Otto von Bismarck; troops began going home in late 1866. Both Maximilian and Carlota tried to persuade Napoleon and even the pope to stop this withdrawal, but nothing worked. Meanwhile, republican forces retook the cities of the north, then the west, then the south, then Mexico City. After leading Mexican royalists at Querétaro for 100 days, Maximilian surrendered and took his chances with Juárez's past history of clemency. Juárez's patience with Mexico's enemies had run out, however, and the deposed emperor faced the firing squad on June 19, 1867. His death, however tragic, followed that of 50,000 Mexicans.

Mexico's next chapter is often called the "Restoration" or "Restored Republic," and it saw the presidencies of Benito Juárez and Sebastián Lerdo de Tejada (author of the Ley Lerdo). Porfirio Díaz, who would unseat the latter president in 1876 by force, was already becoming a political force, but the restoration consisted of more than just a prelude to his rise. This was a period of genuine reforms, particularly in education and economy but also the military. It was during Juárez's first presidency that Mexico's fabled *rurales* were formed, a kind of national guard sent against bandits and other internal threats seen as obstacles to institutionalizing property rights.

Juárez felt that Mexico's economic recovery required a revival in mining, so high taxes and other impediments were trimmed to encourage investment. Along with minerals came an interest in railroads, the universal nineteenth-century symbol of progress. The most symbolic rail line was of course the link between Mexico City and its Atlantic port at Veracruz, a project begun in 1837. It was eventually completed on December 20, 1872, an engineering marvel, and it touched off Mexico's railroad revolution. Only booming Argentina had laid more track by 1913.

Educational reforms inspired by the writings of Auguste Comte, French father of **Positivism**, established a new curriculum throughout Mexico and a public school system. Positivism inspired many Latin American reformers, and its influence would be lasting. In Mexico, modern science, Comte's prescription for all ills associated with the Old Regime, was finally on center stage. Juárez sought a fourth term and won by a hair, only to die of a heart attack on July 19, 1872. Meanwhile, Cinco de Mayo hero Porfirio Díaz was experimenting with coup plots, the first of which failed. He would be back. The liberal stalwart Lerdo succeeded against Díaz in a new election and continued the reform schedule set by Juárez. No nation could be modernized overnight, but by the end of the liberal reforms Mexico seemed well on the march.

CENTRAL AMERICA DIVIDED

Central America at Independence was something of an economic backwater and, perhaps as a result, politically conservative. Liberals initially gained the upper hand, since they were the drivers of independence, but by 1837 conservatives rode a wave of peasant discontent led by José Rafael Carrera, a Guatemalan

---

Positivism   philosophy developed by Auguste Comte that rejects metaphysical speculation and argues that knowledge can only come from actual experience and the strict following of scientific methods

ladino (the local term for mestizo) of humble origins. He seized power in Guatemala by 1840 and dominated the region until 1865. Carrera was a caudillo in favor of continuity—a strong church, a favored land-holding aristocracy, an audiencia-like judicial system. As colonial or retrograde as all this seemed, these policies were widely supported by poor indigenous folks who rejected the liberal break-up of communal ejidos, and by extension native communities.

Central America ceased to exist as a political unit under Carrera, beginning in 1838, but he did his best to influence neighboring states. The galvanizing issue was a proposed canal somewhere in isthmian Central America, particularly interesting to the United States and its investors in the wake of the 1849 California gold rush. British and French capitalists were also snooping around, from Mexico's Isthmus of Tehuantepec to Panama, and one plan proposed making use of Nicaragua's San Juan River and Lake Nicaragua.

Liberal leaders in Nicaragua signed an agreement with American Cornelius Vanderbilt in 1849, but when Conservatives gained power in 1853, they backed British competitors. The Liberals hired Tennessee filibuster William Walker and his band of veterans from the Mexican War, but Walker, contemptuous of virtually everyone involved, took over Nicaragua in 1855, as a kind of gringo caudillo. After bringing slave-holding colonists from the U.S. South, Walker was ousted in 1857, then killed in 1860 when he tried to return. The Walker Affair, or "National War," as it is known in Central America, had the twin effects of humiliating the region's Liberals and sowing lasting distrust of the United States.

Central America's Liberals were down but not out, and as in conservative Andean nations such as Ecuador, they came back with a vengeance between the 1870s and 1890s. Also like their peers in other parts of Latin America inspired by Comte's Positivism, Central American Liberals called for "order and progress," in that order. (The Brazilians went so far as to put the motto on their flag when the monarchy ended in 1889.) The result in Central America was a string of "republican dictatorships," self-perpetuating political machines with armed enforcers, ready to sell the soil and subsoil of the nation to foreign investors. Nicaragua and Honduras, with their ample Caribbean coastlines and perennially weak governments, proved especially vulnerable. Meanwhile the church was stripped of its "colonial" authority over education, marriage, inheritance, and banking, and indigenous communities were progressively stripped of corporate rights. The effect in the latter case was to end official segregation, but not racism. Guatemala, with its indigenous majority, was most profoundly affected by the liberal revival.

THE END OF SLAVERY IN BRAZIL AND CUBA

Change came more slowly in regions dependent on slavery. When the slave trade was officially ended in 1850 (despite having been outlawed by the British in 1808), Brazil counted some three million slaves in a total population of about

---

Ladino   used variously to mean Spanish-speaking or Hispanized; in Guatemala, refers to mestizos (Spanish speakers of mixed racial ancestry)

seven million. The nation was even more dependent on enslaved Africans and their descendants than in colonial times. Sensing that this arrangement was out of touch with the modern world, some Brazilian intellectuals began to call for an end to slavery. The benevolent monarchy did not suppress dissent. Still, when push came to shove, even the most liberal-minded urban whites were reluctant to upset the planter class whose coffee profits fueled Rio's gaslights and trolleys. Thus, it was the slaves themselves, in rebellion, flight, and formal calls for abolition, who pushed hardest for an end to their bondage. Planters responded to abolitionists and slaves alike by predicting an apocalyptic collapse of the nation's economy. They equated abolition with anarchy and labeled freed slaves a menace to society.

Emperor Pedro II, like his father, did not support slavery. He freed his slaves when he took the throne in 1840 at the age of 14. Still, Pedro was more bellwether for the elite planters than activist for abolition, and only in 1867 did he begin to publicly call for gradual emancipation. The 1864–1870 War of the Triple Alliance, which pitted Argentina, Uruguay, and Brazil against Paraguay (see Image and Word 10.1), put the issue on hold but also offered a means of emancipation for some 6,000 slave volunteers. By the end of the war, Brazilians of all political leanings were beginning to hate their image abroad as tyrants and social dinosaurs. In response to the Spanish Moret Law of 1870, which freed children born of slaves in Cuba and Puerto Rico, Brazil passed its own Free Birth Law in 1871. Brazil would continue to follow, not lead, in this trend toward abolition.

Throughout the nineteenth century, abolitionists, many of them Afro-Brazilians, spoke out against the evils of slavery. Among them were José Carlos de Patrocinio (1854–1905), a journalist; Andre Rebouças (1838–1898), organizer of abolitionist clubs and prolific pamphleteer; and Luis Gonzaga de Pinto Gama (1830–1882), a former slave turned lawyer and defender of slaves in the courts; Gama's public statements were quite radical (for example, he claimed that slave homicide against a master was by definition self-defense, regardless of circumstances, and that insurrection was a legal right of slaves, as well). A mulatto abolitionist, Castro Alves (1847–1871), used poetry to further the cause, creating indelible images of the middle passage in his poem "Navio Negreiro." White abolitionists, as in England and the United States, were mostly urban whites who had no personal connection to slavery, but an exception was Joaquim Nabuco (1849–1910), a Pernambuco lawyer. He wrote a polemic on abolitionism that exposed the absurdity and hypocrisy of gradualism in the late 1870s.

The planter class, and to some extent their supporters among the Conservative Party, continued to argue for gradual emancipation and even for a continuation of slavery in spite of everything. They argued that their system was beneficial for those oppressed by it: Through slavery, heathen Africans were brought into the one true faith, acculturated, civilized. The "big house" of the plantation was a metaphor for Brazilian society at large, a patriarchal stronghold bound by ties of god-parentage and even blood, an outpost of Christian civilization in the vastness of the tropical wilderness. The same arguments had been made in colonial times.

It is probably true that slaves in most of Brazil were less brutally exploited than in the French, English, Dutch, or even Spanish Caribbean, much less the U.S. South, but the differences should not be exaggerated. Prior to 1850, slaves brought directly from Africa lived no more than 15 years on average, and possibly as few as seven years, after setting foot in Brazil. Punishments witnessed by foreign visitors in Rio, Salvador, and elsewhere were cruel, unusual, and frequent. Most notorious were instruments of humiliation, such as the belled collar, the tin mask, and time in the stocks. Public floggings and branding simply added to the horror.

But it was neither foreign observers nor homegrown abolitionists who spoke out most strongly for abolition; it was the slaves themselves. The largest maroon communities in the world had formed in Brazil's vast backlands, and some of the most violent and effective slave revolts took place in nineteenth-century Bahia. Slave revolts in this revived sugar region broke out in 1807, 1809, 1813, 1816, 1826, 1827, 1830, and massively in 1835, the so-called Malê Rebellion. News of Haiti's successful rebellion had circulated for years.

The nineteenth-century rebellions of Brazil's northeast were often led by a Muslim minority among the slave population, but they had a broader, more revolutionary appeal. First, Muslim slaves had to overlook or even incorporate West African religious traditions that fundamentalist teachings would have considered fetishistic or simply pagan to attract and organize followers. Islam had a long history in West Africa, as seen in earlier chapters, but it was significant westward advances of interior kingdoms in the early nineteenth century that led to a growth in the number of Muslims enslaved by the Portuguese. Among these were the Hausa, who became leaders of revolts in Bahia after 1807. They allied with a Yoruba majority to challenge slavery directly. Though a full-blown Bahian *jihad* may never have been intended, clearly the Muslim element in leadership was key. Approximately 1,000 slaves and freed persons came close to capturing the city of Salvador da Bahia in 1835.

Slave resistance, whether large in scale or small, the latter including everything from vandalism to suicide, was clearly a motor for change in the history of Brazilian slavery. No matter how masters tried to paint the picture, slaves were always an insult away from rebellion, a veiled threat away from flight. In short, an economy based on violence could not be sustained forever, particularly in an increasingly free and globally connected world.

Slave owners were not unaware of the rising tide and began shifting to wage labor long before abolition. To the surprise of many elites, wageworkers could be exploited in ways that made them preferable to slaves, especially with growing population pressure in Europe and a rise in immigration. Planters in the northeast produced sugar with more wage than slave laborers in the decades following 1850, and coffee producers made the shift as well. The only people screeching in defense of slavery by the 1880s were those hoping for some compensation from the government. Princess Isabel, acting as regent while her father was away on business, issued the famous Golden Law that ended slavery in Brazil on May 13, 1888, to general celebrations. One issue had been left unclear: What were ex-slaves to do now?

Abolition in Cuba, which remained a Spanish colony until 1898, followed a similarly tortuous path. Large-scale plantation slavery had developed later here than in Brazil, but by the early nineteenth century it was the basis for a humming, industrialized sugar economy (see Image and Word 10.3). Enslaved Africans and their descendants in Cuba had always resisted like their brothers and sisters in Brazil through flight, rebellion, and even religious subversion. But after mid-century the struggle against slavery in Cuba became intertwined with a slow-burning independence movement. Cubans of varying social background began to take up arms against Spanish authorities in the backcountry beginning in the 1860s, and one of their arguments against colonialism—and Spain's legacy

---

IMAGE AND WORD 10.3 White Gold, Black Workers

Library of Congress

By 1850, Cuba had approximately one million people, about a third of whom were enslaved. Of the enslaved population, half worked in the sugar mills, Cuba's only capitalized export sector (the photograph above shows Cuban slaves harvesting cane, ca. 1855). Some male slaves were highly skilled technicians in the sugar mills and on railroads, and although many women worked in domestic tasks, a large proportion of enslaved females worked alongside men in plantation agriculture. Other slaves picked tobacco and coffee, which were also sent abroad, and still others staffed port facilities and drove oxcarts connected in one way or another to the business of cash crops. As in Brazil, slave labor had been made to fill many gaps.

in the Americas generally—was its backward embrace of slavery. Although Cuba never developed as sophisticated an abolitionist movement as Brazil or the United States, both enslaved Africans and free people of color were encouraged to join the struggle in the name of "Cuba Libre," or "Free Cuba."

As in Brazil, the government's response was heavily influenced by planters, who sought to maintain the status quo, but momentum was on the side of abolitionists and rebels. The compromise, forced by the enslaved themselves as much as anyone else, was gradual abolition, completed only in 1886. Children born to enslaved mothers after 1870 were declared free by the Moret Law, and a system of so-called patronage, or quasi-freedom with mutual obligations, was established in 1880. Another compromise developed in the midst of gradual abolition, as in Peru in the Guano age, was to import Chinese indentured laborers. This practice began in 1847, and by 1874 125,000 Chinese workers had arrived. The fact that most were men, and many died from tropical diseases, prevented formation of a substantial Chinese community in these years.

As in the United States and Brazil, former slaves in Cuba faced a number of hardships after abolition. Some were trapped in webs of debt by clever plantation owners, which kept them immobile and dependent. Still, demand for former slaves' labor remained high in much of the island, especially as foreign investment in the sugar sector grew dramatically after independence in 1902 (following a four-year occupation by the United States). These factors, not mirrored in contemporary Brazil, allowed some individuals to migrate in search of competitive wages. Former slaves in Puerto Rico largely abandoned sugar plantations in favor of subsistence agriculture or coffee growing in the highlands. There they competed with a wave of European immigrants.

COLOMBIA AND THE STRUGGLE FOR PANAMA

In Colombia, Liberals and Conservatives feuded almost incessantly after independence, and as in the case of Mexico, Colombia would suffer a territorial loss to the United States in part as a result of internal strife. Colombia also shared Mexico's intense struggle over the role and power of the Catholic Church. Indeed, Colombians became so divided over this issue that four civil wars raged across the country between 1876 and 1902. Interestingly, as in Mexico, liberal economic policies and the importance of the export sector were *not* points of dispute between liberals and conservatives after 1850.

The principal Liberal-Conservative conflict of the era, so eloquently evoked by Gabriel García Márquez in *One Hundred Years of Solitude* and other writings, was the so-called War of the Thousand Days, which lasted from 1899–1902. Exports of gold, tobacco, quinine, and, above all, coffee fueled the contention, but mostly as sources of income for the competing factions. No group monopolized them. In the confusion, the Province of Panama, the last relic of Simón Bolívar's Gran Colombia, fell into neglect just as foreign interest in it was growing again after a world depression. France had long wanted to build a canal across the isthmus, and the United States already had a railway.

Liberals such as President Rafael Núñez (1885–1894) had tried to pull Panama more closely into the national fold, economically and politically, but the war delayed such plans. The bloody and highly personal War of the Thousand Days made both the losing Liberals and winning Conservatives look bad in Panamanian eyes, opening the door for independence. President Theodore Roosevelt sent U.S. troops to Panama in 1903 without Colombian approval, but a treaty was signed in haste, the Hay-Herrán Treaty, authorizing a U.S.-built canal. The bill passed the U.S. Congress but was roundly rejected in Bogotá, leading to what one Colombian historian has called "the greatest humiliation in [Colombian] history."

The next step was taken by agent-provocateur Philippe Bunau-Varilla, an engineer for the French firm of Ferdinand de Lesseps, holder of the canal concession since 1878. Bunau-Varilla pushed locals who stood to gain into calling for independence, and when Colombian troops tried to intervene from Cartagena they were blocked by the U.S. Navy. The Spanish-American War of 1895–1898 had just given the United States control of Cuba, Puerto Rico, and the Philippines, and no one seemed capable of stopping Roosevelt from extending his new American Empire in either the Caribbean or Pacific. Panama, with Bunau-Varilla as attaché to Washington, gave up the Canal Zone.

Competition from U.S. canal interests in Nicaragua was stifled by mention of active volcanoes. Thus, the "white man's burden," as imperial apologist Rudyard Kipling called it, was to make Panama an international waterway, and the project, largely staffed by black Caribbeans from Barbados and other densely populated and impoverished British islands, was completed in 1914. Many thousands died of malaria and yellow fever before mosquito eradication programs were implemented. Beginning in 1904, U.S. scientists conducted experiments on workers to see when and where mosquitoes bit in hopes of making the tropics "safe for white colonization." The canal was declared sovereign U.S. territory, while the rest of Panama languished as an underdeveloped puppet state. Conservatives were rewarded for their loyalty.

The era of liberal reform, like the struggle for independence, was marked by great hopes and also measurable gains. Slavery was ended, as was indigenous tribute. Suffrage was expanded and education improved and popularized. Communications, rail lines, and port facilities were modernized, at least in some places. In light of all these changes, plus the overhauling of legal codes, many historians consider the "liberal revolutions" that swept Latin America between the 1850s and 1910s the first clear break with the colonial past.

Yet there were drawbacks and disappointments in this era, too. Liberals proved as liable to corruption as their conservative rivals and predecessors, and most embraced the racist doctrines prevailing in contemporary Europe and the United States. Though hopeful about modernization and its likely benefits, liberals continued to view African-descended and indigenous populations as obstacles to progress, not pools of untapped talent or unique fountains of culture. Not everyone shared these views, as witnessed with the rise of Benito Juárez in Mexico, but there was little room in the liberal world for cultural diversity. The other seemingly paradoxical liberal triumph was in the economy, which

though humming with export activity after 1850 also brought deeper dependency on foreign markets, deepened the exploitation of Latin American workers,
and wreaked havoc on the natural environment. Again it seemed as if Latin
America was trapped in a riddle.

KEEP READING

A classic and accessible work on nineteenth-century literature is Domingo F.
Sarmiento, *Facundo, or Civilization and Barbarism* (e.g., the Penguin edition).

Among many books by historians on nineteenth-century developments
in Spanish America, we recommend Charles Bergquist, *Coffee and Conflict in
Colombia, 1886–1910* (1986); David Bushnell and Neill Macaulay, *The Emergence
of Latin America in the Nineteenth Century* (1988); and Simon Collier and William F.
Sater, *A History of Chile, 1808–1994* (1996) and Peter Henderson, *Gabriel García
Moreno and Conservative State Formation in the Andes* (2008). We also suggest the
volumes in the Cambridge Concise Histories series, such as Brian Hamnett's *Concise
History of Mexico* (2006) and Herb Klein's *Concise History of Bolivia* (2nd ed., 2011)

On Brazil, we suggest Roderick J. Barman, *Citizen Emperor: Pedro II and the
Making of Brazil, 1825–1891* (1999); Zephyr Frank, *Dutra's World: Wealth and
Family in Nineteenth-Century Rio de Janeiro* (2004); Warren Dean, *With Broadax
and Firebrand: The Destruction of Brazil's Atlantic Forest* (1992), Dain Borges, *Family
and Wealth in Salvador da Bahia* (1988), and Emilia Viotti da Costa, *The Brazilian
Empire: Myths and Histories* (1985).

11

✴

Exports and the Problem
of Development

The Scramble for Minerals	**Bananas and Republics: Central America**
Immigrants in Cattle Country	**Culling the Rain Forest**
Tropical Agriculture Expands	**Export-Led Growth and Dictatorship in Mexico**

"The civilized world has been shocked by authenticated reports of the perpetration of atrocious acts by officials of a British rubber company in the Putumayo district of Peru on the upper waters of the Amazon." So begins a brief report in the *American Yearbook* of 1912. The true story of native Amazonian peoples being enslaved, chained, and beaten to produce natural latex for the industrialized world was broken by the Irish journalist and activist Roger Casement. Casement's report on similar atrocities under King Leopold's rule in Congo had forced Belgium to formally take over the colony, and now his report on the Putumayo would shame British investors into reorganizing their affairs in the Amazon.

Sometimes treated as a simple colonial continuity, Latin America's phenomenal growth as an exporter of raw materials in the late nineteenth century was in fact a complex and paradoxical affair. Balls of slave-produced rubber were transported on the most modern steamships, and the rubber-tappers' overseers received rations of canned food and manufactured shotgun shells from the United States. Elsewhere in South America, Argentina grew fabulously rich from exports of refrigerated beef and rushed to join the industrialized world. Export-led growth in the industrial age often proved at once progressive and retrograde, leaving both its harshest critics and strongest backers perplexed.

TIMELINE	
1850	Latin American population passes 20 million
1869–1914	Argentina's population quadruples to eight million, partly due to heavy migration from Europe
1876–1911	The Porfiriato in Mexico
1897	New state capital, Belo Horizonte, built in Minas Gerais (Brazil)
1899	Creation of the United Fruit Company
1900	Latin American population passes 60 million
1906	Brazilian coffee production reaches 20 million bags

What did it mean when Europe's demand for raw materials simultaneously fostered industrialization in Argentina and revived Native American slavery in the Amazon?

If this was not colonialism in disguise, what was it? Certainly, the world economy changed rapidly after 1850, as did the press and the speed with which events could be reported. A transatlantic cable linked Brazil to Europe in 1874. Steamships and railroads made international travel easier than ever for those with money, and the culture of literate and politically active world citizens was ballooning. Spying was not out of fashion despite liberal openness, but gone were the days of closed colonies. Even more than in the independence era, the colonial era was looked on as a kind of Dark Age. Critiques of the new industrial capitalism were multiplying, too, however, and spreading around the globe. These critiques helped generate a new kind of consciousness in the form of international worker solidarity.

With steamships and passports, millions of poor European workers soon made their way to the United States and Latin America's Southern Cone. The total population of Latin America in 1850 was just over 20 million, highest in Mexico and Brazil. By 1900 it had surpassed 60 million. Natural growth was significant, but it was massive European immigration that transformed Argentina, along with Uruguay and southern Brazil, and it continued to profoundly affect Spain's last remaining American colonies of Cuba and Puerto Rico. Approximately 10 million Europeans, the vast majority from Italy, Spain, and Portugal, entered Latin America by the time of the Great Depression. Most sought work in the export sector as meatpackers, sheepherders, wheat farmers, and coffee pickers.

Overland transportation outside the export sectors remained little improved since colonial times even after the turn of the century (see Image and Word 11.1), but internal markets were beginning to be tapped. As in the colonial era, imported manufactures were expensive and a drain on foreign exchange, facts noted by national leaders and businessmen. With rich resources and cheap urban labor, then, one might have expected one or more of Latin America's fledgling nations to industrialize after 1850, perhaps in the areas of textile

---

IMAGE AND WORD 11.1 The White Man as Burden

Courtesy of the John Carter Brown Library at Brown University

The lack of roads and a modern transportation system, combined with exploitative labor systems, made common scenes like the one above. The use of porters was an Andean tradition from before the Inkas, through colonial times, and into the modern era. The picture above is from Colombia at the turn of the twentieth century—and many others like it can be found, depicting native porters in northern Peru, Ecuador, and Colombia carrying men and goods. For example, the first automobiles to reach highland Ecuador were carried on the shoulders of native men.

---

manufacturing or steel-making. Cotton and wool were widely produced, after all, and young women's labor could be exploited as it had been in the factories of England and the United States. Several countries boasted substantial deposits of iron and coal.

As it happened, only Mexico experimented seriously with industrialization before the twentieth century. After early success in producing cotton cloth for the internal market on mechanized mills located in the city of Puebla, government support collapsed amid political chaos. Private investors did not step in to help. Even more than mining, manufacturing required political stability and steady access to capital. Both conditions were lacking in most of Latin America in the nineteenth century. Brazil might have been an exception had not the continued power of merchants under the monarchy discouraged local production in favor of European imports. Chile had capital and stability but lacked a significant internal consumer market and remained at war with potential trading-partner neighbors.

As for technical innovation, another necessary ingredient for industrial revolutions, talented individuals were as common in Latin America as in the United States or Europe, but institutions for research and development, not to mention patent policies, were sorely lacking. Corporations were not yet strong enough to fend for themselves. Without state protection, then, it would have been extremely difficult for any Latin American manufacturer to compete in a low-tariff, globally connected world. Brazil's great pioneer aviator, Alberto Santos-Dumont, worked only in Paris. As European observers such as Karl Marx noted, this predicament echoed that of the late colonial period. Not until the twentieth century would Latin American nations recognize the need to incubate and nurture an industrial sector.

If Latin America was not yet ready for industrialization, it was ready to resume its proven colonial role as a mass exporter of primary products. These included minerals such as gold, silver, copper, and nitrates; animal products such as meat, tallow, and hides; tropical agricultural products such as sugar, coffee, tobacco, cocoa, and cotton; and wild harvested forest products such as hardwoods, rubber, and quinine. In most cases, Latin American countries were able to draw from what optimistic economists called their "comparative advantage."

So why did primary exports alone tend not to bring lasting wealth? Some sectors, such as mining, were simply extractive and prone to run out. Guano was a good example. In other cases, such as that of rubber, foreign development of plantations rendered the old-fashioned and inefficient Latin American version of the industry unprofitable. "Monoculture," as it was sometimes called, was also susceptible to drought, frost, blight, and unstable labor conditions. In the long term, all primary export economies entailed a precarious dependency on unpredictable and often speculative foreign markets. When prices for primary exports were high in London or New York, a country might prosper, but when they crashed, the country crashed, too. Even when export wealth flowed in, few Latin American governments bothered to spend it on social or economic development programs. Kickbacks and other forms of corruption were the more common means of benefiting from export bounties.

THE SCRAMBLE FOR MINERALS

Foreign investors had long been interested in the silver of Mexico, Bolivia, and Peru and the gold of Brazil and Colombia. Industrial minerals were a newer concern, among them Chilean copper and Bolivian tin, as well as fertilizing salts, coal, and petroleum. Throughout the region, and beginning before the dusts of independence settled, old mineral deposits were revived and new ones discovered. The payoff was sometimes considerable, but the human cost was usually high (see Image and Word 11.2).

IMAGE AND WORD 11.2 Mining Life and Strife

The Library of Congress

Mining for precious metals, in particular, was risky business, and all mining for export required substantial investment and access to the latest technologies. Like all extractive industries, mining also tended to consume a great deal of labor (the workers above are in Cerro de Pasco, Peru). Even with a host of modern, labor-saving machines, mining was dangerous and exhausting work—facts workers acknowledged with demand and protest. Indeed, though often geographically isolated from the rest of the nation, mining and oil drilling camps were often the sites where Latin America's first true industrial working classes formed. The scramble for minerals also spawned some of the first strikes.

We have seen how the colonial silver mining sectors of Bolivia and Mexico were revived after 1850, and how Peru and Chile benefited from exports of guano and nitrate deposits. In the last case, the struggle for a few exhaustible minerals sparked an international war that left Peru and Bolivia smaller than they had been before and soured relations in the region for decades to come. No other major Latin American conflicts were fought over minerals, but the late-nineteenth-century export boom highlighted the importance of knowing exactly what resources one had and what rivers or ports might be needed to transport them. Partly for this reason Brazil launched a major exploration campaign that led to the firm delineation of its long and multiple borders.

Chile had produced copper since colonial times, but it was only in the late nineteenth century, when world demand for this metal rose, that the industry took off. Copper was used in many civilian and military applications after the industrial revolution, but concentrated deposits of it were relatively scarce. In the nineteenth century, Chileans lacked the capital and technical expertise to produce copper on a large scale, but foreign investors were quick to help out in exchange for generous concessions. As a result, Chile became the world's top copper exporter after 1850, and despite some fluctuation, it has held this title until recent years.

Initial investment in Chile's copper mines came from Britain, but by 1900 it was U.S. companies such as Anaconda, Braden, and the Chilean Exploration Company (managed by the Guggenheim family) that owned the largest and most productive mines. Aided by engineers trained in U.S. mining schools, these "A, B, C" companies revived the industry by developing technologies to refine low-grade ores. This innovation proved better for American shareholders than for Chile. The new recovery methods required expensive and complex refineries that consumed huge amounts of fossil fuels, and in most cases it proved cheaper to ship raw ore abroad to be refined. What this meant locally was less value added to the export commodity and hence less revenue for the Chilean government. Wages remained depressed compared to the United States, as well, and safety measures lax. As a result, copper camps such as El Teniente and Chuquicamata became crucibles for Chile's labor movement.

Petroleum seeps were exploited for ship tar in colonial times along the coasts of Venezuela, Mexico, Ecuador, and Peru, but it was only with the rise of industrialization in the nineteenth century that Latin America's substantial oil deposits became a prime object of foreign desire. The first big strikes were made by British and U.S. oilmen along Mexico's Gulf Coast, but some of the richest oil fields in the Western Hemisphere, located in and around Venezuela's Lake Maracaibo, would have a more dramatic effect on national development. First British and Dutch and then U.S. oil interests began cutting deals with dictator Juan Vicente Gómez around 1908. Exports ballooned after World War I ended in 1918. Gómez remained in power until 1935.

Venezuela, long a significant exporter of coffee and cocoa, had suffered around the turn of the century from the low prices caused by competition from Brazil and Ecuador. Oil wealth soon changed everything, particularly between 1928 and 1965, when Venezuela was the top global petroleum exporter. By 1928 oil accounted for 75% of exports by value, and by 1944 over half of all state revenues came from oil. The depth of Venezuela's dependency on mineral exports alone soon dwarfed that of copper-rich Chile, which at the time had a similar population. It was as if oil was all there was. Still more of it was found in the lush Orinoco delta.

Social effects followed. Even before the Great Depression, the oil boom led to massive migration of Venezuelans to the Maracaibo Basin. The arrival of foreign engineers and their English-speaking assistants and foremen from the West Indies, derisively called *maifrenes* ("my friends"), generated class and ethnic tensions as well. As in Chile, workers in the mineral sector began to organize and form political alliances that would profoundly alter Venezuelan politics. The capital city of Caracas, meanwhile, expanded and modernized at an extraordinary pace. Even though the lion's share of profits went to the handful of foreign companies that possessed concessions, "petrodollars" funded everything from universities to highways, making Venezuela a shining exemplar of the possibilities of export-led growth. The dark side of Venezuela's oil boom was that it fueled corruption and propped a string of military dictatorships. The truly poor got nothing.

IMMIGRANTS IN CATTLE COUNTRY

Industrial growth and urbanization in Europe caused demand for food to outstrip local supplies, particularly of wheat and meat, and Argentina was well suited to respond. Refrigerated steamships traversed the Atlantic by the 1870s, replacing the old dried beef for which Argentina had previously been known. Railways linked the ranches and wheat farms of the pampas to Buenos Aires, Rosario, Santa Fe, and other cities on the Río de la Plata. Two obstacles typical of Latin America's export sector were the shortage of capital and labor, and here both were met with European solutions.

Capital came from England, labor primarily from southern Europe. English bankers financed Argentina's port improvements, packinghouses, railroads, power grids, and sewers, and with English capital came an elite Anglophilia that persists today. Meanwhile, Italy, Spain, and Portugal underwent population explosions in the countryside after 1850, leading to widespread impoverishment and migration to cities. Argentina alone saw an influx of 3.5 million immigrants between 1857 and 1930, the greatest migratory wave experienced by any nation in the Western Hemisphere in terms of demographic impact. The nation's population swelled from under two million in 1869 to almost eight million in 1914.

The industries that employed these *golondrinas*, or "swallows" (so-called because many made multiple trips back and forth across the Atlantic), were almost entirely oriented toward primary exports. To the chagrin of their employers, some of these transatlantic sojourners harbored radical notions about labor's proper relationship to capital; a few were anarchist organizers exiled from their homelands. Regardless of their political views, the golondrinas moved and milled wheat, worked in construction, cut and packed beef, and even rode herd in the backlands. The hardiest of them grew wheat as tenants and sharecroppers, but homesteading was made impossible by increasingly voracious and politically powerful cattlemen. This confluence of intensive investment, world market demand, cheap labor, and continued availability of productive land (extended by Argentina's Indian Wars of the 1870s) led to an average growth rate of 5% per annum across more than three decades, the highest recorded for any country anywhere.

But sustained growth did not create a more independent Argentina. Instead, it only heightened the nation's dependency on world demand for its limited number of exports. After the onset of World War I, Argentina's fortunes fluctuated considerably, each downturn displacing numerous vulnerable workers, each upswing sucking them back into the export sector, only to have hopes dashed once again at the next drop in prices. Unwise government policies spurred inflation, which for workers meant erosion in the value of wages.

By the second decade of the twentieth century some Argentines began to resent dependence on foreign markets and a new wave of political economists began to talk of "economic nationalism," a drive toward state ownership of key economic sectors, such as transport, electricity, and communications. Industry was to be incubated to meet the basic needs of the nation's consumers. Most talk, and action, was concentrated in the capital city, however, and if times were occasionally hard in Buenos Aires, they were mostly terrible in the interior. As in the days of Rosas, resentment of *porteños*, or residents of the capital, rose as Buenos Aires neglected the hinterland. In the city itself, gaping class differences were compared by one critic to "race track and soccer field." The soccer players would eventually form a winning team.

In other Latin American nations, as will be seen in the case of Mexico, such regional divisions could lead to a convergence of reform demands—some coming from the urban proletariat, others from the rural peasantry. However, with its uniquely rapid, immigrant-driven export boom that did not permit homesteading, Argentina failed to develop a substantial peasantry, so it was urban labor that emerged as the political force to be reckoned with in the twentieth century. Anarchists won hearts and minds by organizing strikes and marches, mostly by way of their Argentine Regional Worker's Federation, or FORA. FORA's efforts were noble, but government repression increased between 1900 and 1910, such that an anarchist counterpoint to the nation's first centennial ended in bloodshed, mass deportations, and general disillusionment.

Labor would rise again in Argentina, but meanwhile, the 1910s saw the emergence of disaffected bourgeois and aristocratic elements in the form of the Radical Party. After a broadening of the franchise by the Conservatives in 1912 (a reaction to the labor unrest of the previous decade), the Radicals came to power in 1916. Attempts to co-opt the labor movement were unsuccessful amid high inflation and a tide of international worker solidarity, and the first global general strike in 1919 ended in harsher repression than before. Anarchism worldwide was crushed.

In Buenos Aires, members of ultra-right paramilitary units shot labor leaders and innocent bystanders in the streets, and a wave of "patriotism" ensued. Right-wing reactionaries labeled all labor organizers foreign agents, not a difficult thing to do in a country whose population was largely foreign-born. A nativist and intensely Catholic nationalism was gaining ground in Argentina, but labor and the left were not broken. The 1920s saw workers enjoying some wage gains due to strong demand for exports and the Radicals managed to co-opt some elements of the newly enfranchised working and emerging middle classes. The result by the time of the stock market crash of 1929 was a state that no longer represented entrenched business interests, a rarity in Latin America. However, as if to revive the ghost of Rosas, these interests called in the military to set things right. Conservatives ruled for more than a decade after a coup on September 6, 1930.

TROPICAL AGRICULTURE EXPANDS

Unlike the Southern Cone and industrialized north, most of Latin America falls within the tropics. This provided the so-called comparative advantage, evident from the beginning of colonial times, for those wishing to grow and export cash crops such as sugar, cocoa, tobacco, and coffee, all of which did best in frost-free environments. Unlike mining, tropical agriculture required relatively little capital investment, at least at first. The key problem was labor. As we have seen, the solution was found not in massive peasant immigration from Europe but rather in the massively inhumane enterprises known as the transatlantic slave trade and large-scale plantation slavery, both of which survived independence and the industrial revolution despite predictions of a natural demise. Exports of tropical products did not lead to industrialization with one exception: Brazilian coffee.

Coffee began to pull ahead of sugar as Brazil's most valuable export only in the 1830s, and as this shift progressed into the early twentieth century, Brazil made the transition from peripheral neo-colony to industrialized nation. Was coffee in the national period somehow different from sugar in the colonial one? Aside from keeping North American and European workers awake for countless extra hours (arguably a kind of stimulus for industrialization elsewhere), coffee pulled Brazil more tightly into the orbit of the North Atlantic, its center of gravity shifting inexorably from London to New York by the turn of the century. It was in the coffee sector that semi-industrial changes took place first, with railroads linking plantations to the coast. In coffee, also, slavery gave way—*very* gradually—to wage work. In the end, however, coffee cultivation was as old-fashioned as it was new and improved. Even in the 1880s planters might live in vibrant cities such as Rio or, increasingly, São Paulo, but they owned vast tracts of land, their *fazendas*, staffed them with slaves and poor immigrants, and ruled them like the patriarchs of old.

Whereas tobacco, cocoa, and even sugar welcomed small to middling producers in Brazil, coffee was less open to farmers with shallow pockets. Coffee had been introduced to the northeastern district of Pará in 1727, but its future lay in the south-center, where it could be found by the last quarter of the eighteenth century. The first boom region was the southern uplands draining into the Paraíba River, which flows northeastward from near São Paulo to the Atlantic. Coffee does best at 800 meters (about 2,500 ft.) above sea level or more, and the central Brazilian highlands, particularly southern Minas Gerais, abounded in temperate hill and terrace country at and above this altitude.

Coffee bushes are understory plants (they grow under the forest canopy); they thus need either shade or long wet seasons and moderate average temperatures to survive. Like sugar, coffee is easily damaged by frost. Enslaved workers cleared forest and brush by slash-and-burn methods, fired just before spring rains in September, and then transplanted bushes from nurseries. These became trees within three or four years and could continue producing for up to 30 years.

Coffee berries were harvested from May to June, stripped off branch tips by hand and collected in wicker baskets, transferred to sacks to be carried to storage sheds, and later taken to drying platforms for the next step of processing. Getting the beans ready for export meant cracking off the shell, done before drying, then removing two subsequent protective layers. On large plantations these tasks were increasingly done by machines. The coffee harvest, like the sugar *safra*, was a time of intense labor; the only difference was that the coffee beans were not nearly as heavy or perishable as the ripe canes. Mules carried coffee to port until railroads encroached in the 1860s.

Once in Rio, which handled the bulk of Brazil's export product up to the turn of the century, coffee was sold by agents to packers, who moved it to warehouses to be sacked. English wholesalers dominated the next step for many years, sending the coffee to various world markets. Unlike the mountain-grown coffee of Colombia and Central America, Brazil's product was generally of low quality, and only North Americans took to it willingly. Volume was what counted; coffee made up about 20% of Brazil's exports at independence in 1822, but by the end of the empire in 1889 it accounted for nearly 70%. Put another way, the value of coffee exports for these 67 years was equal to *all* colonial exports taken together, including gold. Brazilian coffee was exported in such quantities that it created a trade surplus by 1860.

The bounty had social consequences aside from stimulating slavery. Coffee aristocrats emerged in southern Brazil, many of them aspiring and achieving nobility in the court of Dom Pedro II. An example of the success of the large planter was the plantation of Commendador Silva Pinto in Minas Gerais. He possessed 64 square miles of properties producing not only coffee but also all the foodstuffs needed by his more than 700 slaves and other workers. It also grew cotton to clothe them. It was hard to say if this was a colonial survival or something else. However modern or retrograde it may have been socially and economically, the coffee boom's effect on Brazil's natural environment was profound. Coffee was planted over burned virgin forest, retired plants were abandoned, and the cycle of destruction begun again.

Capital from coffee exports provided the base from which Brazil's industrial sector grew. The process was slow and uneven by North American or European standards, but Brazil counted 636 factories of various types in 1889, up from 50 in 1850. These were not the great mill complexes of Manchester or Lowell but rather smaller, less mechanized outfits producing medium- to low-grade textiles, food products (canned goods and the like), and some chemical and metal products. Despite being home to some of the world's best iron deposits, Brazil remained dependent on foreign steel. Even so, Rio was a gas-lit, modern metropolis with a population of roughly half a million by 1868. After 1858 engineers were trained in Rio's Central School, which became the Polytechnic Institute in 1874.

Brazil responded to the end of slavery by recruiting European immigrants. Government-funded efforts, concentrated in Italy, Germany, and Portugal, were mostly a failure in the 1870s; at least half of the immigrants who came to São Paulo in these years returned disillusioned to their homelands, where they spread the word that Brazil was no paradise. By the mid-1880s the planters learned to be more sophisticated in their recruiting efforts, and along with promising to pay passage from Europe to Brazil, inland transport costs, and initial housing and subsistence costs, they promised a chance to homestead a neo-Europe, Brazil's south. Many chose the United States or Argentina instead, but millions took up the offer.

In 1886 the Society for the Promotion of Immigration produced a glossy brochure in Portuguese, German, and Italian, 80,000 copies of which were distributed by state recruiters in Europe. It was an advanced form of propaganda for the time, and as with all propaganda, it is as notable for what it failed to say as for what it claimed as truth. There was no mention of slavery, or even of race, and no mention of tropical diseases or the nature of coffee work. The illustrated promise was of free land, a free house, and room to move and improve. Immigration was subsidized by the national government and, after the Republic was declared, the new state government of São Paulo, in part drawn from a per capita tax on slaves. These efforts worked so well that by the time slavery was about to be abolished, immigrants came to fill the void; 61,000 arrived in São Paulo's coffee region between 1882 and 1887. Evidence of the successful transition from slavery to free labor—now part freed slaves, part immigrants—comes from the figures for the coffee harvest of May through July 1888, the year of abolition: 2.6 million bags were harvested, up from 1.1 million in 1887. No coffee rotted in the fields.

The coffee zones of São Paulo, Minas Gerais, and Rio grew to even greater importance, always dominated by São Paulo (which produced between 45% and 70% of Brazil's coffee after 1900). Coffee fazendas grew enormous as a result, dwarfing the plantations of the imperial era. Like Mexico's largest haciendas in this period, fazendas became like cities, complete with company stores, churches, and lumber mills. Coffee politics in Brazil, unlike Colombia, was a generally peaceful affair. The only problem, aside from labor, was overproduction. Excess supplies after 1900 led to government-funded programs to stockpile, reduce plantings, and otherwise try to come in to hold up prices. The *annus mirabilis* of 1906 saw a bumper crop of 20 million bags, but more than half of that number was already stockpiled in hopes of a price surge. Successive crops were less large, and the government banned new plantings.

A new capital, Belo Horizonte, was built in central Minas Gerais in 1897, Brazil's first modern, planned city. But São Paulo was the nation's new metropolis; it exploded in population from some 65,000 inhabitants in 1890 to more than half a million by 1920, a pace of growth that continued throughout the century. Libraries, opera houses, universities, and other accoutrements of high urban culture suddenly appeared. Rio also doubled in size during the same period, exceeding one million inhabitants by 1920. Urban renewal in the old colonial capital was the job of the Federal District prefect, Pereira Passos. His city was grand, a modern and sanitary "white city" on the bay, a tropical wonder. Swamps were drained on orders of Dr. Oswaldo Cruz, greatly reducing mosquito-borne diseases. No cases of yellow fever were reported for the first time in 1906.

Despite many impediments, São Paulo, rather than Rio, became Brazil's industrial powerhouse. Whereas only 626 factories had been counted in 1889, by 1914 there were some 7,000. Most still produced food products and cheap textiles, but some ventured into more complex things such as metal works. By

1920 more workers labored in factories than for federal, state, or local governments, a real measure of importance in Latin American nations at this time. Still,
by 1920 over 70% of workers labored in agriculture, and 64% of individuals over
15 were illiterate. The economy was still dependent on coffee.

One of the effects of Brazil's industrialization was the **proletarianization**,
or creation of a substantial working class, of women. One immediate result was
unionization, and female- and male-led strikes became increasingly common
after the turn of the century. Government officials, mostly looking after coffee and
growing industrial interests, cast a wary eye on labor organizers, some of whom
were foreign-born communists and anarchists. As a philosophy, anarchism was
extremely radical, but it proved malleable in the hands of organizers, who focused
on immediate needs such as limits on overtime work, higher wages, and safety on
the factory floor.

When government policies favoring immigrants faded after 1920, Afro-
Brazilians joined the urban proletariat, especially in São Paulo. Exclusion from
education and other avenues to middle- or upper-class life through subtle and not-
so-subtle racist means led black Brazilians to create anti-racist organizations plus a
political party called the Black Brazilian Front. The struggle for equality, ignored
by whites who claimed Brazil had no "race problem," was aired and discussed in
more than 25 black-run newspapers in São Paulo alone. Fighting race prejudice in
a nation that did not practice formal segregation and proudly called itself a "racial
democracy" at home and abroad was made even more difficult by the fact that color
gradations (including "black," "dark brown," "light brown," and "yellow") were
recognized by employers such as São Paulo Light, one of the city's largest employers. Unlike in the Jim Crow United States, any hint of African ancestry was not
equated with blackness, making racial solidarity an uphill battle.

Immigration continued to swell Brazil's southern states, totaling some four
million between 1820 and 1930. The majority of newcomers were Italian
(34%), then Portuguese (30%), Spanish (12.2%), and German (3.5%). More like
the United States than Argentina, immigrants were never a large group relative
to overall population, but they contributed greatly to the survival of Brazil's
coffee economy and the shift to industrialization. Some of those who cham-
pioned European immigration espoused then-current doctrines of Aryan
supremacy, but more important was how Brazilians either embraced or rejected
such nonsense. One view is displayed in the famous Brocos painting, "The
Redemption of Ham" (see Image and Word 11.3).

BANANAS AND REPUBLICS: CENTRAL AMERICA

In Central America after the liberal revolutions of the 1870s, coffee was increasingly displaced by bananas as the top export. Bananas, introduced in colonial
times from Africa and Asia to supplement worker diets, were grown increasingly

---

Proletarianization   creation of a substantial working class

IMAGE AND WORD 11.3 The Redemption of Ham

akg-images

This allegorical painting, *The Redemption of Ham*, was created in 1895 by Modesto Brocos y Gómez. It presented an interpretation of progressive "whitening" through immigration and mixing of races. In the painting, the grandmother is black, the parents mulatto, and the child white; implied and invisible is the white planter who must have impregnated the black woman to help create the mulatto generation. This suggestion of a benevolent slavery, whose sexual activities were redeeming, anticipated by several decades Gilberto Freyre's *The Masters and the Slaves* (which became the most famous book to promote Brazil's myth of racial democracy). Although the idea of progressive whitening was popular among people of a certain class, it was likely not shared by anything like a majority of Brazilians. Even some elites had questioned racist ideas such as these, instead celebrating Brazil's African and Native American roots. Silvio Romero was most vehement in his defense of Afro-Brazilians, and nationalists such as Afonso Celso followed suit, rejecting imported ideas that suggested innate inferiority.

on large, foreign-owned plantations, and coffee was grown on small, locally owned plots. The Central American rural working class came to be divided into *colonos*, a kind of sharecropper, and *jornaleros*, or day laborers. In part because of the general fertility of Central American soils, often nourished by volcanoes, neither group developed into a clear-cut rural proletariat. Subsistence agriculture always supplemented work in coffee and bananas.

Foreign interest in Central American exports concentrated on the sphere of exchange in the case of coffee but entered the sphere of production in the case of bananas. In 1870 Lorenzo Baker began shipping bananas to New England from Port Antonio, Jamaica, and soon formed the Boston Fruit Company. Meanwhile, Yankee railway entrepreneur Henry Meiggs, who soon had projects all over Latin America, was developing ties with Costa Rican Liberals. Meiggs's nephews took over the operation, laying track in exchange for banana lands. They formed the Tropical Trading & Transport Co. around 1878. By 1899 this company and Boston Fruit merged to form the United Fruit Company, or UFCO, known throughout Latin America as "La Frutera" (and later less generously as "El Pulpo," or The Octopus).

The governments of Honduras, Guatemala, Nicaragua, Costa Rica, Panama, Colombia, and Ecuador all handed over vast stretches of coastland to United Fruit in exchange for modest promises of tariff income and "development." As in mining and oil operations run by U.S. and European firms throughout Latin America, supervisors were brought from outside, mostly U.S. engineers and agronomists who lived in segregated colonies. Laborers came in part from the local population but increasingly from the English-speaking West Indies: Jamaica, Trinidad, Antigua, Barbados, and other islands. Some visitors to plantations around World War I compared the scene to slavery in the Old South.

Central American banana exporting enclaves, aside from their divisive social implications, did almost nothing to aid local, much less national, development. Profits were paid to U.S. shareholders as Jamaican field hands died of typhoid fever. Bribes financed mansion building and land grabbing by government officials. Although Colombia's story was more complex given its varied economy, most of the nations that gave banana lands to United Fruit and other companies gained precious little and lost autonomy in the bargain.

CULLING THE RAIN FOREST

The Brazilian Province of Amazônas was created by Pedro II in 1850, but it remained essentially free from the ills and boons of capitalist development for some years. By 1853 steamboats connected Belém, on the Atlantic coast, with the interior town and future metropolis of Manaus, eight days upriver. Under pressure from Andean republics and more powerful foreign ones, Brazil opened the Amazon in 1867, allowing access to a vast interior of unimagined biodiversity.

Rubber was one of many forest products ripe for the picking, or tapping, but only rubber was directly connected to the rise of industry. Charles Goodyear's 1840 invention of the vulcanizing process made rubber a versatile, all-weather, impermeable, inflatable, pourable, even wearable substance. It shed rainwater, refused to carry electrical currents, cushioned the ride of previously bone-shattering bicycles, and finally supported the weight of Henry Ford's ubiquitous cars. Some 69,000 lbs. of rubber were counted at Belém in 1827. By 1853 the number had risen to more than 5.2 million.

Hevea brasiliensis was a wild tree that required decades to mature, so collection of its precious sap came to resemble a cross between gold mining and fur trapping. Claimants marked out territories on a map, paid the government a concession fee, then set about locating and tapping trees. The boom drew in hardscrabble folks from Brazil's desert northeast but also speculators from the big cities, foreign merchants, and petty criminals on the lam. In the far interior districts of the Andean piedmont, such as Colombia's Putumayo, Amazonian Indians were forced to work like slaves as tappers (**seringueiros**), porters, and suppliers of food.

As in any gold rush, the rubber boom made millionaires of only a select few. Yet it transformed the Amazon overnight, never to be the same again. Population in the Brazilian Amazon grew from about 250,000 in 1850 to over one million in 1910. Most inhabitants lived in some way off the prosperity that rubber brought or appeared to bring. Even when not enslaved the seringueiros, arguably the backbone of the enterprise, made almost nothing, living as indebted dependents as they wound their way through the immense forests checking their trees and hauling their product on their shoulders. Rubber had to be smoked daily to be saleable, and cups of fresh latex were poured slowly over a turning spit each night, yielding giant balls of raw rubber weighing over 200 lbs.

Staple foods—including, ironically, coffee—cost four times going rates in New York City. Life in the seemingly fecund jungle depended almost wholly on imports supplied by itinerant merchants and wholesalers, some of them Lebanese and Syrian (new ethnic groups in South America at this time). Merchants gained from the labor of others, as did the emerging Republic of Brazil. Indeed, tappers extended Brazil's claims in Amazonia tremendously, and they would be ratified by treaty around the turn of the century. The states of Amazônas and Pará also gained in importance as a result of rubber, mostly in the form of tax revenue. Dependency on rubber, however, like coffee or copper, was dangerous.

Rubber prices peaked at almost $3/lb. in 1910, with production topping out two years later. Rubber even vied with coffee as Brazil's number-one export in 1910 and 1912. Rubber profits built the world-famous Amazônas Theater, one of the most impressive nineteenth-century opera houses in the world, built in the 1890s. The theater, with its mix of classical and **indigenista**, or Indian revival, iconography, is perhaps symbolic of the conquest of the jungle by westerners, or at least of the metropolitan dreams of some Brazilians. Whatever its deeper symbolism, the opera house represented money in the form of raw latex, and raw latex was the darling of the world in the era of the Russo-Japanese War, the rise of Germany as an imperial power, and the growth of

---

Seringueiros   rubber tappers

Indigenismo   indigenism, or "Indian revivalism"

the automobile industry. When rubber was king, Manaus and Belém bustled, saturated with all the conveniences and vices of the age. Unfortunately, the sap wealth would soon run out.

In an early case of industrial spying, an English botanist named Henry Alexander Wickham pocketed hevea seeds during an 1876 Brazilian field trip. He planted them in the hothouses of London's Kew Gardens and observed their development. Seedlings were later taken to Ceylon, where land and labor were both cheap, and the rest, for Brazil, was a history lesson. Asian rubber exploded onto the world scene by 1915 and almost completely displaced Amazonian rubber by 1920. In 1922, 93.1% of all rubber was plantation grown. U.S. automaker Henry Ford tried to copy the British model in the lower Amazon, but his plantation, called Fordlândia, was a dismal failure. A fungus that caused hevea trees to scatter naturally in the primeval forests of the upper Amazon proved deadly when trees were concentrated on a plantation. The British, who had started from seeds, were lucky enough not to have taken the fungus with them.

EXPORT-LED GROWTH AND DICTATORSHIP IN MEXICO

What historians have called the Gilded Age in the United States would have its counterpart in Mexico: the so-called Porfiriato. This period, from 1876–1911, was characterized by strong-armed politics, sharp-eyed reforms, rampant corruption, massive extraction of wealth by foreign capitalists, endemic rural poverty, and other ills. Yet it was also the first prolonged period of stability in independent Mexico's history, and thus one of technological progress in everything from railroads to agriculture, with a bit of manufacturing thrown in. In the spirit of the Gilded Age, the Porfiriato was in some ways amazingly progressive, and in others astonishingly retrograde.

As in other Positivist-inspired regimes, progress in Mexico was expected to result from order, with order established via the rule of law, or at least lawmen. The rurales were expanded and Díaz's methods included a time-honored dictum: Shoot all prisoners (*mátalos en caliente*). Borderlands bandits were suppressed in 1877 after near-war with the United States. In thanks, the Hayes administration recognized the Díaz government. The other time-honored method of achieving order was **clientelism**. The first beneficiary was Manuel González, who succeeded Díaz as president in 1880. Though plagued by financial difficulties, the González regime seems to have been fairly independent of the caudillo's hand. Reelection for Díaz seemed inevitable nonetheless. A 50-something widower after 1880, Díaz soon married Carmen Romero Rubio, 18, and she taught him, at the least, proper upper-class decorum. Together they wowed foreign diplomats at the New Orleans World's Fair.

Clientelism   rule through a patronage system of subordinate friends and allies

M A P 11.1   Mexico and its Railroads, 1910

Mexico after 1884 was Díaz's, and in step with the times, Díaz's Mexico was steam-driven. Improvements in infrastructure included new railroad and tele-graph lines, hydroelectric dams, tramways, and even a renewed drainage system for Mexico City—now undertaken by the British firm S. Pearson & Son at a cost of 16 million pesos (see Map 11.1). If Mexico City had become one of the unhealthiest cities in the world by century's end—its 1910 mortality rate of 42 per thousand, twice that of Buenos Aires or Rio de Janeiro, made it a verita-ble Petri dish of flooding, disease, and crime—this was in part because its growth was extraordinarily rapid. Between 1870 and 1910 the city tripled in size, reach-ing three-quarters of a million inhabitants; the Porifirato laid the foundations for Mexico City to become the world's largest city by the end of the twentieth cen-tury. Construction not only took the form of affluent homes in the west, and slums in the east, but (again like its northern neighbor) Mexico and its capital experienced a public building craze—the darker side of which included a 2.5-million peso panopticon prison (see Image and Word 12.1 in Chapter 12). Not everyone, apparently, was shot on sight.

Educational reform in the liberal mode continued, producing the so-called **científicos**, a class of Positivist accountants and engineers who believed science in its many and elegant forms could fix Mexico. Mexico's financial situation improved through efficient tax collection and wise administration. José Limantour

Científicos   class of accountants and engineers in Porfirian Mexico who believed science could solve all problems, including social and political ones

deserves credit for his fiscal policies, which included a switch to the gold standard from the silver, an important change in an era of high silver production and hence rapid devaluation. Debts were paid and by 1890 a surplus in the treasury even appeared, a stunning turnaround in a nation known only for its empty pockets.

Railroads, almost totally financed by foreign concerns but ultimately purchased by the state, began to link the nation to the outside world and to itself. Mining was still Mexico's hidden treasure, though, and an 1884 law and subsequent revisions made foreigners salivate at the possibilities. The gates of exploitation were thrown open in the name of progress, while the environmental and human costs of industrial mineral production were scarcely considered. In the 1880s three new districts were opened: Coahuila's Sierra Mojada, Chihuahua's Batopilas, and Baja California's El Boleo (aka Santa Rosalía). The first two were large-scale silver-lead producers and the last a copper concern.

Mining investors were mostly North Americans during the Porfiriato, from the United States and Canada, but the British, French, and Germans were well represented. As in Bolivia at this time, silver production grew enormously between 1877 and 1908, from some 25 million pesos to over 85 million. Gold was for the first time a serious byproduct of this bonanza due to new separation technologies. Mercury was still widely used in Mexican refineries, but cyanide leaching was introduced around the turn of the century, fouling streams and killing off fish in a new way.

Big names in mining included the Guggenheim family. They had made their initial fortunes in the lead-silver mines of Lake County, Colorado, and their expansion into Mexico was logical given the appetites of the Gilded Age. Also active in Chile's copper mines, they had mining investments in Mexico of over $12 million in 1902. Another American, Colonel William Greene, became a symbol of the foreign mine operator during the Porfiriato after developing the Cananea Consolidated Copper Co. in Sonora; a claim purchased from a Mexican widow in 1898 became a multimillion-dollar operation employing—some would say exploiting—3,500 men by 1910.

The British were busier in Mexico's untapped oilfields, but Americans were there with them. U.S. petroleum interests were led by a California oilman named Edward Doheny, mostly in the Tampico district of the Gulf Coast. His company's gusher was called El Ebano (the Ebony); the company itself was called the Mexican Petroleum Co. The British were led by Sir Weetman Dickinson Pearson, head of the famous engineering firm that drained Mexico City. His success came more slowly after false starts in Chiapas, San Luis Potosí, and Tamaulipas. Tabasco yielded a gusher that supplied over 100 million barrels of crude in eight years. Pearson's El Aguila Co. and Doheny's Mexican Petroleum pumped tremendous amounts of oil out of Mexico almost duty-free, but Díaz's regime did not suffer.

Industry in the sense of manufacturing was slower to develop under the Porfiriato, but tax incentives and other subsidies to foreign capitalists led to the establishment of a major steel plant in Monterrey, along with a major brewery, José Schneider's Cervecería Cuauhtémoc, founded in 1890. Cuauhtémoc's first big seller was Carta Blanca. Monterrey was also home to numerous textile, tobacco, furniture, soap, and other light industry plants, and by 1910 it was clearly the industrial powerhouse of Mexico—its São Paulo.

What was absent, as in Brazil, was heavy industry, the sort of facilities capable of building ships, railroad engines, or even automobiles. The developed world remained a few crucial steps ahead. Mexican infrastructure was still in great need of improvement, and port facilities were high on the list of priorities. The Gulf ports of Veracruz and Tampico were dredged and docking facilities built, and similar improvements were made in the Pacific ports of Mazatlán, Manzanillo, Puerto México, and Salina Cruz. In part as a result, the volume of foreign trade ballooned. Incredibly, the value of exports exceeded the value of imports after 1895, a trade balance to be envied today.

The *Pax Porfiriana* was a clientelist military dictatorship. Politics was played like chess, only with Don Porfirio on both sides. Uppity politicians were played off one another or snapped out of play altogether. The army was set against the rurales, whose force grew in size and importance. Local political bosses were rewarded for loyalty and punished for disloyalty. The only thing keeping the lid on rural and working-class discontent was the omnipresence of armed forces.

The rhetoric of the científicos was usually progressive, but not when it came to the rural peasantry, particularly those labeled Indians, two million of whom did not speak Spanish in 1910. Here the creole elite espoused European and North American notions of pseudo-scientific racism, eugenics, and, at best, social Darwinism. These same innately intractable Indians, it would turn out, had suffered quite enough—their biggest gripe was that old liberal maxim against corporations, the Ley Lerdo, which led to continued dissolution of ejido lands, by law under the older liberal regimes, but by force under the Porfiriato. An 1883 law allowing foreign surveyors to appropriate or buy land not properly titled greatly exacerbated the problem in a time of rapid population growth and resulting land pressure.

Here, not in the colonial period, is the beginning of the great Mexican hacienda of literary and cinematic fame. Land laws under Porfirio Díaz allowed for the near-complete dissolution of village lands and led directly to the displacement of millions of peasants. By 1894 a fifth of Mexico (more than its arable land total) was re-titled, and by 1910 134 million acres were in the hands of a few hacendado families. Over half the population of the country was living on a hacienda. In 1910 Mexico counted 8,245 haciendas, many over 300,000 acres in extent and concentrated in the hands of a relatively small number of families. Putting even Brazil's richest coffee planters to shame, don Luis Terrazas of Chihuahua owned over 50 haciendas totaling some 7 million acres, plus half a million head of cattle, a quarter million sheep, 25,000 horses, 5,000 mules, and the best *toros* outside Spain. One million-acre-plus hacienda employed 2,000 peons. Beyond this land- and livestock-based wealth, don Luis owned mines, textile mills, banks, and virtually everything else worth owning in Chihuahua—that which he did not own belonged to his relatives, mostly his 12 children and their spouses.

On the other side of this massive land grab were the peasants. For those who worked on the haciendas, the peons, life got worse by the day. Prices rose but wages stagnated, at about 35 cents a day. Theirs was the Mexico of the Spaghetti Western, a desolate, materially poor, and hopeless place where the Don Luises of the world owned even the sombrero on one's head, purchased on unrepayable credit from the tienda de raya, or company store. Hacienda owners were aided by the law, which punished "vagabondage" and indebted persons without means. If liberals like Juárez had hoped to outlaw corporatism by outlawing church and village holdings, they were mistaken. The new states-within-the-state were Mexican-owned haciendas and foreign-owned mines. Liberalism under the conservative Díaz had simply led to a swap of masters but had gone the further step of removing the colonial system of checks.

These wide-ranging examples show how Latin America became a major player in world economic affairs after 1850, principally as a supplier of raw materials and receiver of a huge number of European and Asian immigrants. Economic historians continue to debate the significance of export-led growth (formerly denounced as simple dependency), but it is clear that the wealth generated by exports did little to improve the lives of ordinary Latin Americans. At best, export-led growth took more from the working majority than it gave back. At worst, it revived or reinforced colonial-style patterns of exploitation.

The facts of widespread foreign ownership and government collusion in the export business generated a reservoir of resentment that would eventually overflow, in the most extreme cases in the form of revolution. By the first decades of the twentieth century, Latin Americans working in virtually every export sector were more aware than ever of their collective power to bring about change. Despite their numbers, however, they did not account for everyone. In the backlands and even the urban margins there lurked a huge and growing population of subsistence farmers, freelance prospectors, autonomous indigenous peoples, and social misfits. Their stories are only beginning to be told.

KEEP READING

We recommend the following works on topics related to this chapter: George Reid Andrews, *Blacks and Whites in São Paulo, Brazil, 1888–1988* (1991); William H. Beezley, *Judas at the Jockey Club and other Episodes of Porfirian Mexico* (1987); Charles Bergquist, *Labor in Latin America: Comparative Essays on Chile, Argentina, Venezuela, and Colombia* (1986); Kim Butler, *Freedoms Given, Freedoms Won: Afro-Brazilians in Post-Abolition São Paulo and Salvador* (1998); Paul Dosal, *Doing Business with Dictators: A Political History of United Fruit in Guatemala, 1899–1944* (1993); Judith Ewell, *Venezuela and the United States: From Monroe's Hemisphere to Petroleum's Empire* (1996); Paul Garner, *Porfirio Díaz* (2001); Lowell Gudmundson, *Costa Rica before Coffee: Society and Economy on the Eve of the Export Boom* (1986); Manuel Moreno Fraginals, *The Sugar Mill: The Socioeconomic Complex of Sugar in Cuba*, trans. Cedric Belfrage (1976); June Nash, *We Eat the Mines and the Mines Eat Us: Dependency and Exploitation in Bolivian Tin Mines* (1979); Stanley Stein, *Vassouras: A Brazilian Coffee County, 1850–1900* (1985);

Steve Striffler and Mark Moberg, eds., *Banana Wars: Power, Production, and History in the Americas* (2003); Steven Topik, Carlos Marichal, and Zephyr Frank, eds., *From Silver to Cocaine: Latin American Commodity Chains and the Building of the World Economy, 1500–2000* (2006); Barbara Weinstein, *The Amazon Rubber Boom, 1850–1920* (1983).

12

✳

Rural Majorities, Urban Poverty, and Unconquered Frontiers

The Plight of the Peasant   **Hard Times in Indian Country**

Bandits and Prisoners   **Environmental Degradation**

"Canudos did not surrender. The only case of its kind in history, it held out to the last man." Thus writer Euclides da Cunha ended *Os Sertões*, his epic account of the Brazilian government's destruction of an isolated religious community in the northeast backlands of the state of Bahia in 1897 (see Map 12.1). The leader of Canudos, a mysterious figure known as Antônio the Counselor, was a wandering Catholic mystic who had built a large following among drought-stricken renters and sharecroppers, many descended from slaves, who felt the new Brazilian Republic was a godless monstrosity. These pious folk Catholics gathered together to form a peaceful commune but soon ran afoul of local authorities who resented their withdrawal from the local labor pool. Modern-minded priests who disliked competitors were even more critical.

Believing they were in the midst of an apocalyptic persecution, the residents of Canudos armed themselves and barricaded their settlement. As word of the commune spread, most urban and literate Brazilians failed to sympathize with what appeared to them followers of a dangerous brand of ignorant fanaticism. After several skirmishes, the Brazilian army was ordered to attack Canudos and capture its leader. Instead of losing or surrendering, the residents of Canudos defeated the invaders and killed the colonel in charge. Outraged, Brazilian authorities sent a huge force armed with modern artillery that ended by totally destroying the commune and killing or imprisoning nearly all of its 30,000-plus members.

TIMELINE	
1847–1901	Caste War in Yucatan (most fighting 1847–1855)
1861–1883	Main military campaigns by Chilean government against the Mapuches in Araucanía
1897	Brazilian military destroys backlands religious town of Canudos
1897–1938	Life of Lampião, the Bandit King of Brazil
1900–1908	Mexican government military subdues and enslaves many Yaquis in Sonora
1908	Butch Cassidy and the Sundance Kid shot in Bolivia

For da Cunha, Canudos was a cautionary tale that highlighted the vast gulf separating modern, urban Brazil from its huge and "backward" interior. The interior was not so much colonial as it was prehistoric, a primordial space inhabited by organically adapted creatures whose ways of thinking could barely be fathomed by educated city dwellers. In this persuasive literary imagining, rural people could only be understood in a scientific and detached way, as if viewed through a telescope like the last of a dying species of wild animals. If this was the mentality replacing the old colonial dichotomy of condescending but caring missionaries vs. hateful or dismissive landlords, then the modernizing project, which here turned tragic and bloody, was not off to a promising start.

When one turns to Latin America's vast and densely populated countryside, its indigenous and bandit-ruled frontiers, and even its urban criminal fringes, it becomes clear that the region's celebrated export-led growth and liberal-led projects of modernization were by the turn of the century facing serious limits and contradictions. In copying European models of scientific development, Latin American elites moved sharply away from the old colonial acceptance of social and ethnic diversity—as long as it fit within an established secular and religious hierarchy defined by monarchy and Catholicism—to embrace a racist and exclusionary definition of citizenship. Rather than seeking to embrace precisely that which made each nation unique—its African or indigenous heritage, say, or its peasant cuisine and music—this new ethos sought to punish or eliminate all that was nonwhite, "irrational," deviant, and marginal.

The folk, as the case of Canudos demonstrates, did not sit idly by. Although many were victimized by newly expanded military and police forces, and increasingly housed in prisons, the "marginal" masses of Latin America fought back with their own visions of what it meant to be a citizen. Indigenous groups found dignity in the struggle to maintain territorial and cultural autonomy, even when faced with the considerable firepower of the modern state. Some rebelled openly, and others returned to colonial practices of playing missionaries off government officials to gain advantage. New on the scene by the late nineteenth century were anthropologists, some of whom sought only to record native lore

M A P 12.1 Rebellion in the Backlands

or physical types before they disappeared, but others who became advocates for cultural survival.

Rural and urban law-breakers found themselves special objects of state attention in the liberal era, but not with the aim of "regeneration" or personal redemption touted by contemporary European and U.S. criminologists. Instead, many states, like Porfirio Díaz's Mexico, openly sought to exterminate alleged criminals, which did nothing to inspire confidence in the justice system. Many outlaws responded to authoritarian attempts at dehumanization and exclusion with clever tactics of evasion and even solidarity. Some outstanding criminals became folk heroes. Less capable of fighting back against the liberal onslaught was the natural environment, which underwent profound changes during the scramble for resources and attempts to link city to country and coast to interior. The liberal project was framed in terms of a struggle against nature, not an attempt to find harmony within it.

THE PLIGHT OF THE PEASANT

Slavery and indigenous tribute regimes ended in much of Latin America by the 1850s, but this did not lead to improvement in the everyday lives of the rural majority. Even where poor whites predominated, good land was rare and those who owned most of it demanded labor in exchange for even the most meager of rights, such as the sharing of irrigation water or collection of firewood. Share-cropping was a common successor to colonial labor arrangements, but **debt peonage**, or the advancing of merchandise or cash to the poor in exchange for promises to work through a harvest season, quickly became the most common means of de facto enslavement. Marked-up goods were sold on credit at the so-called **tienda de raya**, or company store.

As seen in Porfirio Díaz's Mexico, national and local governments made sure debt peonage worked—that is, that those who resisted or ran away were punished or returned to their "masters." Efforts to turn Yucatan's Maya peasants into sugar workers soon after independence contributed to a massive revolt and civil war, which left much of the peninsula outside the nation-state until the twentieth century (see Image and Word 12.1 and Map 12.1). As a result, when prosperity came to Yucatan's elite during the henequen (rope fiber) boom of the Porfiriato, the henequen workers of Yucatan's northwest were kept firmly under thumb. The system of debt peonage, enforced by violence or its threat, took root throughout Latin America, being most developed in regions where arable land was scarce and population density relatively high, as in highland Ecuador or El Salvador. In places where country folk could escape to work in a city or mining town as an alternative, such as in Peru or Chile, coercive mechanisms could be harsher, often violent. Some hacienda owners took their assumed patriarchal duties of protection and reciprocity seriously, but in many places the hacienda became a kind of prison camp run by cruel underlings.

Aside from violent mistreatment from overseers and agents of the state, Latin America's millions of peasants suffered from malnutrition, lack of education, inadequate health care, and poor housing. High birth rates coupled with the expansion of export agriculture led to diminishing pools of land and other resources for a growing number of people. The plight of peasants seemed to point to a colonial continuity in desperate need of correction and was increasingly denounced by political activists such as Peru's José Carlos Mariátegui and writers of fiction such as Ecuador's Jorge Icaza. It was the peasants themselves, however, who fought most consistently for their rights, if mostly on no more than local terms. As will be seen in the next chapter, this was to change into nation-wide revolutionary struggles in Mexico, and later in Cuba, Nicaragua, and elsewhere.

Debt peonage   the advancing of merchandise or cash to the poor in exchange for promises to work

Tienda de raya   company stores where goods were sold at inflated prices, often on credit, to rural workers

IMAGE AND WORD 12.1   The Caste War of Yucatan

© Gordon Sinclair/Alamy

In 1846, Yucatan seemed poised to realize a noble destiny. Having broken away from the Spanish Empire, along with the rest of greater Mexico, in 1821, it now claimed independence from the Mexican republic. Two decades of a sugar boom seemed to assure its future prosperity. But the new nation was short-lived; built on a fragile foundation, it was torn apart by a bloody civil war in 1847. Because most of the protagonists were Mayas, and the elite felt so threatened by the rebellion of native villages, the war was dubbed *La Guerra de las Castas* (the Caste War). In fact, it was much more than a simple race war, with people of Spanish, African, and Maya descent on all sides. The above painting of the conflict is from the Palacio de Gobierno de Mérida in Yucatan. By 1855, when the war ended in the northwest, some 200,000 people had been killed, succumbed to the cholera epidemic, or displaced—almost half the total population. Many captured Maya fighters were sent to work as slaves in Cuba. Although the peninsula's west had been forced back into the Mexican republic, the east remained an independent zone of small, loosely connected Maya states. These rebels were called **cruzob** (Spanish *cruz*, cross; Maya plural ending *–ob*), after the religious and political cult of the Talking Cross, which kept many of their leaders in power. Not until 1901 did Mexican forces finally subdue their capital, deep in what is today the state of Quintana Roo, and there remained independent villages into the 1930s.

Despite worsening times, popular culture in Latin America proved surprisingly rich. Many people found refuge, if not escape, in a range of cultural

Cruzob   Maya rebels in late-nineteenth-century Yucatan

expressions, from dance to ballads to poetry. Most of the dance forms now considered typical of Latin American nations or regions, such as the tango, samba, and salsa, first became popularized in the era of liberal reforms. Some were urban, others rural. Uptight elites tended to view these dances and songs as lewd expressions of uncultured ignorance, and turned instead to Europe for cultural guidance. Religious songs and festivities were often equated with an outmoded and superstitious colonial piety. New quasi-religious traditions of spiritism and folk healing, some developed locally by descendants of Africans, such as Haitin **vodun** and Cuban **santería**, and some imported from Europe, such as the teachings of Frenchman Allan Kardec, also spread widely after 1850.

All over Latin America new musical forms were developed by fusion of lively African rhythms with traditional European instrumentation. In the Andes and parts of Central America, folk music took on a more melancholic, indigenous cast. In the dry northeast of Brazil, folk poets emerged alongside folk healers and visionaries to find the poignant and humorous in what was otherwise a fairly harsh rural life. Northern Mexican balladeers gave rise to the mariachi and folk *corrido* traditions. Whether in dance, poetry, or song, storytelling and ribald humor were everywhere at the core of folk entertainment. In coastal Brazil, even funerals were occasions for exuberant cultural expression. In most homes there were no phonographs or even radios in the era before 1930—only campfires, hearths, and the rich imaginations of elders, nighttime dancers, and virtuosic musicians. Among the favorite topics of storytellers and balladeers were regionally famous bandits, the prototypical peasant antiheroes.

BANDITS AND PRISONERS

The Latin American countryside had been famous for its bandits since colonial times, but the phenomenon seems to have grown significantly in the national period. Weak central governments, ruthless regional caudillos, and grinding rural poverty all contributed to the rise of banditry, as did the growth of the primary export sector. Most bandits preyed on travelers and merchants making their way through mountains, rain forests, swamps, and deserts, areas where victims were most vulnerable and hideouts were abundant. Roads were universally bad in the rugged backcountry in the nineteenth century, and police or military presence almost zero.

Most rural bandits were motivated by greed, but some came to be regarded as Robin Hood figures. Historians disagree sharply as to whether the liberal era's celebrated highwaymen drew on peasant solidarity or simply exploited it for personal ends, but it is clear that word of their activities got around, and their power was widely admired. As with Lampião in Brazil (see Image and Word 12.2), complex networks linking rural criminals and powerful landholders developed in various countries, including Mexico and Colombia. Banditry often emerged in the interstices of state power, and since it tended to draw media attention a

---

Vodun, santería   quasi-religious traditions of spiritism and folk healing, developed in Haiti and Cuba, respectively, by descendants of Africans

IMAGE AND WORD 12.2 The Bandit King of Brazil

Autor: Alexandre José Felipe Cavalcanti
d'Albuquerque Saboia Dilla - 445 D 17.
"MARECHAL do Cordel de Cangaço"

LAMPIÃO E
MARIA BONITA

DILLA

© Roger-Viollet/The Image Works

Born in the *sertão* or arid backlands of Pernambuco in 1897, a young leather-worker named Virgulino Ferreira da Silva took to banditry after seeing his father killed by the police. His band of outlaws (**cangaçeiros**), at times as many as 50 strong, terrorized farms and small towns in seven Brazilian states. He became known as the "Bandit King"

(continued)

Cangaçeiros   Brazilian outlaws or bandits

IMAGE AND WORD 12.2   The Bandit King of Brazil (continued)

Reuters/Corbis

Lampião, and his girlfriend Maria Déa was nicknamed María Bonita (Beautiful Mary, depicted on the previous page in a contemporary print). Lampião survived in part because he was well connected to local ranchers and bosses, or "colonels," who sheltered him and used his power against political foes. In 1938 he, his girlfriend, and nine of his *cangaçeiros* were killed and their severed heads put on public display in Bahia (above). Family members were not able to claim and bury the heads until 1971.

---

great many deals were made for which liberal authorities could not be proud. Yet peasants still claimed these outlaws as their own, or at least approximate reflections of their wildest fantasies of reprisal or socioeconomic gain.

If rural banditry seemed a colonial survival, urban crime struck many Latin Americans as a genuinely new and modern phenomenon. Rural to urban migration, the end of slavery and indigenous draft labor, the arrival of waves of immigrants, the expansion of civil liberties under liberal rule—all these and other factors contributed to rising crime rates in Latin American cities. It is impossible to know how much urban crime actually increased since we have scant statistics from the late colonial and early national periods, but the perception among elites was that it was exploding after 1850 and had to be confronted.

This apparently modern ill demanded modern, scientific solutions. Among liberals, especially, but also some conservatives, modern crime was to be fought in other ways than the typical colonial strategies of public corporal punishment, humiliation, and (for women, at least) religious rehabilitation. Criminals were now to be carefully identified, tracked, and incarcerated. Some, particularly the young, were to be reformed through education and constant surveillance. All were exploited with hard labor. Perhaps most importantly, urban crime was by the 1870s blamed on the innate characteristics of certain types of human beings. It was no longer a matter of sin, in other words, but rather genetics. Unsurprisingly, people of African, Asian, or indigenous descent were often singled out by educated elites for their "bad genes." Others were blamed for the size of their brains, the "asymmetry" of their faces, and other physical characteristics thought to reflect criminal tendencies.

Institutional responses to urban crime followed developments in Europe and the United States, among them professionalization of police forces, expansion of detective units, and construction of sanitary, "panopticon" prisons, or penitentiaries (see Image and Word 12.3). Not only liberals were on the cutting edge of crime fighting. One of the first panopticons in Latin America was built in Ecuador by conservative president Gabriel García Moreno, and it is still in use today. Police work was treated as a science worthy of respect in this age of Sherlock Holmes, and courts began to hear evidence from chemists and other highly trained specialists. Fingerprint records and mug shots were soon kept on file, and "all points bulletins" were issued by telegraph and rail service.

Some police information was shared internationally, allowing for the capture and extradition of foreigners, many of them accused of spreading anarchist, communist, and other dangerous doctrines. In this era of improved communication and cheap steamship travel, U.S. bandits Butch Cassidy and the Sundance Kid escaped to Argentina, then Bolivia, only to be killed in a shootout with government forces in 1908 after stealing a payroll shipment from the powerful Aramayo family, heavy investors in Potosí and other silver districts. For the truly incorrigible, among them high-profile political prisoners, penal colonies were established in remote locations, frequently on offshore islands such as Fernando de Noronha in Brazil and Isla Gorgona in Colombia. Devil's Island, off the coast of French Guyana, served to "correct" criminals from both France and its colonial holdings in the Caribbean.

Most responses to urban crime focused on men, but women were also blamed for the alleged moral rot of modern cities, and they were similarly treated to new, scientific approaches to deviance. Prostitution was one crime that drew considerable attention from reformers, and in rapidly growing cities crawling with transient young men, such as Buenos Aires and Rio de Janeiro, it was a particularly widespread phenomenon. Mining towns were similarly "plagued." Seen as a moral failing in colonial times, now the crime of prostitution was tied to disease. In the years before the discovery of penicillin, which made syphilis treatable only after 1945, prostitution was considered a serious public health hazard. Men were almost never blamed, much less prosecuted for their sponsorship of prostitutes, but the women involved were frequently rounded up and incarcerated, and sometimes subjected to medical experimentation. Patriarchal laws also did nothing to protect sex workers, or women in general, from physical abuse perpetrated by clients, pimps, or the police.

In all of these approaches to criminality, Latin America's educated urban elites, liberal and conservative, reinforced an exclusionary and often racist and

IMAGE AND WORD 12.3 Putting Prisoners in Panopticons

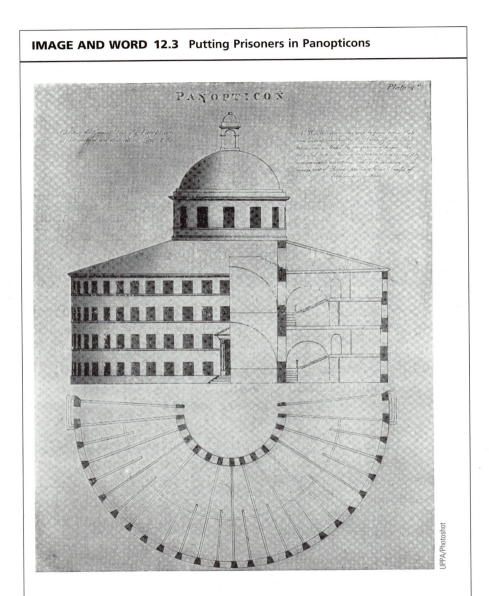

UPPA/Photoshot

Originally designed by English philosopher Jeremy Bentham in 1785 (see drawing above), the panopticon prison allowed guards and criminologists to observe (-*opticon*) all (*pan*-) the prisoners without them being able to see their observers. The concept (or variants on it) became popular throughout Latin America in the late nineteenth century. Some of Latin America's panopticon prisons are now open to voluntary visitors: Bogotá's former Panóptico, built in 1874, is now the National Museum of Colombia; the Lecumberri penitentiary built in Mexico City in 1900 was converted into the National Archives in 1982; and the Presidio Modelo on Cuba's Isle of Pines (renamed Isla de la

Presidio Modelo
Isla de Pinos
El gran comedor

Juventud), built in 1926–28 and a prison for Fidel Castro in 1953–55, is now a museum (see photograph above).

sexist vision of progress. It was hoped that these societies' "bad elements" could be sifted or weeded out, cut off and separated from the mainstream and hopefully made extinct within a few generations. Modern Latin America, in this vision, had no place for the poor, especially if female or brown in color. Criminality was bred in the bone, not a product of social inequity or Satan's urgings, and thus had to be excised with surgical precision. Unfortunately, most Latin American justice systems remained too corrupt, inefficient, or weak to protect marginal groups from persecution by state and elite interests.

HARD TIMES IN INDIAN COUNTRY

Modern Latin America in the liberal era had even less room for unassimilated Amerindians than it did for petty criminals. In Argentina and Chile, the late nineteenth century was marked by vicious military campaigns against nomadic indigenous groups such as the Ranqueles and Mapuche who had long thrived beyond the margins of colonial rule in Patagonia, Araucanía, and other southern districts. The wars to exterminate them in the 1870s and 1880s resembled those of the post–Civil War United States, and a similar racist language was used to describe them (see Image and Word 12.4). In upper Amazonia, as seen in the last chapter, in a region stretching from Colombia to Bolivia, indigenous groups who had successfully resisted European missionaries and conquerors since the sixteenth century fell victim to seekers of rubber, quinine bark, palm ivory, and

IMAGE AND WORD 12.4 Mapuche Persistence

©The Print Collector/Heritage/The Image Works

The Chilean government invaded the Mapuche lands of Araucanía, at Chile's southern end, in a series of military campaigns between 1861 and 1883. Officially called "the Pacification of the Araucanía," the campaigns were aimed at ethnic "cleansing" to seize Mapuche lands. Some 10,000 Mapuches had been killed in the war by the 1890s—the above image of a Mapuche chief and mounted headmen is from 1895. Anti-Mapuche violence continued through the twentieth century as Mapuches attempted to resist full incorporation into the modern Chilean nation. Despite over a century of persecution, the Mapuche persist. Some, like the Mapuche woman healer pictured here, proudly display symbols of cultural survival—which include silver jewelry, most likely adopted in the colonial period.

DAVID ALAN HARVEY/National Geographic Stock

other forest products. As if to further echo colonial times, many others were felled by smallpox and other foreign diseases.

Post-1850 gold rushes and oil strikes transformed indigenous–controlled regions in the backlands of Mexico, Venezuela, Colombia, Brazil, the Guyanas, and Panama, as did the building of roads, canals, and telegraph lines all over the hemisphere. Accused of banditry and sedition, the Apaches and Comanches of the Texas–New Mexico borderlands found themselves hunted by federal authorities on both sides of the U.S.-Mexico border during the Porfiriato. The Yaqui of Sonora, on the Arizona border, were forcibly subdued from 1900–1908, many of them sent to work on henequen fiber plantations in faraway Yucatan. The many hunter-gatherer groups of South America's Gran Chaco region found themselves displaced by Mennonite homesteaders from Russia and Canada in the 1920s, and then caught in the midst of a vicious war between Paraguay and Bolivia in the 1930s. For educated whites the period from 1870–1930 was a heroic age of exploration and modernization, but from most indigenous perspectives it was a time of genocide.

The largest "unexplored" area of Latin America, and home to the greatest number of autonomous indigenous peoples, was the Amazon basin, or Amazonia, much of which fell within the borders of Brazil. Though it is everywhere warm and wet, Amazonia is characterized by numerous sub-climates, differences in altitude, and seasonal variations. As a result of these natural factors as well as historical forces, including slaving expeditions and missionary endeavors in the colonial period, indigenous groups of widely varying ethnicity have settled and adapted to this vast ecosystem. Mixed peoples also emerged. Along the Amazon's extensive shores a large number of indigenous people joined the descendants of African slaves and others to form "hybrid" cultures built around farming, nut gathering, fishing, river transport, and gold mining.

Among the many groups that maintained autonomous territories, languages, and ways of life were the Shuar and other Jivaroan peoples of Amazonian Ecuador and Peru (see Image and Word 12.5 and Map 12.1). Both groups resisted outside incursion, but it was an uphill battle against the onslaught of everything from Bibles to rifles; modernity lurked everywhere in the forest by this time, alongside colonial-style barbarity. Just to the north, Quechua-speaking lowlanders were caught up in the Amazon rubber boom. Many were enslaved for debts and sent to Iquitos, Peru's thriving Amazonian capital.

ENVIRONMENTAL DEGRADATION

Deforestation, overgrazing, and fouling of streams with toxic metals were all legacies of the colonial period, but things got much worse after the mid-nineteenth century. With the explosive growth of cities, the expansion of mining and other extractive industries, and the rise of cattle ranching and commercial agriculture for export came numerous new environmental ills. City sanitation and contamination of urban water supplies cried out for attention. Outbreaks of cholera and yellow

IMAGE AND WORD 12.5   **Believe It or Not**

CBS/Landov

Mireille Vautier/Alamy

The Shuar were famously bellicose and renowned for shrinking heads. This fearsome reputation had helped them stave off would-be conquistadors and missionaries for many centuries. It was only after 1900 that missionaries from several of the Catholic Church's newest orders, such as the Salesians, made inroads among the Shuar. Both liberal and conservative governments in Ecuador permitted this activity since it offered the possibility of cheap expansion of the state into long-claimed but never controlled territory. The Shuar proved resistant to missionary efforts, but small numbers of converts who managed to survive unwittingly introduced disease epidemics began to gather around the lowland trading outpost of Macas. Anthropologists from as far away as Finland arrived on the heels of the missionaries to study these "pristine savages." Interest in the practice of Shuar head shrinking became a popular obsession in Europe and the United States, and a trade in **tsantsas**, or trophy-heads, rapidly developed (see Robert Ripley with tsantsas in 1934). Shuar warriors, long dependent on wooden lances, traded heads for shotguns and repeating rifles. Despite outside forces, including a long border conflict between Ecuador and Peru, the Shuar, like the Mapuche, are alive and well, and undergoing a cultural revival. Pictured above is a modern Shuar warrior demonstrating the traditional blowgun.

fever were both hazardous and embarrassing. Less noticeable to city dwellers were things such as deforestation caused by charcoal making and soil erosion due to overgrazing. As in the western United States and Canada, the "taming" of the Latin American frontier for the benefit of the metropolis came at tremendous cost.

Tsantsas   the heads of enemies shrunken and kept as trophies by the Shuar

Water supply and sanitation were ancient urban concerns, but like railroads and telegraph lines, upgrading them to modern scale and sophistication required the intervention of foreign engineers. These problems were not small. Mexico City had since colonial times relied on a massive, hand-excavated canal to drain the landlocked valley in which it sat, but it was not until 1900, during the administration of Porfirio Díaz, that the Gran Canal was expanded, lined with concrete, and made reliable, "a massive toilet in constant flush," as one historian describes it.

Beginning around the turn of the century, rivers were canalized and re-routed through many Latin American cities, including Lima, Santiago, Medellín, and Caracas, and everywhere (as in colonial times) they were treated as sewers. Residents of Quito filled in numerous gulches to reclaim building space downtown in the 1910s, only to see the Machángara River gain in volume and erosive power. Little was done outside the building of urban park spaces to preserve the natural beauty of these streams. The picturesque Tequendama Falls that drain the verdant Sabana of Bogotá, for example, quickly became fouled with urban waste and as a result less fun to visit. Despite the best of intentions and scientific efforts, many cities remained vulnerable to floods, landslides, earthquakes, and even volcanic eruptions.

Massive reservoirs were built to supply growing cities with water, displacing tens of thousands of peasants and pastoralists. Cities also increasingly demanded electricity, and by the first decades of the twentieth century numerous hydro-electric projects and their associated dams and reservoirs were either planned or underway. These projects, such as the ingenious damming of the Pinheiros River near São Paulo by U.S. engineer Asa Billings, provided not only urban lighting but also the means for industrialization. The reservoir was full by 1925, which soon gave rise to the enormous industrial wasteland known as Cubatão. Dams also inundated huge tracts of forest, farms, and grazing land, and even swallowed up many ancient towns.

In the countryside, environmental concerns varied even more. Commercial logging was slow to develop except in parts of the Amazon basin, but massive deforestation followed the expansion of rail lines and opening of new farmlands and mines all over Latin America. Livestock herds grew into the millions in the grasslands of Colombia and Venezuela, the arid north of Mexico, and the pampas of the Southern Cone. They drove out other species (many of them, especially predators, hunted by ranchers and cowboys) and in some places led to desertification. More fragile still were the dry Andes and Mexican sierras, where sheep nibbled sparse grasses and intensified erosion. Mining and oil drilling left toxic lakes and fouled streams for miles around, and refineries emitted clouds of unfiltered smoke. To those at the top of the export food chain, pollution smelled like money; to those unfortunates who lived down-wind, it smelled like death.

Ordinary Latin Americans were not unaware of these ugly and destructive byproducts of modernization, but most, including the poor, took them to be the natural price of change. Social mobility meant earning enough money to avoid having to live beside a sewer or scrounge in the town dump. City-dwellers of all classes had little love for the countryside, which in the liberal era they still associated with barbarism and savagery. Aside from rare villagers or autonomous indigenous groups who protested the direct destruction of their livelihoods when a rail line plowed through or a dam was built, virtually no voices were raised in favor of conservation for either aesthetic or practical reasons. State protection of wild species or natural wonders, of which Latin America has many, were even more exotic concepts. Exceptions included Mexico's "Apostle of the Tree," Miguel Ángel Quevedo (1862–1946), who avidly promoted reforestation and protection of primary forest from the Porfiriato until his death, but only in recent years have environmental causes gained wide advocacy in Latin America.

Latin America in the era of liberal reforms remained a land of contradictions and riddles. As educated urban elites embraced scientific European and U.S. approaches to everything from criminology to sewer systems, the mass of folk remained almost entirely outside the fold of genuine citizenship. Only in exceptional countries such as Argentina was education made widely available. Many rural folk became trapped in the webs of dependency and exploitation typical of the export agriculture sector, including the most modern-looking haciendas and cattle ranches. Meanwhile others, such as forest- or desert-dwelling indigenous groups, struggled to remain beyond the reach of the nation-state. This became increasingly difficult with the advance of resource frontiers and the emergence of government-sponsored "civilizing" missions.

Closer to the center, those who failed to find honest work in the city could increasingly count on being picked up, documented, incarcerated, and even exiled to a penal colony. Female sex workers were similarly monitored and treated more as a public health hazard than as human beings. All of these examples serve to illustrate how "modern" Latin America was not turning out to be the land of equal rights and opportunities promised by liberal leaders. Instead, it was becoming a region dominated by oligarchies, or clusters of wealthy and powerful families, who used the state as a means of reinforcing an exclusionary social order for their own benefit. At the heart of the riddle of widespread poverty in a land of natural bounty lay the short-sighted attitude of the rich toward the masses. Before long, the policies of the elite would prove to be detrimental to nations as a whole. But, as the chapters of Part V show, Latin Americans in the twentieth century proved to be persistent and creative in seeking solutions to these problems.

KEEP READING

We recommend the following works by historians: Carlos Aguirre, *The Criminals of Lima and Their Worlds: The Prison Experience, 1850–1935* (2005); Peter Beattie, *The Tribute of Blood: Army, Honor, Race, and Nation in Brazil, 1864–1945* (2001); Katherine E. Bliss, *Compromised Positions: Prostitution, Public Health, and Gender Politics in Revolutionary Mexico City* (2001); John Charles Chasteen, *National Rhythms, African Roots: The Deep History of Latin American Popular Dance* (2004); Warren Dean, *With Broadax and Firebrand: The Destruction of the Brazilian Atlantic Forest* (1995); Todd A. Diacon, *Stringing Together a Nation: Cândido Mariano da Silva*

Rondon and the Construction of a Modern Brazil, 1906–1930 (2006); Donna Guy, *Sex and Danger in Buenos Aires: Prostitution, Family, and Nation in Argentina* (1991); Paul E. Little, *Amazonia: Territorial Struggles on Perennial Frontiers* (2001); Lucio V. Mansilla, *A Visit to the Ranquel Indians*, trans. Eva Gillies (1997); Shawn W. Miller, *The Environmental History of Latin America* (2006); Richard Price, *The Convict and the Colonel* (2006); Terry Rugeley, *Of Wonders and Wise Men: Religion and Popular Cultures in Southeast Mexico, 1800–1876* (2001); Ricardo Salvatore, Carlos Aguirre, and Gil Joseph, eds., *Crime and Punishment in Latin America: Law and Society since Late Colonial Times* (2001); Lane Simonian, *Defending the Land of the Jaguar: A History of Conservation in Mexico* (1995); Richard Slatta, ed., *Bandidos: The Varieties of Latin American Banditry* (1987); Michael Taussig, *Shamanism, Colonialism, and the Wild Man: A Study in Terror and Healing* (1989); Paul Vanderwood, *Disorder and Progress: Bandits, Police, and Mexican Development*, 2nd ed. (1992).

PART V

*

Reorientations and Reactions
(1910–2010)

These final three chapters bring us through the past century of the Latin American experience and up to the present. In Chapter 13, we outline the region's two most famous revolutions, those of Mexico (1910) and Cuba (1959); neither can easily be given end dates, and their impact has been widely felt ever since. Both are placed within the context of other nationalist and revolutionary movements and key events. Although nationalism was even more dominant a theme in the twentieth century than it had been in the nineteenth, the influence of Europe and the United States remained significant. Thus while the rise of dictatorships in Europe in the 1920s and 1930s meant that authoritarian regimes were as prominent as democracies in Latin America in those decades, the outcome of World War II helped push Latin America toward democracy in midcentury.

However, starting in the cold war era of the 1950s, a return to military intervention and authoritarianism shook Latin America; Chapter 14 explores the forms this took in Mexico, Central America, the Caribbean, and the southern cone nations. The final chapter of the book (Chapter 15) briefly outlines the turn back toward democracy in recent decades. We also discuss new environmental concerns and the rise of urbanism—as Latin American capitals joined the ranks of the world's megacities. The riddle of the twentieth century derives in part from the dramatic shift between various manifestations of democracy and authoritarianism. Which won where, and why? It also springs from the dynamic interaction between, on the one hand, nationalism and the development of local solutions and distinct local cultures, and on the other hand, complex relationships between Latin American nations and the outside world—political, economic, cultural, sometimes violent, sometimes creative and productive. Will twenty-first-century Latin America break free from dependency on primary exports or will new Asian players complicate the old Atlantic-centered, North-South dynamic?

13

✳

Riding a Revolutionary Tide

The Mexican Revolution

Economic and Other Nationalisms

The Cuban Revolution

The Nicaraguan Revolution

Failed Revolutionary Movements

"The nation's future, the solutions to its problems, cannot continue to depend on the selfish interests of a dozen big businessmen nor on the cold calculations of profits that ten or twelve magnates draw up in their air-conditioned offices." With these words, student leader Fidel Castro outlined his country's inequalities at his trial in 1953 and predicted a popular upheaval that would address them.

By 1959, Castro and several companions, including the Argentine medical student-turned-revolutionary Ernesto "Che" Guevara, were at the head of a new Cuban government. They had successfully overthrown the corrupt, U.S.-supported regime of President Fulgencio Batista. The Cuban Revolution of 1959 was arguably the most profound break with the past witnessed in Latin America since the Conquest, yet it was also a culmination of a long-accumulating revolutionary tide, one that stretched back to the turn of the twentieth century.

Discontent with corrupt government and gaping social inequity had long been voiced in Latin America, but it was only in the twentieth century that reflexive reactions to bad policies gave way to full-blown revolutions. Mexico was first, although its revolution was far from unified ideologically—followed much later by Bolivia, Cuba, and Nicaragua. These later upheavals were directly inspired by European socialism and Soviet-style Communism, and both Cuba and Nicaragua sought and received Soviet military and economic aid. Failed revolutionary movements, meanwhile, rose and fell in virtually every Latin American country beginning in the 1950s and 1960s. They were inspired by the writings of Marx, Lenin, Trotsky, and Mao, as well as those of José Carlos Mariátegui, Fidel Castro, and Che Guevara.

TIMELINE	
1910–1917	Mexican Revolution
1929	Founding of ruling party in Mexico, later renamed PRI
1930–1945	Presidency of Getúlio Vargas in Brazil
1938	President Lázaro Cárdenas nationalizes Mexican oil reserves
1946–1955	Presidency of Juan Perón in Argentina
1952	Bolivian Revolution
1954	Jacobo Arbenz overthrown in Guatemala
1959	Cuban Revolution
1961	U.S.-organized "Bay of Pigs" invasion of Cuba fails
1968	Military coup in Peru
1973	President Allende overthrown and killed in CIA-backed military coup in Chile
1979	Nicaraguan Revolution
1992	Capture of Shining Path leader Abimael Guzmán in Peru

Most Latin American countries did not experience revolutions in the twentieth century, but all underwent profound political and economic adjustments, often spurred by the economic shocks of the Great Depression and World War II. As it became more and more evident how dependent Latin America had become on world commodity prices, a mix of urban intellectuals, labor leaders, and politicians began to respond by calling for greater economic independence. The idea was not entirely new, but by the 1930s economic nationalism entailed state appropriation and management of natural resources and basic services, worker protection through expanded social welfare programs, and high tariffs on imported manufactured goods to stimulate local production. This last feature of economic nationalism, known as Import Substitution Industrialization, or **ISI**, was adopted by nearly every Latin American country by 1950. Though most clearly articulated in Argentina and Brazil, policies of **economic nationalism** had already been tested by the revolutionary government of Mexico.

THE MEXICAN REVOLUTION

In the last years of Porfirio Díaz's rule, upper-crust Mexican society became richer through land grabs and foreign trusts, while the poor majority languished

---

ISI   Import Substitution Industrialization, a self-explanatory element of economic nationalism

Economic nationalism   state appropriation of natural resources and basic services, worker protection through social welfare, and high tariffs on imports

in unequivocal squalor. If the fermented agave sap known as pulque offered some escape, toxemia was the price to pay. In unperceived irony, the rich celebrated Bastille Day (July 14), complete with filet mignon dinners at the Maison Dorée, as the masses ate corn tortillas. Dissent bubbled up just after the turn of the century, first in the form of liberal attacks in the press, then in plans for rebellion. The Mexican Revolution was not a Marxist revolution, but many of its leaders were well-read radicals.

A mining engineer from San Luis Potosí and three Mexico City journalists, the Flores Magón brothers, were the first to feel Díaz's wrath after they reported abuses by clergymen and political bosses in the newspaper *Regeneración*. After several arrests between 1901 and 1904 the brothers moved to San Antonio, Texas, where they wrote even more scathing exposés. An elite sympathizer and financial supporter was Francisco Madero, son of a Coahuila hacienda owner. An assassination attempt by Porfirian agents pushed the Flores Magón brothers north to St. Louis, Missouri; there, thanks to the influence of U.S. investors in Mexico's booming export economy, they were not universally welcomed.

Still, the printed attacks continued, each time with more socialist and even anarchistic elements. The reform push was catalyzed by the great Cananea Mine strike of 1906, an event that brought to the fore the injustices wrought by unrestrained foreign capitalist enterprise on Mexican soil. Conditions in the old silver mines of Guanajuato might have been objectively worse, but at Cananea Mexican laborers could see their North American counterparts receiving preferential treatment on a daily basis. Here the subjective conditions were aided by the distribution of copies of *Regeneración* and violence ensued. The strike was crushed by both Mexican and U.S. forces, particularly Arizona Rangers, prompting some to think of revolution as the only means to end the suffering.

Strikes at numerous Mexican textile factories followed, and a massacre at Río Blanco in 1907 made clear the position of Don Porfirio; he was no friend of the working classes. The other catalyst for revolution was Díaz's claim that he would not seek reelection in 1910, a promise made in 1908 to a U.S. journalist. When it became clear that Díaz was insincere, Francisco Madero launched a campaign on a non-re-electionist platform—Madero had split from the now-radical Flores Magón brothers and was at best a reformer, mostly interested in suffrage, not land redistribution. Madero became a hero when he was jailed by Díaz in 1910, on the eve of the election that should never have been. The Díaz regime celebrated 100 years of independence and 80 years of Porfirio's presence on earth, but trouble was brewing.

The Plan of San Luis Potosí was Madero's answer to defeat. The first to fight the dictator were the Aquiles Serdán family of Puebla, but Chihuahua soon became the crucible of revolution. The first figures of note, besides Madero, who did not fare well on the battlefield, were Pancho Villa and Pascual Orozco Jr. The latter is remembered for routing *federales* and sending their uniforms to Díaz with the taunt, "*Ahí te van las hojas; mandame mas tamales*" ("Here are the leaves, send me more tamales"). The tide turned in favor of the rebels with the seizure of Ciudad Juárez in early 1911, but the rebels were hardly of one mind. In the confusion Díaz resigned on May 25, 1911, to cheering crowds. Meanwhile, in the south a great leader emerged in the person of Emiliano Zapata, a small landholder, mule-skinner, and town official of Anenecuilco, Morelos. Unlike his northern counterparts who knew much about Yankee imperialism and the power of industry, Zapata knew the plight of landless Indians and even addressed them in Nahuatl. Thus Zapata, in his first meeting with Madero in Mexico City, cut to the crux of the issue with his constituency. The cry of his followers was "Land or Death!"

Madero won the 1911 presidential race, but the Zapatistas continued in revolt with their own Plan de Ayala. Madero was deposed and executed on orders of Victoriano Huerta, who in turn was ousted with U.S. pressure by 1914, after a violent U.S. attack on Veracruz. From this point onward the three key players, all presidents, were Venustiano Carranza (1914, 1915–1920), Alvaro Obregón (1920–1924), and Plutarco Calles (1924–1928). The United States intervened again, in 1916, after the murders of U.S. mining engineers in northern Mexico and finally a Villista raid on Columbus, New Mexico. The response to this attack was a punitive force under John J. Pershing, but it failed to find Pancho Villa. With Europe in flames, President Woodrow Wilson decided to leave Mexico alone in 1917.

The revolution was at last codified in the Constitution of 1917, which established a range of guarantees for labor, including an eight-hour workday and the right to strike. Peasants were rewarded with the elimination of debt peonage and the company store, and indigenous communities were restored communal lands. Economic nationalism appeared in the form of articles declaring the nation owner of all mineral wealth and water rights, sharply limiting foreign ownership. The state did not threaten to confiscate foreign businesses for the time being, but the groundwork for expropriations was laid in the form of Article 27. The promise to break up haciendas, however, was not kept.

The violence that had taken the lives of hundreds of thousands of Mexicans was not over. Carranza, who served as president after 1917, had Zapata killed in 1919. He, in turn, was murdered while trying to leave the country in 1920. Tempers calmed under Obregón, who took office in 1920, but during his term, in 1923, Pancho Villa was murdered. Many other scores were settled, and surviving bandit-warlords sought to consolidate their personal gains. Obregón and his successor, Plutarco Calles, who ran Mexico like a mob boss from 1924–1934, concentrated on rebuilding and "institutionalizing" the revolution. Mostly they manipulated labor and the peasantry with empty promises. In 1929 Calles formed the National Revolutionary Party, later renamed the Institutional Revolutionary Party. The **PRI**, as this vast political machine was known, ruled Mexico until 2000.

One institution that felt the blows of revolution most directly was the Catholic Church, long an object of both liberal and leftist hatred. Obregón fought the church by establishing schools and promoting a secular "indigenism," or nationalist

---

PRI   Institutional Revolutionary Party, ruled Mexico 1929–2000

pride in Mexico's native American heritage. Church authorities not only denounced public education but also backed an attempt to overthrow the government so that Calles could not take office. Calles survived only to face Church rejection of the Constitution of 1917. He sought revenge by enforcing the document's harshest anticlerical measures, including the shutting of Catholic schools. The bloody 1926–1927 Cristero Rebellion resulted, but Calles won. Obregón succeeded Calles in 1928, only to be assassinated by a Cristero fanatic right after his election. Calles ran Mexico as "maximum boss," fronted by three weak presidents until 1934. As he and his elite friends grew rich in the name of revolution, the poor masses went back to eating tortillas and wondering what everyone had died for. Artists such as the famous muralist Diego Rivera openly depicted the betrayal.

The Great Depression interrupted the feast of the so-called socialist millionaires and helped promote the program of reformer Lázaro Cárdenas, former governor (1928–1932) of Michoacán and head of the revolutionary party. Cárdenas was supported by Calles and handily won the presidency in 1934. He immediately set a new standard by halving his own salary and living modestly; he also slowly disempowered Calles and his supporters in the military. When the "maximum boss" reacted in 1936 he found himself on a plane to the United States as an exile. Cárdenas pursued land redistribution and restoration of ejidos as none of his predecessors had, but his most memorable act came on March 18, 1938, when he expropriated all of Mexico's oil reserves. This was economic nationalism of a truly revolutionary sort, and it provoked strong reactions from the United States and Great Britain. With the Depression not yet over and war looming in Europe, only words flew.

ECONOMIC AND OTHER NATIONALISMS

Resentment of foreign ownership of everything from oilfields to telegraph lines was hardly unique to revolutionary Mexico, and state takeovers of port facilities, railroads, power grids, and other key utilities were widespread in Latin America after 1900, though much more common during and after the Great Depression. The first takeovers were enacted in Uruguay and Argentina when exports filled state coffers just after the turn of the century, but the high tide of economic nationalism came after 1929, when Latin American nations dependent on primary exports watched their celebrated "comparative advantage" go up in smoke.

One observer of this phenomenon was Argentine economist Raúl Prebisch, who by working in the national treasury in the 1930s and studying trade statistics in the 1940s reached the conclusion that developing nations such as his suffered from "unequal exchange." The industrialized "center," he argued, whether Britain or the United States, was structurally fated (or so it seemed from observed patterns in wages, prices, and flows of capital) to recover from cyclical economic downturns far more rapidly than the primary goods-producing "periphery." The peripheral nations of Latin America therefore had to move closer to industrial self-sufficiency and state-managed finances to escape dependency on a progressively less rewarding international market. This market was much freer in theory, he argued, than it was in practice. Prebisch's thesis and recommendations, adopted by the U.N. Economic Commission for Latin America after 1950, had a profound impact throughout Latin America.

In Argentina, Prebisch's recommendations were only slowly and fitfully embraced, in part because he had served in government under the hated conservatives from 1930–1943. The new face of government at the end of this so-called Infamous Decade, and of compromise, belonged to Juan Domingo Perón, a military colonel and secretary of labor. He deftly shifted the potentially radical momentum of the urban working voters toward a more conservative, nationalist end. To many it was fascism with a populist veneer. Perón was a vocal admirer of Benito Mussolini, whom he had observed during a visit to Italy in the 1930s. After Perón was jailed during a 1945 coup, his supporters took over the streets of Buenos Aires and demanded his release. He promptly dropped the uniform on getting out and easily won the 1946 presidential election. None of the traditional players in Argentine politics knew what to make of this new phenomenon, which seemed neither radical nor conservative, nor entirely in the hands of its namesake. Whatever it was, **Peronism** became the most potent political force in Argentina after World War II. With "Juanito" came a cultural icon that eventually outshone him, his dear mistress (whom he married in 1945), Evita.

As a military man, Perón liked order. He preferred an Argentina where everyone was in his or her proper place, doing the assigned job, and not making waves. Dissenters, as during the Infamous Decade, were treated to cattle prods, high-pressure hoses, and other tortures by the Special Section of the Federal Police. Such harsh treatment of protesters was practically expected, as Argentina, like most Latin American nations in this period, was neither culturally accustomed nor judicially prepared to guarantee its citizens' basic civil rights. Under Perón, patriotism meshed with policy in the form of five-year economic plans. These included the kinds of state takeovers of utilities recommended by Prebisch but fell far short of punishing foreign investors as Cárdenas had in Mexico. Industry grew and with it a newly empowered working class happy to consume its own products. Pensions and other benefits kept both the working and middle classes on Perón's side. The very poor received charity from Evita's popular foundation.

Argentina's budget surplus of 1947 was used to pay off the entire national debt, which raised hopes for this new model of "inward-directed development." Unfortunately, 1949 marked a sharp reversal, with drastic jumps in inflation, drops in income, and droughts in the pampas. It appeared that Argentina's gains had only been possible due to the postwar restructuring of Europe and the United States. Despite denunciations of Yankee imperialism to stoke voters, Perón's brand

---

Peronism   Argentine political movement based on the ideas and programs of Juan Perón and his second wife Evita; also called Justicialism (mixing justice and socialism)

of economic nationalism had not gone so far as to nationalize key export industries such as meatpacking, still in the hands of Swift, Armour, and other multinational corporations, and virtually no attention was given to long-range concerns
such as agricultural efficiency, adequate transport infrastructure, and energy
self-sufficiency.

Still popular, Perón sought a second term, which required a constitutional
amendment. The press hounded him on this and other matters, so Perón, true
to his fascist leanings, took over the leading national paper, *La Prensa*. Having
granted women suffrage in 1947 at Evita's urging, Perón now counted on the
female vote. Leaner years were made sadder by the death of Evita from cancer
in the election year of 1952. Her cult became one of the few religious elements
of Peronism, which tended to clash with the Catholic Church.

Economic troubles, as well as Evita's death, eroded Perón's power, but he
retained a fiercely loyal core following. It would be their job to keep Peronism,
if not Perón himself, politically alive. Its essence he called *justicialismo*, something
like "social justice." After a series of unpopular policy reversals that included inviting foreign capital and freezing wages, plus more violent repression of dissenters than ever before, Perón was forced out by the military in 1955.

What followed were two decades of political and economic turmoil
marked by a steady rise in murderous violence, both by the state and its opponents. Peronists were kept at bay by the military while the formerly popular
Radical Party supplied weak presidential candidates who could be removed as
the armed forces saw fit. Perón's attempts at economic nationalism in the 1940s
may have been half-hearted, but they were almost entirely reversed after 1958,
in part thanks to pressure from a new post–World War II institution whose
influence was being felt all over Latin America: the International Monetary
Fund (IMF).

The U.S.-based IMF lent money to developing countries in exchange for
policies that limited inflation, reduced social spending, and opened the door
to foreign capital investment. With massive currency devaluation after 1966,
Argentina's industrial sector was rapidly eviscerated, wages dropped, and unemployment rose. This extraordinary reversal of the nation's fortunes made Raúl
Prebisch, still active in the academic world, seem like a prophet.

Strikes spread across the country, and insurgent violence took on a multi-
tude of forms. It was met with the kinds of repression and extrajudicial killings
that would only intensify in years to come. After a coup in 1970, and a subsequent military failure to calm the country, elections were called for 1973. Perón
was allowed to return, though not as a candidate. A Peronist won, however,
and he soon resigned to allow the people to choose their leader. They picked
Juan Perón in September of 1973, along with his third wife Isabel as both first
lady and vice president. Perón died in July 1974, leaving the untested Isabel in
charge of a boldly interventionist economic policy. Opposition erupted from all
sides as Argentina faced the aftermath of the 1973 global oil shock. Amid widespread bombings, kidnappings, and raids by right-wing death squads, Isabel was
removed by the military in 1976. As will be seen in the next chapter, the results
were grim both socially and economically.

Chile's trajectory in these same years offers some contrasts and parallels to Argentina's. Political and economic instability were both hallmarks of the era, but instead of a turn to a nationalist or "populist" leader or ideology, Chileans hewed more closely to traditional categories of right, left, and center. Even more so than in Argentina, economic nationalism was a core issue that divided the nation into pro- and anti-expropriation camps. There were other matters on the table, to be sure, but as in Argentina the resulting stalemate was resolved by an army takeover followed by years of harsh repression.

Back in 1920, Liberal president Arturo Alessandri had managed to absorb some of Chile's working-class elements in the mining and urban industrial sectors, but his outmoded ideas did not seem to please anyone. Few protested when the military took over in 1924, even though the coup leaders sharply curtailed labor rights. Alessandri returned with military support in 1925 but soon resigned in protest. The new regime crushed a nitrate workers' strike later that same year, and by 1927 it produced its own candidate, Colonel Carlos Ibáñez. As expected, he spent lavishly on the military and other pet projects until the stock market crash of 1929. Ibáñez was forced out by popular demand in 1931. A brief Socialist interlude was followed by the return of Arturo Alessandri, president from 1933–1939, now more authoritarian and economically liberal than ever. With his invitations to foreign capital, the export sector began to bounce back.

The normally fractious left formed a coalition, called the Popular Front, and put forth a candidate named Pedro Aguirre Cerda. Aguirre Cerda, a leader of the Radical Party, had only two years in the palace, resigning due to illness in 1941, but the Popular Front continued in power until 1948. Chilean politics meanwhile had taken a sharp left turn, mostly led by labor. Strikes in 1946–1947 crippled industry and transportation. The Radicals, in response to increasingly shrill demands from Communists and even the traditionally moderate Socialists, reacted with violent measures—although levels of violence never came close to those in Argentina, much less Colombia at this time (see Image and Word 13.1).

The far left was not so easily silenced, and after 1948 Chile entered a prolonged period of competitive party politics, dominated by such figures as the old military favorite, Carlos Ibáñez, who courted the IMF as Chile's economy suffered wild swings after World War II, and Jorge Alessandri, son of Arturo. The younger Alessandri was elected in 1958 on a joint Conservative-Liberal ticket (evidence of how little these parties now differed in approach). Other contenders were Salvador Allende, backed by a Socialist-Communist alliance, and Eduardo Frei, a Christian Democrat.

Like his father, Jorge Alessandri was a true economic liberal, but he did push for U.S. copper interests to invest more capital in processing plants in Chile (to add value to the product before it left the country, hence improving state revenues). This effort failed, and when it did it pushed the left to call for full nationalization of the copper industry, the kind of solution Mexico's Cárdenas or Argentina's Prebisch might have called for. Alessandri faced new pressures as the United States launched its own kind of preemptive aid program called the Alliance for Progress. Funds from this and other Washington-based anti-Communist initiatives were invested in highways, dams, and ports. A 1962 land

IMAGE AND WORD 13.1   The Bogotazo

In 1948, leading Colombian presidential candidate Jorge Eliécer Gaitán was assassinated in Bogotá, sparking riots by his supporters. Although the apparent killer was caught and slain by the mob, rumors spread that the government of President Ospina Pérez was responsible. Thousands died in the capital that night, and then the bipartisan violence spread across the country in waves, leading to a decade of torturing, assassination, and mass murder—known as *La Violencia* of 1948–1958. As in colonial times, urban riots were seen as highly symbolic. The riots that began La Violencia became known as the *Bogotazo*. A 1969 riot in Córdoba, Argentina, became known as the Cordobazo, and the worst riots in Venezuelan history, which also led to the death of thousands in Caracas in 1989, thus became known as the *Caracazo*.

reform bill was probably the most radical measure taken by Alessandri's government, but it hardly broke up the great haciendas of the Central Valley. Growing poverty in the countryside spurred massive migration to the cities, creating great slums in the capital.

With woman suffrage in 1949 and urban migration on the rise, Chilean voters became far more numerous and outspoken than ever before. They chose from rightist Conservative/Liberals, centrist Radicals, leftist Socialist/Communists, and reform-minded centrist Christian Democrats. The 1964 election was viewed by foreigners and Chileans alike as the first serious opportunity for the far left to win power. The right sensed this and went in with the Christian Democrats to paint Allende and his coalition as extremists with closer ties to Moscow and Havana than to average Chileans. The CIA lent Eduardo Frei's Christian Democratic campaign a hand, as did U.S. copper interests. Anaconda and Kennecott did not want to lose their mines to economic nationalists and with their help, the center-right, not the left, took the day. Frei's Christian Democrats pushed for modest reforms in the export structure (the state purchased a stake in Kennecott and Anaconda, for example) and land tenure, but the results of this so-called Revolution in Liberty were limited.

The 1970 election saw the center-right alliance fall apart, creating a new opportunity for the left. Allende, backed by the Socialist-Communist Popular Unity coalition, vigorously denounced the sellout policies of the Christian Democrats. The right put forth Jorge Alessandri again, but he had to contend not only with Allende but also a new Christian Democratic face, Radomiro Tomic. The result of this three-way race was a narrow plurality for Allende, just 36% of the popular vote. The question on everyone's minds was: Could this elected Marxist president survive in a hemisphere dominated by the fiercely anti-communist United States?

For three tumultuous years the answer was yes. Allende immediately used the power of the state to ensure that the economy yielded better living for most Chileans. Wages rose, public health care became available, schools were improved, and prices stabilized. The issue of copper nationalization had become popular, so much so that many Chileans called for the outright expulsion of the companies, not buyouts. It was accomplished in 1971. As nationalization in other sectors of the economy progressed, foreign investment (and aid money) disappeared.

Though the Nixon administration, and in particular Secretary of State Henry Kissinger, liked to portray it otherwise, Chile under Allende was no totalitarian state. Allende might have wished for more power, but he was a popularly elected president faced with an opposition congress. The result was something of a hamstrung revolution by 1972; the right was stunned but hardly dead, the centrists glib but still unsure of the future. The economy, feeling the spurs of the state for the first time, was bucking like a wild bronco. Copper prices fell, inflation soared, and a black market flourished as state price controls diverged from market dictates. Members of the old guard were happy to see Allende's try at economic nationalism fail.

Allende was an ambitious and arguably revolutionary leader, but he was no fool. Having survived for years in Chilean politics, he sought an alliance with the Christian Democrats. They turned him away. He then tried to reorganize the military to back him, but he was again rejected. His best military ally, Carlos Prats, a staunch constitutionalist, was forced to resign by fellow officers by mid-1973. He was replaced by General Augusto Pinochet. Courted by the CIA since at least 1972 and certain of U.S. support, Pinochet made his move and deposed Allende by force. (Prats was murdered while living in exile in Argentina in 1974.) What followed was nearly two decades of brutal repression under a right-wing police state that tortured, detained, and killed thousands of Chileans,

IMAGE AND WORD 13.2 **Father Vargas**

Leonard Mccombe/Time & Life Pictures/Getty Images

Getúlio Vargas governed Brazil in many different guises. First he was the military leader of a temporary government (1930–1934); second, he was a constitutional president elected by Congress (1934–1937); third, as fascism rose up in Europe, he ruled as a dictator (1937–1945); finally, he returned as a popularly elected constitutional president (1951–1954). The official photograph above was taken at the start of this final term of office. Vargas committed suicide while still president in 1954.

while throwing open the doors to foreign capital and ignoring social services. Economic nationalism had again been foiled.

Brazil, which also drifted in and out of military rule in the twentieth century, offers yet another interesting set of contrasts. The story begins with a man. Like Argentina's Juan Perón, Getúlio Vargas was a master politician, able to reinvent himself as the times demanded (see Image and Word 13.2). Yet even in his dictatorial phase, Vargas was an easy-going pragmatist, not an intolerant despot. With no clear platform of his own, Vargas tended to follow the reformist lead of Brazil's young military officer corps, the so-called *tenentes*, and although they fell apart as a political unit, their calls for nationalization vs. internationalization, public health and education initiatives, land and labor reform, and social security came to be the goals presented by Vargas. Such initiatives were hard to finance in the midst of a global depression, however, when coffee exports fell to approximately one third of pre-1929 levels. Prices more than halved and competition from Colombia and Central America, not to mention British East Africa and Dutch Indonesia, grew.

The first Vargas administration faced the hard times head on, careful to tend to the needs of the old São Paulo elite without giving them back their power. Valorization, or government hoarding of coffee to boost prices, continued, and some coffee was even burned in hopes of boosting prices more. Meanwhile, a shift toward other cash crops, such as cotton, became evident, even in traditional coffee states. Significantly, industrialization began to displace coffee in the overall scheme of things, a trend never reversed from this time forward in Brazil, even after coffee prices rose again during World War II. Industrialization was not quick enough to create a large proletariat ripe for communist teachings, but a powerful Communist group called the National Liberation Alliance called for "Bread, Land, and Liberty" after 1935, headed for a time by an old military rebel, Luis Carlos Prestes. When Vargas outlawed the movement a series of bloody incidents ensued, leading to a kind of "red scare" and persecution of Communists and suspected Communists.

Not to be outdone, a Fascist party appeared on the scene at about the same time, the so-called **Integralists**, with patriotic green shirts, sigma-inscribed armbands, upraised arms, and a shout of *ananê!* (something like "Hiawatha!"). Their motto was simple and ultra-nationalist: "God, country, and family." Democrats, Communists, Masons, and Jews were their sworn enemies. The Integralists had a strong base in immigrant-heavy São Paulo, and their principal spokesman was a Paulista novelist, Plinio Salgado, who beat Albert Camus to the title "The Stranger," his 1926 novel.

For Vargas, always a pragmatist, politics of this diverse kind was messy and distracting. He concocted a Communist, potentially Jewish plot to overthrow the government by violence, and on November 10, 1937, he declared a state of emergency. Even the fascists were appalled. Vargas now styled himself "the Father of the Poor," the populist dictator as the nation's dad. The family was now called the Estado Nôvo, or "the New State," and its internal enemies, such as the Communists and fascists, were sent to the prison island of Fernando Noronha.

"Father" Vargas's weapon was the military, which swelled with well-paid officers and enlisted men, absorbing state militias and consolidating federal power. Vargas himself sounded half-fascist, half-communist when he made statements such as, "The New State does not recognize the rights of the individual against the collective. Individuals do not have rights, they have duties. Rights belong to the collective!" Brazil became a close partner with Nazi Germany in the late 1930s, but when the United States entered World War II against the Axis powers, Brazil followed suit. The fascist streak was diffused by this course of events, and Vargas was due for a makeover.

Integralists   Brazilian fascist party of the 1930s

World War II was an important watershed in Brazilian history in ways that it was not in other parts of Latin America. Whereas Brazil had only marginally participated in World War I, it entered World War II with some force. Brazilians fought the Axis on land, at sea, and in the air, both in Europe and in the South Atlantic, and participants grew to admire the individualist grit and technological superiority of their giant neighbor to the north.

The road to Fordlândia was not an easy one, but war needs fueled industrialization. Industrialization fueled urbanization, and both trends created for the first time a genuine middle class and proletariat, two nontraditional power bases that Vargas exploited wisely. Workers were co-opted by the Ministry of Labor soon after the coup of 1930, while the middle class benefited from the policies of the Ministry of Education and by federal employment. The reforms proposed by the *tenentes* paid political dividends, particularly in these emerging sectors.

Brazil's population grew prodigiously under Vargas, from some 33 million in 1930 to nearly 46 million in 1945. Educational opportunities for a modern nation were expanded accordingly, and standards rose with the creation of the University of Rio de Janeiro in 1920 and, under Vargas, the University of São Paulo in 1934 and Federal University of Brazil (Rio) in 1938. Schools and universities were, in Vargas's mind, laboratories for nationalism, and national history and Portuguese language instruction were heavily emphasized. The new technologies of radio and cinema were similarly used to influence the illiterate majority, and a Department of Press and Propaganda busily filled the airwaves and screens with pro-government pronouncements. Despite manipulation of the press, Vargas was never the ham-handed dictator that his opponents made him out to be.

Industrialization took off, and one early champion of economic nationalism through industrial growth was Alberto Torres, a popular essayist who linked Brazil's (relative) backwardness to dependency on foreign markets, banks, and multinational corporations. Right or wrong, this economic nationalism argument, which would later lead to ISI policies, was a wave Vargas was willing to surf. It was easy to argue that Brazil must harness its resources and talent to join the league of industrialized nations as an equal rather than a dependent; it also gave Brazilians from every region a common (though undefined) foreign "enemy" to vanquish. Tariffs rose to nearly 40% by 1933, and moves toward nationalization of resources were well under way. The example of the Itabira iron ore deposits is illustrative: In the 1920s a North American named Percival Farquhar gained a vast concession in the iron fields, but the Brazilian government took it over in the 1930s, developing, after 1942, the state-owned Companhia Vale do Rio Doce. This one was a success, although it helped speed deforestation for charcoal production.

Another nationalization effort concerned petroleum. Unlike its neighbors, Brazil did not possess large or easily tapped oil reserves, but the issue was treated in a fashion similar to Bolivia and Mexico's nationalization campaigns of the late 1930s. Vargas made oil nationalization his platform in the early 1950s, and Petrobras was formed as a result in 1953. The first steel plant in Brazil was also a national endeavor, built during the previous Vargas administration at Volta

Redônda during World War II, going into operation in 1946, the year after Vargas's ouster.

Industry grew and diversified, such that Brazilian textiles began to be exported for the first time in quantity during World War II, exchanged for cash from war-needy developed nations. Brazil's large and growing internal consumer market was also an obvious target for industrial producers. Still, much of this population was too poor to buy much of anything, particularly expensive things, and transportation networks failed to keep pace with output. The first road linking Salvador da Bahia to Rio was only opened in 1939. A peculiarly Brazilian form of regionalism, partly a colonial legacy, seemed responsible for the country's uneven development riddle: industry was a southern states phenomenon, the northeast remained moribund, and the backcountry was still largely wilderness.

It was Vargas who first pushed for government aid in "taming" the interior, calling for a "March to the West" as early as the 1930s. One colonization scheme entailed 50-acre homesteads for willing families. The momentum established here would continue into the twenty-first century, with unprecedented environmental destruction and the elimination of native peoples as its most negative consequences. Vargas knew all too well that Brazil, in spite of its ambitious industrial program, was still a nation of peasants. In 1945, the end of Vargas's Estado Nôvo, 75% of Brazilians lived in the countryside, longing for land of their own to work and develop.

If authoritarianism and economic nationalism had been deemed necessary by most Brazilians during the Depression and World War II, a more popular, open-market approach was called for by war's end. Vargas seemed to be setting the stage for another coup in spite of elections set for December 1945, but the military instead removed him from office so that he could not interfere. Vargas retired to his country estate in Rio Grande do Sul to reinvent himself for the more civilian, cosmopolitan 1950s.

Vargas's new support base rested in two parties he helped form, the Social Democrats and the Workers' Party. His enemies congregated in the National Democratic Union party. It was a Social Democrat and ex-tenente, Eurico Dutra, who took the presidency in 1945, and since Vargas was linked to this party, he also won senate representation. Dutra reduced his presidency to something like a Communist witch-hunt, and Brazil's venerable communist party was outlawed by 1947 (it had only been legalized in 1945). Though successful in creating an atmosphere of hostility worthy of Joseph McCarthy, no one backed a second term for Dutra. The obvious candidate, though now nearing 70, was Getúlio Vargas.

For Brazil's favorite twentieth-century patriarch, autumn would not last long. Life as a democratically elected civilian, Vargas discovered, was nothing like that of an authoritarian *caudilho*. Policies could not be steamrolled across the nation, money could not be spent or borrowed freely, and critics could not be silenced without consequences. One such critic, Carlos Lacerda, was nearly assassinated on August 5, 1954, in Rio. His friend, an air force major, was killed by a stray bullet. An investigation pointed to Vargas, or at least the chief of his personal guard, and the military stepped in—as a matter of honor on behalf of one of their own—to depose the president on August 24. Vargas, not wanting to face humiliation, committed suicide. His rambling suicide note revealed a conflicted personality and an ego the size of Amazônas. Vice President João Café Filho served the remaining 17 months of Vargas's term.

The 1955 elections saw Vargas's spirit ("Getulism," never as strong as Peronism) live on in the presidency of Juscelino Kubitschek and Vice President João Goulart. "JK," as Kubitschek was known, was a native of Minas Gerais with support from the Social Democrats. Goulart was supported by Labor. The two came into office with a comfortable margin of the popular vote, but the transition had to be guaranteed by the armed forces, a sign of democracy's weakness. This was a time of intense conflict between the army, navy, and air force, presaging trouble to come. JK's first job was placating the military with posts in Petrobras and other favors and calming down the labor unions. Getulism was at this stage more about interests created under Vargas hanging onto gains than any particular ideological concerns such as economic nationalism. Like Vargas himself, Getulism was about survival through clientelism, or cementing personal loyalties, not ideas.

Still, JK was a visionary and a highly effective politician. He fought bureaucracy the only way he could, by creating more bureaucracy, mostly through his "Programa de Metas," or Program of Goals. (Goals were especially appealing in a soccer-obsessed society. Led by Pelé, Brazil won the World Cup in 1958 and 1962.) One of JK's worries was the northeast, a region of grinding poverty and corrupt elites. As in the western United States, the northeast became the site of massive water control projects aimed at reviving agricultural production. Locals began to rely on the state for aid, but they also blamed it for failure. JK was more ambivalent on such matters than Vargas; he was a strong advocate of state intervention in the economy but not of total state control. He liked foreign investment and technology.

Unfortunately, the expanding Brazilian electorate was still unskilled in the business of civics. Education remained an urban conceit while the population remained rural—urban parents sent their kids to school, the rural majority kept them home to help keep food on the table. The result was that illiteracy, though declining into the 1960s, remained pitifully high, especially in the depressed northeast.

Through it all, the Catholic Church, always a key player in Brazilian life, began to push for social reform. The movement known generally as Liberation Theology, discussed in the next chapter, was a product of the 1950s and 1960s, and it stirred some peasants to call for land and labor reforms (birth control was not on the list of desiderata). In 1962 Ação Popular (AP, or Popular Action) grew out of a blend of the new nationwide student movement and the JUC, or Catholic University Youth, movement. Ranking churchmen were mostly in support of these trends, although some conservatives saw them as too radical.

Kubitschek and Goulart's "developmental nationalism" amounted to moderate state intervention aimed at dealing with rapid population growth and other problems. The Superior Institute of Brazilian Studies (ISEB), founded in 1955, sought solutions to dependency and remedies for rural poverty. Academics of the ISEB split on ideological grounds, some leaning toward radical solutions involving such un-Brazilian notions as Maoist purges, and others following a more neo-classical, yet still nationalist, reforming approach. Many read and admired Raúl Prebisch. The split in opinions would in many ways play out in Brazilian politics up to (and after) the coup of 1964.

Economically, Brazil rode a wave of prosperity in the later 1950s, and the government spent like there was no tomorrow. The optimism of those years was epitomized by the construction of the new capital, Brasília, begun in 1957 and completed in 1960. The winged city of the future was designed by Lúcio Costa, and many of its buildings were the product of one of modern architecture's greatest minds, Oscar Niemeyer. Brasília, following the dream of earlier presidents and intellectuals, was located in the interior state of Goiás, closer to the geographical center of the nation. After 1960, due in part to the growth of highways in the wake of Brasília, the nation would be a nation on wheels and a major producer of cars. The effects of this process were disastrous for the natural environment, and the policies of colonization that emerged from these years would lead to the massive destruction of the Amazon rain forest.

None of this was yet on people's minds, and profits from industry rose 80% between 1955 and 1961. Steel production doubled. Much higher gains were made in the electricity, communications, and transportation sectors. Brazil's per capita Gross Domestic Product in the 1950s was far ahead of the rest of Latin America, which, when added to the 1958 and 1962 World Cup victories (see Image and Word 13.3), prompted many rumors of miracles.

Much capital was invested in making cars in the São Paulo suburbs, and soon Brazil was supplying not only its own market but also those of most South American neighbors. Brazil's big three were Volkswagen, Ford, and General Motors. The rise of the automotive industry had the same effect as in the postwar United States: It freed individuals and killed public transportation and the railroads. Politically, autoworkers rose to prominence, albeit slowly. It took time to adapt strategies. What upset workers were government plans to trim benefits in response to inflation, among other things. What kept them from acting out too much was JK's break with the IMF in 1959. Communists came in to join the celebrations, but this only signaled problems down the road. Interestingly, the overall political tide had turned against JK and his team, who were now seen as corrupt clients of a fat but irresponsible state.

Growing pains were felt elsewhere. The backcountry, particularly the moribund northeast, continued to be an overpopulated sea of poverty; the government rushed to implement development programs, but this came during the 1961–1964 Goulart presidency, which was cut short by a coup. The main political innovation here was the formation of peasant leagues, many of them influenced by Pernambuco lawyer Francisco Julião. Most fought against sharecropping demands, eviction, and other abuses. Goulart came through in 1963 with laws protecting the rural proletariat, at least. Big landholders were meanwhile encouraged by higher prices for their goods due to massive urban growth. The cities produced their own horrors, and hunger and desperation were never described so poignantly as in Carolina Maria de Jesús's 1960 *Child of the Dark*. Most Brazilians, in a word, did not share the postwar bounties in spite of some fairly radical government initiatives.

IMAGE AND WORD 13.3 The King

Robert Riger/Getty Images

Edson Arantes do Nascimento, known worldwide as Pelé, won his first World Cup as a striker for Brazil in 1958, when he was 17. He is the only soccer player to have played for three World Cup–winning teams. Called King Pelé or simply The King, he is a global ambassador for soccer and for Brazil and is viewed as a national treasure at home. Although some have criticized him for his optimistic views on Brazilian race relations, he has been credited with helping to open doors for Afro-Brazilians in the second half of the twentieth century.

Some of this effort was derailed during the brief presidency of Jânio da Silva Quadros, an anti-Vargas candidate who won with a wide popular base of support in 1960. Quadros was an oddball and self-styled outsider who promised to clean up. He started off with the grave mistake of outlawing bikinis, though this bogus moralizing gesture did not seal his fate. Quadros is best remembered for his policy of disengagement in the era of the cold war, but his support of Castro's Cuba v. the U.S. Bay of Pigs invasion in 1961 raised heckles from some, including that hard-bitten journalist that Vargas's people had failed to kill, Carlos Lacerda.

When Quadros honored a visiting Che Guevara with the Order of the Southern Cross, Lacerda, governor of Guanabara State (which surrounds Rio), denounced the president on national television as a subversive. Quadros surprised everyone by abruptly resigning. Even Brazilian historians remain unsure why, but probably this gesture amounted to a bad political bet on Quadros's part. He thought he'd be asked back, but he wasn't. Vargas's protégé, João "Jango"

Goulart, stepped into the void after some negotiating with the army and soon led the nation down the path to conflict.

It was not that Goulart was a fool, but he got off to a bad start and only continued to miscalculate. He came to the presidency at the height of the cold war, and as luck would have it, he was in China when the office became his. He only got in because of a brother-in-law from Vargas's home state, and he did not possess full executive power until 1963. Inflation hit harder each year, and parties and factions hardened in their positions. Goulart swung left just as the country swung right. Attempts at Vargas-style publicity stunts just made him appear desperate, and unions looked more and more like bully clients. If ever "powerful forces," as Vargas had liked to say, conspired against a Brazilian president, it was now. By early 1964 a widely supported military coup was seen almost as a relief. As in Argentina and Chile, Brazilian politics hit an impasse thanks to a widespread disinclination to compromise. The country would now have to live under repressive military rule for more than 20 years.

THE CUBAN REVOLUTION

Cuba had long produced the world's best cigars, but even in the twentieth century the big money was still in sugar. The island met 10%–25% of world demand in the first decades after the Spanish-American War, but monoculture, as we have seen elsewhere, entailed dependency on world markets and problems of instability. Profits, as in other export sectors, were mostly taken by U.S. corporate investors in the sugar sector, leaving little behind to help develop the island. By 1912 big sugar companies such as the American Sugar Refining Company (later renamed Domino) owned 10% of Cuba, by 1925 almost 18%, and now 184 massive mills operated. U.S.-owned mills produced 75% of Cuban sugar by 1928, and about the same amount went to U.S. markets. This was agribusiness at its most efficient, but it was in no way structured to benefit the Cuban people.

An unintended consequence of king sugar's reign was the formation of a Cuban working class with shared interests and goals. Whereas nations such as Peru remained divided between highlands and lowlands, Quechua speakers and Spanish speakers, conservatives and radicals, Cuba experienced a unifying trajectory that linked urban and rural interests and cut across racial lines. This is not to say that Cuba, which had by U.S. standards a black majority, was free of racism, but class issues could and did prevail. U.S. companies' consolidation of the sugar industry replaced the traditional peasantry with a wage-dependent but chronically unemployed rural proletariat. As a result, urban slums often were home to rural cane workers trying to make it through the off-season. The harvest took them back to the fields for about three months, there to meet with workers living in rural shantytowns called *bateyes*. This punishing seasonal displacement and itinerancy laid the groundwork for the rise of a revolutionary consciousness.

The first conflicts came in the 1920s, when post–World War I prices for sugar plummeted. Workers absorbed much of the shock. Then, in the midst of the Great Depression, tariff agreements were restructured. At issue were U.S. sugar beet production, refinery competition, and Republican jingoism, and the Smoot-Hawley tariff was passed in 1930, punishing Cuban sugar (workers) again. President Franklin Roosevelt and the Democrats largely reversed this policy with a Reciprocal Trade Agreement in 1934, but the new policy cut both ways. Cuba now had a guaranteed share of the U.S. sugar market, but the price to pay for it was political and monetary domination from outside. Embers of discontent were fanned by increasingly corrupt politics. Nattily dressed U.S. tourists in search of rum, rumba, and sex only added to the insults.

The first caudillo of the sugar years was Gerardo Machado, elected president in 1925. Machado set a pattern of dictatorship that survived his ouster in 1933. In essence, Machado represented the status quo, and all opposition, including students, workers, and stymied entrepreneurs, was put down violently. The United States, which still effectively controlled the island, did nothing. A general strike in 1933 coincided with FDR's assumption of power, and Machado saw the writing on the wall and left town. Ramón Grau San Martín, a leftist university professor, emerged at the top of the new political wave, backed by young Turks in the military such as Sergeant Fulgencio Batista. But as U.S. ships took up positions offshore, Batista aborted the revolution. A turncoat, Grau San Martín returned to serve as president under the watchful eye of Batista from 1944–1948. The anger of the left, the middle, and even some on the right was only contained by the brutal repression unleashed by Fulgencio Batista, particularly in his years as dictator, 1952–1959.

One of many dissidents was Fidel Castro, educated son of Spanish immigrants. After some experience abroad, most notably in Colombia in the midst of the 1948 *Bogotazo*, the urban riot that followed the assassination of Jorge Eliécer Gaitán (see Image and Word 13.1), Castro launched a rather amateurish attack on a military barracks in Santiago, on the southeast coast (see Map 13.1). Fidel and brother Raúl were later tried and jailed for the Moncada barracks attack, and its date, July 26, 1953, and defense, the "History Will Absolve Me" speech, would become revolutionary icons.

Released less than a year later in a whimsical amnesty act by Batista, the Castro brothers went to Mexico to plan the next move. They set out for Cuba in 1956 in a broken-down yacht called the *Granma*, accompanied by a young Argentine radical and physician named Ernesto "Che" Guevara, who, like Fidel, had traveled Latin America and witnessed his share of injustice (see Image and Word 13.4). Of 82 men landed, 70 were killed or captured. The remainder, including the three leaders, escaped to the Sierra Maestra mountains of Cuba's southeast. Batista led everyone to believe that the rebels were dead, but in early 1957 a 57-year-old reporter for the *New York Times*, Herbert Matthews, filed an interesting series of dispatches. Suddenly the world saw photos of Fidel and his comrades, alive, armed, and smiling. Matthews was sympathetic to the rebel cause, and his reports breathed new life into the movement.

The rebels slowly gained the tacit support of surrounding peasants, but Fidel and his followers knew the movement's success was in the cities. A planned

M A P 13.1 Central America and the Caribbean in the Twentieth Century

strike in Havana in April 1958 did not take place, so the rebels decided to make their move. They were aided by the collapse of Batista's forces in the Sierra Maestra, along with cross-class resentment of the government's increasingly repressive tactics in the cities. The campaign waged by the 26th of July Movement, as it came to be known, was in many ways a war for public opinion. A last-ditch effort by Batista to have a front man elected in his stead in late 1958 failed as most voters stayed home. The United States again did nothing. Batista stuffed an airplane with money and relatives and celebrated the New Year in the Dominican Republic. Fidel and his bearded band of guerrillas then marched in, entering Havana amid jubilant celebration.

Punctuated by public relations coups in the United States and brutal retaliation against Batista supporters, 1959 was a curious year. Fidel was acutely aware of U.S. fears of communism, so he was careful not to bring his politics to the fore. As elections were canceled and agrarian reform took on radical appearances, however, many initial supporters began to express grave doubts. Conflict with the United States was on the horizon.

With an eye to the north, Castro boldly aligned with the Soviet Union, nationalized resources and industries, and set about launching programs for land redistribution, education, health care, and many other things. This extreme economic nationalism resulted in a U.S. trade embargo, offset somewhat in 1960 by

IMAGE AND WORD 13.4   **The Castro Brothers**

In these symbolic photographs: Raúl Castro (top center) looks to his brother Fidel (top left), who is talking to Che Guevara (ca. 1959); a half-century later, as Fidel's health began to fail him, he turned increasingly to Raúl (seen above, right, in 2007; the following year, Fidel turned power over to his brother). (See Image and Word 15.1 for more Guevara and Castro images.)

Soviet offers. On the home front, support for the new regime was reinforced by the formation of Committees for the Defense of the Revolution, and a new civil defense militia swelled to 500,000 in a population of 6.7 million in 1960. Literacy campaigns, wage increases, price freezes, and other such boons cemented support among the poor.

Meanwhile, U.S. politics began to reflect growing concern about Cuba. The 1960 presidential race between Richard M. Nixon and John F. Kennedy included fierce debate about containing Soviet influence in the hemisphere, and the defining moments of Kennedy's subsequent presidency included the abortive Bay of Pigs invasion of April 1961 (planned in Eisenhower's administration) and the missile crisis of October 1962, a showdown that ended with Nikita Khrushchev's reluctant withdrawal of missile installments in Cuba. To Castro's dismay, Cuba was reduced to the status of pawn in a bigger chess game between superpowers.

At home, the Revolution focused on economic change, but it would come neither easily nor cheaply. Che Guevara, the great guerrilla fighter, proved less adept at managing the economy—keeping in mind that the U.S. trade embargo was no small obstacle. The idea was to move away from sugar monoculture and into industry, as prescribed by Marx and his followers in Europe, not to mention Raúl Prebisch, but the move made little economic sense, even within the Soviet bloc.

In what seemed an ironic twist, Soviet economists pushed Cuba back into sugar. Che resigned his post and Fidel committed the nation in 1963 to a distant goal: to reach 10 million tons of sugar production by 1970. The goal would prove a chimera, as would Che's goal of internationalizing the Cuban Revolution, particularly in Latin America. The pragmatic approach of economist Carlos Rafael Rodríguez was tried for a time, then replaced in 1966 by Che Guevara's more stridently idealist, quasi-Maoist approach. Che met his death in the Bolivian backcountry in 1967 while trying to repeat the Cuban uprising, but Fidel still pushed for the 10-million-ton year, compensated by "moral rewards." The harvest was massive, yielding 8.5 million tons, but the disappointment was almost as heavy.

After this disappointment, Fidel took responsibility with an exhausting mea culpa speech entitled "Let the Shame Be Welcome." He then decided to take a more Soviet approach to the economy, building in incentives for skilled and innovative personnel, opening up some new trade ties with the West, and investing in education and medicine. The U.S. embargo still stung deeply, however. In political terms, openness was not the order of the day, and critics were silenced or made to confess "crimes against the Revolution" in public humiliation ceremonies. Cuba in the 1970s was totalitarian in the Orwellian sense, and many foreign sympathizers became less hopeful of the nation's future.

By the 1980s Cubans were so steeped in revolutionary thought and policy that one could genuinely argue for a near-totalizing cultural transformation. It soon became evident this was not quite the case, but both pro- and anti-Castro propaganda played up robot-like conformity. Economically, Cuba was more dependent on Soviet markets and aid than ever, and though it remains to be proved more adequately by historians, Cuba became a political dependency as well. Cuban troops were sent to Angola and Ethiopia in the 1970s and 1980s in response to Soviet initiatives, and some have argued that the price of dependency on the USSR was as taxing as previous ties to the United States. The difference, of course, was that the Soviets never owned Cuba or tried to subject it to imperial rule.

On the positive side, Cuba under Castro succeeded in wiping out illiteracy, improving education, providing all citizens with basic health care, and meeting basic nutritional requirements across the board. In a region still marked by high infant mortality, grinding urban and rural poverty, endemic disease, chronic malnutrition, and appalling shortcomings in education, Cuba was, by the 1980s, a miracle of development. All this was accomplished despite the U.S. embargo. Much, though not all, was lost with the break-up of the Soviet Union after 1989 and subsequent economic crisis. The availability of food, housing, and energy all became chronic problems, and these and other shortcomings fueled the 1980 exodus known as the Mariel boatlift, in which over 100,000 Cubans fled to the United States, with aid from the exile community of Miami. A brief opening for small-scale agricultural entrepreneurialism was reversed in 1986 (a policy that seemed to hearken back to Mao when Russia was poised to drop Marxism altogether). Still, the 1980s was a lost decade for Latin America generally, and average Cubans continued to live longer, healthier lives than most Brazilians or Mexicans.

The 1990s brought hard times to Cuba, but despite the evaporation of Soviet aid and strengthening of the U.S. trade embargo in 1996, the Castro regime held on. Other nations did not share the U.S. policy of strangling Cuba, and investment flowed in from many quarters, much of it in mining and tourism. Canada and Europe began sending jets full of sun-, rum-, and sex-starved tourists, and Venezuela replaced the Soviet Union as the key supplier of oil. Relations between Cuba and Venezuela became increasingly close after the rise of President Hugo Chávez, who in 2006 began trying to take his "Bolivarian Revolution" hemispheric (see Chapter 15). As his health began to decline considerably, Cuban President Fidel Castro began paving the way for a successor. His younger brother Raúl officially took over in 2008, nearly 50 years after the start of the revolution.

THE NICARAGUAN REVOLUTION

U.S. interference in Nicaragua dated to the William Walker episode of the mid-1850s, but it took new shape in 1909 when Liberal dictator José Santos Zelaya was unseated. Nicaragua thus joined Haiti, the Dominican Republic, Cuba, and Panama on the list of effectively occupied zones under Theodore Roosevelt's "rough-riding" corollary to the Monroe Doctrine. Resistance was sporadic but most vehemently led by Augusto César Sandino, who headed a temporarily successful guerrilla war, then a political war, until his murder in 1932. He became an instant national hero.

The responsible figure was the head of the U.S.-supported Nicaraguan National Guard, Anastasio "Tacho" Somoza García. Somoza removed a sitting Liberal president in 1937 and took the reins of power. The next four decades were dominated by Somozas, ending with the Sandinista-led Nicaraguan Revolution of 1979. Tacho was assassinated in 1956, but his son, Luis Somoza Debayle, was quickly elected in 1957. An insider named René Schick was elected in 1963. When Luis Somoza died of a heart attack in 1967, his brother, Anastasio Somoza Debayle, head of the National Guard, took over. This Somoza was as corrupt and hated as any dictator in the hemisphere, but only a 1972 earthquake undermined Somoza's remaining support base. A cross-class alliance was in the making.

As in Cuba under Batista, the tyrannical ways of the dictator made armed resistance both necessary and popular, and given the U.S. tendency to support such leaders for their anti-communist commitment, the movement was likely to swing far to the left. Three groups, the peasant-led Prolonged Popular War (or GPP), the more urban Proletarios, and the moderate Terceristas, joined to form the Sandinista National Liberation Front, or FSLN, after the 1972 earthquake. Under pressure from numerous fronts and with few friends in his own camp, Anastasio Somoza took a vacation in Miami in 1979. He was assassinated in Paraguay in 1981.

At first, the United States was sympathetic to the Sandinistas and even sent aid to the new government. As in the Dominican Republic under Trujillo, the dictator himself owned so much land that land reform was made easy for the Sandinistas. Implementing educational and health programs was first on the list of desiderata, and initially this was done with a unique blend of U.S., Western European, and Cuban (but not Soviet) aid. But Jimmy Carter's good neighbor politics were soon replaced with the old-fashioned anti-communism of Ronald Reagan.

The Reagan years were like a dreamy 1950s time warp for many Americans, but for Nicaraguans they were a time of great struggle, warfare, and extreme economic hardship. The long and bloody Contra War, based in Honduras and funded by the United States, drained the treasury and annoyed many of the Sandinistas' early supporters with its turn to martial law and Soviet alignment. An election in 1990 saw Violeta Barrios de Chamorro, of the National Opposition Union, elected president. This was much to the Sandinistas' chagrin, but it was to their credit that their armed revolution had spawned a democracy and that they stepped peacefully into the role of opposition party.

Barrios de Chamorro met with limited success in turning things around, and despite massive inputs of foreign aid and efforts at demilitarization, old disputes festered openly. With democracy already weak, Hurricane Mitch, which hit in 1998, just after Barrios de Chamorro's term ended, was more than insult to injury. Thousands died in massive mudslides in Chinandega Province, and hundreds of thousands fled the country, some through Guatemala and Mexico to the United States, others to neighboring Costa Rica (see Map 13.1). Discontent with government responses to this and other disasters, as well as the failure of neoliberal policies to improve living standards, helped former Sandinista leader Daniel Ortega win reelection by a narrow plurality in 2006. Ortega also managed to reinvent himself as an anti-abortion, born-again Catholic. In 2008 he openly embraced Venezuelan president Hugo Chávez, broke ties with Colombia's president Álvaro Uribe, and offered medical support to FARC guerrillas wounded in a Colombian air attack in Ecuador. In some ways a symbol of Latin American politics in the first decade of the twenty-first century, Ortega the one-time guerrilla had managed to refashion himself as a civilian president with his own mix of leftist, rightist, and celebrity credentials.

FAILED REVOLUTIONARY MOVEMENTS

Revolutionary movements sprouted all over Latin America in the wake of the Cuban Revolution of 1959. Most advocated violence, although a few were peaceful. Rebels and other opposition movements in Argentina and Chile were nearly exterminated by the military and police during the Dirty Wars, as were those of El Salvador and Guatemala. Others emerged but faced less organized or effective opposition in Mexico, Venezuela, Colombia, Bolivia, Peru, Uruguay, and Brazil. Some, such as the ERP of Argentina and neighboring Tupamaros in Uruguay and ELN in Bolivia, maintained with each other contact across international borders and provided each other refuge. Cuba also helped, and Che Guevara's attempt to foment revolution in rural Bolivia led to his death in 1967. Ferreting out and destroying these international revolutionaries was a major aim of the U.S.-funded and Chile-based Operation Condor, begun soon after the 1973 coup.

Who were the revolutionaries? As a general rule, they did not come from the peasantry or working classes but rather the educated and urban middle class. Many were college students; this was true at least of the leadership. In cases that met with some success, such as the Shining Path of Peru and Colombia's National Liberation Army, rank-and-file revolutionaries were effectively recruited from among peasants and urban workers. Women joined men in nearly every case and not just in noncombat positions. Several outstanding female guerrilla leaders, such as the Colombian FARC's "Karina," who gave up arms in 2008 after 20 years of fighting, became legendary in their own time. Former leftist guerrilla leader Dilma Roussef was elected president of Brazil in 2010.

According to many observers, what caused most of Latin America's late-twentieth-century revolutionary movements to fail was their inability to establish common goals—and therefore trust—with the poor masses they sought to liberate. Peasants were particularly difficult to convince when it came to "raising class consciousness." Most country folk, indigenous, black, and mixed, were wisely reluctant to risk their lives for a utopian cause proposed by idealistic, young city slickers who might suddenly change their minds and leave the consequences to those stuck on the land. Barriers of language and culture, furthermore, not to mention widespread devotion to Catholicism, if not always Church authorities, often obscured what outsiders took to be natural solidarities of class.

Peaceful revolutionary movements were rarer. Although its epitaph may be premature, a Catholic revolutionary movement known as Liberation Theology rose and fell in Latin America between 1968 and about 1991. Beginning in the

1960s, young and energetic members of the Catholic clergy started to call for a return to Christianity's earliest roots. They argued that the Church in Latin America had become more an instrument of the rich than an advocate of the poor. Some even regarded this as a colonial legacy that needed to be overcome. Others were more interested in the future of the Church. Rather than let the region's urban and rural masses suffer in silence or join atheist rebels, the Church should step in to go beyond simple charity and focus on sustained class uplift in some organized way.

The response after a 1968 conference of Latin American bishops held in Medellín, Colombia, was to create "Christian Base Communities" in both city and countryside (similar to those in El Salvador and elsewhere; see Image and Word 13.5). Priests in these communities, which sprouted all over Latin America, from the *favelas* of Brazil to the coffee farms of Nicaragua, mixed orthodox Catholic teachings with Marxist-inspired analysis of political economy. Most priests did not espouse violence as a means to achieve their ends, but some recalled the spirit of Mexican independence leaders Miguel Hidalgo and José María Morelos, activist priests who had felt compelled to urgent action in desperate times.

In retrospect, the right's reaction to liberation theology seems surprisingly harsh, but at the time anyone who advocated programs for the poor while denouncing hacienda owners and foreign capitalists ran the risk of being branded a subversive. Priests throughout Brazil were jailed and tortured by the military regime that ran the country from 1964–1985, and similarly violent reactions swept Central America beginning in the late 1970s. When proponents of liberation theology joined the revolution in Nicaragua, some in the region felt their worst fears were being realized. The oligarchy in El Salvador felt so threatened by Archbishop Romero's critique of their corruption, violence, and connection to U.S. military forces that he was assassinated while holding mass in 1980 (see Image and Word 13.5). The decline of liberation theology came about not as a result of repression but rather the fall of the Soviet Union and general discrediting of Marxism and revolutionary socialism. Pope John Paul II, who died in 2007, proved to be a major force in eliminating liberation theology's supporters throughout Latin America and other parts of the developing world.

Latin America's twentieth-century revolutions, failed or successful, reveal a pattern of growing popular discontent with both the conservative and liberal projects of the nineteenth century. The first century after Independence had been marked by political chaos and disenfranchisement, the wholesale export of resources to benefit foreigners, and the stunning enrichment of tiny oligarchies. The liberal promise of improved fortunes for all as a result of comparative advantage had not panned out. Responses to this failure, made painfully evident by the Great Depression, ranged from revolutionary insurrection in Mexico to a massive co-opting of the working class in Argentina. Despite apparently radical changes, both departures from the past entailed new betrayals.

Economic nationalism, whether in large, industrializing countries such as Brazil or tiny, underdeveloped ones such as Nicaragua, also failed to live up to promises. State management of resources and utilities was not always corrupt or inefficient, but just as often it was both. The dearth of competition encouraged cronyism and gave no incentive to good service. Industrialization for the internal

IMAGE AND WORD 13.5   Death of an Archbishop

AP Photo

Although most of the church hierarchy in El Salvador continued to support the ruling oligarchy and its army-backed regime, a number of priests embraced what Archbishop Oscar Romero (above) called "the preferential option for the poor." In the late 1970s, hundreds of Christian Base Communities sprouted up, combining religious study with discussion of social and economic problems. In response, leaflets appeared in the capital with the slogan "Be a Patriot! Kill a Priest!" Right-wing death squads and governmental security forces murdered seven priests between 1977 and 1979, and in 1980 Romero himself was assassinated while delivering a sermon, probably murdered by a military officer. Massive demonstrations at his funeral were met with yet another massacre of civilians by the military. This was followed by the slaughter of the population of the entire village of El Mozote by a U.S.-trained battalion in 1981. Nevertheless, Romero's martyrdom for the opposition cause catalyzed the struggle against the regime. Despite the massive influx of U.S. military and financial support under the Reagan-Bush administrations (1980–1992), and the brutalization of Salvadorans by their own government, the opposition (led by the FMLN) were able to gain and hold territory and fight the government to a stalemate by 1990. A 1992 peace treaty did not produce the revolution that many in the FMLN had sought, but it brought the civil war to an end, demilitarized the country, made possible the kinds of popular mobilization and activism that had been suppressed for 60 years, and went a long way to emancipating women. Converted into a political party, the FMLN were finally elected to power in 2009.

market alone was rarely worth the trouble, especially when multiple economic shocks exacerbated wage instability and spurred inflation. Often state monopolies and protectionist policies only stimulated contraband trade, which in turn eroded popular respect for state agents. It is difficult to say what path would have worked best, but even the celebrated Argentine economist Raúl Prebisch had trouble solving the riddle of twentieth-century Latin American economics.

KEEP READING

Two superb novels of the Mexican Revolution are Mariano Azuela, *The Underdogs* (written in 1915) and Carlos Fuentes, *The Death of Artemio Cruz* (written in 1962).

Recommended works by historians include Ann Farnsworth-Alvear, *Dulcinea in the Factory: Myths, Morals, Men, and Women in Colombia's Industrial Experiment, 1905–1960* (2000); James P. Brennan, ed., *Peronism and Argentina* (1998); Gustavo Gorriti, *The Shining Path: A History of the Millenarian War in Peru* (1999); Jeffrey L. Gould, *To Lead as Equals: Rural Protest and Political Consciousness in Chinandega, Nicaragua, 1912–1979* (1990); Alan Knight, *The Mexican Revolution*, 2 vols. (1986); Robert M. Levine, *Father of the Poor? Vargas and His Era* (1998); William Beezley and Colin MacLachlan, *Mexicans in Revolution, 1910–1946: An Introduction* (2009); Steven Niblo, *Mexico in the 1940s: Modernity, Politics, and Corruption* (1999); Steve J. Stern, *Shining and Other Paths: War and Society in Peru, 1980-1995* (1995); Perez-Stable, Marifeli, *The Cuban Revolution: Origins, Course, and Legacy*, 2nd ed. (2003); Timothy Wickham-Crowley, *Guerrillas and Revolution in Latin America: A Comparative Study of Insurgents and Regimes since 1956* (1992); John Womack Jr., *Zapata and the Mexican Revolution* (1968); Thomas C. Wright, *Latin America in the Era of the Cuban Revolution* (1991); Mark Danner, *The Massacre at El Mozote* (1994); Greg Grandin, *Fordlandia: The Rise and Fall of Henry Ford's Forgotten Jungle City* (2009).

14

✳

Authoritarianism
and Its Discontents

The Dirty Wars of the Southern Cone

**Insurgency and Repression
in Central America**

**One-Party Rule and Repression
in Mexico**

**Dictatorship in Haiti and the
Dominican Republic**

Creative Counterpoints

"If and when the Chilean military decided to undertake a coup, they would not need U.S. Government assistance or support to do so successfully nor are they likely to seek such support." So concluded members of a secret CIA meeting on Chile in October 1972. U.S. embassy officials in the capital of Santiago had just offered an assessment of a likely leader of such a coup, General Augusto Pinochet. They found him ambitious and small-minded, a potentially malleable ally. On September 11, 1973, the day on which Pinochet and others toppled the regime of democratically elected President Salvador Allende, a CIA official sent a memo to U.S. Secretary of State Henry Kissinger that began: "We are forwarding for your information the attached memorandum on a possible request for U.S. Government aid from a key officer of the Chilean military group planning to overthrow President Allende."

U.S. support for the Pinochet regime and similar right-wing Latin American dictatorships from the 1950s to the 1990s remains a subject of intense debate. Documents, memoirs, and exhumed corpses are still coming to light, and charges are still being filed. In 1998 Spanish judge Baltasar Garzón nearly managed to have Augusto Pinochet extradited from Great Britain, where he was being treated for cancer. Had the British honored the Spanish request, Pinochet would

TIMELINE	
1929–1961	Trujillo dictatorship in the Dominican Republic
1954	U.S.-organized coup in Guatemala, leading to decades of civil war and military rule
1956–1986	Dictatorships of Papa Doc and Baby Doc Duvalier in Haiti
1960s	Dawn of the Latin American Boom in literature, the New Song and MPB in music, and the Third Cinema movement
1964–1985	Military-backed dictatorship in Brazil
1965	United States invades the Dominican Republic
1968	The Tlatelolco Massacre in Mexico City
1973–1988	General Pinochet's dictatorship in Chile
1976–1983	Military dictatorship in Argentina
1980s	Civil war in most of Central America
1982	Gabriel García Márquez wins Nobel Prize for Literature
1982	Malvinas/Falklands War between Britain and Argentina

have been tried for the murder of Spanish citizens who were detained in the military sweeps he ordered in the 1970s and 1980s. In Chile and many other countries where such repression took place, the search for truth and reconciliation continues.

The riddle of late-twentieth-century Latin American politics is how a region so accustomed to popular protest, open debate, and accommodation slipped into a pattern of violent repression not seen since the worst days of the nineteenth-century caudillos. How was it that citizens' civil rights evaporated so quickly and thoroughly, to resurface only after decades of violence and intimidation? The authoritarian regimes that typified the region in the era of the cold war seem an aberration in retrospect, but for a time they appeared to all but define politics in Latin America since independence. One question that concerns modern researchers: How important was the U.S. role? Would all of this have happened if U.S. anti-communist policies had not led to financial and political support for dictatorship?

THE DIRTY WARS OF THE SOUTHERN CONE

Under General Augusto Pinochet, Chile's military chose the role of self-styled, U.S.-backed national savior. The coup was finalized on September 11, 1973. Democratically elected President Salvador Allende remained in La Moneda, the downtown presidential palace, as it was bombed by air force jets. He was killed—his attackers said he committed suicide—as his office was stormed by army troops.

What emerged from the ashes of the coup was the Pinochet regime, a bureaucratic-authoritarian state purged of popular politics. A Pinochet-led junta suspended civil liberties, outlawed unions, overturned agrarian reforms, and hunted down dissenters. Chile became, for the first time, a repressive police state operating under state-of-siege conditions. Chile's rough equivalent of the FBI, known as DINA, was in charge of rooting out all potential communists and "subversives." Individuals suspected of antigovernment activity, particularly young people and those associated with organized labor or the Allende regime, but also some foreigners who found themselves in the wrong place at the wrong time, were rounded up and detained in soccer fields, then selectively "disappeared" and murdered. More permanent interrogation centers and concentration camps were also built and quickly became the sites of torture and extrajudicial punishment. Some were designed and run by former German Nazis.

Even enemies of the regime who had fled the country for Europe or the United States were not safe, made clear when former Allende official Orlando Letelier was killed by car bomb in Washington, D.C., in 1976 (Pinochet underlings were convicted of the crime in 1993). Earlier, in 1974, Neo-fascist gunmen were hired in Italy to assassinate Chilean exiles including Christian Democrat Bernardo Leighton. He and his wife survived being shot at close range in 1974 but were permanently brain-damaged and paralyzed.

Operation Condor, an agreement among South American dictatorships to share intelligence on alleged subversives, was founded in Chile in 1975. Chile was joined by Argentina, Paraguay, Uruguay, Bolivia, Brazil, and eventually Ecuador (Map 14.1). With Operation Condor came Operation Colombo, an effort to persuade foreign media that missing Chileans and foreigners were not being killed by the Chilean secret police but rather fellow "subversives" in Argentina and other countries. As part of the strategy, Chilean identity papers and notes claiming responsibility by Argentine rebels were placed on mutilated corpses in and around Buenos Aires. Many other exiles were captured by cooperating "Condor countries" and either murdered or returned to Chile.

The only thing open about Pinochet's Chile was the economy. Led by a team of University of Chicago–trained economists, the project of dismantling all the accumulated institutions of economic nationalism was immediately underway. Wages dropped and unemployment rose as Chile's industries collapsed in the face of foreign competition. Inflation eventually dropped to manageable levels by the early 1980s and export diversification diffused copper dependency. The nation became known for its high-quality fish, timber, fruit, and wine. Silenced workers were stripped of benefits and few could have afforded to purchase the table grapes they produced, had the best of them not been reserved for export.

Crisis struck again in 1982 as oil prices plummeted and interest rates rose, causing Mexico to default on its external debt. The reverberations were profound throughout Latin America. The response in Chile was an even sharper neoliberal economic turn. Mostly this entailed selling off remaining state enterprises and natural resources and borrowing money from foreign banks to subsidize high living by a small oligarchy, now joined by Pinochet and his cronies. Other countries were by this time swearing off so-called debt-led growth, but in

MEXICO

Gulf of
Mexico

Mexico City

CUBA   HAITI

BRITISH
HONDURAS   JAMAICA
(Gr. Br.)

HONDURAS

PUERTO
RICO

ATLANTIC
OCEAN

Caribbean
Sea

GUATEMALA
EL SALVADOR
NICARAGUA

Panama

TRINIDAD
(Gr. Br.)

COSTA RICA

PANAMA

Caracas
VENEZUELA

Bogotá

COLOMBIA

GUYANA
Georgetown
Paramaribo

Orinoco

FRENCH
GUIANA

SURINAME

Quito
ECUADOR

Negro

Amazon

Belém

Madeira

Brazil, 1964–1985

PERU
Lima

B R A Z I L

São Francisco

Salvador

Lake
Titicaca
La Paz

Araguaia

PACIFIC
OCEAN

Chile, 1973–1989

BOLIVIA

CHACO

Paraguay

São Paulo

Asunción

Rio de Janeiro

PARAGUAY

Paraguay, 1954–1989

C H I L E

Santiago

A R G E N T I N A

Paraná

URUGUAY

Buenos
Aires

Montevideo

Uruguay, 1973–1984

Argentina, 1976–1983

0   250   500 Km.
0   250   500 Mi.

M A P 14.1 Dictatorship in the Southern Cone

opposition-free Chile, the advice of Milton Friedman was still being followed. Chile's foreign debt was soon among the highest per capita in Latin America (as it still was in the year 2000), and a third of working-age adults were unemployed.

Pinochet became an institution not easily dismantled in his own right, especially after an assassination attempt in 1986 that killed virtually everyone else around him. Many began to think he would never die. A plebiscite in 1988 changed things at last; Chileans wanted a return to democracy. Even the old Marxist-Leninists got out and cleared their throats after a near-20-year hibernation. Christian Democrat Patricio Aylwin won, but the specter of Pinochet loomed large. He had changed the constitution to allow himself and a junta to "co-rule" the country even after the elections of 1989, and a further clause named him senator-for-life. Only slowly did his grip on the country loosen in the early 1990s, and with the return to democracy and the rule of law Chileans began to grapple with the tangled legacy of authoritarian rule. The Chilean Truth Commission Report of 1991 was the basis for Spanish judge Baltasar Garzón's indictment of General Pinochet, but he was never extradited despite being under house arrest in Britain for over a year and a half. He served as head of the armed forces until 1998 and died unrepentant, still "senator-for-life," on Human Rights Day, 2006.

Argentina's military dictatorship began much less dramatically than Chile's, but it proved at least as murderous and repressive. Following the death of Perón in 1974 and the collapse of his widow's government, the military seized power in 1976. The pretext was terror. Well before Perón's restoration his supporters had split into numerous wings, including the leftist Montoneros who advocated armed struggle after the manner of Cuba's insurgents. They were even inspired by Che Guevara's *foco* strategy. After 1968 they began robbing banks, bombing foreign-owned chain stores, killing police and army personnel, and kidnapping high-ranking generals and wealthy industrialists.

When their leader unexpectedly returned to office in 1973, Peronist guerrillas backed off under an amnesty offer. Peace might have come had there not also been several leftist guerrilla groups active by this time in Argentina even more directly inspired by Che Guevara and willing to kill and die for a Cuban-style revolution. Most important of these was the People's Liberation Army, or ERP, formed in 1968. The military was soon back in power, in any case, and generals such as President Jorge Videla branded all armed rebels "terrorists."

Terror was certainly among the guerrillas' many violent, revolutionary methods, whether Peronist or Marxist, and by 1976 both the Montoneros and ERP were experienced, well armed, and deeply embedded in Argentine society. Both groups counted on thousands of supporters and sympathizers, and their robberies and kidnappings had generated considerable funds. They were not the only rogues on the streets with political aims, however. Those not called terrorists by the government included ultra-nationalist paramilitary death squads and official police and armed forces units who used comparable and even identical tactics to intimidate their enemies. No one could claim the moral high ground since all sides engaged in the murder of innocents.

As in Chile, democracy was suspended by the ruling military junta, which saw itself as national savior. What replaced it was a politics of state terror, heavily influenced by French counterinsurgency doctrines developed in Vietnam and Algeria. All individual rights were effectively suspended, and anyone accused of aiding or harboring alleged subversives could be taken and detained without warning. Unidentified men in Ford Falcons roamed the streets of Buenos Aires,

Córdoba, and other cities, picking up labor organizers and even high school students without arrest or charges being filed. Prisoners were held in secret jails, tortured, and executed without a word to their relatives or access to lawyers. Some 340 secret detention centers have since been identified. In all, tens of thousands of Argentines were "disappeared" in this fashion between 1976 and 1982, when the military regime began to crumble. The armed forces claimed victory as both the ERP and Montoneros were defunct by 1979.

The fall of Argentina's military regime did not result from popular outrage over repression, although it began to emerge thanks to the Mothers of the Disappeared (see Image and Word 14.1). Argentina under military rule was an economic catastrophe. Essentially neoliberal policies of privatization and opening of domestic markets to foreign competition destroyed what was left of the nation's industrial sector. High interest rates and soaring fuel costs related to the oil crisis of 1973 made matters worse, driving inflation through the roof and eroding wages to their lowest levels since the nineteenth century.

Cracks in the junta appeared by 1980, but in 1982 General Leopoldo Galtieri tried a last, desperate measure to regain popular support. He sent Argentine armed forces to the Malvinas Islands, long occupied by the British and known to the rest of the world as the Falklands. Britain's Prime Minister Margaret Thatcher surprised the generals by calling for the islands' defense, which was effected with great speed. The disastrous 10-week Malvinas War effectively brought down the Argentine dictatorship and ushered in a chaotic and morally fraught return to democracy. Few of those responsible for the worst atrocities, military or guerrilla, were brought to justice in the aftermath.

Brazil's era of military dictatorship predated that of both Argentina and Chile, but it took on a similar, repressive character. As later happened in Chile, the military took control of the federal apparatus in 1964 in the midst of what they saw as a radical leftward shift in democratic politics. Leftist insurgents were not yet active. In this cold war environment, anyone who even squeaked about social and economic reform was instantly branded a communist and censured, sometimes violently, sometimes by way of exile. Popular politics was reduced to a charade between the hard-line ARENA party and the so-called Democratic Movement Party, or MDB (not to be confused with MPB, or Brazilian Pop Music, which emerged in protest). Genuine opposition came mostly from so-called nationalists, who criticized the military's courting of U.S. investment at any cost.

The early hard-line government of General Humberto Castelo Branco ended in 1967, followed by a handpicked successor, Marshal Artur Costa e Silva. During his years in office Brazilians from many quarters began to call for reforms, including free speech, and the Catholic Church was for the first time an outspoken advocate of state social policy reform for the benefit of the poor. Costa e Silva was overwhelmed by hardliners in December 1968, and Congress was dissolved. Protest emerged in pop culture, particularly music but also in the form of armed guerrilla bands, never as numerous as in neighboring Argentina or Uruguay but increasingly effective and deadly.

IMAGE AND WORD 14.1 The Mothers of the Disappeared

In 1977, the mothers and grandmothers of those who had been "disappeared" (arrested and never heard of again) by Argentina's military regime began to gather every Thursday in the Plaza de Mayo in Buenos Aires. Many held up photographs of their missing family members (as in the image below). Some of the women were themselves disappeared by the military. Argentine army officers have since admitted that up to 10,000 civilians were kidnapped, tortured, and executed, but the Mothers insist the number is closer to 30,000. With the bodies of many still unaccounted for, the Mothers continue their Thursday meetings and marches. For many in Latin America—and indeed worldwide—the Mothers of the Disappeared, or Madres de la Plaza de Mayo, have become a symbol of popular political participation, female empowerment, and resistance to authoritarianism.

TravelStockCollection-Homer Sykes/Alamy

In September 1969 guerrillas calling themselves Action for National Liberation (ALN) kidnapped the U.S. ambassador in Rio, and the military was helpless to stop them. Their leader, who was soon after shot and killed by police, was Carlos Marighela, former head of the Communist Party in São Paulo. The ambassador, Burke Elbrick, was released and the guerrillas captured, jailed, and tortured. Marshal Costa e Silva had fallen ill from a stroke and was incapacitated, so he was replaced by hard-line general Emilio Garrastazú Médici. Médici ran Brazil as a virtual fiefdom from 1969 to 1974, advocating tortures and disappearances of so-called subversives, many of them students calling for such mild reforms as new textbooks. Médici was followed by Ernesto Geisel, the milder of the two but still an authoritarian military man. Geisel's policy of "relaxation," or *distenção*, was a tease, and he proved it by shutting down congress in 1977 when things failed to go the way of his party, the ARENA.

Only under General João Baptista Figueiredo, "elected" in 1979 for a six-year term, was the option of democracy seriously discussed. *Abertura*, or aperture, included political amnesty, freer speech, and formation of new political parties. It was in the early 1980s that the Workers' Party, or Partido dos Trabalhadores (PT), emerged as a new political force. Its leader, metalworker Luís Inácio "Lula" da Silva, was persecuted by the military regime but survived to become a two-term president. Meanwhile, the return to democracy in 1985, following a 1983 plebiscite against the military, took place in a climate of global economic turmoil. As will be seen in the next chapter, the 1988 election proved to be a huge disappointment.

As in Chile and Argentina, Brazil's age of the generals had offered a feast for foreign capital and a famine for the mass of Brazilians. Foreign investment poured into the export and utilities sectors, but profits went right back out. Land became overwhelmingly concentrated in the hands of small numbers of ranchers, loggers, and other individuals and families with military connections. Landless peasants, meanwhile, flowed into the cities in droves from the country-side. Poverty in cities such as São Paulo and Rio was stunning in depth and extent, and crime began to get out of control as if it were a new form of popular insurgency.

INSURGENCY AND REPRESSION
IN CENTRAL AMERICA

If canal politics and U.S. threats helped shape twentieth-century Panama and Nicaragua, Honduras emerged as a colony of the United Fruit Company. A true "banana republic," Honduras was dominated by its U.S.-supported military after 1950. Coups and counter-coups reversed democratic gains leading up to the 1980s, when civilian presidents (mostly from the pro-business Liberal Party) returned. With only occasional banana worker strikes to suppress, the Honduran armed forces sought U.S. support in helping "contain" their potentially communist neighbors.

Whereas Costa Ricans have always prided themselves on not being like Nicaraguans, Hondurans have always cast a jaundiced eye toward neighboring El Salvador, Latin America's most densely populated nation. An example of the tension between the two nations was the Soccer War of 1969–1970, which involved reprisals from Honduran military forces for a loss to El Salvador in a World Cup elimination round. More serious causes included landless Salvadorans who had moved across the border into Honduras and disagreements over a regional trade pact.

The 1980s were a time of war in a different sense, as Honduras's close links to the United States and proximity to Nicaragua led almost naturally to involvement in the so-called Contra War, the Reagan administration's years-long attempt to overthrow the Sandinista regime. Civilian government survived throughout this period in Honduras, but always in the shadow of the army, which received tens of millions of dollars annually in U.S. aid. Many Hondurans were unhappy with this arrangement, but few wanted to risk their lives by declaring U.S. use of Honduran territory as a base for war with Nicaragua as a violation of national sovereignty. There were other consequences of cooperation. U.S. aid for the Contra War propped drug-trafficking elements in the Honduran army, some of whom had ties to Panama's rogue president, Manuel Noriega, deposed in 1989. Again, it was Honduras's poverty and convenient location that allowed outside elements, this time Colombian drug kingpins, to penetrate. Airstrips controlled by the military allowed Colombian planes on the way to Mexico to refuel.

If Honduras became a classic banana republic under the thumb of the military, neighboring El Salvador became a coffee republic under the thumb of a small landed oligarchy. Salvadorans, among them many more Amerindians than in Honduras, Nicaragua, and Costa Rica, had mostly to grapple with land issues rather than foreign investors. Hard-line policies promoted by the so-called 14 families drew resistance, which became revolutionary by the late 1970s. Civil war and repression raged throughout the 1980s.

As if a reflection of nature, El Salvador's social volcano blew for the first time in the early 1930s. Allowance of Communist Party participation in town elections by newly elected president Arturo Araujo led to a military takeover. The poor responded in kind, raiding lands, estate buildings, and shops. Some were led by Agustín Farabundo Martí, a veteran of similar conflicts in Nicaragua with Sandino. A kind of race war emerged, with the military essentially targeting Maya-speaking Indians for extermination. Between 10,000 and 20,000 Salvadorans died by 1932. The aftermath included 12 years of authoritarian rule followed by a series of military regimes. The only blip on the screen for a long time was José Napoleon Duarte, who won the presidency by popular election in 1972. Fearing even his Christian Democratic form of change, the military removed, jailed, tortured, and exiled him. Not surprisingly, many Salvadorans concluded that the old elite, allied with the military and supported by the U.S. government, would never permit democracy to function and so would opt for the bullet instead of the ballot.

Salvadoran politics after 1972 disintegrated into violent struggles between competing camps, with a more militant right committing atrocities of every kind and a more militant left, particularly the Farabundo Martí National Liberation Front, or FMLN, displacing thousands of peasants as it took over parts of the backcountry. Duarte reemerged as a potential leader of reform, but he proved nearly powerless in this atmosphere of violence and recrimination. The 1980s were marked by bitter fighting, wrangling in Washington over aid to known killers of U.S. nationals, including four nuns, and economic disaster compounded by a massive 1986 earthquake. Only after the signing of the Esquipilas Peace Accord in 1987, brokered by Costa Rican President Oscar Arias, did disarmament receive consideration. In spite of continued human rights abuses up to 1990, arms were laid down by 1992. The FMLN subsequently became a legitimate political party in a democratic system (see Image and Word 13.5 in the previous chapter).

In some ways El Salvador resembled its larger neighbor to the north, Guatemala. Guatemala's history has been marked by dictatorship-type regimes since independence and by violence in the countryside, most of it perpetrated against indigenous peoples. The period between mestizo strongman Rafael Carrera and the 1940s, roughly a century of Guatemala's history, was dominated by only three major figures, all of them linked to a small number of land-holding families. Coffee was Guatemala's main export, but unlike Costa Rica, coffee fincas were not all mom-and-pop operations; instead, many were staffed by indebted Maya Indians who lived in virtual slavery. Among the first Guatemalan politicians to recognize the explosive potential of this arrangement was the vehemently anticommunist General Jorge Ubico, in power from 1931–1944. Ubico was Perón-like in his efforts to build support bases among workers for an essentially fascist state.

Ubico was forced to resign in 1944 amid worker and peasant protests. The so-called October Revolution of 1944 led to the 1945 election of Juan José Arévalo Bermejo, a socialist inspired by Mexico's 1917 Constitution. Arévalo is among the few successful examples of a university professor turned politician, and he survived numerous attempted coups to hand over power to popularly elected Jacobo Arbenz Guzmán in 1950. Arbenz was a military man, but one with progressive ideas. Aided by his Evita-like wife, María Villanova, Arbenz wanted reform, not revolution. He built highways, port facilities, and the like, but colonial legacies could not always be avoided; the defining issue was land reform. This time the colonial elites were not just locals, however.

The 1952 Arbenz land reform program soon upset La Frutera, the massive U.S. banana concern. UFCO by this time essentially owned the Caribbean lowlands of Guatemala, and the idea of forced expropriation and redistribution was ignored. The government's offer of a little over $1/2 million for the 85% unused portion of UFCO's lands was countered by a U.S. State Department appraisal of some $15.8 million. The U.S. responded by attempting to isolate Guatemala via the Organization of American States, but other members were not easily bullied by the rabid anti-communist rhetoric of U.S. Secretary of State John Foster Dulles. The response was then to move for covert action, and CIA director Allen Dulles, brother of the secretary of state, began to put together a small invasion force in Honduras, to be led by a disgruntled Guatemalan Army colonel, Carlos Catillo Armas. The summer of 1954 saw Arbenz ousted by force, stripped and humiliated before the international press, and U.S. interests, protected in the name of anti-communism, preserved.

This ugly chapter in Guatemala's history had manifold consequences. One of the witnesses of the takeover was Che Guevara, who went on to fame in Cuba and to lead attempted uprisings throughout Latin America until his death in 1967. The United States would go on to lead covert takeovers and other such intrigues in Ecuador, Chile, and numerous other Latin American nations through the 1980s. Worst of all, for Guatemalans, the takeover of 1954 would usher in a period of violence unmatched in Central America in scope and duration. Between the takeover and the 1990s between 80,000 and 100,000 Guatemalans were killed in fighting, much of it carried out by paramilitary death squads. Most of the victims were Mayas and other Guatemalans of indigenous descent, people such as Nobel Peace Prize winner Rigoberta Menchú. Menchú came under fire over the naming of names in her harrowing account of violence in the 1970s and 1980s, but the truth remains that she lost most of her immediate family members in a series of attacks. Her story would be repeated many times before peace agreements, again resulting in part from the Esquipulas Peace Accord of 1987, began to stick by the mid-1990s after the fall of the Soviet Union.

ONE-PARTY RULE AND REPRESSION IN MEXICO

The presidency of Manuel Ávila Camacho was marked by World War II more than anything else, and it turned out to be something of an economic blessing. Mexico only reluctantly entered the war in a small way after some Mexican freighters were torpedoed by German submarines in the Caribbean in 1942; allying with the United States was an embarrassment for nationalist Mexico, but one group of fighters was proud—Escuadrón 201, flying tigers in the Philippines and Taiwan. Mexico's industrial raw materials brought an influx of cash from the Allies and Mexican labor flowed north to bring home exchange money as well. The so-called Bracero Program, which continued off and on into the early 1960s, would have all sorts of unintended consequences for Mexico and the United States.

The ruling PRI continued to pass the presidency down from one handpicked politico to another, each serving a six-year term without reelection. The existence, even encouragement, of a growing number of small opposition parties helped give the PRI's dictatorship a veneer of democracy. The 1950s—the presidencies of Miguel Alemán (1946–1952), Adolfo Ruiz Cortínes (1952–1958), and Adolfo López Mateos (1958–1964)—witnessed dramatic economic and population growth, contributing to the idea that PRI-led Mexico was politically stable and successfully modernizing. But the era also saw major corruption and public projects aiding large landholders who also happened to be politicians. Precious little aid went to small farmers and indigenous communal landholders, or ejidatarios. Laws requiring 51% Mexican ownership did not keep industrialization from occurring; they just kept the deal-making more secretive and corrupt.

Like his predecessors, Gustavo Díaz Ordaz, president through the late 1960s, ensured the continued growth of the Mexican economy—inflation was kept down and the peso devalued, along with other measures promoting foreign investment. But this was achieved at the expense of the kind of social justice for which the Revolution had supposedly been fought. Electoral fraud was widespread, with the conservative PAN (National Action Party) emerging as a genuine opposition. Strikes by railroad workers, teachers, and doctors were crushed, with protesters fired and leaders arrested. The brutal, open crackdown on the student movement in 1968 went one step too far (see Image and Word 14.2). The international scandal brought down neither Díaz Ordaz nor the PRI, but for the next 30 years the party had to fight hard to maintain its legitimacy. The question was not whether the PRI would ever cede power, but when and how. That the PRI became a peaceful opposition party in the first decade of the twenty-first century

IMAGE AND WORD 14.2   The Tlatelolco Massacre

AP Photo

AP Photo

On October 2, 1968, 10 days before the opening of the Olympic Games in Mexico City, the police and military opened fire on student demonstrators in the Plaza de las Tres Culturas in the Tlatelolco district of the capital (the images on the previous page and below are from international newspapers of the time). The numbers of those arrested and killed remain controversial, and some insist there were thousands of victims, but the death toll was certainly several hundred. The demonstrations were the culmination of months of unrest over police tactics and the detention of political prisoners. The Tlatelolco Massacre exposed the authoritarian underpinnings to Mexico's one-party rule. Thirty years later, Luis Echeverría Alvarez, interior minister in 1968 and Mexico's president from 1970 to 1976, admitted that the massacre had been a preplanned attempt to crush the student movement. In 2006, the 84-year-old Echeverría was charged with genocide and placed under house arrest—but soon released before his trial on the grounds that the statute of limitations had expired.

AP Photo

is a tribute to the endurance of the system forged by the party over 60 years, and to the commitment of the Mexican people to the democratic process—even if the transition was not, as we shall see in the next chapter, an easy one.

DICTATORSHIP IN HAITI AND THE DOMINICAN REPUBLIC

The Haitian economy since independence has remained mostly subsistence-oriented. Only in the early twentieth century did U.S. sugar interests attempt a return to plantations, but they soon moved to the neighboring Dominican Republic, Cuba, and Puerto Rico. Haitian politics since 1900 have been dominated by foreign, mostly U.S., intervention (including a military occupation from 1915–1934) and a mulatto minority, a kind of French-speaking mini-bourgeoisie. U.S. aid to dictators and the Haitian military has had disastrous effects for the mass of black Haitians.

Black politicians such as Dumarsais Estime emerged in the 1940s and 1950s with populist agendas, but economic instability and armed political opponents always seemed to win out. A 1956 coup unseated President Paul Magloire, and into the void stepped Francois Duvalier, perhaps Latin America's most bizarre dictator of the twentieth century. Terrorizing opposition with his army of henchmen, the Tontons Macoutes, Duvalier became president for life. Papa Doc, as he came to be known, smoothly manipulated the black vs. mulatto divide in Haiti and even pushed for ties with newly independent African states to back his alleged love of blackness. Utilizing Haiti's vodun tradition to political ends, Duvalier co-opted the symbol of Baron Samedi, a kind of lord of the dead. Meanwhile politics devolved to clientelism balanced by death squads. Voting for the United States at the UN and OAS kept aid dollars flowing until Papa Doc's death in 1971.

Duvalier was succeeded by his 18-year-old son, Jean-Claude, who came to be known as Baby Doc. Baby Doc followed in Papa's footsteps, with occasional faux-pas such as marrying a light-skinned mulatto, until his ouster in 1986. Three decades of Duvaliers left Haiti in worse shambles than before: 75% illiteracy, 20% infant mortality, and per capita income (annual) of only $300. Politics were no better, with violence and periodic revivals of Duvalier tactics of intimidation and murder to 1990.

In 1990 a mild-mannered priest and advocate of liberation theology, Jean-Bertrand Aristide, won two-thirds of the popular vote. He was soon ousted by rightist military men, led by General Raoul Cédras. This regime was only pressured to recognize Aristide as president after three years of chaos and repression. The re-installment of Aristide was an early test of the Clinton presidency but was only carried out due to what the rap group Public Enemy has labeled America's "fear of a black planet." Too many Haitians were trying to sail or float to Miami. To the dismay of many, Aristide and his Lavalas Party became associated with repressive violence during his 2001–2004 term as president. He was ousted after a popular uprising that he blamed on the United States and the Haitian military. Aristide's successor, René Preval, did prove more responsive to U.S. Government dictates than to Haitian popular demands, and he virtually disappeared amid Haiti's greatest natural disaster, the devastating January 12, 2010, earthquake that killed nearly 300,000 people.

The neighboring Dominican Republic has had a similarly rocky trajectory in the last century. U.S. marines occupied this half of the island of Hispaniola from 1916–1922, in part to put down insurgents in the hilly backcountry who hated U.S. sugar interests and the local politicians they owned. Trainees included Rafael Leonidas Trujillo, soon a rival with Papa Doc Duvalier and Cuba's Fulgencio Batista as "most ruthless tyrant in the Caribbean." U.S. intervention ended with the election of Horacio Vázquez in 1922, but when Vázquez sought to extend his term in 1929, Rafael Trujillo stepped in to take his place. Remembered in Haiti for the 1936 massacre of thousands of sugar workers, Trujillo ruled the Dominican Republic with an iron fist until his assassination (by disgruntled insiders) in 1961.

The election of journalist Juan Bosch in 1962 featured land reform as the core issue; the land to be redistributed was that hogged by old Trujillo himself. Fearing a Castro-like turn to the left, conservative elites removed the president in 1963. This action sparked a civil war, pitting conservatives against students, workers, and peasants who favored Bosch. Fueled by the same cold war paranoia that led to Vietnam, and with the Cuban missile crisis a recent memory, the United States sent 22,000 marines to calm things down in 1965.

The U.S. occupation of the Dominican Republic was viewed as unjustified meddling throughout Latin America, and U.S. attempts to gain support through the OAS only led to widespread ridicule of that institution. In stepped an ex-Trujillo man, Joaquín Balaguer, and U.S. influence was only softened by massive aid. Aside from brief breaks in the 1970s and 1980s, Balaguer was the dinosaur of Dominican politics until 1996. Part of his staying power was linked to periodic reopening of old wounds with Haiti, and racist denunciations of black opponent Francisco Gómez Peña, an orphaned Haitian raised by Dominican parents, were par for the course. Repressive politics have faded since 1996, and sugar exports and tourism have become important sources of foreign exchange. Still, in spite of neoliberal attempts to turn the economy into a "Caribbean Tiger," the Dominican Republic has succeeded mostly in exporting talented citizens, notably major league baseball players.

The wounds left by authoritarian repression all over Latin America in the late twentieth century have yet to heal, and the tangled legacies of so many regimes and their violent opponents yet to be sorted out. History, especially a history of torture and mass murder of one's own people, requires time and the release of information for perspectives to become clear. As emotions settle and evidence accumulates, perhaps it will be possible to solve the riddle of how a region known for accommodation and tolerance became a theater of repression. It will also become possible to assess the undeniably significant role of the United States in fomenting it.

It was once popular to claim that Latin America's near-ubiquitous repressive right-wing regimes could be traced to colonial patterns of caudillismo, Inquisition-style torture, land-concentration in the form of haciendas, and generalized racism. It may be just as correct to suggest, however, given the observable Latin American tendency to forgive and accommodate with surprising speed, that the age of the dictators was a blip in the region's history, a kind of accident helped along by a blundering giant to the north far too obsessed with the specter of global communism to accept that its neighbors to the south might be capable of choosing their own path to the future.

CREATIVE COUNTERPOINTS

Whether the era of dictators was a blip in Latin America's history or not, it should certainly not be taken as a sign that the region slipped into a modern dark age. The major political developments of the twentieth century—the rise of nationalism, the chain of revolutions, the turn to dictatorship, and the revival of democracy (discussed in the next chapter)—all provided a backdrop for an extraordinary cultural and artistic florescence. Although European and U.S. cultural products found growing audiences in Latin America, the nations of the region developed unique styles in painting and sculpture, fiction and poetry, music and dance, and moviemaking.

Much of the time, artistic heights were reached not just despite political turmoil and repression, but because of it. The Mexican Revolution inspired a vibrant subgenre of novels—from *The Underdogs* (*Los de abajo*), written by Mariano Azuela during the violent first decade of the revolution, to Carlos Fuentes's *The Death of Artemio Cruz* (1962), which encapsulated a lifetime of Mexican history in a fictional biography. Fuentes was part of the literary movement of the 1960s and 1970s known as the Latin American Boom; other contributors achieving international renown were Argentina's Julio Cortázar, Peru's Mario Vargas Llosa (who ran for his country's presidency in 1990, and won the Nobel Prize for Literature in 2010), and Colombia's Gabriel García Márquez (who won the Nobel Prize for Literature in 1982). Their works were experimental but gripping, often politically provocative and sometimes calling for social action. Perhaps the most strident writer of this generation, Uruguayan Eduardo Galeano, inspired millions with his potent works of fiction and political economy. At the fifth Summit of the Americas meeting in Trinidad in 2009, Venezuelan president Hugo Chávez handed U.S. president Barack Obama a copy of Galeano's 1970 articulation of dependency theory, *Open Veins of Latin America*.

As in political and economic affairs, nationalist artistic expressions often struggled against the overwhelming influence of the giant to the north. Cinema, for example, was highly popular in Latin America since its inception there in the 1890s; by 1902 there were already 200 movie theaters in Mexico alone, and at the late century peak there were thousands of screens across the continent. The rise of Hollywood and the U.S. home market advantage (there have always been more movie screens in the United States than in all Latin America) meant that by the 1920s some 95% of movies shown to Latin Americans were Hollywood productions, a dominance that has declined only barely in the past century. Nevertheless, a series of important national cinema movements allowed Latin American filmmakers to more than offset that economic influence with artistic and cultural capital. The Mexican film industry exploded in the 1940s and 1950s, known as its Golden Era; actors such as singing cowboy Jorge Negrete, the stunning Dolores del Río, and comedian Cantinflas achieved international fame. Argentina's film production also grew during this time, and directors such as Fernando Solanas and Octavio Getino spearheaded the Third Cinema movement in the late 1960s. Argentine filmmakers bounced back after the repression of the 1976–1983 military dictatorship with movies such as *The Official Story* (which won the Oscar for Best Foreign Language Film in 1985). Since the 1950s filmmakers in Cuba, Bolivia, Colombia, and Brazil have also produced award-winning movies, often laced with political and social commentary; by the end of the twentieth century Brazilian cinema in particular had gained international audiences and critical acclaim.

An early export of Brazilian cinema, Carmen Miranda, also helped bring samba and other Latin American music to foreign audiences. The cultural stew

---

IMAGE AND WORD 14.3 Bombshells and Poets

Transcendental Graphics/Getty Images

EL MERCURIO de CHILE/Newscom

A Portuguese-born samba singer and actress with the stage name Carmen Miranda became a huge star in Brazil in the 1930s, performing in musicals that promoted national styles of music and dance. Her sensual moves and outrageous costumes—featuring hats and headdresses made of tropical fruit—were rooted in Afro-Brazilian carnival traditions. In the 1940s she took on Broadway and Hollywood roles and rapidly became an international superstar (she was allegedly the highest-paid woman in the United States in 1945). Although nicknamed "the Brazilian Bombshell," her Hollywood image was more that of a generic, even stereotypical, "hot Latin" woman, spreading a mix of Mexican, Argentine, and Brazilian rhythms and sounds to U.S. and European audiences.

Violeta Parra's image was different. A Chilean artist, poet, and folk musician, Parra renewed and revived Chilean folk music and the tradition of the peña—community arts centers also used for political activism—in the 1960s. She is usually credited as the founder of the New Song movement of protest music, which took root most notably in Havana after Parra's death but whose influence was felt throughout the Americas. Peñas were banned by the Pinochet dictatorship following the 1973 coup but survived among Chilean exiles abroad.

Born in Baranquilla, Colombia, in 1977, Shakira started writing poetry at the age of 4, belly-dancing at 8, and recorded her first album at 13. In the late-1990s she exploded onto the musical scene, first in Colombia and then rapidly in the rest of the Americas and worldwide. By the end of 2009 her eight studio albums had sold tens of millions of copies, making her the world's best-selling Colombian artist of all time. She is the only Latin American singer to have reached the number-one spot on

(continued)

IMAGE AND WORD 14.3   **Bombshells and Poets** (Continued)

MIGUEL MEDINA/AFP/Getty Images

the popular music charts in the United States, Canada, Australia, and Britain. While her music has obvious local roots (Andean folk music, Colombian rhythms, Latin rock), it also reflects the Middle Eastern influence of her father's Lebanese ancestry. She has recorded in Spanish, Portuguese, and English. Shakira's image is controversial; some claim she uses her sexuality to sell her music, promoting old gender stereotypes (reminiscent, perhaps, of Miranda), while others hail her as a powerful feminist role model with progressive political and philanthropic ideas (someone Parra would have admired).

These women are just three examples, taken from the world of music, of the dynamic interplay in modern Latin America between national culture and international commercialism, gender and racial stereotypes and the breaking of boundaries, political repression and the liberating impact of music. Miranda died of a heart attack in 1955 at age 46; Parra shot herself after learning of Che Guevara's death in Bolivia in 1967 at age 50; and thankfully Shakira is still very much alive.

---

of musical traditions from Europe, western Africa, and Native America had simmered for centuries across the region, creating a wide range of distinctive national and local musical styles. The rise of the modern recording industry in the early twentieth century stimulated an extraordinary cross-fertilization of these styles both within and outside Latin America. Simply put, popular music today would not be the same without the influence of bossa nova, samba, salsa, bachata, rumba, cumbia, Andean panpipes, Latin rock, reggae, and reggaeton; the classical compositions of Heitor Villa-Lobos; and the New Song protest music that stretched from Chilean folklorist Violeta Parra to Cuba, Mexico, Nicaragua, and back to Chile (see Image and Word 14.3).

The sum of all this creative activity not only added layers of distinction to Latin American civilization, but it also projected the region's cultures onto the world. Consumers across the globe, from Canada to Germany to Japan, listened to bossa nova and salsa, danced the tango, read the novels of Fuentes and García Márquez, and watched Oscar-nominated movies from Brazil and Argentina. The stereotype of a land of banana republics, brutal dictators, and guerrilla warfare was offset by images of cultural dynamism. The world discovered that it had much to learn from Latin American civilization.

KEEP READING

We suggest the following historical works relevant to this chapter: Martin E. Andersen, *Dossier Secreto: Argentina's Desaparecidos and the Myth of the "Dirty War"* (1993); Ian Guest, *Behind the Disappearances: Argentina's Dirty War against Human Rights and the United Nations* (1990); Juan Corradi, et al., eds., *Fear at the Edge: State Terror and Resistance in Latin America* (1992); Joan Dassin, ed., *Torture in Brazil: A Report by the Archdiocese of São Paulo* (1986); Susan Eckstein, ed., *Power and Popular Protest: Latin American Social Movements* (1989); Peter Kornbluh, *The Pinochet File: A Declassified Dossier on Atrocity and Accountability* (2004); Paul H. Lewis, *Guerrillas and Generals: The "Dirty War" in Argentina* (2002); Rigoberta Menchú, *I, Rigoberta Menchú: An Indian Woman in Guatemala* (1984); David Rock, *Authoritarian Argentina: The Nationalist Movement, Its History and Its Impact* (1993); Steve Stern, *The Memory Box of Pinochet's Chile*, 3 vols. (2004–2008); Greg Grandin, *Empire's Workshop: Latin America, the United States, and the Rise of the New Imperialism* (2007); Elena Poniatowska, *Massacre in Mexico* (1992).

We also recommend John King, *Magical Reels: A History of Cinema in Latin America* (2nd ed., 2000); and the biopic *Carmen Miranda: Bananas is my Business,* directed by Helena Solberg (1995); Betsy Konefal, *For Every Indio Who Falls: A History of Maya Activism in Guatemala, 1960–1990* (2010).

15

✳

Democracy, Urban Life, and Neoliberalism

Democracy Revived

Political Awakenings

The Rise of Mega-Cities

Exports and the Environment

"I am a woman, a socialist, separated, and agnostic—all the sins together," said Michelle Bachelet, Chile's first female president, as she described herself on her election in 2006. That Chileans would choose a woman as their leader was surprising to many, but perhaps more so that they elected an avowed socialist. Chile was still emerging from the long shadow of right-wing dictator Augusto Pinochet, who ruled the country with an iron fist and persecuted individuals like Bachelet for nearly 20 years. But for historians, Chile's long and mostly peaceful democratic heritage and strong leftist parties made Bachelet's victory less a novelty and more a continuity. It is now the Pinochet regime that appears out of place.

Since the collapse of the Soviet Union in the early 1990s, most Latin Americans have been freed from the U.S.-funded cold war proxy struggle that defined a generation. Dictatorships and one-party systems have largely disappeared in favor of open-field, multi-party democracy. In Brazil's 2002 presidential election nearly as many people voted, about 100 million, as in the U.S. presidential election of 2000—and there were no "hanging chads" or other glitches thanks to computer standardization of voting machines. Voting is mandatory in Brazil, but high rates of participation in the democratic process are nearly as common in parts of Latin America where it is not. Also, despite a range of populist tricks and occasional intimidation, widespread voting fraud and rigged elections are increasingly seen as a thing of the past.

Yet not all about the cold war struggle has been forgotten, as the survival of communist Cuba and revival of a self-styled revolutionary left in Venezuela and

TIMELINE

1992 Failed military coup led by Hugo Chávez in Venezuela

1994 Zapatista Rebellion in Mexico; NAFTA signed

1999 Election of Hugo Chávez in Venezuela

2000 Election of first non-PRI president in Mexico, Vicente Fox

2005 Election of first indigenous president of Bolivia, Evo Morales

2006 Election of Michelle Bachelet in Chile

2008 Ingrid Betancourt freed in Colombia

2010 Election of Dilma Roussef in Brazil

other countries suggest. Latin America's recent leftist revival, though hardly uniform in message or style, grew in part out of a questioning of neoliberalism, the first global economic current to sweep Latin America in the wake of the cold war.

As seen in the last chapter, neoliberalism, in part a revival of nineteenth-century free trade and comparative advantage arguments, and in part a knee-jerk rejection of any form of economic nationalism, seemed appealing at first. Having suffered years of corruption, bad services, and high prices, most Latin Americans agreed that government was inherently bad at running any sort of business. Unfortunately, the sell-offs of state enterprises and general opening of markets rarely brought the lower prices, better services, and, most importantly, jobs predicted by international advisers. Instead, many countries were simply plundered of resources and accumulated infrastructure by foreign multinationals and millions of state employees were laid off. Economic instability and abrupt drops in living standards through the 1990s prompted millions to migrate to the United States, Canada, and Europe. Others, including Mexico's Zapatistas, rose in revolt.

Abrupt economic shocks and the expansion of commercial agriculture and ranching at the expense of peasants and indigenous forest dwellers combined to make Latin America predominantly urban, a trend greatly accelerated in the last two decades. As of this writing, the percentage of Latin Americans living in cities is higher (82%) than in the United States (80%). Although cities provided a much wider range of employment opportunities than rural areas for many migrants, rapid urban growth generated numerous new problems, including uncontrolled crime, pollution, and traffic congestion. The lack of services in outlying slums prompted citizens to organize and become active in politics.

Other political awakenings have occurred in Latin America's recent past among indigenous, African-descended, and other ethnic and racial groups. The trend of organization along ethnic lines has been most marked in the Andean countries, where millions speak Quechua and Aymara, but smaller groups such as Panama's Cuna and Chile's Mapuche have also become far more vocal participants in the democratic process. People of African descent in Colombia, Brazil, and Ecuador have long sought recognition of land claims and other rights but have gained more representation in high government in the last two decades than ever before. Other traditionally persecuted groups, such as gays and lesbians, have also begun to organize and win legal guarantees, although in traditionally Catholic (and even increasingly evangelical) Latin America, their struggles have been uphill.

With new political enfranchisement, especially of widely scattered indigenous communities, came growing awareness of the environmental costs of primary exports. Logging, ranching, mining, oil drilling, and commercial farming all brought increasing amounts of foreign exchange to certain members of the business elite, but often at the expense of autonomous indigenous peoples, peasants, and large expanses of wilderness. International awareness of Latin America's tremendous and growing environmental problems grew in the 1980s thanks to activists such as Brazil's Chico Mendes, but the destruction has only accelerated in subsequent decades with the global rise in commodity prices. The riddle here may be how in a truly globalized world Latin America's legendarily rich resources can be harnessed to create something other than greater income inequality and degraded landscapes. This may be too pessimistic.

DEMOCRACY REVIVED

With the end of the cold war and the discrediting of authoritarian regimes, most Latin American countries returned to democracy with high hopes. Unfortunately, due to economic woes brought on by the world recession of the early 1980s, the fledgling democracies of the era struggled to gain legitimacy. Inflation ran rampant in Brazil, Peru, and Argentina through much of the 1980s and 1990s, hitting the poor harder than anyone else. From the confusion there emerged several new leaders who promised to bring the chaos under control. Carlos Saúl Meném came to power in Argentina and Alberto Fujimori in Peru at about the same time. Neither was a traditional figure from the left or right, and both presented themselves as something fresh.

Democracy proved unpredictable throughout Latin America in the 1990s and 2000s. Negative reaction to the Sandinista regime in Nicaragua brought Violeta Barrios de Chamorro to power, then returned the presidency to Sandinista leader Daniel Ortega. The post-Duvalier era witnessed the rise of Haiti's Jean-Bertrand Aristide but only brought worse violence and instability than before. In Ecuador, post-military democracy set records for instability, with three presidents driven from office—by the people, rather than the military—between 1997 and 2007. Bolivia underwent wide swings, electing neoliberal friends of the United States, then more autonomous, leftist, and pro-indigenous leaders. Bolivian regionalism has exacerbated the divide. More authoritarian democratic regimes emerged after 1990 in countries with a new or continued leftist guerrilla presence. More open politics reigned in countries such as Uruguay, where guerrillas long ago laid down arms and joined the democratic fray. An outlier of sorts, Guatemala is only just becoming more than a virtual military dictatorship beneath a democratic facade.

Although leftist guerrillas remain a force to be reckoned with in Colombia as of this writing, the left in most of Latin America has reclaimed a share of political power since the late 1990s by way of electoral politics. Reconciliation has proved viable. Former armed rebels were handily elected from El Salvador to Brazil, but it has been the rise of former army colonel Hugo Chávez in Venezuela that has drawn the most attention outside the region. Backed by popular support and enormous oil wealth, Chávez reached out not only to Cuba but also many Latin American and Caribbean neighbors (see Image and Word 15.1). Allies since the early 2000s included Nicaraguan president Daniel Ortega, Ecuadorian president Rafael Correa, and Bolivian president Evo Morales. Other left-leaning politicians such as Brazil's president Inácio Lula da Silva and Argentina's president Christina Kirchner maintained a bit more distance, as did Michelle Bachelet of Chile. Hugo Chávez's desire to create a regional bloc capable of dealing with the United States on more equal terms has not yet come into being, and his support for leftist guerrillas in neighboring Colombia has drawn sharp criticism. At home, Chávez has revived economic nationalism at a level not seen anywhere else in the region, although Bolivia is a close second.

IMAGE AND WORD 15.1 The Bolivarian Revolution

JUAN BARRETO/AFP/Getty Images/Newscom

Hugo Chávez first attempted to break Venezuela's long tradition of democratic rule in 1992, when he led a military coup against the elected government of Carlos Andrés Pérez (president in 1974–1979 and 1989–1993). Released from prison in 1994, Chávez visited Fidel Castro in Havana. Subsequently elected president in 1999, Chávez has frequently visited his mentor in Cuba, who, he readily admits, "is like a father, like a beacon" (Castro and Chávez are included in the murals and banners above and on the next page; both photographs were taken in Caracas). Since 2000, Chávez has built a regime in the tradition of the populist caudillo. He sees himself as Simón Bolívar's heir, his virtual reincarnation (Bolívar can also be seen above and on the next page; the fourth figure in the mural above is Cuban poet José Martí, and on

JORGE SILVA/Reuters/Landov

the banner above is Che Guevara). Chávez had dismantled Venezuela's old institutions of democracy and replaced them with new ones; the country is officially "the Bolivarian Republic of Venezuela." He controls the military, runs his own ruling party, has nationalized much of the nation's vast oil industry, has taken full control of PDVSA (the state oil company), and directly or indirectly controls all major media outlets. When in 2007 he lost a referendum to change the constitution to allow him to remain in power, both his supporters and opponents seemed surprised that he had not simply fixed the results.

Chávez has also adopted a colorful, confrontationist anti-U.S. position, much of it a rhetorical stance for public audiences in Venezuela and other Latin American nations: the United States is "the Empire"; his Bolivarian Revolution is proclaimed as profoundly anti-imperialist (he famously called President Bush "the Devil" in a speech to the United Nations in New York); in 2004 he founded ALBA, a trade and political bloc with Cuba, now extended to other countries with leftist regimes (see Map 15.1); he supports the Colombian guerrillas, FARC, and threatened and taunted Colombia's President Uribe as a U.S. puppet, "coward," and "mafia boss"; and he has courted close relations not just with Castro's Cuba but also with Saddam Hussein's Iraq, Iran, China, and Russia.

Chávez has therefore worked hard to build an empire of influence in the region. The rise in oil prices increased Venezuela's budget from 7 to 56 billion dollars during Chávez's first decade in power, permitting him to buy influence abroad (he spent six times as much on foreign aid to the rest of Latin America than did the United States under George W. Bush). The oil boom has also partially disguised the inefficiency and corruption of the Chávez regime; even as he has tripled spending on social programs, poverty has risen and crime is rampant; with a murder rate of 2,200 a year, Caracas is one of the world's most dangerous cities.

Chávez in many ways embodies the riddle of Latin America. He is both a democrat and a dictator, a nationalist and a regionalist, a populist and a maverick proud of his own personality cult. Whether his Bolivarian Revolution can survive the rise and fall in oil prices, his own fall from office, or his authoritarian tendencies remains to be seen. Whether his rule represents the revival of democracy in Latin America in this century, or presages a return to the dictatorial dark days of the last century, also remains to be seen.

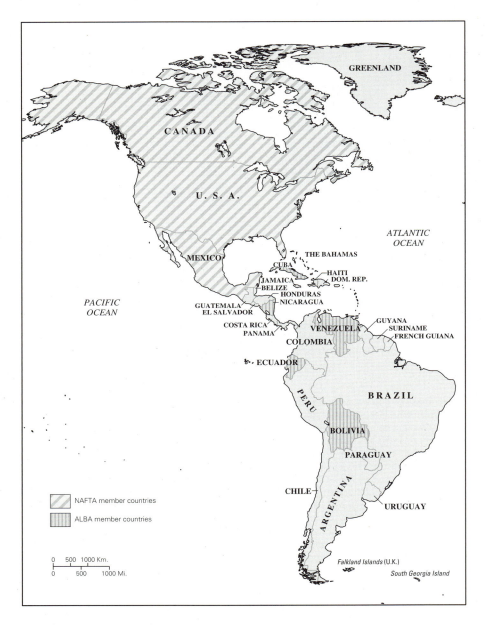

M A P 15.1   NAFTA and ALBA

Brazil's return to democracy was not initially cause for celebration and emerged nearly stillborn. The first candidates were chosen not by the people but by 686 members of the electoral college. One came from the Social Democratic Party, São Paulo Governor Paulo Salim Maluf, and the other from the Brazilian Democratic Movement, Tancredo Neves. Neves had strong support and an untried and therefore interesting running mate, José Sarney, and he was slated to take the helm in March 1985. Neves died during an emergency operation on the night of his inauguration and Sarney inherited the presidential mantle, only to sink beneath its weight.

Brazil was faced with crushing poverty, massive debt, a huge population, environmental degradation, and rampant inflation. The fledgling democracy was swamped, and it was a lot easier to point fingers of blame at elected civilians than at military dictators. Brazilian democracy was not a total sham, however, as candidates emerged for the first time from truly popular sectors. Benedita da Silva, a black *favela* dweller (see Image and Word 15.3), won a position in the Chamber of Deputies, one of the first women of any class or color to do so.

Brazil's shift to democracy came when inflation was over 200% a year and foreign debt totaled about $91 billion. Like Mexico, Brazil had suffered from wild swings in energy prices during the 1970s and 1980s and was now at the mercy of the IMF to remain solvent. Fortunately, the worst times were passing and a slow recovery was noticeable. Sarney followed his economic team and unveiled a new currency, the Cruzado, to replace the old Cruzeiro. The Cruzado Plan proved too rigid, and by 1987 it was bust. People soured on what now seemed like stupid miracle cures and called for a new constitution. It appeared in 1988, and like many Latin American constitutions from these years, it was clearly the work of a bickering, poorly led committee. It even proposed its own obsolescence within five years. In 1993, Brazilians were to choose between a strong presidency, a parliamentary system, and monarchy (yes, monarchy).

A worse disaster struck. In Brazil's first open presidential race since 1960 a suave young made-for-TV personality, Fernando Collor de Mello, governor of Alagôas state, beat the hard-working man of the people, Lula da Silva. After promising to end corruption, Collor proved more corrupt than most. His sidekick, "P.C." Farias, made the president look both better and worse by comparison. Collor resigned amid impeachment proceedings in 1992 and retired to his estate outside Miami. (Brazil's power of forgiveness, or forgetfulness, was well demonstrated when he returned to Alagôas in 2006 and was elected senator.)

Vice President Itamar Franco faced renewed inflation and other woes, but it was up to Treasury Secretary Fernando Henrique Cardoso to engineer a major overhaul. Cardoso produced the Real Plan, again introducing a new currency (the Real) but this time in an era of good feeling about the U.S. dollar. Brazilians went for it and thanked Cardoso by electing him president in 1994. Cardoso had his work cut out for him, and despite a still fragile economy, he won reelection in 1998. His first term was marked by major economic policy changes, essentially undoing all the economic nationalism of the Vargas era. Foreign capital was legitimized and warmly invited into every sector, including the old political honey pot of petroleum, but just as importantly the former untouchables such as foundries, transportation, and telecommunications. The huge Vale do Rio Doce iron concern was sold in 1997, and as of this writing it is among the largest multinational mining companies in the world.

These neoliberal moves, put in place by someone from the left, or at least with strong leftist credentials, struck a strange new chord that would have been almost unimaginable in the cold war years. Where Cardoso had trouble was in trimming social security (such as it was), government pensions (which were fat), and other government responsibilities that had become entitlements among the urban middle class. These entitlements included generous pensions to university professors, so protest quickly snarled the country's higher education system.

As in much of Latin America at this time, huge state companies sold for billions of dollars to foreign consortiums. Brazil's were just bigger than anyone else's by several orders of magnitude. Because of their scale this proved good for consumers, as competition, equipment upgrades, and greater efficiency led to lower phone, electricity, and other utility prices. Many state industries had become massively corrupt machines, and since most people knew it—and suffered from it—protest was muted. Protectionist tariffs also came down, and an economic pact with neighboring Argentina and other Southern Cone nations (MERCOSUR/MERCOSUL) helped cushion losses in the industrial sector by opening nearby markets.

Lula da Silva, Brazil's once and future president since the mid-1980s, was finally elected in 2002, then again in 2006. Much had changed since 1988, and Lula was no longer a young rebel with world-renewing dreams (actually, he had always seemed like a middle-aged, pot-bellied autoworker, which was central to his appeal). He chose, despite radical-sounding rhetoric to the contrary, to keep going with the economic policies established by Cardoso, taking an "if it ain't broke, don't fix it" approach. Investors held their breath and then sighed with relief and kept pouring money in and, of course, taking it out. Critics howled that here was the old revolutionary, making Brazil safe for foreign capital.

After weathering the global economic meltdown that began in 2007 with surprising resiliency, Brazil continued to look promising through the end of Lula's second term in 2010 – this despite continued and deep-seated problems of political corruption, human rights abuses by the police, rampant tax evasion, violent crime, and, most of all, one of the most unequal wealth distribution ratios in the world. As in the United States, the gap between the rich and the poor in Brazil is huge and widening fast. Such gapingly unequal wealth distribution is at great variance from most European nations, plus Canada and Japan. Still, Brazilians have come further faster than any Latin American nation by most measures (infant mortality, literacy, home ownership, Internet access). Economic growth under Lula's first administration broke records, and government fiscal restraint surprised foreign and domestic experts alike. It is premature to say if current trends mark a major turning point in Brazilian history, but despite genuine unrest and considerable growing pains, there is a sense of realization of long-held dreams and optimism for the future not felt since the late 1950s.

Argentina's return to democracy under Raúl Alfonsín, a Radical Party stalwart, was at least as tortuous as Brazil's, but despite severe economic shocks it survived. Alfonsín at first sought to hold the military responsible for the atrocities of the Dirty War, but he backed off in the face of resistance in the ranks and economic troubles. The latter were as profound as any in Argentine history. Throughout the 1980s unemployment kept rising, inflation was out of control, and production in virtually every sector was either stagnant or declining. The country's debt was so huge it could not be serviced except with more borrowed money.

IMAGE AND WORD 15.2 Chico Mendes

SINDICATO

DOS TRABALHADORES RURAIS DE XAPURI · ACRE

REUTERS/Str Old/Reuters Limited

Eye Ubiquitous/SuperStock

(continued)

IMAGE AND WORD 15.2   Chico Mendes (continued)

Francisco Alves Mendes Filho (1944–1988), better known as Chico Mendes, was a Brazilian rubber tapper from Acre state who became a hero of the international environmental movement when he was shot and killed in 1988 by hired gunmen working for a local rancher (the photos on the previous page were taken shortly before his murder). After campaigning tirelessly at the local, regional, national, and finally international levels, Mendes died protecting the Amazonian rain forest. The movement to preserve the forest grew tremendously since Mendes's death, yet the pace of deforestation to plant soybeans and other export crops has not slowed.

Into this maelstrom stepped a Peronist provincial governor named Carlos Saúl Meném, a child of Syrian immigrants who won the presidency in 1989. Meném drew support from the working class but proved an instant enemy of any form of economic nationalism. He ordered all remaining state companies, including profitable ones such as the state oil concern, YPF, sold to the highest (read: foreign) bidder. The Argentine peso was tied to the U.S. dollar, though much more rigidly than in the case of Brazil, and every possible state service and pension was cut to the minimum. Beaten by years of hard times and government repression, Argentines were loath to protest. The foreign debt was renegotiated and amid all the neoliberal excitement Meném managed to have the constitution altered so that he could run again.

Meném handily won reelection in 1995 but soon proved both a repressive and corrupt figure. His flashy personal style kept him in the news, but his pardon of the ruling members of the military junta and subsequent talk of admiring their resilience drew increasing criticism. Some claimed to see a pattern pointing to an authoritarian streak, suggested also by Meném's creation of a new national police force. Meném also seemed uninterested in solving the deadly bombings of Jewish institutions in 1992 and 1994 (considered especially significant since Argentina has the largest Jewish population in Latin America). Many Argentines still supported him despite his flaws, but Meném failed to have the constitution altered again so that he could seek a third term, partly due to growing suspicion of corruption. Meném's economic policies went sour in 2001, leading to a three-year meltdown worse than the Great Depression.

Few wanted to be president in these circumstances, but Néstor Kirchner, another Peronist governor from the provinces, was elected in 2003. With great difficulty he began to pull Argentina from the rubble and was succeeded by his wife, Christina Kirchner, in 2008. She immediately faced a massive rebellion from farmers who resisted a government tax on grain exports. Kirchner was surprised to find that Argentines overwhelmingly supported the farmers rather than her administration. She and her husband, who clearly retained a great deal of his former power until his death in 2010, were forced to back down. Mindful of what had hit them in 2001, Argentines accepted government austerity measures a bit more peacefully when the scale of the global economic crisis became clear.

While still one of the largest economies in Latin America and its fourth most-populous nation, Argentina has yet to hit on a stable economic policy that capitalizes on its considerable potential beyond primary exports and rewards its nearly 40 million citizens with something other than poverty and repression. Economic instability has kept the matter of Dirty War truth and reconciliation on the back burner, but the Kirchners proved far more willing to prosecute known perpetrators than their predecessors.

Chile's return to democracy was also halting and troubled as dictatorship faded, but with fewer economic woes than its Southern Cone neighbors. Under Patricio Aylwin Chile became less of an international pariah, which drew the attention of formerly reluctant international investors. Divesting in dictatorships had been a minor movement in the developed and sanctimonious north, but it had never stopped the flow of dollars, marks, and pounds. Aylwin followed the lead of his neighbors by sticking to neoliberal policies, and soon Chile was pumping out more copper, timber, wine, and fruit than ever before. The Patagonian toothfish, known in U.S. supermarkets and restaurants as Chilean sea bass, was nearly fished to extinction within a decade.

Aylwin was followed in 1994 by Christian Democrat Eduardo Frei Jr. Frei handily beat Arturo Alessandri, grandson of the great early-twentieth-century politician of the same name. Frei continued with the same policies of neoliberal export-led growth and slow reconciliation with the armed forces pioneered by Aylwin until he left office in 2000. As a bonus Pinochet legacy, his retirement came with the office of senator-for-life.

Frei was succeeded by former rival and Social Democrat Ricardo Lagos, who only slowly pushed for prosecution of former Pinochet officers but left the economy alone until his term ended in 2006. Growing frustration with the government's inattention to social services and social justice helped bring avowed leftist and victim of repression Michelle Bachelet to office in 2006. Like Lula in Brazil, she did little as president to suggest that she remembered what being poor and powerless was like, but high commodity prices, then the global economic crisis (which Chile also weathered with relatively minimal damage), diverted attention. Billionaire business-man Sebastián Piñera was elected in 2010.

Mexico's return to democracy followed yet a different pattern. Luis Echeverría, who served as another of many PRI presidents from 1970–1976, was an activist and liberal of sorts, but despite efforts at reform, he got nowhere (see Image and Word 14.2). Rampant inflation and leftist guerrillas continued to un-dermine his ambitious social agenda, and in the end there was neither the money nor the will within the PRI to turn things around. Meanwhile, Mexico's rich, in-cluding officials of the state oil company, Pemex, took billions abroad. Devaluation of the peso effectively taxed poverty; the process would be repeated. Mexico's economy, in short, entered freefall in these years, to be saved only by a brief oil boom in the late 1970s under José López Portillo, president from 1976–1982.

The bubble burst, and quickly. The late 1970s oil boom came too late and at enormous cost. Pemex had to purchase equipment from U.S. and European man-ufacturers on credit, only to watch oil prices plummet to their lowest levels in many years. On his way out, López Portillo nationalized banks, and the IMF and other

creditors asked Mexico to swallow the usual harsh medicine—cuts in already minimal social services, education, and the like—in exchange for a bailout. What this
meant for poor folks, as usual, was higher food, fuel, and consumer-goods prices.

Under President Miguel de la Madrid (1982–1988) things went from bad to
worse. Amid the economic turmoil came the Mexico City Earthquake of
September 19, 1985, which killed thousands and revealed the depth and extent
of government ineptness and corruption in everything from relief efforts to
building inspection. By 1988 Mexico's foreign debt reached $105 billion.
Inflation ran above 100% some years, with no end in sight. As a result of these
compounding factors, the 1980s were remembered as the Lost Decade in
Mexico. On the positive side, Mexican politicians retained the moral high ground
with regard to U.S. intervention in Central America. No thanks to Ronald
Reagan's belligerent, interventionist policies, peace talks based in Mexico City
finally ended and resolved civil wars in Guatemala, El Salvador, and Nicaragua.

Carlos Salinas de Gortari, president from 1988–1994, followed a new, techno-
cratic model. His defeat of Cuautéhmoc Cárdenas, a socialist and leader of the National Democratic Front (FDN), was widely regarded as fraudulent, but once in
power, Salinas confidently played auctioneer to the world. A true believer in what
he had learned at Harvard, his presidency marked the triumph of neoliberalism in
Mexico and the last sellout of the Revolution. Article 27 of the 1917 Constitution
was amended to allow dissolution of ejidos in 1992. Given that this was the 500th
anniversary of Columbus's landing, indigenous folks took this as a slap in the face.
Privatization of state industries and resources and building of tax-exempt foreign as-
sembly plants, or maquiladoras, were the order of the day. One result was the creation
of many low-wage jobs for young women. As a crowning achievement of this
approach, NAFTA went into effect January 1, 1994. Ominously, the Zapatista rebels
of the southern state of Chiapas declared war on Mexico's government on exactly the
same day. Many Mexicans, having gained little from the changes, were sympathetic to
the rebels. Serial murders of female maquiladora workers remain unsolved.

Salinas de Gortari was shamed out of the country by the end of his term (he
went back to Harvard for a while to teach). His brother Raúl was discovered to
be deeply involved in drug trafficking and other illegal enterprises—a forewarn-
ing of the battle against the international drug trade that would later bedevil the
Mexican government. Ernesto Zedillo was elected in 1994 after the PRI's preferred candidate, Luis Donaldo Colosio, was assassinated in Tijuana under suspi-
cious circumstances. Zedillo carried on with Salinas's neoliberal program,
essentially selling off what was left of the government's assets and embracing
NAFTA in hopes of some reward from the powers to the north.

Instead of marked gains in productivity or industrial growth, Mexico got a
Wal-Mart next to the ancient ruins of Teotihuacan. Peasant farmers were driven
out of business by cheap, imported corn. The Zapatista rebels who challenged
the neoliberal model and the PRI head-on were cautiously approached with car-
rots and sticks. Those in power hoped that with time the group's intellectual
leader, Subcomandante Marcos, would disappear. Meanwhile, the economy
crashed again, prompting a regionwide wave of divestment known as the "te-
quila effect." NAFTA partners stepped in to help, and with no social spending

to keep it down the country rebounded until another banking crisis hit in 1998. Neoliberalism was not bringing stability, much less the promised prosperity and development.

The crises and blatant corruption of the 1990s prompted Mexican voters to reject the PRI for the first time since the 1920s in the 1999–2000 presidential election. Conservative candidate Vicente Fox, of the National Action Party (PAN), came to power amid great expectations. Despite the apparent failure of neoliberal policies, the Mexican left was in disarray, and Fox had only the PRI machine to fight with. It remained highly formidable, and left the president hamstrung by 2003. Neoliberal policies continued to make the rich richer while yielding minimal gains for the mass of Mexicans. Millions migrated to the pre-housing crisis United States in search of work, mostly without visas. This left the undocumented vulnerable to human traffickers as well as unscrupulous employers, but despite their difficulties, migrant workers remitted billions of dollars to relatives in Mexico, a major source of foreign exchange felt most acutely in small towns.

By 2006, the Mexican left had regained some of its former legitimacy, and was represented in presidential elections by Mexico City Mayor Andrés Manuel López Obrador. López Obrador faced PAN candidate Felipe Calderón in a race tighter than that between Salinas and Cárdenas in 1988. (The PRI remained strong at the local and state level.) Calderón won by a hair and quickly turned his attention to an escalating crime crisis fueled by the international drug trade.

Using billions of dollars to bolster the army and police and coordinating efforts with the U.S. Drug Enforcement Administration, Coast Guard, and other government bodies, Calderón sought to bring down the massive cartels of northern Mexico's Pacific and Gulf coasts. By 2008, Mexico's drug-related violence resembled a small-scale civil war, with thousands of casualties and hundreds of assassinations of high-ranking police and military officers. Seizures and public burning of hundreds of tons of cocaine were far from reassuring evidence of the government's "winning" of the war on drugs. Meanwhile, other forms of crime, including kidnapping and ransoming middle-class urbanites, a favorite tactic of 1990s gangs, spiraled out of control. Calderón's "law-and-order" conservatism drew many critics who wanted tax money spent on other projects, but most Mexicans agreed that decades of corruption and collusion among the PRI, state police, and armed forces had generated a criminal state-within-a-state. Calderón was not helped by the fact that Mexico's close economic ties to the U.S. and Canada made it suffer more than most Latin American nations as a result of the global economic crisis that began in 2007.

The balance between civil liberty and security has nowhere been more challenged than in Colombia, where decades of civil war meshed with intense involvement in the international drug trade to produce Latin America's most dangerous country. The leftist guerrilla insurgency led by the Fuerzas Armadas Revolucionarias de Colombia (FARC; the Colombian Revolutionary Armed Forces) and other groups, such as the Ejército de Liberación Nacional (ELN; the National Liberation Army), began in the early 1960s and continues as of this writing. These groups lost support from the Soviet Union after the end of the cold war but quickly found a new source of funds in the emerging international cocaine trade, greatly expanded in the 1980s by criminal master-minds such as Pablo Escobar, who was killed in a U.S.-supported shootout in Medellín in 1993.

The history of the relationship between drug traffickers such as Escobar and guerrillas such as the FARC is a complex one. The guerrillas had long used kid-napping as a means of gaining funds, and with time they began to capture and ransom not only prominent industrialists and ranch owners but also the family members of drug kingpins, who were rich in cash and legally vulnerable. Escobar, who painted himself as an outraged businessman and also a friend of the people, formed a paramilitary organization known as MAS (from the Spanish acronym for "Death to Kidnappers"). MAS began to gain ground against the FARC in Colombia's Department of Antioquia and the Magdalena Valley. Escobar went on to challenge the Colombian nation-state directly with a terror and assassination campaign. This bold strategy to disrupt and capture the machinery of the state prompted a series of events that ended in his death, but the anti-guerrilla paramil-itary phenomenon he helped found flourished. The FARC, meanwhile, made peace with many of Escobar's competitors and shifted to taxing the production and transport of coca leaves, cocaine base, and refined cocaine.

By the early 1990s, rural Colombians and some city dwellers were being ter-rorized by the thousands either by the FARC or the paramilitaries, and sometimes by both. Others who entered the fight included the Colombian Army, local and national police forces, and the private armies formed to protect competing drug cartels. Three- and four-way bloodbaths were frequent, as were many odd alli-ances of convenience. As in Mexico, U.S. involvement in what was insufficiently titled the "War on Drugs" included training the Colombian Army in antinarcotics and anti-guerrilla tactics; providing intelligence information collected by the Drug Enforcement Administration and other agencies; and supplying planes, pilots, and chemicals to destroy coca plantings. National political leaders such as Liberal Ernesto Samper (president 1994–1998), whose receipt of campaign contributions from the Cali cartel led to Colombia being "decertified" by the U.S. government, and Conservative Andrés Pastrana (president 1998–2002), whose concession of a demilitarized zone to the FARC in the Amazon only revitalized the guerrilla, proved powerless in the face of this multidimensional, drug-fueled violence.

Initially funded by prominent businessmen and landowners, but increasingly by direct involvement in the drug trade, the paramilitaries began to take over vast areas of the countryside. Anyone suspected of aiding the guerrilla was murdered on sight, and soon the killings extended to town council officials, union leaders, schoolteachers, and eventually homeless youths, homosexuals, and prostitutes. The term used by members of the United Self-Defense Forces of Colombia (AUC), as the paramilitaries called themselves, was *limpieza*, or "cleansing." Meanwhile the FARC, also increasingly funded by direct production and distribution of cocaine rather than taxation, turned from attacks on police and army installations to attacks on civilians, often in the poorest rural districts of Colombia. A string of kidnap-pings and murders of poor Colombians, including native Americans, and unarmed foreign human rights advocates followed. Whatever sympathy the guerrillas' cause had won over the years instantly evaporated.

In 2002 the former Governor of Antioquia, Álvaro Uribe Vélez, won the presidency on a new platform. A former Liberal whose cattle-ranching father had been kidnapped and murdered by the FARC, Uribe argued for a far harder line against the guerrillas than even most Conservatives had pondered. He quickly courted support from the administration of U.S. president George W. Bush, and, by cleverly adding timely "War on Terror" rhetoric to that of drugs, quickly gained it.

Long in the making, "Plan Colombia" entailed increased satellite surveillance and coca eradication programs but mostly focused on strengthening the army to fight the FARC. A small number of expensive helicopters constituted much of what was touted in the U.S. press as "billions of dollars in aid." Army units were stationed along major highways and even in the heart of cities such as Bogotá, Medellín, and Cali. Instead of martial law, however, the government offered amnesty to any insurgent willing to lay down arms and reenter civil society after spending some time in a halfway house. The offer of "reinsertion" under the so-called Law of Justice and Peace of 2005 was extended to paramilitaries as well. Several of their most prominent leaders had been indicted in U.S. courts for international drug trafficking and faced extradition if captured (see Map 15.2 on the next page).

What followed was a massive demobilization of paramilitary organizations and a much smaller demobilization of leftist insurgents, mostly individual desertions by members of the FARC and ELN. The ELN, which swore off involvement in the drug trade from the start, struggled to survive, and the FARC suffered a number of blows, including, in 2008 alone, the death of founder Manuel Marulanda, aka Tirofijo ("Sure-shot"); the bombing of a FARC camp just across the border in the Ecuadorian Amazon that killed a high-ranking leader known as Raúl Reyes; the desertion of "Karina," FARC's legendary female commander; and finally, the rescue of Ingrid Betancourt and other hostages by the Colombian Army. Three of the freed hostages were U.S. defense contractors whose plane went down while reconnoitering coca fields. Evidence surfaced suggesting that Venezuela's President Chávez had been supporting FARC with funds and guns; Chávez denied this while threatening Uribe with military action. Tensions abated somewhat when Colombia's Supreme Court rejected Uribe's bid to run for a third term as president in 2010. His successor, former Defense Minister Juan Manuel Santos, started his presidency by trying to calm tensions with Chávez.

It remains to be seen whether or not the ELN and FARC can survive the blows dealt by the Uribe administration, but it seems clear that the related problem of paramilitaries is likely to persist for some time. Indeed, the only viable threat to Uribe's highly popular "democratic security" policy was his and his "Uribista" party's many connections to paramilitaries, nearly all of them deeply involved in the drug trade. A number of ranking leaders were extradited to the United States in 2008 amid government victories against the FARC, but soon after a younger generation of paramilitaries burst violently onto the scene, some under the name "Black Eagles." As long as such illegal armed groups rule the countryside, Colombians will continue to suffer from arbitrary murders, extortion, corrupted politics, and the consequences of mass displacement.

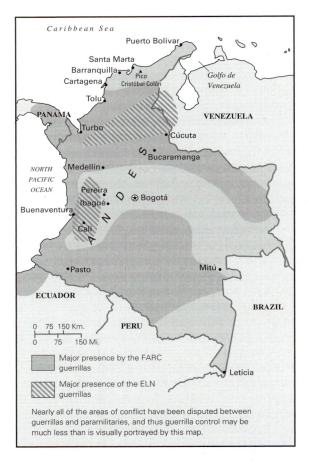

M A P 15.2 Colombia in 2008, showing the roughly 40% of territory in which guerrillas and paramilitaries freely operated

THE RISE OF MEGA-CITIES

Urbanism is an ancient phenomenon in the Americas, but it is only in recent times that cities have swelled to absorb large proportions of Latin Americans. Latin America's two largest cities, São Paulo (20 million inhabitants) and Mexico City (20 million inhabitants) are among the most populous in the world (see Image and Word 15.3). Unlike New York, Paris, or London, both had well under half a million inhabitants in 1900 and only surpassed one million in the 1930s. The explosive growth of these and many other Latin American cities in recent decades is a result of several factors, including rural population growth, commercial land concentration, urban industrialization, and in some cases displacement due to violence or natural disasters.

Capital cities such as Managua, Santo Domingo, Caracas, and Bogotá have long drawn immigrants because of access to political power, higher education,

IMAGE AND WORD 15.3   Skyscrapers, Favelas, and Ranchos

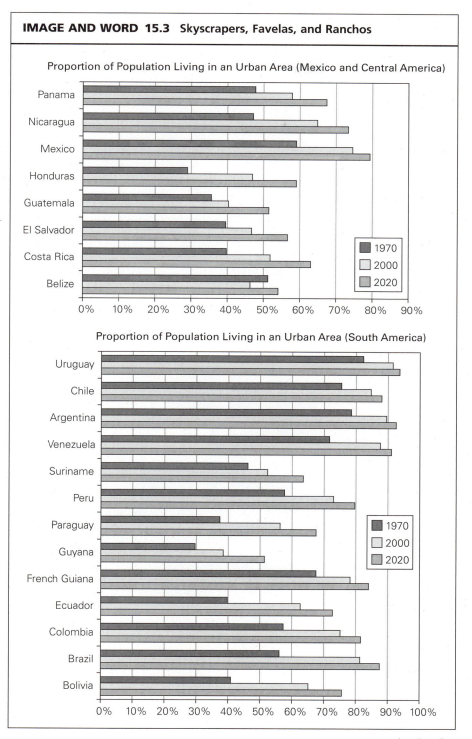

Proportion of Population Living in an Urban Area (Mexico and Central America)

Proportion of Population Living in an Urban Area (South America)

(*continued*)

IMAGE AND WORD 15.3   Skyscrapers, Favelas, and Ranchos (continued)

Robert Fried/Alamy

PAULO WHITAKER/Reuters/Landov

Dramatic urban growth in Latin America (see the charts on the previous page) has consistently outstripped the provision of housing, services, and jobs—from Mexico's Ciudad Juárez on the U.S. border down to Buenos Aires—generating massive slums

(continued)

IMAGE AND WORD 15.3   Skyscrapers, Favelas, and Ranchos (continued)

where illness, crime, and grinding poverty remain entrenched. In many mega-cities, the majority of the population live in dangerous, crowded slums that sprawl around the business and affluent sections of town—as in Caracas (previous page, top), where the slums are called *ranchos*, and in São Paulo (previous page, bottom), where they are called *favelas*. Still, slum-dwellers have not been silent about their needs, and many have organized successful political campaigns to bring water, electricity, increased police presence, and schools to their neighborhoods. Some former slums have even become gentrified within a generation.

---

and cultural institutions, but newer port cities such as Barranquilla and Manaus, as well as older ones such as Guayaquil, Salvador da Bahia, and Valparaíso, have grown tremendously with the rise in long-distance shipping and light industry. Havana, Lima, Buenos Aires, and Rio de Janeiro are all examples of colonial capitals that doubled as major ports, but Panama City is perhaps the only national capital with a colonial pedigree entirely dependent on international trade. Regional capitals and industrial hubs such as Medellín, Santa Cruz de la Sierra, Belo Horizonte, and Monterrey have also expanded dramatically since 1950, offsetting somewhat the power of the old centers. Favorite "colonial" tourist destinations such as Fortaleza, Cartagena, Acapulco, and San Juan have also grown, absorbing far more people than the service sector requires.

Latin America's cities have highlighted one of the riddles of the region in that they continue to represent both promise and misery. The city is a place of hope and desperation at the same time. Yet all is not sadness. Medellín, Colombia, one of the most violent cities in the world in the 1980s and 1990s, emerged in the 2000s as a model of reconciliation thanks to concerted efforts by citizens of widely varying social and economic circumstances. Inadequate services, pollution, traffic congestion, and other urban ills have not disappeared, but optimism returned to Medellín for the first time in decades.

A grimmer picture has emerged in the last decades in Mexico City, Buenos Aires, Rio de Janeiro, and São Paulo. The wealth generated in part by privatization and other neoliberal policies, coupled with the massive expansion of the drug trade, have created huge opportunities for kidnapping rings and slum-based gangs. In the absence of an authoritarian state and goaded by official corruption, criminals have been clever at manipulating the legal system to avoid punishment.

Private citizens have responded to growing urban crime by investing heavily in private security measures, and some have supported formation of police and paramilitary death squads. Rather than go after high-ranking criminals, these death squads have targeted poor urban youths who often get recruited to commit crimes due to their relative impunity before the law. Escaping such a vicious cycle of violence and the social inequity that generates it will clearly be one of the greatest challenges of Latin America in the near future.

POLITICAL AWAKENINGS

One of the most notable Latin American trends beginning around 1990 was the emergence of indigenous and other ethnic or "race-based" political movements. Native peoples had always been active and vocal, often at great cost, as in Guatemala during the cold war, but it was only in the 1990s that pan-indigenous parties were formed that were capable of upsetting older balances of power. The trend was most notable in Ecuador, Peru, and Bolivia, all of which counted large indigenous populations, but important movements have also formed in Chile, Brazil, Colombia, Venezuela, Panama, and Mexico. Indigenous cultural survival, sometimes coupled with environmental concerns, has become a pressing global issue. A number of indigenous representatives from Ecuador's CONAIE confederation and Pachakuti Party have held cabinet posts since 2000, but the 2005 election of former indigenous coca grower Evo Morales in Bolivia marked perhaps the greatest watershed in Latin American politics since at least the days of Benito Juárez. Morales handily won a referendum on his continuance in August 2008.

Latin Americans of African descent have also developed stronger political organizations than ever before in recent decades. Black activism had emerged in countries such as Brazil and Colombia in connection to abolition and later moves to industrial cities, but since no Latin American nation adopted official segregation policies like those in the United States or South Africa, no similar movement for civil rights or against apartheid emerged. Leftist politicians and guerrillas influenced by Marxism had long argued that class differences were the significant divides, not those based on color, and thus attempted to address Afro-Latin American grievances in these terms. In the wake of the cold war the failure of many neoliberal promises of equality in a free market has helped spur greater awareness of racial injustice. Countries with significant African-descended populations, such as Brazil, Colombia, and Ecuador, have witnessed the rise of black power movements and a general revitalization of black culture (see Image and Word 13.3 in Chapter 13).

EXPORTS AND THE ENVIRONMENT

After World War II, all Latin American economies developed and diversified, but most continued to rely on primary exports for foreign exchange. The four most populous countries, Brazil, Mexico, Argentina, and Colombia, were the only ones to develop significant manufacturing sectors that served both internal demand and that of neighboring countries. Cars made in Brazil were sold in Bolivia and Peru, for example, and those made in Mexico were sold in Guatemala and the United States. State enterprises that survived neoliberal reforms included massive oil companies such as Mexico's Pemex, Venezuela's PDVSA, and Brazil's Petrobras. Other state-controlled enterprises managed tin, copper, iron, and coal production. Although some state enterprises hung on, the rush to export primary materials soon engulfed the region, at great environmental cost.

The 1990s witnessed the rise of a number of Latin American environmental groups, some spurred by the deaths of activists such as Chico Mendes and others by the plight of indigenous groups such as the Cuna Cuna of Panama and the Huaorani of Ecuador. Other activists included biologists and other scientists who had long been documenting the loss of habitat, erosion of vital river basins, pollution, and other consequences of unrestrained exploitation of the natural world. Disastrous chemical spills at mines and petroleum plants got serious press coverage for the first time, and ordinary urban dwellers who had generally ignored the idea of wilderness began to appreciate the scope of the problem. Environmental awareness remains, as in the United States, a far more marginal concern than in contemporary Europe or Japan. How or if this will change as demands for primary materials in fast-developing countries such as India and China continue to grow remains to be seen.

The key riddle of Latin America in the current era of neoliberalism and hyper-globalization is yet to be determined, much less solved. Most countries faced rocky transitions to democracy after years of authoritarian rule. Cyclical economic woes challenged these fragile new regimes, helping to propel leftist politicians and opportunistic business celebrities alike back into the limelight. Only in countries where order and security were deemed higher priorities than social equity, as in Colombia and Mexico (and possibly Panama), did conservatives win out.

Relatively high commodity prices resulting from economic expansion in Asia buoyed many Latin American nations that had struggled to service their debts as recently as the early 2000s, but as in the past, these globally dictated prices were always subject to drastic and unpredictable fluctuation. High oil prices stoked the socialist and internationalist ambitions of Venezuela's President Hugo Chávez in the mid-2000s, much to the consternation of the United States, only to drop radically after 2007, causing him to scale back his plans. The smaller riddle here is: How is it that for the first time in memory leftist politics and economic good times have proved compatible, or at least coincided? But whether the seemingly fortunate conjuncture of leftist leaders and economic buoyancy survives or not, the old challenge remains paramount: Will the mass of Latin Americans benefit over the long term? Thus the larger riddle of the twentieth century is this: Which of the political and economic solutions and experiments explored by Latin Americans will reveal themselves in this century to have been of lasting success and significance?

KEEP READING

We recommend the following: Marc Becker, *Indians and Leftists in the Making of Ecuador's Modern Indigenous Movements* (2008); Sinclair Thomson and Forrest Hylton, *Revolutionary Horizons: Past and Present in Bolivian Politics* (2007); Charles Bergquist, ed., *Violence in Colombia, 1990–2000* (2001); Olwyn Blouet, *The Contemporary Caribbean* (2007); Steve J. Stern, *Battling for Hearts and Minds: Memory Struggles in Pinochet's Chile, 1973–1988* (2006) and *Remembering Pinochet's Chile: On the Eve of London 1998* (Duke University Press, 2004); John Lindsay-Poland, *Emperors in the Jungle: The Hidden History of the U.S. in Panama* (2003); John Womack, *The Zapatista Reader* (2004); Susana Sawyer, *Crude Chronicles: Indigenous Politics, Multinational Oil, and Neoliberalism in Ecuador* (2004); Michael Taussig, *Law in a Lawless Land* (2003).

Conclusion

History may not be regarded as it once was—a straightforward chronicle of human progress—but the discipline remains centered on explaining patterns of continuity and change. Historians and other observers of Latin America have long puzzled over a series of questions that we have cast here as riddles: Why did the collision of worlds that took place in the Américas after 1492 happen in the way it did? How were Iberians able to establish and maintain vast colonies for hundreds of years? Why did this vast, populous, and promising region not develop and grow wealthy soon after Independence when it had at least as much potential, if not more, than the early United States, and later Canada? Do the political upheavals of the twentieth century reflect a failure by Latin Americans to find political stability, economic prosperity, and social equality? Or have the region's people struggled successfully in the face of structural obstacles and outside interference to create a unique civilization and a relatively peaceful network of nations?

Many nineteenth-century Latin American observers blamed their nations' persistent poverty on the many and seemingly unshakable legacies of the colonial past, among them slavery, indigenous segregation, political corruption, a too-powerful Catholic Church, regional feuding, and technical and financial dependency on Europe. Later observers, including many nineteenth- and early-twentieth-century liberals, blamed Latin America's racial diversity for economic backwardness. The same people of color who had borne the worst burdens of colonialism and its long aftermath were now being treated like a dying and degenerate race. Some elites, such as the coffee barons of Brazil, sought to "whiten" their societies by encouraging European immigration. Others, most notably the governments of Chile and Argentina, hoped to exterminate intractable indigenous peoples.

Twentieth-century Latin American observers, including some socially conservative nationalists and military officers, started to turn these arguments around, blaming what eventually became known as "underdevelopment" on repeated

European and U.S. interventions, both military and economic. The foreigners, as in colonial times, had been aided by Latin American elites who profited from the sell-out. Colonialism I had simply been replaced by Colonialism II. Escaping the cycle of dependency required embracing racial and cultural diversity, breaking ties with foreign capitalists and bankers and harnessing each nation's resources to the task of modernization. "Economic nationalism," as this trend became known, would kick-start industrial revolutions and lead the masses of Latin America, not just elites, to a brighter, more equal future.

Still, the riddle was not solved. Whether in revolutionary Cuba or Peronist Argentina, economic nationalism failed to live up to expectations by the last quarter of the twentieth century. How could this be explained? Punishing cold war U.S. economic policies, often supplemented with military threats or intervention, were certainly no help. Cheap goods from more industrialized nations inevitably snuck in as contraband. Yet even where the United States and other foreign nations played only a minor role and the internal economy was large enough to absorb huge quantities of national products, economies that were heavily state-managed fared poorly. Experts disagreed on details, but by the 1990s most blamed the model rather than the managers. A return to free-market principles would save the day. "Neoliberalism," as this doctrine of dismantling and auctioning state assets was labeled, was preached even by the U.S. Democratic and British Labour Parties, which helped win converts all over Latin America.

Some military dictatorships, most notably Chile's, embraced neoliberal practices before the end of the cold war, but soon after the war's end the selling off of state enterprises and wholesale cutting of social spending were standard everywhere but Cuba. Politics and economics, some said, were like oil and water. Even Cuba was forced to open up to gain foreign exchange as its populace sunk into extreme poverty after the end of Soviet aid. Yet again, however, it seemed the riddle of "underdevelopment" could not be solved. Spectacular economic shocks followed the passage of NAFTA, and these were repeated all over Latin America throughout the 1990s. Argentina, at first held up as a miraculous example of turnaround, collapsed entirely in 2001. By this time many Latin American intellectuals, politicians, and the public at large began to wonder what had happened. The rising tide of post–cold war globalization, as the new gurus of development had predicted, was not "lifting all boats."

Both the old and new left called for a quick abandonment of neoliberal policies, but older leftists who came to power after years of struggling proved slow to reverse course. For countries such as Brazil and Chile, the waters seemed to calm, but those who had benefited from neoliberal policies had also become firmly entrenched; they worked hard to persuade new leaders to compromise. Only Venezuela, with its tremendous oil wealth in a time of high prices, seemed capable of charting an alternative course. The long-term effects of President Hugo Chávez's lurching return to economic nationalism remain to be seen; but after more than a decade in power, the achievements of the Bolivarian Revolution are limited, a shortcoming that Chávez blames on "the Empire" (that is, the United States). Colombia and Mexico, by contrast, remained in the hands of conservatives after 2000 despite—or perhaps because of—the continued threat of armed leftist insurgency. More pressing in both countries was the meteoric rise of drug trafficking and associated crime. Despite the popularity of Colombia's President Uribe, the state's ability to crush a thriving subterranean economy under his watch proved just as pathetic as its attempt to manage a legitimate one.

At the start of the second decade of the twenty-first century, Latin Americans remain sharply divided over the causes of persistent poverty at the national and regional levels. The most radical leftists argue that only armed revolution will unseat the entrenched and corrupt interests that hold the people down, while the most radical conservatives, including neo-Nazi paramilitaries, argue for a return to strict social hierarchies, military discipline, and the unblinking faith of the conquistadors. In between are a wide range of more flexible—and far more numerous—moderates, including politicians such as Brazil's Lula da Silva who seem capable of swinging back and forth between the interests of business and the interests of the masses with an agility unimaginable before 1990.

Foreign observers and analysts have continued to ponder this paradox, what we have called "the riddle of Latin America." A common argument in the twentieth century blamed Latin America's uneven progress on the caudillo culture, which allegedly permeated not just politics but the whole civilization. In this view, "personalism" and "the habit of not cooperating" were the most important characteristics of the region's people. As recently as 2008, acclaimed political scientist Francis Fukuyama argued in *Falling Behind* that it was not culture, geography, race, or even foreign intervention but rather poor institutions that had set Latin America back. Examples of fragile, corrupt, or poorly conceived institutions were not hard to find. As seen in the matter of trying perpetrators for Dirty War crimes after the fall of dictatorships in the 1980s and 1990s, weak judiciaries remained a significant problem all over Latin America into the late twentieth century, but what might such an institutional failure have to do with economics? Would the problem of high-level criminal impunity undermine, for example, the confidence of so-called micro-entrepreneurs in the civil courts?

The riddle of Latin America in the early twenty-first century may be how its nations will adjust to a world in which the United States, despite its military power, is only one of several sizeable nations (or blocs of nations) in need of primary exports. As of this writing, steady demand in China, India, and other parts of the developing world, not the United States or Europe, keeps fueling a new wave of export-led growth. Since the early 2000s, relatively high oil prices have stimulated expansion of drilling operations as well as the use of biofuels, in particular ethanol derived from sugarcane. High metals prices have buoyed Chile's copper mines and revived silver, gold, platinum, tin, and iron in Colombia, Peru, Bolivia, Brazil, and elsewhere. Gold became especially attractive as investors scrambled for safe havens after the global economic meltdown of 2007; massive mining pollution followed suit. Asian demand for soybeans, mostly to feed animals, has driven massive expansion in the Brazilian Amazon, at the expense of the forest and remnant indigenous populations. These are just a few examples of how emerging global centers of economic activity are affecting Latin America. Thus far, most of Latin America is doing simply that—being affected by changes abroad.

Only Brazil has moved into new spheres of economic activity in the decades since dictatorship's end, manufacturing not only cars but also midsize jets capable of competing with giants Boeing and Airbus. Brazil has also begun a modest space program and developed massive offshore oil deposits at tremendous depths. It has repeatedly won disputes with the United States and Canada over tariffs on steel, orange juice, and other commodities before the World Trade Organization, and it remains the world's top producer of sugar and coffee, as well as ethanol for fuel. Latin America's next largest economy, that of Mexico, has less to show despite (or perhaps because of) signing the North American Free Trade Agreement with the United States and Canada in 1994. Mexico shared the burden of the 2007 U.S. housing bubble collapse more than any other Latin American country. If even joining a huge regional trade bloc has not improved the lives of most of Mexico's citizens, what then might be the solution to the greater riddle of Latin America? Perhaps the solution lies with a new generation of Latin American leaders more representative of ordinary citizens. The Conquest and centuries of colonial rule were made possible by the contributions of the non-elites—less-privileged Iberians, mixed-race peoples, Africans, Native Americans—whose descendants built independent nations in the nineteenth century, modern economies in the twentieth, and one of the world's most vital and fascinating civilizations. The future of Latin America is in their capable hands.

Index